COLONIAL
AMERICAN
∽ English ∽

COLONIAL
AMERICAN
~ English ~

Words and Phrases Found in
Colonial Writing, now Archaic, Obscure, Obsolete,
or Whose Meanings Have Changed.

Richard M. Lederer, Jr.

A Verbatim Book

A VERBATIM® BOOK
Essex, Connecticut 06426
U.S.A.

Designed by Peter K. Good

Library of Congress Cataloging-in-Publication Data

Lederer, Richard M., 1916–
  Colonial American English, a glossary.

  Bibliography: p.
  Includes index.
  1. Americanisms--Dictionaries. 2. English language--
Archaisms--Dictionaries. 3. English language--Obsolete
words--Dictionaries. 4. English language--18th century--
Glossaries, vocabularies, etc. 5. English language--
Early modern, 1500-1700--Glossaries, vocabularies.
6. English language--United States--Glossaries, voca-
bularies, etc. I. Ashley, Leonard R. N. II. Title.
PE2838.L43 1985   427'.973   85-50954
ISBN 0-930454-19-7

Contents

Introduction

Language changes and so writings of any period contain many words and phrases whose meanings are unknown or unclear to scholars and other readers of a later date. Some definitions for these difficult words and expressions may be found in unabridged and historical dictionaries; but often the early or pertinent meaning is not given or is not readily apparent. Occasionally a specialized reference book will yield the sought-after meaning, but the hunt can be exhausting, and takes all the fun out of reading.

Here is a handy glossary that lists and defines many words and phrases, the meanings of which are now obscure, that were used in America during the period from 1608 to 1783, the Colonial period.

I have built this glossary by poring over patents, deeds, laws, newspapers, letters, memoirs, diaries, songs, plays and public records. There are inevitably sources that I did not cover, hence words and phrases I have not included, but I believe that there is enough here to satisfy the questions of many who have an interest in the English of the period.

This glossary obviously does not pretend to replace the *Oxford English Dictionary* [*OED*], *Webster's New International Dictionary* [*WNID*], Craigie and Hurlbert's *A Dictionary of American English* [*DAE*], Mathews' *A Dictionary of Americanisms* [*DA*], Partridge's *A Dictionary of Slang and Unconventional English* [*DSUE*], Wentworth and Flexner's *Dictionary of American Slang* [*DAS*], or Mencken's *The American Language* [*AL*]. The specialist will still have to go to these and other works listed in the bibliography—and beyond. My purpose is to treat some 3000 words and phrases that are likely to need explanation so that modern readers can better understand and enjoy writing of Colonial times.

Much consideration was given to the selection process. No rigid rule was possible, so the result is subjectivity. I used my own vocabulary and judgment. Some words have many meanings; in some cases these are still current, well-known meanings. Here are defined only those words which appeared in Colonial usage and which are now obsolete or which had meanings then that are not known today. Certain legal, medical, military and nautical terms, familiar to lawyers, doctors, soldiers, and sailors, modern or past, are included because these terms may not be familiar to those knowledgeable in other fields. Where examples of usage add to clarity or may be interesting in themselves, they are supplied. Useful etymologies are included, some quite surprising. If a word brings to mind an unusual fact or if an interesting sidelight was discovered in researching the word, it is provided. I hope you find this ancillary information as interesting as I did.

Introduction

Pronunciation is not indicated, primarily, because it is not within the purposes of this book. Sometimes an indication of how a word was probably pronounced is reflected in its spelling as, "two payer of shoes," "a town clark," "a boat with owers," "silver slive [sleeve] buttons," and "trunnels" for "tree nails."

For the most part I have used the modern spelling for an entry even if the source used a variant spelling. If the modern spelling is close, the reader will find it; if it is not, I have indicated the variant spelling and have shown other spellings in cross reference. If you have any difficulty with a word, say it out loud; that will help you to hear the other spelling. When reading original documents, one must beware the long "s" that looks like an "f." One researcher did not when transcribing a John Cotton 1630 document and wrote, "Will not recompense the wrongs done in a peaceful fort [sort]."

Sources of the definitions are listed in the Bibliography. The vast majority were culled from the above-named *WNID,* the *OED* and the *DAE.* Many specialized books, however, were needed and a word of gratitude is due to the fine resources and staffs of the New York, Scarsdale, and White Plains Public Libraries and the libraries of The New York Academy of Medicine, The Cooper-Hewett Museum, and The Fashion Institute of Technology.

The publication of a glossary such as this cannot be done without the counsel, criticism, involvement, and generous help of many people. I would like to acknowledge warmly those whose gracious and helpful correspondence made this research a delightful learning experience: Don H. Berkebile, Gerald Carson, Frederic G. Cassidy, Christopher Davis, John Drew, J. B. Ecklund, Robert Feder, John Feulner, James J. Fuld, Victor S. Gettner, Charles Ghering, Dr. Henry F. Graff, Rev. J. Scottie Griffin, Lise Halttunen, Dr. Florence M. Hetzler, Gertrude Hofheimer, Oliver Jensen, Winthrop D. Jordan, Marguerite S. Kane, Ardie L. Kelley, Bruno Kisch, Howard R. Lamar, Vera Brodsky Lawrence, Lester B. Levy, Richard Maass, Julie Mirsberger, Mrs. Charles F. Montgomery, Eric P. Newman, Judith Ozment, Harry Partridge, John S. Reynolds, Roger E. Ritzmann, Rabbi Lawrence W. Schwartz, Nicholas T. Smith, Milton Sonday, Jess M. Stein, Dr. Harold Speert, Marion Tinling, Walter W. Weinstein, Ellen B. Wells, James Harvey Young, and Ronald E. Zupko.

A special note of gratitude goes to the painstaking, meticulous and demanding editing of Leonard R. N. Ashley, Professor of English at Brooklyn College of the City University of New York.

This book is intended as a reference book, but I hope it is also a "reading book."

Richard M. Lederer, Jr.

Scarsdale, New York
Spring 1985

Bibliography

Academy of Play. London: F. Newberry, Pub., 1755.

Alexander, J. H. *Universal Dictionary of Weights and Measures*. New York: D. Van Nostrand, 1867.

American Fabrics Magazine. *Encyclopedia of Textiles*. Edgewood Cliffs, N.J.: Prentice Hall, 1960.

American Heritage Cookbook and Illustrated History of American Eating and Drinking. New York: American Heritage Press, 1980.

Andrews, Charles N. *Colonial Folkways*. New Haven: Yale Univ. Press, 1919.

Apel, Willi. *Harvard Dictionary of Music*. Cambridge: Harvard Univ. Press, 1944.

Appleton's Cyclopedia of American Biography. 6 vols. New York: D. Appleton, 1891.

Ash, John. *New and Complete Dictionary of the English Language*. 2 vols. London: E. and C. Dilly, 1775.

Babbidge, Homer D., Jr., ed. *Noah Webster: On Being American*. New York: Frederick A. Praeger, 1967.

Baker, Ernest A., Ed. *Cassell's New French-English; English-French Dictionary*. New York: Funk and Wagnalls, 1950.

Baker, William A. *Colonial Vessels*. Barre, Mass.: Barre Pub. Co., 1962.

Barck, Oscar Theodore, Jr. and Hugh Talmadge Lefler. *Colonial America*. New York: The Macmillan Co., 1968.

Barnes, Harry Elmer. *The Story of Punishment*. Montclair, N.J.: Patterson Smith, 1972.

Barrère, Albert and Charles G. Leland. *A Dictionary of Slang, Jargon and Cant*. The Ballentyne Press, 1890. (Reprinted, Detroit: The Gale Research Co., 1967).

Bartlett, John Russel. *Dictionary of Americanisms: A Glossary of Words and Phrases Usually Regarded as Peculiar to the United States*. New York: Bartlett and Welford, 1848.

Bate, George. *Bate's Dispensatory*. n.d.

Benton, William. *The Annals of America*. Chicago: Encyclopedia Brittanica, 1968.

Berg, Fred Anderson. *Encyclopedia of Continental Army Units*. Harrisburg, Pa.: Stackpole Books, 1972.

Berrey, Lester V. and Melvin Van den Bark. *American Thesaurus of Slang*. New York: Crowell, 1953.

Bilebofketz, Louise, ed. *Dictionary of American History*. 8 vols. New York: Charles Scribner's Sons, 1976.

Black, Henry Campbell. *Black's Law Dictionary, 4th Ed.* St. Paul: West Publishing Co., 1968.

Blanton, Wyndham Bolling. *Medicine in Virginia in the 17th Century*. New York: Arno, 1930 (Reprinted, Salem, N. H.: Ayer Co., 1976).

Blanton, Wyndham Bolling. *Medicine in Virginia in the 18th Century*. New York: A M S Press, 1976 (A reprint of a 1931 edition).

Boatner, Mark Mayo III. *Encyclopedia of American Idioms*. New York: Davis McKay Co., 1966.

Bibliography

Boatner, Maxine Tull and John Edward Gates. *A Dictionary of American Idioms.* Woodbury, N. Y.: Barron's Educational Services, 1966.

Bolitho, Hector. *The Glorious Oyster.* New York: Horizon Press, 1961.

Boorstin, Daniel J. *The Americans: The Colonial Experience.* New York: Random House, 1958.

Boucher, Jonathan. *Glossary of Archaic and Provincial Words.* London: Black, Young and Young, 1832.

Bouvier's Law Dictionary. New York: West Publishing Co., 1914.

Brackenridge, Hugh. *The Battle of Bunkers Hill, 1776.*

Brewer, E. Cobham. *Brewer's Dictionary of Phrase and Fable.* New York: Harper and Row, 1976.

Bridenbaugh, Carl. *The Colonial Craftsman.* Chicago: Univ. of Chicago Press, 1950.

Budd, Thomas. *Good Order Established in Pennsylvania and New York.* Readex Microprint, 1966.

Bullock, Helen. *The Williamsburg Art of Cookery.* Williamsburg: Colonial Williamsburg, 1952.

Caruba, Rebecca. *Colonial Cooking.* Maplewood, N.J.: Hammond, 1975.

Caulfield, S. F. A. and Blanche C. Seward. *Dictionary of Needlework.* London: L. Upcott, n.d.

Chapelle, Howard I. *American Small Sailing Craft.* New York: W. W. Norton & Co., 1951.

Chapelle, Howard I. *The History of the American Sailing Navy.* New York: W. W. Norton & Co., 1949.

Chapelle, Howard I. *The History of American Sailing Ships.* New York: W. W. Norton & Co., 1935.

Clabburn, Pamela. *The Needleworker's Dictionary.* London: Macmillan, 1976.

Coggins, Jack. *Ships and Seamen of the American Revolution.* Harrisburg, Pa.: Stackpole Books, 1969.

Copeland, Peter F. *Working Dress in Colonial and Revolutionary America.* Westport, Conn.: Greenwood Press, 1977.

Craigie, Sir. William A. and James R. Hulburt. *Dictionary of American English.* 4 vols. Chicago: Univ. of Chicago Press, 1938.

Culpeper's Complete Herbal. London: Foulsham and Co., n.d. (Culpeper died in 1654.)

Cunningham, Anne Rowe, ed. *Letters and Diary of John Rowe.* Boston: W. B. Clarke, Co., 1903.

Cunnington, C. W. and P. E. *Dictionary of English Costume, 900-1900.* London: A. & C. Black, 1916.

Dann, John C., ed. *The Revolution Remembered.* Chicago: Univ. of Chicago Press, 1980.

Denton, Daniel. *A Brief Description of New York.* New York: Readex Books, 1966.

Earle, Alice Morse. *Colonial Dames and Good Wives.* New York: Houghton Mifflin & Co., 1895.

Earle, Alice Morse. *Colonial Days in Old New York.* New York: Charles Scribner's Sons, 1896.

Earle, Alice Morse. *Costume of Colonial Times.* New York: Charles Scribner's Sons, 1894.

Earle, Alice Morse. *Curious Punishments of Bygone Days.* Montclair, N. J.: Patterson Smith, 1896.

Earle, Alice Morse. *Stage Coach and Tavern Days.* New York: The Macmillan Co., 1900.

Earle, Alice Morse. *Two Centuries of Costume in America, 1620-1820.* New York: The Macmillan Co., 1903.

Eddis, William. *Letters from America.* Cambridge: Harvard Univ. Press, 1969.

Edmunds, John, ed. *A Williamsburg Songbook.* New York: Holt Rinehart and Winston, 1964.

Encyclopedia Brittanica. Chicago: Chicago Univ. Press, 1947.

English, Mary O'Connor, ed. *Early Town Records of Mamaroneck, 1697-1881.* Mamaroneck, N. Y.: Town of Mamaroneck, 1979.

Farrand, Max, ed. *Benjamin Franklin's Memoirs.* Berkeley: Univ. of California Press, 1949.

Fithian, Philip Vickers. *Journal and Letters of Philip Vickers Fithian.* Williamsburg: Colonial Williamsburg, 1943.

Flexner, James T. *States Dyckmanm: An American Loyalist.* Boston: Little Brown, 1980.

Fox, Dixon Ryan. *Yankees and Yorkers.* New York: New York Univ. Press, 1940.

Franklin, Benjamin. *The Autobiography of Benjamin Franklin.* Garden City, N. Y.: Garden City Pub. Co., 1916.

Funk, Wilfred. *Word Origins.* New York: Funk and Wagnalls, 1950.

Gaynor, Frank. *The New Military and Naval Dictionary.* New York: Philosophical Library, 1951.

Gonzalez, Ambrose E. *The Black Border.* Columbia, S. C.: The State Co., 1922.

Goodwin, Maria Wilder. *Dutch and English on the Hudson.* New Haven: Yale Univ. Press, 1920.

Grieve, Maud. *A Modern Herbal.* New York: Harcourt Brace and Co., 1931.

Griffenhagen, George B. and James H. Young. *Old English Patent Medicines in America.* Washington: Smithsonian, 1959.

Grose, Francis. *A Classical Dictionary of the Vulgar Tongue.* London: 1788.

Grose, Francis. *A Provincial Glossary.* London, 1790.

Guinagh, Kevin. *Dictionary of Foreign Phrases and Abbreviations.* New York: H. W. Wilson Co., 1972.

Haggard, Howard W. *Devils, Drugs and Doctors.* New York: Harper and Row, 1929.

Halliwell, James O. *Dictionary of Archaic and Provincial Words.* London: 1850.

Harder, Kelsie B. *Illustrated Dictionary of Place Names.* New York: Van Nostrand Reinhold, Co., 1976.

Hargrave, Catherine P. *A History of Playing Cards.* Boston: Houghton Mifflin Co., 1930.

Heath, William. *Memoirs of Major General Heath.* Boston: L. Thomas and E. T. Andrews, 1798.

Hervey, George F. *The Complete Illustrated Book of Card Games.* Garden City: Doubleday and Co., 1973.

Hess, Karen. *Martha Washington's Booke of Cookery.* New York: Columbia Univ. Press, 1981. (Referred to throughout as "A seventeenth-century cookbook").

Hopkinson, Francis. *An Exercise Containing a Dialogue and Ode.* 1762.

Hoyle, Edmond. *Mr. Hoyle's Games of Whist, Quadrille, Piquet, Chess and Backgammon Complete.* London: J. Brambles, 1807.

Isham, Norman Morrison. *Early American Houses and A Glossary of Colonial Architectural Terms.* New York: Da Capo Press, 1967.

James, Robert. *A Medicinal Dictionary.* 3 vols. 1743.

Jameson, John Franklin. *Privateering and Piracy in the Colonial Period.* New York: Macmillan, 1923.

Jensen, Merrill, ed. *English Historical Documents. Vol. IX: American Colonial Documents to 1776.* New York: Oxford Univ. Press, 1955.

Johnson, Samuel. *A Dictionary of the English Language.* London: 1755.

Johnstone, William D. *For Good Measure.* New York: Holt, Rinehart and Winston, 1975.

Katcher, Philip R. N. *Encyclopedia of British Provincial and German Army Units, 1775-1783.* Harrisburg, Pa.: Stackpole Books, 1973.

Kramer's Dutch Dictionary. New York: Dover Pub., 1946.

Krochmal, Arnold and Connie. *A Guide to the Medicinal Plants of the United States.* New York: Quadrangle, 1973.

Bibliography

La Wall, Charles Herbert. *4000 Years of Pharmacy.* London: Lippincott, 1927.

Lawrence, Vera Brodsky. *Music for Patriots, Politicians, and Presidents.* New York: Macmillan, 1975.

Lee, Francis Cook and Richard Lander. *North Castle/New Castle Historical Records.* Chappaqua, N.Y.: Towns of North Castle and New Castle, 1975.

Lewis, Charlton T. and Charles Short. *Harper's Latin Dictionary.* New York: American Book Co., 1879.

Linton, George E. *The Modern Textile and Apparel Dictionary.* Plainfield, N.J.: The Textile Book Services, 1954.

Maass, Richard. Personal collection of manuscripts, newspapers and almanacs.

Marchwardt, Albert H. *American English.* New York: Oxford Univ. Press, 1958.

Marks, Stephen S. *Fairchild Dictionary of Textiles.* New York: Fairchild Publications, 1959.

Mathews, Mitford M. *A Dictionary of Americanisms.* 2 vols. Chicago: Chicago Univ. Press, 1951.

Mawson, C. O. Sylvester. *Dictionary of Foreign Terms.* New York: Thomas Y. Crowell Co., 1975.

Mac Donald, John M. *The Mac Donald Papers, 1844-1851.* Unpublished manuscript at The Hufeland Library, New Rochelle, N.Y.

Mead, Robert Douglas. *Colonial American Literature.* New York: New American Library, 1976.

Mencken, Henry Louis. *The American Language, 4th Edition.* New York: Alfred Knopf, 1936.

Miller, John C. *The Colonial Image.* New York: George Braziller, 1962.

Morris, Anna Cary, ed. *The Diary and Letters of Gouveneur Morris.* 2 vols. New York: Charles Scribner's Sons, 1888.

Morris, William and Mary. *Morris Dictionary of Word and Phrase Origins.* New York: Harper and Row, 1977.

Moses, Montrose. *Representative Plays by American Dramatists. Vol. 1. 1765-1819.* New York: Benjamin Blom, 1964. (Contains plays by Thomas Godfrey, John Leacock, Robert Mumford, Robert Rogers and Mercy Warren.)

Motherby, G. *A New Medical Dictionary, Third Ed.* London: 1791.

Murray, James A. H., Henry Bradley, W. A. Craigie, C. T. Onions. *The Oxford English Dictionary.* 13 vols. London: Oxford Univ. Press, 1933.

Newman, George C. and Frank J. Kravic. *Collectors Illustrated Encyclopedia of the American Revolution.* Harrisburg, Pa.: Stackpole Books, 1975.

Norton, Mary Beth. *Liberty's Daughters.* Boston: Little Brown and Co., 1980.

O'Callaghan, E. B., ed. *Documents Relative to the Colonial History of the State of New York.,* 13 vols. Albany: State of New York, 1856.

O'Callaghan, E. B., ed. *The Documentary History of the State of New York.,* 4 vols. Albany: Weed, Parsons & Co., 1849.

Oxford English Dictionary Department, comp. *The Oxford Dictionary for Writers and Editors.* Oxford: Clarendon Press, 1981.

Oxford Dictionary of Quotations, Second Edition. London: Oxford Univ. Press, 1955.

Partridge, Eric. *A Dictionary of Catch Phrases.* New York: Stein and Day, 1977.

Partridge, Eric. *A Dictionary of Slang and Unconventional English.* New York: The Macmillan Co., 1970.

Partridge, Eric. *Macmillan Dictionary of Historical Slang.* New York: The Macmillan Co., 1975.

Patents for Inventions: Abridgements of Specifications Relating to Medicine, Surgery and Dentistry, 1620-1866. London: Commissioners of Patents, 1872.

Payton Geoffrey, comp. *Webster's Dictionary of Proper Names.* Springfield, Mass.: G. & C. Merriam, 1970.

Perry, William. *The Royal Standard English Dictionary.* Brookfield, Mass.: E. Merriam & Co., 1809.

Picken, Mary Brooks. *The Fashion Dictionary.* New York: Funk and Wagnalls, 1957.

Pickering, John. *Vocabulary or Collection of Words and Phrases Which Have Been Supposed to be Peculiar to the United States of America.* Boston: Cummings and Hilliard, 1816.

Randolph, Mary. *The Virginia Housewife or Methodical Cook.* New York: Hurst & Co., n.d.

Riley, Edward Miles, ed. *Journals of John Harrower.* New York: Holt, Rinehart and Winston, 1963.

Rinzler, Carol Ann. *Dictionary of Medical Folklore.* New York: T. Y. Crowell, 1979.

Ruffner, James A., ed. *Eponyms Dictionary Index.* Detroit: Gale Research Co., 1977.

Scharf, J. Thomas. *History of Westchester County, New York.* 2 vols. Philadelphia: L. E. Preston & Co., 1886.

Shipley, Joseph T. *Dictionary of Early English.* New York: New York Philosophical Library, 1955.

Shumway, George, Edward Durrell and Howard C. Frey. *The Conestoga Wagon.* York, Pa.: American Industries Assn., 1964.

Singleton, Esther. *Social New York under the Georges, 1714-1776.* New York: D. Appleton and Co., 1902.

Skeat, Walter W. *A Concise Etymological Dictionary of the English Language.* New York: Capricorn Books, 1963.

Sloane, Eric. *A Museum of Early American Tools.* New York: Funk and Wagnalls, 1964.

Sloane, Eric. *A Reverence for Wood.* New York: Funk and Wagnalls, 1965.

Smith, Al. *Dictionary of the City of London Street Names.* Newton Abbott: David and Charles, 1970.

Smith, E. *The Compleat Housewife.* London, 1742.

Smith, John. *A Little Teatable Chitchat.* 1781.

Smith, William. *The History of the Province of New York from the First Discovery to the Year 1732.* London: T. Wilcox, 1757.

Sollmann, Torald. *A Manual of Pharmacology.* Philadelphia: W. P. Saunders Co., 1917.

Street, John Phillips. *The Composition of Certain Patent and Proprietary Medicines.* Chicago: The American Medical Assn., 1917.

Swan, Susan Burroughs. *Plain and Fancy.* New York: Holt, Rinehart and Winston, 1977.

Talbot, William, trans. *The Discoveries of John Lederer.* London, 1672 (Reprinted, New York: Readex Books, 1966).

Thornton, Richard. *An American Glossary.* New York: Lippincott, 1912.

Tunis, Edwin. *Colonial Living.* Cleveland: World Publishing Co., 1957.

Tunis, Edwin. *Wheels.* Cleveland: World Publishing Co., 1954.

Ukers, William H. *All About Tea.* New York: The Tea and Coffee Trade Journal, 1935.

Van der Donck, Adriaen. *A Description of the New Netherlands.* The Hague, 1653 (Reprinted, Syracuse: Syracuse Univ. Press, 1968).

Van Doren, Carl, ed. *The Letters of Benjamin Franklin and Jane Mecom.* Princeton: Princeton Univ. Press, 1950.

Warwick, Edward, Henry C. Pitz and Alexander Wycoff. *Early American Dress.* New York: Bonanza Books, 1965.

Washington, George. *The Diaries of George Washington 1748-1799.* 4 vols. Boston: Houghton Mifflin Co., 1925.

Webster, Noah. *A Compendious Dictionary of the English Language.* Hartford and New Haven, 1806.

Webster, Noah. *An American Dictionary of the English Language.* New York: S. Converse, 1828.

Webster's Biographical Dictionary. Springfield: G. & C. Merriam Co., 1956.

Bibliography

Webster's Geographical Dictionary. Springfield: G. & C. Merriam Co., 1949.

Webster's New International Dictionary of the English Language, Second Ed. Springfield: G. & C. Merriam Co., 1949.

Webster's New International Dictionary of the English Language, Third Ed. Springfield: G. & C. Merriam Co., 1961.

Weekley, Ernest. *An Etymological Dictionary of Modern English.* New York: Dover Pub., 1967.

Wentwort, Harold and Stuart B. Flexner. *Dictionary of American Slang.* New York: Thomas Y. Crowell, 1975.

White, Andrew. *A Relation of Maryland.* London, 1635. (Reprinted, New York: Readex Books, 1961).

Whitney, William Dwight and Benjamin E. Smith. *The Century Dictionary and Cyclopedia.* 12 vols., New York: The Century Co. 1889.

Whittaker, Otto. *Such Language.* Anderson, S. C.: Drake House, 1969.

Wilcox, R. Turner. *The Dictionary of Costume.* New York: Charles Scribner's Sons, 1969.

Wingate, Isabel B. *Fairchild's Dictionary of Textiles.* New York: Fairchild Pub., 1979.

Wolley, Charles. *A Two Year Journal of New York, 1678-1680.* Cleveland: The Burroughs Bros. Co., 1902 (Reprinted, Harbor Hill Books, 1973).

Woodfin, Maud H., ed. and Marion Tinling, decoder. *Another Secret Diary of William Byrd of Westover, 1739-1741.* Richmond: The Deitz Press, 1942.

Wooton, A. C. *Chronicles of Pharmacy.* London: Macmillan, 1910.

Wright, Louis B. and Marion Tinling, eds. *The Secret Diary of William Byrd of Westover, 1709-1712.* Richmond: The Deitz Press, 1941.

Wright, Louis B. and Marion Tinling, eds. *William Byrd's London Diary, 1717-1721 and Other Writings.* Toronto: Oxford, 1958.

Wright, Thomas. *Dictionary of Obsolete and Provincial English.* London: Ball & Doldy, 1869.

Yardley, J. H. R. *Before the Mayflower.* New York: Doubleday Doran & Co., 1931.

Yoshpe, Harry B. *The Disposition of Loyalist Estates in the Southern District of the State of New York.,* 1939. (Reprinted, New York: A. M. S. Press, 1967).

Zupko, Ronald Edward. *A Dictionary of English Weights and Measures.* Madison, Wisc.: Univ. of Wisconsin Press, 1968.

COLONIAL
AMERICAN
∽ English ∽

abatis (*n.*) A military obstacle of live or dead trees with their butt ends facing the enemy. From French *abatis* 'mass of things thrown down.' When Maj. John Andreé was captured, in 1780, in his possession was found a description of West Point in Benedict Arnold's handwriting. Arnold had written that Fort Webb at West Point was:
"without defense save a slight abatis."

abroad (*adj.*) Out of doors. Dr. Alexander Hamilton, in 1744, wrote of the women of Boston:
"Pretty women who appear rather more abroad than they do at York."

absinthe *See* **wormwood.**

abuse (*v.*) **(1)** To add other material. In 1709 the Virginia House of Burgesses:
"drew up a bill against the masters that abuse hogsheads of tobacco."
(2) To deceive. A 1718 author prayed:
"That we may not profane the name of God . . . nor abuse ourselves into Eternal Perdition."

accommodate (*adj.*) Fit, suitable. In 1643:
"The Colledge [Harvard] was . . . appointed to be at Cambridge (a place very pleasant and accommodate)."

accustomed (*adj.*) As usual. A 1754 bill of lading provided for:
"They paying freight for the said goods . . . with primage and average accustomed."

ace of hearts A card game. In 1718 William Byrd wrote:
"[I] played at the ace of hearts and lost 3 guineas."

acetum *See* **vinegar.**

Adamite (*n.*) A member of a religious sect that worshiped while naked. In 1656 Connecticut legislated that:
"No Towne within this Jurisdiction shall entertain any Quakers, Ranters, Adamites, or such like heretiques."

address (*n.*) **(1)** Skillful management. In 1775 Gen. Heath, describing troops, wrote:
"great address and gallantry were exhibited."

(2) A petition. In 1719 William Byrd:
"moved an address to the Governor" in the Virginia House of Burgesses.

ad libitum *Latin.* 'At pleasure.' The 1767 South Carolina *Remonstrance* deplored,
"Thus they live ad libitum, quitting each other at pleasure."

adrat *(interj.)* A mild oath, evolved from *God rot.* Robert Mumford used the word in a 1770 play:
"Here's at ye, adrat ye, if you're for a quarrel."

advantage *(n.)* An increase or surplus. A 1776 Connecticut newspaper advertised:
"a two year and advantage steer," one that was two-plus years old.

adventure *(v.)* To risk; place in jeopardy. In a 1625 proclamation the King advised:
"all our loving subjects not to adventure the breach of our royal commandments."

adventurer *(n.)* One who engages in commercial ventures. The 1625 Virginia Charter was given to:
"a company of adventurers and planters."

advertisement *(n.)* A notice given; notification. In 1631 Thomas Dudley wrote,
"We received advertisement from our friends in England."
It was also used in today's sense of a public notice.

advowson *(n.)* The right of the lord of a manor to name the local clergyman; who pays the fiddler calls the tune. The 1697 Manor Grant gave Stephanus Van Cortlandt:
"the advowson and right of patronage."

afflatus *(n.)* An inspiration. In 1721 Cotton Mather wrote that he received:
"an afflatus from heaven."

afterclap *(n.)* An unexpected subsequent event. In 1775 Edward Johnson recorded in his memoirs,
"I desired a receipt to prevent any afterclaps."

agitate *(v.)* To discuss; to debate. Gouverneur Morris wrote,
"He desires a further conversation when the matter shall be agitated."

agitation *(n.)* A discussion, debate.

alamode *(n.)* A thin silk fabric for scarfs, etc. A 1775 Boston newspaper advertised,
"Persons may be supplied with muslins, lute-strings, alamodes."

alb. *(adj.)* An abbreviation of Latin *albus* 'white.'

Albion *(n.)* The Celtic name for England, Scotland, and Wales. From Latin *albus* 'white,' referring to the white cliffs of Dover.

alfogeo *(n.)* The cheek pouches where a tobacco chewer stores his quid. From Spanish *alforja* 'saddlebag.' School mistress Sarah Knight wrote in 1704,
"In comes a tall country fellow with his Alfogeos full of tobacco."

Algerine *(n.)* A native of or a ship belonging to Algiers, particularly the Barbary Coast pirates. In 1678 J. Hull entered in his diary,
"James Elson was taken by the Algerines."

alien *(v.)* To transfer property. The 1683 deed to Stephanus Van Cortlandt read:
"bargain, sell, alien, enfeof."

alkermes *(n.)* The scarlet grain insect that was once thought to be a berry. In 1616 Capt. John Smith recorded,

"Fruits are of many sorts and kinds as Alkermes, Currans, Mulberries." Ground and boiled with sugar, it made a cordial for sweetening medicine.

allemande (*n.*) One of various German dances, older forms resembling the minuet, later ones, the waltz. After Yorktown (1781) Cornwallis was satirized in a song, "Now hous'd in York, At minuet or all'mande."

all fours A card game for two, named for the points that counted. In 1755 Samuel Johnson explained,
"The all four are high, low, Jack and the game." Philip Fithian in 1775 wrote,
"In our dining room companies at cards, Five & forty, whist, Alfours, Calico-Betty, etc."

allize (*n.*) A variant of *alewife*, the fish.

allodial (*adj.*) In absolute ownership, free of rent or service to a feudal overlord. Although feudal tenure was abolished in 1660, grants, patents, and deeds after that date often spelled out that the transaction was not subject to feudal law. The New Jersey Legislature in 1787 stated,
"Tenure . . . shall . . . be . . . Allodial and not Feudal."

alopeen (*n.*) A silk and wool cloth used for men's clothing. Named for Aleppo, Syria. Foster & Thomas Hutchinson advertised in a 1765 Boston newspaper,
"Tammy, Shaloons, Camblets, Alopeen, Bombazeen, Silk Ferrets, Ticks."

amain (*v.*) To signal surrender by lowering a topsail. From French *emener* 'to surrender.'

amaranth (*n.*) A legendary flower that never fades, generally used poetically. Hugh Brackenridge used the word in a 1776 play.

amber (*n.*) A distillate of ground amber prescribed as a cure for epilepsy and hysteria. A 1737 writer referred to:
"Not hartshorn, nor spirit of amber, nor all that furnishes the closet of an apothecary's widow."

ambersune (*n.*) A variant of *embrasure*. Col. Nicholas Fish in 1776 wrote to Richard Varick,
"The old battery . . . with a sufficient number of ambersunes."

amerciament (*n.*) A fine or penalty at the discretion of the court, usually imposed on an officer for misconduct or neglect; amercement. The 1697 Courtlandt Manor Grant provided,
" . . . and all Fines, Issues and Amercements at the said Court Leet."

American Legion The body of Loyalist troops raised by Benedict Arnold after he fled to the British in 1780. He was successful in enlisting only 212 men, who participated in the raid on Ft. Griswold and New London the following year.

Ames Medulla A statement of Calvinist doctrine written by William Ames (1576–1633).

amusette (*n.*) A light field piece. From French *amuse* 'a toy.' In 1775 John Adams reported,
"They are carting patarares and making amusettes."

amygd. (*n.*) Almond. An abbreviation of *Amygdalaceae*, its Latin botanical name.

Anabaptist (*n.*) A member of a Baptist sect which did not baptise its members until they reached adulthood.

anagreeta (*n.*) Corn picked before ripening and then dried. Probably from an Indian word.

Anamaboe (*n.*) Anamabu, in present-day Ghana. In 1756 Captain David Lindsey noticed:
"the Schooner Sierra Leone from Anamaboe" carried a cargo of 44 slaves.

anatomy (*n.*) An anatomical study. The Massachusetts Body of Liberties in 1641 prohibited,
"the body be unburied twelve hours unless it be in case of anatomy."

anchor (*n.*) A frequent misspelling of *anker*, about ten gallons. In 1719 William Byrd admitted that:
"a smuggler brought some brandy and I bought two half anchors."

ancient (*n.*) A flag or streamer.

Anderson's Pills A laxative containing aloes and jalap. Anderson's Scotts Pills were first produced by Patrick Anderson in 1630. In 1739 William Byrd wrote that he'd:
"had five stools from Anderson's Pills."

angel (*n.*) An English coin issued between 1470 and 1634 with the image of St. Michael slaying the dragon. In 1619 the Virginia General Assembly passed a law stipulating that servants caught trading with the Indians were to be punished by whipping,
"unless the master redeem it off with the payment of an angel."

anis. (*n.*) An abbreviation of Latin *anisum*, 'anise.' Anise oil was used to relieve colic and to flavor alcoholic and oily liquids.

anker (*n.*) A liquid measure of about ten gallons; a dry measure of one-third barrel. Frequently misspelled *anchor*.

an't (*v.*) An abbreviation of *am not*. In his 1766 diary, John Adams wrote,
"Come, come, Mr. Veasey, says Master Joseph Cleverly, don't you say too much; I an't of that mind."

antic (*adj.*) Odd. In 1684 Increase Mather complained that:
"the boy was growing antic as he was on the journey."

antimo. (*n.*) An abbreviation of Latin *antimonium*, 'antimony,' prescribed to counteract numbness or pains in the limbs.

Antinomian (*n.*) A member of the Protestant sect which opposed the doctrine that the moral law is obligatory.

apartment (*n.*) **(1)** A room in a building. In 1760 John Galt wrote,
"Mr. Robinson conducted the artist to the inner apartment."
(2) A place separated; a compartment. Washington, in his 1760 diary, reported that he:
"mixt my compost in a box with ten apartments."

aperto prelio *Latin.* In open battle.

apostle (*n.*) A short statement of a case sent on appeal to a higher court, together with a statement that the entire record will follow. From Latin *apostolus* 'something or someone sent out.'

apparel (*n.*) The equipment of a sailing vessel: masts, rigging, sails, etc. The Naval Act of 1660 referred to:
"a vessel with all its guns, furniture, tackle, ammunition and apparel."

apparitor (*n.*) An officer of the ecclesiastical court. In 1771 Franklin wrote,
"He saw the apparitor coming, who was an officer of the spiritual court."

apple leather A food made from apples that have been boiled into a paste, which is rolled out to dry in the sun. The resulting sheet was the color and toughness of leather.

apple pomace The residue of apple cider. In 1768 Washington:
"saved Apple Pumace in the New Garden from Crab Apples."

apprehend (*v.*) To learn about. In 1760 Washington wrote,
"apprehending the herring were come."

appurtenance (*n.*) Something that is accessory to something else; an adjunct, such as a right of way, an easement, or a small building. The 1701 grant of Scarsdale, N. Y. to Caleb Heathcote read,
"William The Third . . . doe . . . grant . . . profitts, benefits, advantages and appurtenances."

a quanto . . . a tanto *Latin.* By how much . . . by so much. In the 1640s John Winthrop wrote,
"The Governor was excused a quanto but not a tanto." That is, apparently he was excused, but not quite in the manner or degree he had expected.

aqua vitae *Latin.* [Literally, 'water of life.'] Spirituous liquor, especially brandy.

argent viv. An abbreviation of Latin *argentum vivum*, 'quicksilver.'

ark (*n.*) A large barge used to carry freight on rivers; a descendant of Noah's. A 1659 magazine reported,
"Our great boat called the ark, being near 80 foot long and 30 wide."

armadillo (*n.*) A small armed vessel that got its name from the diminutive of Spanish *armada* 'armed.'

Arminianism (*n.*) The doctrine of a Protestant sect created by Dutch theologian Jacobus Arminius (1560–1609). Their tenets were the basis for Methodism in America.

arni (*n.*) A shortened form of *arnica*, a liniment made from the herb of that name. It was also used for dissolving coagulated blood.

arrack (*n.*) A distilled rum with fresh fruit added. William Byrd and his friends drank:
"a bowl of rack punch" in 1733.

arroba (*n.*) A Spanish or Portuguese measure of weight of from 25 to 36 pounds. An Arabic word meaning 'quarter,' it being a quarter of a Spanish *quintal.*

arrow-wood (*n.*) Viburnum and dogwood, whose straight, thin branches made them particularly desirable for arrows. In 1709 John Lawson wrote,
"Arrow-wood, growing on the banks, is used by the Indians for arrows and gunsticks."

arsesmart *See* **ass smart.**

article (*v.*) To bind by articles of covenant or stipulation. After the 1676 Bacon Rebellion, the leaders:
"articled for themselves and whomelse they could."

artist (*n.*) Anyone with a special skill or knowledge, as an artisan, surveyor, expert seaman, scientist, etc. In 1649 John Winthrop wrote,
"they sent out a pinnace well manned . . . under the conduct of a good artist." In

1658 the citizens of Lancaster, Mass. asked,
"Iff wee may choose an artist . . . to lay our towne bounds."

asafetida (*n.*) A foul-smelling gum resin prescribed as a sedative in hysterical and nervous conditions.

ash cake Corn pone, wrapped in cabbage leaves to keep it clean, and baked in hot ashes.

asinucoe (*n.*) A spelling for *ass* 'donkey' used by the Virginia House of Burgesses in 1631.

asmart *See* **ass smart.**

Assembly of the XIX The body governing The West India Company, and therefore New Netherland from 1609 to 1664. It was made up of delegates from five Dutch provinces and the States General.

assignation (*n.*) A making over by transfer of title; an assignment, not a tryst. In 1650 the Connecticut Colony stated,
"Assignation is when simply any thing is ceded, yielded and assigned to another."

assize (*n.*) A standard of weights and measures. This word is the precursor of both *excise* and *size*, the latter being is a shortened form of it. A 1749 South Carolina law:
"made and provided for regulating the price and assize of bread."

Assize, Court of The supreme court of the Province of New York from 1674 to 1684, which was also a legislative body. The term was also used in Maryland and Virginia.

ass smart Smartweed or water pepper. According to Manasseh Cutler in 1784,
"Arsmart occasions severe smarting when rubbed on the flesh."

assumpsit (*n.*) A legal action in which the plaintiff claims damages owing to a breach of contract by the defendant. From Latin for 'he has assumed.'
"Assumpsit is a voluntary promise made by word by which a man assumeth. . . to perform or pay any thing to another." [1641, *Termes de la Ley*]

astragalus (*n.*) A gummy exudation of a plant related to the pea, used to increase the size of pills and to soothe tickling coughs.

asunder (*adj.*) Apart in time. In 1737 Jonathan Edwards worried that:
"our sacraments are eight weeks asunder."

a tiptoe Anticipatory. In his 1766 diary John Adams described a Braintree, Mass., man as:
"a tiptoe for town meeting."

auditory (*n.*) Any sort of audience.

aur. (*n.*) An abbreviation of Latin *aurum* 'gold.'

aurigation (*n.*) A wagon or a carriage ride. From Latin *aurigare* 'to drive a chariot.' In 1679 Charles Wolley reported from New York that,
"The diversion used by the Dutch is aurigation."

auripigment (*n.*) Trisulfide of arsenic, a bright yellow pigment used in paint. From Latin *auripigmentum* 'gold coloring matter.' In 1672 John Lederer met:
"Five Indians whose faces were covered with auripigment."

Avalon (*n.*) A tract in southeastern Newfoundland which was not successfully colonized. George Calvert, Lord of Baltimore, was proprietor of the provinces of Maryland and Avalon. Everybody knows where Maryland is, but not many know where Avalon was.

average (*n.*) **(1)** Miscellaneous charges such as port duty. From French *avarie* 'port dues.' A 1754 bill of lading provided,
"goods with primage and average accustomed."
(2) A payment to the master of a vessel, over and above the regular freight charge, for his care of the goods transported. A 1740 letter offered,
"5% more for the average."
(3) Pasturage found after the harvest; stubble. In 1679 Charles Wolley reported,
"Horses . . . nourish themselves with the barks of Trees, and such average and herbage as they can find."

ax (*v.*) A spelling reflecting one pronunciation of *ask*. A song protesting the stamp tax in 1765 rhymed it with *tax*:
"I shant do the thing that you ax."

azile (*n.*) Probably a misreading of *asylum*. In 1693 the Huguenots of New Rochelle, N. Y., sent a petition to Gov. Fletcher,
"Their Majesties, by their proclamation of ye 25th of April 1689, did grant them an azile in all their dominions."

babyhut (*n.*) A badly designed covered carriage. Also called a *booby hutch*. Anna Winslow's 1772 diary recorded:
"She might have sent either one of her chaises, her chariot or her babyhutt."

bafta (*n.*) A cotton fabric from India. From Persian *baft* 'woven.'

bag holland A coarse linen cloth used for bags. Samuel Sewall's 1693 letter book referred to:
"One piece of Shepard's Holland or coarse Bag-Holland."

bailiwick (*n.*) The area under the administrative jurisdiction of a bailiff. A 1700 New Jersey document instructed:
"the Sheriffe summon twenty foure of good & lawful men in his bailewick."

bait (*v.*) To feed an animal. From Middle English *baiten* 'to feed.' In 1744 Dr. Alexander Hamilton wrote,
"I baited my horse," referring to feeding it.

baize (*n.*) A coarse woolen material with a long nap. From French *baie* 'bay colored.' A 1787 Philadelphia newspaper advertised a:
"jacket lined with green baize."

baldric (*n.*) A shoulder strap used to support a sword.

balk (*n.*) **(1)** A ridge of land left unplowed between furrows or at the end of the field. In 1788 Washington wrote,
"All hands went to Hoeing up the Balks between."
(2) A great beam in a chimney from which utensils were hung.

ballafon (*n.*) A musical instrument like a marimba. Probably an African word.

ballarag (*n.*) A variant of *bullirag* 'bullying language.' A 1774 Connecticut document read,
"If I can't answer them by ballarag, I can by small sword."

ball play A game that was the forerunner of lacrosse, played by both male and female Indians. Henry Timberlake in his 1765 memoirs recorded,
"I was not a little pleased likewise with their ball-play . . . especially when the women played."

balm (*n.*) The herb melissa from which a tea was brewed. Thomas Morton in 1637 mentioned:
"Honeysuckles, balme and divers other good herbes."

bals. *Latin.* (*n.*) An abbreviation of *balsamum,* 'balsam.'

band (*n.*) A collar. There were *standing bands* and *falling bands.* They were fastened with a *band string,* and clean ones were kept in a *band box.* Hence the expression:
"right out of a band box" means something fresh and clean, and *band box* is still used in reference to a small baseball field. John Winthrop in 1649 described an unkempt man:
"He came in his worst clothes . . . without a band."

banjor (*n.*) A variant of *banjo.* In 1781 Jefferson observed,
"The instrument proper to them is the Banjor which they brought hither from Africa."

banker (*n.*) A man or ship that fished the Newfoundland Banks. A 1710 Boston newspaper reported,
"A French Banker of fourteen guns, laden with Fish, arrived there from Newfoundland."

bank oil Menhaden oil. John Rowe in 1760 requested,
"I desire it may be of the pale sort of bank oil."

banquette (*n.*) A platform inside the outer wall of a fort for defenders to stand on when firing weapons. A 1766 report from Albany stated,
"There is only a stockade round the place with a large banquet."

banyan (*n.*) A loose-fitting garment for men, women, and children, copied from an Indian costume. In 1744 Dr. Alexander Hamilton described someone as being:
"wrapped up in a banyan."

Baptist (*n.*) A member of the sect that led the opposition to the established church in all the colonies.

bar (*n.*) An athletic contest in which men competed at throwing a heavy bar of iron or wood, forerunner of today's Scottish sport of tossing the caber. In 1656 John Winthrop deplored men:
"in the street at play openly some pitching the bar."

barber (*n.*) One who performed blood letting and minor surgery, as distinguished from a surgeon. A 1722 memoir reported,
"No surgeon to be had but a sorry country barber."

barco longo *Spanish.* 'long barge.' A fishing boat with two or three masts. A 1711 South Carolina document reported,
"Having then a brigantine and barco longo mounted with cannon."

bardan (*n.*) A variant spelling of *bardane* 'burdock.'

bargain (*v.*) To make small talk. Philip Fithian in 1773 wrote of:
"several assembled to dine and bargain."

barilla (*n.*) Saltwort, or the sodium carbonate that is produced by burning it. William Stork in 1765 described:
"salt water marshes full of the barilla."

bark[1] (*n.*) A two-masted vessel, square rigged on the foremast, fore-and-aft rigged on the mainmast.

bark² (*n.*) **(1)** A bed of cyprus bark. In 1733 William Byrd reported:
"I slept very comfortably upon my bark."
(2) Peruvian bark; cinchona from which quinine is derived. In the sixteenth century it was purported to have cured the Countess of Chinchon of malaria. In 1733 William Byrd reported:
"taking another ounce of bark."

barkentine (*n.*) A three-masted vessel, square-rigged on the fore- and mainmasts, fore-and-aft on the mizzenmast.

barleycorn (*n.*) As a measure of length, one third of an inch; as a measure of weight, one gram.

barley water Barley water was used for inflammatory disorders. In 1679 Charles Wolley observed,
"The women are not so busie . . . with the strong barley water."

barm (*n.*) The scum that forms on the top of fermenting beer. A seventeenth-century cookbook refers to a:
"full quart of ale barm."

barnish (*v.*) To grow fat. Goodwife Charles of New Haven reported in 1649 that:
"Ther was a maide that satt neare her at meeting that did barnish apace." She was probably as big as a barn.

barony (*n.*) A political division of a county in Pennsylvania and South Carolina. In 1669 the Constitution of Carolina provided that:
"each county shall consist of eight signories, eight baronies and four precincts."

barracan (*n.*) A thick, strong stuff, like camlet. From Arabic *barrakan* 'camlet.' In 1638 a lady bequeathed:
"my petticoat of barracan."

barrow (*n.*) A castrated hog. In 1763 Washington counted:
"12 lambs, 2 sows, 5 barrows, 15 pigs."

Barrowist (*n.*) A member of a Puritan sect having Congregationalist views; for Henry Barrow (1589–1593).

barvel (*n.*) A fisherman's leather apron. A 1639 Maine document reported,
"Our men lost many of their thinges in the bootes, barvells . . . buckets."

bashaw (*n.*) An honorary Turkish title, later pasha. In 1776 Hugh Brackenridge complained,
"Thrust in Bashaws and Viceroys to rule."

basilicon (*n.*) An ointment of beeswax, rosin, and lard that would not melt at body temperature. It was applied to alleviate wounds and ulcers.

bason (*n.*) A work-bench with a heated metal plate, used in making felt for hats.

basset (*n.*) A card game similar to faro, said to have been invented in Venice by a nobleman who was banished for introducing it. In 1710 William Byrd said that he:
"played at basset."

bastard (1) (*n.*) A sweetened wine. A 17th-century recipe instructed,
"put in a pint of basterd white wine."
(2) (*adj.*) Unusual; differing from the normal. In 1753 a Maryland engraver made
"bastard carving."

Bateman's Drops Dr. Bateman's Pectoral Drops, patented by Benjamin Okell in

1726, contained opium and camphor. They were prescribed as a cure for rheumatism, agues, and hysterics.

bath (*n.*) A body of water adequate for bathing. The royal grant of Morrisania in New York in 1697 included:
"brooks, rivulets, baths, inlets."

bath metal A brass alloy, originally developed in Bath, England. Its sale was advertised in a 1729 Philadelphia newspaper.

bat horse A horse that carried the baggage of an army officer. From French *bat* 'pack-saddle.' In 1757 Washington stated that:
"the officers provided bat horses at their own expense."

bat money A monetary allowance for carrying military baggage. In 1758 Washington wrote,
"As your troops are allowed bat money."

battalia (*n.*) Troops arranged as for action. In 1772 Joseph Warren said that troops were:
"drawn up in a regular battalia."

batteau (*n.*) A flat-bottomed boat, tapering at both ends, propelled by oars, poles, or square sails. An adopted French word. Benedict Arnold's treasonous estimate in 1780 of the troops at West Point was:
"inclusive of 166 batteaux men at Verplanks."

batter (*v.*) To beat. When William Byrd wrote in 1709,
"I ate battered eggs," he meant 'scrambled.'

battle hammed Having thick buttocks. An obsolete word, unrelated to 'fight,' *battle* meant 'to grow fat.' A 1727 Boston advertisement described a runaway slave as,
"A young negro servant . . . battle hammed and goes somewhat waddling."

battle kneed Having thick knees. *See* **battle hammed.** A 1743 thief in New Jersey was described as of:
"ruddy complexion, light hair, battle kneed."

bavin (*n.*) Kindling; a bundle of small sticks.

bawbee (*n.*) A British halfpenny. Possibly from the Laird of Sillebawby, 16th-century mintmaster. John Leacock used the word in a 1776 play:
"I care not a bawbee for them all."

bay gall Swampy ground covered with sweet bay. A 1775 description of Florida included,
"savannahs, swamps, marshes, bay and cypress galls."

Bay line In Rhode Island, the boundary line of the Massachusetts Bay Colony. The 1725 Providence Records refer to:
"the highway from Town to the Bay Line."

Bayman (*n.*) **(1)** One who lived near Massachusetts Bay. In 1643 Gov. Shirley of Massachusetts wrote,
"Pay Mr. Andrews or the Bay men, by his order."
(2) A sailor on a ship from the Bay of Honduras:
" . . . as Capt. Lyde was afterward inform'd by some of the Bay-men" appeared in a 1723 Boston newspaper.

bays (*n.*) A variant of *baize.* The Woollen Act of 1699 spells it this way.

bay salt Salt produced by evaporation of sea water. Whether the *bay* refers to the site of evaporation or to the brownish color of the salt is a matter of dispute. In the 1774 Massachusetts Provincial Congress they referred to:
"the method used in that part of France where they make bay salt."

beak (*n.*) A metal-clad ram on the prow of a vessel. In John Trumbull's 1774 poem, *An Elegy on the Time*:
"But hostile beaks affright the guarded shore."

beak horn A variant of *bickern*, an anvil with a beak or point. In 1636 John Winthrop wrote,
"Here was an anvil with a beak horn at the end of it."

beareager (*n.*) Vinegar made from soured beer.
"With any Beare or Beereager" appeared in a 1639 Maryland document.

bear garden Originally a place for bear baiting, later any place of uncouth conduct. In 1647 Samuel Ward wrote,
"If the state of England shall . . . tolerate [other religions] the civil state [will become] a bear garden."

beastlings (*n.*) Rich milk produced immediately after calving; beestings; beastings. A woman was described in 1723:
"She does not know . . . how to boil a skillet of Beastlings . . . without letting it turn."

beat (*v.*) **(1)** To beat a distinctive signal or command on a drum. In 1781 Gen. Heath reported,
"They beat a parley," meaning 'They signaled for a conference with an enemy.'
(2) To crush. Washington in 1768:
"began to beat cyder at Doeg Run."

beat up To search thoroughly. In 1776 William Smith wrote,
"Officers were sent to beat up for volunteers."

beaver (*n.*) A hat made of beaver fur; also called a *castor*. A 1739 *Poor Richard's Almanac* advertised,
"William Reynolds . . . makes and sells all sorts of Hats, Beavers, Castors and Felts."

beaverette (*n.*) Rabbit fur dyed to look like beaver. A 1731 Boston newspaper offered,
"Several sorts of English goods, as Bevers, Beaverette, Castor Hats."

beaver maker One who made beaver hats.
"Theodore Atkins of Boston . . . beaver maker," advertised in a 1652 Boston newspaper.

beaver mineral *See* **castor.**

bed case Mattress ticking.

beetle ring A metal ring around a beetle, or heavy mallet, to keep it from splitting.

beforehand (*adv.*) In advance; early. Franklin wrote in 1771,
"I now began to think of getting a little money beforehand."
See also **behindhand.**

beggar's velvet An inexpensive fabric similar to velvet. A Philadelphia newspaper (1721) reported,
"He had a pair of spare breeches of beggar's velvet."

behindhand (*adj.*) In arrears; in debt. In 1771 Franklin wrote,
"Harry went continually behindhand."
See also **beforehand.**

behindments (*n.*) Arrearages. In 1758, Gloucester, Mass., had a problem,
"the behindments of the Parish taxes."

behoof (*n.*) An advantage, profit. The 1697 patent for Bedford, N.Y., states,
"the only proper use benefit and behoofe."

beldame (*n.*) An ugly old woman; a shrew. Charles Lee, in writing to Robert Morris in 1776, referred to England as:
"A beldame step mother whose every act is cruelty."

ben (*v.*) To repair. In 1660 in Huntington, L.I., a man:
"did get a workman in the spring to ben the mill."

benefit of clergy Originally, exemption of the clergy from trial by an ordinary court; later, from capital punishment; still later, the exemption was extended to all clerks and those who were literate. At no time did the exemption apply to high treason.

bengal (*n.*) A fabric from Bengal, India, made of silk and hair. It was advertised in a 1774 Philadelphia newspaper.

benne (*n.*) Sesame. In 1775 Bernard Romans wrote,
"The negroes use it as food . . . they call it benni."

bergamotte (*n.*) A fruit produced by grafting a citron to a pear tree. It was used to produce a fragrant medicinal oil. A 1782 Hartford newspaper advertised,
"quill Jesuits Bark, opium, essence of Bergamotte."

Berlin needle work *See* **Dresden work.**

berme (*n.*) A narrow space between the moat and the wall of a fortification. If the wall fell down, it would fall on the berme and not fill the moat. In 1775 Richard Montgomery wrote,
"By the time we arrived the frais around the berme would be destroyed."

beryllan (*n.*) Probably *barmellion* or *bermillion*, a kind of fustian. A 1729 Philadelphia newspaper advertised,
"beryllan and plain Calamanco."

beset (*v.*) To arrange for. In 1718, William Byrd complained that he,
"sat in the gallery about an hour but none of our tickets came up though I beset [them] myself this morning."

besom (*n.*) A broom. In 1698 Cotton Mather reported,
"A besom gave him a blow on the head."

bespeak (*v.*) To order or engage beforehand. In 1770 Washington complained that the:
"millstones . . . were thinner by two inches than what were bespoke."

best hand, at the Cheapest. In 1739, William Byrd recommended to:
"ransack the fripperies of Long Lane . . . for finery at the best hand."

Bethlehemite (*n.*) A member of the Moravian Brethren at Bethlehem, Pa.

bettering house A poor house where work habits were taught. In 1774 Silas Deane described:
"What is called a Bettering House, in other words a poor house."

betty lamp (*n.*) A shallow, metal, grease-filled dish with a lip on which lay a linen wick. From Early English *bettyngs* 'oil or fat.'

bever (*n.*) A small repast between meals. In 1646, Harvard College decreed:
"No scholar shall . . . be absent from his studys . . . above . . . halfe an houre at afternoone Bever."

bez. miner. An abbreviation of *bezoar mineral*, antimony oxide. The stone is a concretion found in the intestines of ruminants. Ground, it was taken to promote perspiration.

bib (*n.*) The upper part of an apron. Anna Winslow in 1772 wrote,
"I was dressed in my yellow coat, my black bib and apron."

bickern (*n.*) An anvil ending in a beak, or point.

bien venue A sum assessed on a newcomer. [French, lit. 'welcome'] Franklin encountered this custom when he started as a printer in Philadelphia in 1723:
"A new bien venue or sum for drink."

bigoted (*adj.*) Blindly attached to some creed or opinion. Gouverneur Morris wrote,
"He is bigoted to it."

bilboes (*n. pl.*) A long, heavy bolt with shackles that slide along it and are locked around a prisoner's legs above the ankles. The etymology is uncertain.

bill[1] (*n.*) An official list of births and deaths, published weekly. Franklin in 1751 wrote,
"an observation made upon the bills of mortality, christenings, etc."

bill[2] (*n.*) A battle axe on a long staff. The Anglo-Saxon word for *sword*. The Provincial Congress in New York in 1776 raised two companies for the Continental Army and moved,
"It is expected that each man furnish himself with a good gun and bayonet . . . and two bills."

billa vera A true bill. [From Latin].

billet[1] (*n.*) A small stick of wood cut to fuel length; sometimes used as a club. In 1630 Francis Higginson wrote that in Salem, Mass. wood was:
"cheaper than they sell billets and faggots in London."

billet[2] (*n.*) A ticket or pass. In 1789 Jefferson received:
"a billet for the audience."

billingsgate (*n.*) A fishmonger, generally foul-mouthed, named for the London market celebrated for fish and foul language near a gate in the old London wall named for an early property owner. Edward Ward in 1699 wrote,
"Rum, alias Kill Devil, is as much ador'd by the American English, as a dram of brandy is by an old Billingsgate."

Bill of Rights A restatement of the laws dealing with the relationship between the British Parliament and the Crown enacted in 1689.

bilsted (n.) *See* **boilsted.**

binder (*n.*) A garment like a cummerbund, worn by children and adult males. In 1688 Samuel Sewall noted,
"Shifted my linen this day, shirts, drawers, wastcoat, binder." He apparently didn't change them often.

birchen (*adj.*) Made of birch, as a *birchen broom.*

Birching Lane A street in London, known for the Cockney fripperers, dealers in cast-off clothing; it was named for one Birchouer, a former landowner William Bradford wrote from Plimouth Plantation in 1646 that:
"there was sent over som Birching Lane suits in the ship." The Pilgrims wore second-hand clothing.

bird's-eye stuff A worsted cloth with small diamond design; sometimes also known as diaper cloth.

bishop (*n.*) **(1)** A half-circular pillow stuffed with horsehair, used as, but larger than, a bustle.
(2) A drink concocted by adding oranges or lemons to wine.

bissextile (*n.*) Leap year. From Latin *bissextus* 'twice six.' The sixth of the calends of March (February 24) was the intercalated day every fourth year.

bistoury (*n.*) A surgical instrument similar to a scalpel.

bit (*n.*) A Spanish *real*, one eighth of a Spanish *peso*. Two bits were a quarter of a *peso*.

bitch (*v.*) To botch. Indentured servant Elizabeth Spriggs in 1756 was whipped for bitching.

bite (*n.*) A cheat. A 1755 Massachusetts document confided,
"I'm told horse dealers here are great bites."

bittern (*n.*) A liquid the Indians made from roots; it was used to drug fish so that they might be caught easily. James Adair in 1775 instructed,
"til the water is sufficiently impregnated with the intoxicating bittern."

bitters (*n.*) Quinine. In 1773 Philip Fithian took:
"half a Gill of bitters to qualify my humours."

bitter wort (*n.*) The yellow gentian. A brew made from its leaves was taken to counteract fever. In 1739 William Byrd suffered,
"and then my fever began to come. However I ate bitter wort."

black (*adj.*) Brunette. When William Byrd in 1710 described:
"a pretty black girl" he meant she was not a blonde.

black coat A disparaging term for a minister. Edward Johnson in 1654 wrote,
"I'le bring you a woman that preaches better gospell than any of your black coats."

black fish The tautog; also a small kind of whale about 20 feet long.

black frost A frost so severe that vegetables turn black. Washington wrote in his 1787 diary,
"This morning there was a small white frost and a black one which was so severe as to stop brick laying."

black jack A large drinking mug made of leather with a tar coating. A 1775 Massachusetts document said,
"We left a pint black jack abt half full of water."

blackroot (*n.*) *Veronocastrum virginicum*; taken to induce vomit. In 1710 William Byrd reported that:
"Dick Cox sent to me for two or three purgatives. I sent him some blackroot sufficient for three doses."

blasting (*n.*) **(1)** A blight to crops. In 1642 the Governor of Virginia was warned of:
"relying on one single harvest, drought, blasting or otherwise."

(2) Flatulence. An 18th-century book observed that:
"Oyle of rue is good for wind in ye side & against blasting."

blazing iron A gun. Thomas Anburey in 1778 wrote of:
"a New Englander riding in the woods with his blasting iron (the term they give to a musket or a gun)."

bleaching ground The area on which cloth was bleached by exposure to sunlight. In 1767 the citizens of South Carolina remonstrated that:
"It is therefore in vain for us to attempt the laying out of vinyards, sheep walks or bleaching grounds."

bleed (*v.*) To remove blood. During the Colonial period the cure for many ailments was the removal of liquids (which they called *humours*) from the body by bleeding, cupping, and purging. In one instance where quantity was mentioned, ten ounces of blood were drained.

blister (*n.*) A plaster that caused blisters. Removing serum from blisters was one way to remove liquid from the body. *See also* **bleed.** In 1710 William Byrd reported that:
"Old Moll continued to have the headache and I put a blister behind her neck."

blonde lace Lace made from silk.

bloodroot (*n.*) A plant named for the color of its roots; also called *puccoon, turmeric* and *red root.* In 1722 Thomas Dudley recommended,
"Remedies for the sting of a rattlesnake . . . is . . . bloodroot."

bloody back A derogatory name for a British soldier, a redcoat. A 1770 Boston newspaper reported that the mob taunted,
"Come you Rascals, you bloody backs, you lobster scoundrels."

bloody flux Dysentery; a disease in which the discharges from the bowels have a mixture of blood.

bloomery (*n.*) The first forge through which iron passes after it is melted from the ore into a *bloom*, a mass of wrought iron. A 1757 document reported that:
"there were two Furnaces in the Mannor of Cortland & several Bloomeries."

blossom hemp Hemp with pollen, that is, male hemp; *seed hemp* is female. Washington in 1766:
"Began to pull hemp . . . to late for the blossom hemp."

blue (*adj.*) Obscene. Perhaps from the color of burning brimstone.

blueskin (*n.*) A zealous rebel. A 1783 poem went,
"James Rivington, printer of late to the king,/But now a republican./ Let him stand where he is/ And he'll turn a True Blue-Skin."

blue wing A kind of duck. In 1709 William Byrd:
"ate blue wing for dinner."

Board of Trade and Plantations A board made up of several lords of the Privy Council to whom the supervision and management of the British colonies were entrusted. Created in 1696, it functioned until the Revolution.

bobbin lace Lace made by knotting threads on bobbins around pins.

bobbinet *See* **bobbin lace.**

bodies (*n.*) A bodice. This ladies' outer garment looked like a corset, laced both in front and in back. A 1674 book on plants observed,

"A flower without its Emplacement would hang as uncouth and tawdry as a Lady without her Bodies."

bodkin (*n.*) A dagger. Capt. John Smith reported a 1608 punishment,
"A bodkin was thrust through his tongue."

Body of Liberties A code of laws largely drafted by Nathaniel Ward (1578–1652) adopted by the General Court of the Massachusetts Bay Colony in 1641.

bogue (*v.*) To walk. In 1775 one Rauck admitted,
"We were four days boguing in the woods seeking the way."

bohea (*n.*) A coarse, low-priced black tea from the Wu-i hills in China. Pronounced *boo-hee*. A 1773 song threatened,
"We will throw your bohea into the sea."

boilsted (*n.*) A variant of *bilsted*, maple wood. A 1776 inventory included:
"1 large boilsted table."

bole[1] (*n.*) A dry measure; six bushels of oats, corn, barley or potatoes; four of wheat or beans.

bole[2] (*n.*) A variant spelling of *bolus*, a soft mass of anything medicinally made into a large pill. A Virginia doctor's 1658 bill asked 36 pounds of tobacco:
"for a bole as before."

bolster (*n.*) The padding worn under a skirt to enlarge the hips and buttocks. In impolite language it was known as a 'bum roll.' In 1731 Swift wrote:
"Off she slips The bolsters, that supply her hips."

bolt (*v.*) To separate wheat from chaff by sifting it through coarse silk, linen, or hair cloths in a bolting mill.

bolts (*n.*) Leg irons. A form of punishment. In 1619 The Virginia General Assembly, as a punishment for drunkenness, decreed that an offender must:
"lie in bolts 12 hours in the house of the provost marshal."

bombazine (*n.*) A twilled dress fabric of silk and worsted.

bonavist (*n.*) A variety of bean. In 1682 Thomas Ash reported that in Carolina:
"they have a great Variety . . . beans, pease . . . and Bonavist."

bond slave An indentured servant. The Massachusetts Body of Liberties in 1641 provided that:
"There shall never be any bond-slavery, villenage or captivity among us."

bone lace Bobbin lace. The first bobbins were small bones. A 1636 Massachusetts law provided that:
"No person . . . shall make or sell any bone lace, or other lace, to bee worn upon any garment."

bonnyclabber (*n.*) Thickened sour milk. [From Irish *bainne* 'milk' and *clabar* 'the dasher or lid of a churn']. In 1731 a Massachusetts document recorded:
"Today we dined on roast mutton . . . mixed with bonnyclabber sweetened with molasses."

booby (*n.*) Baby. [Sense derived from the context, but not found in any dictionary in this sense.] *Poor Richard's Almanac* quoted John Gay (1685–1732),
"Where yet was ever found the mother, Who'd change her booby for another."

booby hutch *See* **babyhut.**

boodle (*n.*) Personal effects. [From Dutch *boedel* 'estate, possession']. A 1699 document stated,
"Elisabeth had the Boedel of Jan Verbeek, desceased, in hands.''

booger (*n.*) A pronunciation spelling of *bugger*. In low English it merely means a man, a person, not a sodomite. A 1770 Boston newspaper reported that the mob taunted,
"Where were the boogers, where were the cowards''

book (*n.*) **(1)** The Bible; in this case representing benefit of clergy. A 1639 Maryland document read,
"Then was read the Bill . . . for allowing Book to certain felonies.''
(2) A cloth so called because it was folded like a book. *See* **kenting** and **muslin.**

boor (*n.*) A farmer in New Netherlands. [From Dutch *boer* 'farmer']. In 1701 Charles Wolley wrote that he heard quarreling:
"betwixt two Dutch Boors.''

boot (*n.*) An extremely painful form of punishment. Four pieces of wood tied by wet thongs encased the leg; when the thongs dried and shrank an excruciating pressure was created. In 1711 William Byrd:
"put the boot'' on a slave.

boothose (*n.*) Stocking hose or spatterdashes.

boot top To coat the underwater part of a vessel with tallow and sulfur to prevent the growth of barnacles.

borage (*n.*) A plant of the genus *Borago*, used medicinally and in salads.

borderer (*n.*) A person who lives on or near a border. In 1722 William Byrd wrote,
"nor were these worthy borderers content to shelter runaway slaves.''

borough town A self-governing town which could send representatives to a provincial assembly.

bosom bottle A small flask, tucked into a stomacher, to hold flowers.

bossloper (*n.*) An inhabitant of the woods. [From Dutch *boschlooper* 'wood runner']

boston (*n.*) A card game for four using two decks, similar to whist. French officers created it and named it for the siege of Boston.

bottom (*n.*) **(1)** A ship. A 1696 Virginia law stated,
"He hath power to enter into any Ship, Bottome, Boat or other Vessell.''
(2) A ship in its figurative sense. Boston's instructions to its delegates to the Massachusetts Legislature in 1764 observed,
"Other Northern American colonies are embarked with us in this most important bottom.''
(3) Flat land adjoining a river. In 1765 George Croghan described land in Ohio,
"this creek . . . between two fine rich bottoms.''
(4) The foundation or groundwork of anything. In 1774 Richard Henry Lee recommended to:
"lay our rights upon the broadest bottom.''

bounty (*n.*) A payment by a government as an inducement to do something. In addition to the well-known meaning of a payment for killing wolves, etc., in 1723 it was proposed that a bounty be paid to encourage the production of white pine trees for masts and for tar.

bouting rows The rows made by the round-trip of a plow. In 1767 Washington:
"sowed the bouting Rows at Doeg Run with 1½ Bushels.''

bouwerie (*n.*) A farm. The Dutch word from which *The Bowery* in New York came.

bowl (*n.*) An American Indian game for two. Six or eight small bones were tossed into the air and caught in a bowl.

bowse[1] (*v.*) To pull or haul hard. John Leacock used the word in a 1776 play.
"I must bowse taught there, or we shall get at loggerheads soon." *Also* **bouse.**

bowse[2] (*v.*) To drink too much; to stagger drunkenly. In 1774 Philip Fithian told of a friend,
"up he bowses with a bottle of rum in his hand."

bowyer (*n.*) **(1)** An archer.
(2) One who makes bows. There was a 1697 law:
"concerning Bowyers and the making and keeping of bows."

box (1) (*n.*) A cut in a tree from which to collect sap or resin. In 1720 P. Dudley observed,
"The box you make may hold about a pint."
(2) (*v.*) To make such a cut. In 1700 Springfield, Mass., enacted a law stating that:
"no Stranger . . . shal box any trees . . . for turpentine."

brace (*n.*) Wrist armor.

bracket shoes Snow shoes. A 1648 report from New England stated,
"Hunters persue with bracket shooes."

brake[1] (*n.*) A tool used in breaking flax or hemp. John Winthrop wrote in 1634,
"We . . . have need of . . . a brake for hemp."

brake[2] (*n.*) **(1)** Fern.
(2) An area where fern grows. In 1748 Jared Eliot wrote,
"next to the salt marsh . . . then large Brakes and Bushes."
(3) Any thicket. In 1757 J. Carver recorded,
"I threw myself into a brake."

brand (*n.*) **(1)** The mark of a criminal. Branding was a widely used punishment. A Quaker in Connecticut was branded for engaging in business without a license. The practice of instructing a witness in court to raise his right hand has its root in the former practice of determining thereby if the witness had been branded as a criminal and, if so, what kind.
(2) The word was also used in a figurative sense. An anonymous 1705 Virginia writer explained:
"I advised him to be very wary for he saw the Governor had put a brand upon him."

brandlet (*n.*) A cooking utensil for broiling.

brase (*v.*) To burn; cause food to stick. A 17th-century cookbook instructed,
"Set them on the fire in a pan or pot that will not brase."

brawn (*n.*) Pig flesh, rolled and tied with a string. A 17th-century recipe instructed,
"then roule it up like a coller of brawne."

brazier (*n.*) One who works in brass. In 1771 Franklin went to:
"see joiners, bricklayers, turners, braziers, etc. at their work."

braziletto (*n.*) A kind of red dyewood, inferior to brazilwood, imported from Jamaica. A 1790 newspaper advertised,
"For sale by John Leamy . . . Braziletto Dye wood."

breach (*n.*) An opening along a coastline. In 1624 Capt. John Smith wrote,
"We found many shoules and breaches."

breachy (*adj.*) Apt to break fences. In 1780 Ebenezer Parkman complained,
"My oxen have been breachy."

break (*n.*) **(1)** A variant of *brake* 'a baker's kneading trough.'
(2) The annual quantity of hemp. *See also* **brake**[1].
(3) Ground meal. In 1771 Franklin wrote,
"My breakfast was a long time break and milk."

break the Pope's neck An indoor game played by a "Pope" and "friars" in which
a plate was spun. Philip Fithian played it in 1773.

breast horn button A coat button made of horn.

breathe (*v.*) To exercise. In 1710 William Byrd wrote,
"I ran to breathe myself."

breeches (*n.*) A baggy garment tied below the knees and fastened to a doublet. A 1661
diarist recorded that he:
"put both his legs through one of his knees of his breeches."

breviate (*n.*) A brief account; a summary. From French *brève* 'short.' A 1665 New
York document said,
"of which ye comrs [commissioners] made a breviat."

bridewell (*n.*) A jail, after the one of this name in London. The jail, built in 1688 and
demolished in 1864, was on the site of the Palace of Bridewell near the well of St.
Bride's [Bridget's] Church. In 1767 it was recorded,
"We have not a bridewell, whipping post or a pair of stocks in the province."
[South Carolina]

brig (*n.*) A square-rigged, two-masted vessel. A 1722 newspaper reported,
"[the pirates] promise him his Brig again when they have taken a better Vessel."

brigand (*n.*) Probably a variation of *brigantine*. In a 1718 letter William Pepperill
wrote,
"We have a large brigand which went to Barbados."

brigantine (*n.*) A vessel similar to a brig, but without a square mainsail.

brilliant (*n.*) A silk material. [1774 Philadelphia newspaper.]

Bristol stone Rock crystal from near Bristol, England. In 1699 Lord Bellomont wrote
about Captain William Kidd to the Board of Trade,
"There was in it [an enameled box] a stone ring, which we take to be a Bristoll
Stone."

Bristol water Water from the warm springs at Clifton, near Bristol, England. It was
prescribed for dropsy, internal hemorrhages, immoderate menses, dysentery, scrofula, diabetes, and gleets. William Byrd used it in 1740.

bristowman (*n.*) A ship from Bristol, England. *Bristow* was the early name of *Bristol*.
In 1685 Samuel Sewall wrote,
"A Bristow-man comes in this day and fires five Guns at the Castle."

britania (*n.*) A cloth of cotton, or cotton mixed with linen, made in Brittany. A
1783 Philadelphia newspaper offered:
"Platilla & Britania."

britch (*n.*) The large end of a musket. From German *britsche* 'club.' A Revolutionary War veteran reminisced,
"Every man was ordered on his right knee and the britch of his gun on the ground."

broad arrow A sign used to mark the property of the Crown. It is still used in England to mark military supplies and the clothes of convicts. In Maryland in 1642 it was recorded:
"The sheriff . . . shall mark it with a broad arrow."

broadcloth (*n.*) A fine, plain-woven woolen cloth used mainly for men's clothing. So called because it was woven double-width. In 1691 Samuel Sewall requested,
"Send me an end of coloured Broad-Cloth . . . rather inclining to sad than light colour."

broad seal The great seal of England. The 1701 Charter for Pennsylvania included:
"set my hand and broad seal."

brockle (*adj.*) White and black. Joshua Hempstead in 1749 referred to:
"my cattle . . . 1 black brockle faced."

broglio (*n.*) A silk and wool fabric with small geometric patterns.

broken days Among American Indians, the length of time agreed upon for the performance of some act. In 1775 James Adair wrote,
"Seventeen were the broken days . . . when the Choktah engaged to return with the French scalps."

brooklime (*n.*) A tea from the leaves and young stems of this herb, used to counteract scurvy.

broomrape (*n.*) A plant of the genus *Orobranche*. In 1729 Mark Catesby reported from North Carolina,
"Broomrape . . . risen to the height of eight to ten inches, and is of flesh colour."

Brother Jonathan Any Yankee or American. The phrase was frequently used by Washington to refer to Gov. Trumbull of Connecticut. It was later replaced by *Uncle Sam*.

Brownist (*n.*) A follower of Robert Brown who, around 1580, proposed a system of Puritan church government.

Brunswicker (*n.*) *See* **Hessian.**

brush away To lose. In 1647 William Bradford deplored that:
"Many of them had brushed away their coats and cloaks at Plymouth."

brussels (*n.*) A fine bobbin lace.

buckra (*n.*) A white man. Probably from Gullah (an Afro-American language used by southern blacks). See **Gonzalez**, in bibliography.

buckskin (*n.*) A country bumpkin. John Harrower in 1774 referred to:
"a buckskin, a lubber, a thick-skull."

budget (*n.*) A bag or sack. From French *bougette*, diminutive of *bouge* 'leather bag.' A 1677 book referred to:
"a Budget or Pocket to hang by their sides."

buhrstone, burrstone (*n.*) [*pl.* **burze**] The rock used for millstones. In 1652 in Dedham, Mass., a document referred to:
"the burze brought to make a new millstone."

bul, bul[l]-beggar, bulbeggar (*n.*) A bogey; a bugbear. William Byrd uses this word in his essay "The Female Creed" in 1725,
"having been terrified in the nursery with bul beggars and apparitions." The footnote in *Another Secret Diary of William Byrd of Westover 1739–1741* says *bul* is a 'falsehood.' This is true, but Byrd's shorthand probably intended *bull*.

bulles (*n.*) A variant of *bullace* 'a wild plum.' A 17th-century cookbook said to:
"Take bulles & boyle them."

bully (*n.*) A ludicrous jest. In 1766 Gov. Bernard of Massachusetts wrote,
"for New England to threaten the mother country with manufactures is the idlest bully that ever was attempted."

bum (*n.*) Buttocks. From Dutch *boem* 'bottom.'

bumbo (*n.*) A drink of rum, sugar, and water. From Italian *bombo* 'a child's word for drink.' In 1733 William Byrd had:
"a Capacious Bowl of Bombo."

bumkin (*n.*) A small, water barrel. From Dutch *bommekijn* 'lttle barrel.' In 1680 an anonymous pirate went ashore:
"to fill our Bumkings with water."

bumper (1) (*n.*) A filled cup or glass to be drunk as a toast. In 1768 some Loyalists sang,
"This bumper I crown for our Sovereign's health."
(2) (*v.*) To toast with a bumper.

bum roll A bolster or bishop. See **bum**.

bunch (*n.*) The hunch on a bison's neck, considered a delicacy. In 1733 William Byrd commented:
"a rarer morsel, the Bunch."

bundle (*v.*) Of young courting lads and lasses, to occupy the same bed, with the clothes on, for warmth. Sometimes a *bundling board* was used to separate them. A 1777 song suggested:
"better bundle than fight."

bunter (*n.*) A low, vulgar woman. A 1768 song referred to:
"your brats and your bunters."

burden grass Burden's grass; redtop. Franklin in 1749 wrote,
"I threw in the following seed . . . a peck of Burden grass."

burdock (*n.*) A plant from the root of which a brew was made and prescribed for scurvy and rheumatism.

burgair (*n.*) A large upholstered chair. A variant of French *bèrgere* 'easy chair.' In 1773 E. Singleton announced: "[Joseph Cox] makes all sorts of . . . settees, couches, burgairs."

burgess (*n.*) A representative of a borough to a legislature. In Maryland and Virginia the Colonial legislature was called:
"The House of Burgesses."

burgher (*n.*) A freeman of New Amsterdam.

burgomaster (*n.*) A burgh-master, the chief magistrate of New Amsterdam.

burgoo (*n.*) Burgout, oatmeal porridge, eaten chiefly by seamen. In 1787 P.M. Freneau

wrote,
"If I had him at sea . . . a bowl of burgoo."

burgoynade (*n.*) A surrender; coined after Burgoyne's surrender at Saratoga in 1777. A 1779 Charleston, S.C., newspaper reported,
"He has made a very sudden and precipitate retreat to escape a burgoynade."

burial cake A cake about four inches square, marked with a deceased's initials and kept as a souvenir.

Burlington gammon Bacon from the capital of West New Jersey, famous for its quality.

burnet (*n.*) A garden plant resembling sainfoin. Washington's 1786 diary reported,
"Began to plow a piece of gr[oun]d in the Neck for Burnet."

burning (*n.*) The distillation of tar from wood. A 1646 Springfield, Mass., document said,
"Shall joyne with him in the burninge of tarr."

burrstone *See* **buhrstone.**

burthen (*n.*) Burden, the cargo capacity or weight of the cargo of a ship.

burthenage (*n.*) A tax on goods carried. A 1725 traveler reported,
"The traders are obliged to pay double burthenage."

burthensome (*adj.*) Able to carry a large cargo. A 1763 Boston newspaper offered:
"a very good and burthensome schooner for sale."

burze *See* **buhrstone.**

bushel bean A very common variety of bean. A 1709 traveler to North Carolina wrote,
"so called because they bring a bushel of beans for one which is planted."

bush harrow A harrow with branches rather than discs or spikes. In 1770 Washington recorded,
"The grass Seed was sowed and harrowed with a Bush Harrow."

bushloper (*n.*) A variant of *bossloper.*

busk (*n.*) A removable stay in the center of a corset; sometimes applied to the whole corset. One source, from 1688, speaks of it as:
"wood, or whalebone thrust down the middle of the Stomacker."

buss (*n.*) A two- or three-masted, square-rigged fishing vessel. Adapted from Dutch *buis.*

butler (*n.*) A college officer at Yale or Harvard; among his duties was the charge of the buttery. From Old French *bouteillier* 'bottler.' Harvard in 1734 ruled:
"The butler shall take care that all fines imposed by the President . . . be fairly recorded."

butt (*n.*) A cask or barrel varying in size from 108 gallons for beer to 140 gallons for Spanish wine, depending on its use. It was generally two hogsheads.

butter whore A scolding woman who sells butter. A 1776 play used the description,
"Like a parcel of damned butter whores."

buttery (*n.*) The place where liquor, fruit, and refreshments are sold. From Old French *boterie* 'place for keeping bottles.' Harvard regulations of 1790 decreed:
"Every Scholar . . . shall enter his name at the Buttery."

button (*n.*) A guessing game in which penalties are assessed for guessing wrong. In 1733 Philip Fithian bragged that:
"We played button to get pawns for redemption . . . in the course of redeeming my pawns I had several kisses from the ladies." Buttons were used as the pawns, given by wrong guessers to those asking questions, who could then redeem the pawns in some agreed manner.

buttonbush (*n.*) *Cephalanthus occidentalis*, a shrub with globular, white flowers. A *button* is any small, rounded body; a globe.

by (*adj.*) Incidental, in its sense of *near*. When Gov. Lovelace of New York instituted the first post he wrote to Gov. Winthrop of Massachusetts,
"Only by-letters are in an open bag, to dispense by the wayes."

by inch of candle An adverbial phrase referring to the fact that the bidding at a public auction was stopped, when an inch-long candle, used as a timing device, burned out.

caboose (*n.*) The kitchen of a ship. John Rowe's 1764 diary reported,
"Capt. Dashwood's Brigg caught on fire occasioned by the tar boiling over the caboose."

cachexie (*n.*) A sickness caused by cancer or tuberculosis. From Latin *cachexia* 'a consumption; wasting.' Robert Beverley's 1705 description of Virginia stated:
"disorders grow into a cachexie on which the bodies overrun with obstinate scorbutic humours."

cacique (*n.*) An indian chief. The word is of Arawak Indian origin and is found in many variations. In 1609 Richard Hakluyt wrote,
"The cacique had done the same to learn his mind."

caetus (*n.*) Probably a misprint of *caucus*. William Smith in his 1757 *History of the Province of New York* wrote:
"In several of their late annual conventions at New York called the caetus."

cag (*n.*) A small cask. *Cag* was used in the Plymouth Colony records in 1653.

cain (*n.*) The rent for land paid in its produce. A Celtic word. Robert Rogers used it in a 1777 play:
"if you are but secure and have the cain in hand."

calamanco (*n.*) A woolen or worsted fabric resembling camel's hair cloth.

calamin. (*n.*) An abbreviation of *calaminaris lapis* 'zinc carbonate,' the basic ingredient for an eyewash.

calculate (*n.*) A computation, reckoning. In 1740 Robert Dinwiddie reported.
"The calculate is taken from the years of 16 to 60."

calenture (*n.*) A fever affecting people in hot climates. From Spanish *calentura* 'fever.' The treatment was rest, bleeding, barley water, an emetic, and then a blister. In 1649 W. Bullock reported,
"Being over-heated he is struck with a Calenture or Feaver, and so perisheth."

calibogus (*n.*) A rum drink with spruce beer and molasses added. It is suggested that the *-bogus* comes from *bagasse* 'the residue of crushed sugar cane.'

calico betty A card game. Philip Fithian in 1775 wrote,
"In our dining room companies at cards, Five & forty, whist, Alfours, Calico-Betty, etc."

calipash (*n.*) The edible, greenish, fatty meat of a turtle attached to the upper shell, considered a delicacy.

calipee (*n.*) The light-yellow delicacy attached to a turtle's lower shell.

calker (*n.*) An iron addition to a shoe heel. In 1740 William Byrd indelicately wrote,
"She'll unavoidably run a calker into her thrummy breech."

caltrop (*n.*) A metal instrument with four one-inch points so that three rest on the ground and one always points up. They were strewn on the ground to pierce the feet of horses. Also called 'crow's feet.' From *calk* 'a pointed piece on a horseshoe' and *trap*.

calumet (*n.*) The ceremonial tobacco pipe used by the Indians as a symbol of peace and war. From a French form of Latin *calamus* 'reed.'

Calvinist (*n.*) A member of the group which tried to "purify" the Church of England by simpler forms of worship. Founded by French theologian John Calvin (1509–1564), the majority of the early New England population belonged to this sect.

Cambridge Platform The rules for church conduct formulated by the New England Puritans in 1648. They were very similar to the Westminster Congress of the year before. Cotton Mather noted,
"A synod assembled at Cambridge . . . framed, agreed and published, 'the Platform of Church-discipline.'"

camlet (*n.*) A fabric made originally from camel's hair, later from Angora goat hair and other materials. In 1713 Samuel Sewall wrote,
"Send a pattern for a cloak of good black hair camlet."

camphor (*n.*) A substance extensively used as a mild irritant in liniments.

Canary (*n.*) Wine from the Canary Islands which tasted much like Madeira. In 1722 Samuel Sewall recorded that Mrs. Winthrop:
"gave me a glass or two of Canary."

cancerroot (*n.*) A root parasite.

cancr. An abbreviation of Latin *cancer* 'crab.'

Candlemas (*n.*) February 2. Candles for the altar are blessed at mass to commemorate the purification of the Virgin Mary.

candlewood (*n.*) Splinters of pitch pine used as candles or to start a fire. A 1694 Massachusetts law referred to:
"Our best pine wood alias candle wood."

candy (1) (*n.*) Any crystallized substance resulting from evaporation; it looks like crystallized sugar.
(2) (*v.*) To crystalize by evaporation. In 1629 William Bradford referred to:
"salt which they found candied by the sun."

cane (*v.*) To form a scum during the fermentation process. A 17th-century cookbook described:
"laying a clean course ragg upon ye pickle w[hic]h will keepe them from canneing."

can hooks Hooks with which to lift barrels. A corruption of *cant hook*; a *cant* is a segment forming a sidepiece in the head of a cask.

canker (*n.*) A variant of *cancer*. William Robinson in 1659 deplored the persecution of Quakers which:
"eat you up as doth a canker."

canoewood (*n.*) The wood of the tulip tree, from which Indians made dugout canoes.

canticoy (*n.*) A ceremonial Indian dance. An Algonquian word. In 1670 Daniel Denton wrote of New York Indians,
"At their Canticas or dancing Matches."

canton[1] (*n.*) A fabric from Canton, China. The word is generally used in combinations, such as Canton crepe.

canton[2] (*n.*) **(1)** A division of a county. In 1796 Jefferson wrote,
"In the retired canton where I live."
(2) An Indian tribe. Instructions to the Governor of Virginia in 1771 said,
"there are several nations, cantons or tribes of Indians." (*v.*)
(3) To assign quarters for bodies of troops. In 1752 James MacSparran recorded,
"Four Independent Companies . . . are cantoned in York, Albany, Schenectady."

cap a pie From head to foot. From French *cap à pied* 'head to foot.' Thomas Morton in 1632 writing on Puritan intolerance said,
"I will draw their pictures cap a pe that you may discuss them plainly head to toe."

capcase (*n.*) A small covered case. Jeremy Taylor wrote metaphorically,
"A woman should be the capcase of friendly toleration."

capelin (*n.*) A small fish, about six inches long, related to the smelt.

cape merchant The head merchant. From Italian *capo* 'head.' All goods sent to Virginia in its early days were kept in a common store run by a cape merchant.
"The President's and Capt. Martin's sickness constrained me [Capt. John Smith] to be cape merchant." [1608]

caper (*n.*) A Dutch privateer. From Dutch *kaper* 'privateer.' In 1672 J. Hull wrote,
"ships . . . were taken by the Dutch capers."

capias (*n.*) An arrest warrant. From Latin 'you may take.'

capital (*adj.*) Principal. It applied to laws as well as cities. The Massachusetts School Law in 1642 referred to:
"the capital laws of the country."

capite (*n.*) Land held directly of the king. The ablative of Latin *caput* 'head.' This tenure was abolished in 1660.

cappewee (*n.*) A spelling based on one pronunciation. *See* **copivi, Balsam of.**

capsill (*n.*) The top beam of a structure. A 1681 Boston document mentions,
"a survey of the North Battery wharf . . . only wanting of good Cap-Sills."

captivity (*n.*) Slavery. Massachusetts Body of Liberties in 1641 provided that,
"there shall never be any bond-slavery, villenage or captivity among us."

capuchin (*n.*) A woman's garment resembling a Capuchin monk's habit. An advertisement in a 1754 South Carolina newspaper offered,
"The ladies . . . covered their lovely necks with cloaks . . . the capuchine."

carbonado (*v.*) To broil over coals. From Latin *carbon* 'charcoal.' Capt. John Smith wrote regarding Starving Time in Virginia in 1608,

"And one among the rest did kill his wife, powdered her and had eaten part of her before it was known; for which he was executed, as well he deserved. Now, whether she was better roasted, boiled or carbonaded, I know not; but of such a dish as powdered wife I never heard."

carcajou (*n.*) A wolverine. From Algonquian *karkajoo*.

carcass (*n.*) A canvas container with metal hoops and filled with combustible material that was fired from cannon to set fire to buildings or defenses. A 1775 Boston letter said,

"The carcasses, bombs, and red-hot balls . . . fired into the town had little or no effect."

card. benedict. (*n.*) An abbreviation of *Carduus benedictus* 'blessed thistle,' the salt of which was used to induce vomiting.

cardinal (*n.*) A short, hooded, scarlet, woman's cloak. A red riding hood.

card wires The wires that move guide threads through the control cards in the loom invented by the Frenchman Joseph Marie Jacquard (1752–1834).

career (*n.*) A running charge made at high speed. William Smallwood wrote in a 1776 letter,

"The enemy might be checked in their career."

carf (*n.*) A kerf; a cut in a tree by an axe. From Old English *cyrf* 'a cutting off.' The word is cognate with *carve*.

cariole (*n.*) A small, one-horse carriage. From French *carriole* 'small, covered carriage.'

Carlisle Road (*n.*) The roadstead, or anchorage, of Bridgetown, Barbados.

Carolina (*n.*) The colony of Carolina, granted by Charles II in 1663 to eight proprietors and named for him. It was not separated into North and South until 1729. In 1722 Daniel Coxe wrote *A Description of the English Province of Carolina*.

carpenter (*n.*) The workman who did the heavy framing of a house. A *joiner* did the finish work.

carriage (*n.*) **(1)** The manner of carrying oneself; bearing. The 1650 Connecticut Blue Laws referred to:

"contemptuous carriages."

(2) A means for conveying. In 1784 Franklin wrote,

"Braddock halted at Frederick, Maryland for carriage."

carry log A pair of wheels with which to move heavy things. A 1781 Virginia document described:

"want of wagons and a carry-log."

cartel (*n.*) **(1)** An agreement in writing to exchange prisoners.

(2) A ship carrying such agreements or other proposals under a safe-conduct. In Gen. William Heath's 1798 *Memoirs* he wrote,

"I take the earliest opportunity by Lt. Carter, in the Harbor Cartel, to inform you of the arrival of the transports."

cartouche (*n.*) A cartridge. A roll of paper containing one charge of powder and ball for a gun or pistol. The 1720 Statutes of Virginia provided for:

"each man to be provided with . . . a horne or cartouche box suitable ammunition and a snapsack."

caruel (*n.*) Caraway seeds, used medicinally to alleviate flatulence.

carver (*n.*) One who cleans fish for market. In 1765 Robert Rogers, later famous for Rogers' Rangers, wrote,
"the carver . . . splits the fish open."

case (*v.*) To strip off the skin (case) of an animal. A 1796 cookbook instructed,
"Take a full grown hare and let it hang four or five days before you case it."

cask (*n.*) A loosely used term for keg, barrel, butt, hogshead, pipe, tun, etc.

cass. (*n.*) An abbreviation of *cassia fistula*, the dried pods of the drumstick tree, used to treat acute constipation.

casse tete An Indian war club. From French *casse tête* 'break [the] head.' In 1778 Jonathan Carver mentioned:
"bows and arrows, and also the casse Tete or war club."

cassimere (*n.*). A thin, twilled woolen cloth used for making men's clothes. From Kashmir, India.

cassine (*n.*) A black tea, concocted from the leaves of a southern holly. The word applied to both the plant and the drink. In 1587 Richard Hakluyt wrote,
"Baskets full of the leaves of Cassine, wherewith they make their drinks."

cassock (*n.*) A loose, smocklike garment with buttons down the front, for men, women, and children, now worn only by clergymen. In 1624 Capt. John Smith referred to a:
"Sailers canvas Cassoke."

cassop (*n.*) An alkaline salt related to potash.

cast (1) (*n.*) Help to a traveler by giving him a ride; a lift. In 1710 William Byrd's sister:
"gave us a cast over the river."
(2) A throw of good luck. In 1774 John Harrower prayed,
"God grant that such a cast may happen to you."
(3) A slight degree; a taste. William Byrd in 1722 commented,
"If a person came in their way they will crave a cast of his office."
(4) (*v.*) To thrust, as a man into prison. The 1641 Massachusetts Body of Liberties stated,
"It shall be in the liberty of every man cast, condemned or sentenced."
(5) (*adj.*) Discarded; cast-off. Benjamin Tompson in 1675 wrote of:
"comlier wear . . . than the cast fashions from all Europe brought."

casting voice The deciding vote to break a tie. A 1638 Connecticut document provided that:
"The Governor . . . shall have the casting voice."

castor (*n.*) **(1)** An abbreviation of *castoreum*, the dried reddish-brown substance taken from the cods in the groin of a beaver. It was prescribed as a stimulant and antispasmodic. Also called *beaver mineral*.
(2) A beaver; a hat, originally made of beaver fur, later of rabbit fur. A 1688 newspaper offered,
"2 black hats, one a Beaver, the other a new Caster."

cat (*v.*) To apply the first coat of plaster. A chimney is *catted* when it has *cat-sticks* in the clay filling and is ready for plaster. A 1665 Southampton, N.Y., document noted:
"a chimney catted and fit for daubing."

catamaran (*n.*) A raft. From Tamil *katta-maram* (tied tree). By 1800 it came to mean two boats lashed together. A 1758 Rhode Island newspaper reported,
"one brass 24 pounder was lost . . . by slipping off the Catamarin."

catch (*n.*) A rondo; a song for three or more voices. A 1725 song praised a man who
"heartily quaffs, sings catches, and laughs."

cate (*n.*) Store-bought food as contrasted to homemade. A shortened form of *acate* 'a purchase' from French *acheter* 'to buy.' In 1675 Benjamin Thompson described,
"when men fared, hardly without complaint, on vilest cates."

catholicon (*n.*) A remedy for all diseases; good-for-what-ails-you pills; panacea.

caudle (*n.*) A kind of warm broth, a mixture of wine and other ingredients for sick people. A 1659 diary recorded,
"Went to bed and got a caudle made me, and sleep upon it very well."

caul (*n.*) A membrane covering most of the lower intestines. A 17th– century cook-book suggested using:
"some of the best of the kell shred amongst it."

causey (*n.*) A variant of *causeway*, a way raised above the natural level of the ground. In 1637 a Dedham, Mass., document recorded,
"the making of a Causey & bridge over the little River."

cautery (*n.*) A hot iron used to cauterize, or destroy tissue by burning. From Latin *cauterium* 'branding iron.'

caution (*n.*) The security or bond posted to insure performance. A 1793 report stated,
"this coin . . . they giving caution for the performance of the trust reposed in them."

cavallo (*n.*) A food fish. The word is adopted from Italian.

censure (*v.*) To condemn by a judicial sentence. In the 1640s John Winthrop wrote,
"being convict . . . was censured to be whipped, lose his ears and [be] banished."

centaur (*n.*) A brew of the flowering tops of the knapweed *Centauria nigra* or milk-wort; used as a tonic.

cent per cent A very high interest rate, 100 Charles Wolley in 1697 wrote that in New York,
"They were fain to give after the rate of cent per cent."

centrical (*adj.*) Central. In 1763 William Roberts described,
"From the excellent and centrical position of this fine port."

cephalic (*n.*) A medicine good for headache. A 17th-century Virginia doctor pre-scribed treatment:
"with cephalic powders."

cerv. (*n.*) An abbreviation of Latin *cervus* 'deer.' Deer or hart. *See* **hartshorn.**

chafery (*n.*) A forge in which a square mass of iron was forged into a bar. In 1679,
"Forges are of two sorts . . . [one is] the chafery."

chafing dish (*n.*) A wire container holding burning coals. A 1612 book advised,
"Have ever ready a chaffen-dish with fire . . . to warm clouts."

chain (*n.*) A linear measure used in surveying, Gunter's chain; four rods; 66 feet. *See* **Gunter.** Ten square chains equal one acre.

chair (*n.*) A two-wheeled, one-horse carriage. Also spelled 'chaise,' 'cheer,' 'shay.'

Used in combining form as, *chair horse* 'a horse suitable for drawing a chair'; *chair house*, 'a carriage house for a chair'; *chair road; chair saddle; chair wheel.*

chaise (*n.*) A carriage. Depending on where and when, two- or four-wheeled, one or two horses, covered or uncovered.

chaldron (*n.*) A measure of coal varying in size from place to place. In New York it was 2500 pounds. In London it was 36 bushels.

chamade (*n.*) A drum beat or trumpet signal to invite a parley with the enemy. From French *chamar* 'to call.' *See also* **beat** (1) .

chamoiser (*n.*) One who works with chamois leather. A 1732 South Carolina newspaper reported,
"The Skins are then returned from the Mill to the Chamoiser, to be scoured."

champain (*n.*) Also, **champaign.** Flat, open country. In 1680 Charles Wolley wrote:
"the island it stands on all a level and champain."

champerty and maintenance A legal action in which a party not naturally concerned in a law suit engages to prosecute or defend it with an agreement to share in the proceeds.

chancer (*v.*) To make a fair settlement, as would a court of chancery.

chandelier (*n.*) A movable parapet serving to support fascines for the protection of men digging trenches. In 1775 Gen. Heath ordered:
"Chandeliers, fascines, etc. to be made."

chandler (*n.*) An artisan who makes or deals in candles. A 1711 law referred to a:
"chandler or maker of candles."

channel (*n.*) A groove in the sole of a shoe in which lie the stitches that fasten the sole to the upper.

chapel ghost The gremlin who mixes things up in a printing house. When type was messed up Franklin said in 1771 it was:
"all ascribed to the chappel ghost." A printing house is called a *chapel* because William Caxton did his printing in a chapel connected to Westminster Abbey in 1476.

chapman (*n.*) A seller or marketman. From Old English *ceap* 'to trade.' In 1642 it was said,
"It is not meete that a man be both chapman and customer."

character (*n.*) A shorthand symbol. Franklin used the word,
"If I would learn [to read] his characters."

charge, be at To be financially responsible for. *Poor Richard's Almanac* preached,
"Craft must be at charge for clothes, but Truth can go naked."

charger (*n.*) **(1)** A device for loading a charge into a musket.
(2) A large dish. A 17th-century cookbook instructed,
"roule it out thin & as bigg as a charger."

chariot (*n.*) An ornate, four-wheeled carriage drawn by four, six, or even eight horses. In 1765 Cadwalader Colden complained that:
"they broke open the Lieutenant Governor's coach house . . . carried his chariot round the streets."

charlock (*n.*) A weed often pernicious among grain.

charter party The agreement made between a merchant and the master for the charter of a ship setting forth all arrangements. From French *charte-partie* 'a divided charter.' It was written in duplicate on one sheet, then the sheet was cut irregularly so that the pieces could be uniquely matched together.

chase lane A narrow road. Apparently wide enough for only a chaise. A 1639 Connecticut document referred to:
"A Chasse lane leading from the little Riuer to the meeting house."

chasery (*n.*) A hearth where cast iron is heated in order to chase it (emboss it or cut away parts). A 1748 newspaper advertised,
"To be sold . . . a Good Forge, or iron work, having three fires, viz. two finerys and one chasery."

chasseur (*n.*) A term used of a light infantryman in the French and British armies. From the French word for 'huntsman.'

cheat (*n.*) A weed resembling and often growing among wheat. Also called **chess.** In 1786 Washington complained that the wheat:
"was mixed exceedingly with cheat."

chechinquamin (*n.*) Chinquapin, the dwarf chestnut. From an Algonquian word.

check (*n.*) (1) The squares formed by furrows, and the points at which they cross at right angles, in a plowed field. It resembled a checker board. In 1787 Washington recorded,
"In each of these checks or crosses, a root, when it was large and looked well, was put."
(2) A snack. In 1775 Philip Fithian wrote,
"This is an Irish settlement . . . will you just take a check? She meant a late Dinner."
(3) A counter or chip used in certain games. In 1774 Philip Fithian observed,
"Often the girls play at a small game with peach stones which they call checks."
(4) Restraint. Gen. William Heath in his memoirs wrote,
"to the check and disappointment of the enemy."

cheek music (*n.*) Eloquence. In a song William Pitt's was described as:
"cheek music." (By 1836 the phrase had become *chin music*.)

cheer[1] (*n.*) A variant of *chair*, the vehicle.

cheer[2] (*n.*) Provisions; food. When Mary Rowlandson was captured by the Indians in 1675 she subsisted on:
"poor Indian cheer."

cheesefat (*n.*) Cheesevat, the vat in which curds are confined for pressing. A 1650 document listed:
"One cherne, 3 cheesfatts."

cheespan (*n.*) A sieve. A 17th-century cookbook advised:
"put ye curds into yr cheespan."

chelloe (*n.*) A variant of *challis*. Henry Remsen spelled it this way in a 1775 letter.

chemistry (*n.*) A mental process. In 1645 Nathaniel Ward described,
"such are fittest to mountebank his chemistry into sick churches and weak judgements."

chersonese (*n.*) A peninsula. From Latin *chersonesus* 'dry island.' The 1632 charter for Maryland mentioned,
"all that part of the peninsula or chersonese."

chess (*n.*) *See* **cheat.**

Chesterfield's Plan Although the advice of Lord Chesterfield in his *Letters to His Son* (1746–1753) reflected the manners and morals of a man of the world at that time, many people considered them immoral. As Dr. Samuel Johnson put it, "They teach the morals of a whore, and the manners of a dancing master." Nabby Adams, daughter of Abigail and John, refused to marry actor Royall Tyler because he had a reputation for: "practicing upon Chesterfield's Plan."

cheval-de-frise (*n.*) On land, a large log with spikes, used to bar roads and supplement fortifications. In rivers, it was used to rip bottoms out of ships. From French *cheval* 'horse' *de Frise* 'of Friesland,' in Holland, where they were first used. Benedict Arnold's description of West Point said that there was: "a chevaux de frise on the West Side" of Fort Putnam.

cheyney (*n.*) A variant of *china*. A 17th-century cookbook directed, "put all these together in a cheney pot."

Childermas Day December 28, Holy Innocent's Day, in commemoration of the children of Bethlehem slain by Herod. In 1740 William Byrd recorded that, "the children every Childermas Day go to St. Paul's Church."

chilly (*adj.*) Cloudy. In 1775 John Rowe complained that: "the last Madeira was chilly."

chimney glass A mirror over a mantelpiece. A 1715 Boston newspaper advertised, "New Fashion Looking-Glasses and Chimney-Glasses."

china (*n.*) A woolen material. In 1747 in Virginia Lyman Chalkley remarked: "They were robbed of . . . one orange-colored sitting gown, a pale china gown."

china briar A variety of smilax from the East Indies, with no smell and little taste. A 1745 observer wrote, "and for greens, boiled the tops of China Briars, which eat almost as well as Asparagus."

chinae (*n.*) China root 'smilax china,' prescribed to promote perspiration and urination.

chincomen (*n.*) One of the many variant spellings of *chinquapin*.

chine (*n.*) The spine of an animal. From French *échine* 'spine.' When in 1710 William Byrd wrote: "I ate chine and turkey," it was probably saddle of pig and wild turkey.

chinquapin (*n.*) The dwarf chestnut. An adaptation of an Algonquian word. In 1709 John Lawson observed: "Chinkapin is a sort of Chestnut, whose Nuts are most commonly very plentiful; insomuch that the Hogs get fat with them."

chip hat A hat or bonnet woven of thin strips of wood or palm fiber. A 1776 Boston newspaper advertised a: "sale of chip hats."

chirk (*adj.*) In lively spirits, cheerful. As early as 1789 in his *Dissertations on the English Language* Noah Webster deplored that: "this word is wholly lost except in New England."

chirurgeon (*n.*) A surgeon. A 1711 North Carolina document told of:

"the petition of Edmond Ellis praying to be admitted Chyrurgeon for the expedition."

chitterling (*n.*) A frill on the breast of a shirt. Such a frill resembled the mesentery which connects the intestines to the abdominal cavity. A 1776 New Jersey document referred to:
"A fine shirt with chitterlings on the bosom."

choice (*adj.*) Holding dear; using with care. In 1775 Abigail Adams wrote John regarding some articles he sent her,
"I shall be very choice of them."

chop[1] (*n.*) The sides of a river's mouth, especially in reference to the turbulent water often encountered there. In 1765 Robert Rogers wrote,
"We entered the chops of a river."

chop[2] (*v.*) To thrust suddenly. A 17th-century cookbook directed,
"Chop him into a hot mash, or hot water."

chop-fallen (*adj.*) Dejected, dispirited. Having the lower jaw or chap fallen. Gouverneur Morris wrote,
"His friends appeared chop-fallen."

chopin (*n.*) A French liquid measure equal to a pint; a Scottish liquid measure of wine equal to a quart. John Harrower, who had emigrated from Scotland, referred to:
"One chopin sweet milk" in 1774.

chopine (*n.*) A shoe with a thick sole. From Spanish *chapin* 'a clog with a cork sole.' A 1645 letter referred to:
"their high chapins."

choque (*n.*) A shock. In 1740 William Byrd wrote that:
"she is able to sustain the choque of Bad with the greater security."

chunky (*n.*) An Indian game played with a stone and crooked sticks. Bernard Romans referred to it in 1775:
"their favorite game of chunke."

cider oil *See* **cider royal.**

cider pap A porridge of crushed corn and cider. In 1708 Ebenezer Cook sneered at,
"Homine and Syder-pap,/ (which scarce a hungry dog wou'd lap)."

cider royal A type of cider, first concentrated by boiling or freezing, then sweetened with honey.

cinnamoni (*n.*) *Latin* 'cinnamon,' referring to cinnamon water, a stimulating and invigorating drink.

circiter (*adv.*) *Latin.* Roughly. In 1729 William Douglass wrote,
"Boston is in west longitude 71° 29′ circiter."

circumferentor (*n.*) An instrument used by surveyors for taking angles, now superseded by the theodolite. A 1744 Maryland document referred to:
"One Light Circumferenter for Surveying Land."

circumvallation (*n.*) A surrounding with a wall or rampart.

citizen (*n.*) The word applied only to males in Colonial times.

cive (*n.*) A variant of *chive*, a species of leek. John Lawson in 1709 wrote of:
"Garlick, Cives and the Wild-Onions" in Carolina.

clame (*v.*) To daub. A 17th-century cookbook directed,
"Take a trencher and clame it."

clamp (*n.*) A brush. In 1774 Philip Fithian in Virginia wrote,
"Sometimes they get Sticks & splinter one end for Brushes, or as they call them here Clamps."

clash (*n.*) Any opposition. In 1770 Robert Mumford in a play wrote,
"I can vote for him without your clash."

classis (*n.*) A governing body of the Dutch Reformed Church. From Latin *classis* 'a class or division of the Roman people.' William Smith in 1732 wrote of:
"the majority being inclined to errect a classis, or ecclesiastical judicatory."

clavel piece A mantelpiece over a fireplace. From Old French *clavel* 'keystone of an arch.' John Wynter used the word in 1634.

clerk (*n.*) A clergyman. Today the word is *cleric*. In 1744 Dr. Alexander Hamilton sneered at:
"the ignorance and stupidity of our Presbyterian clerks."

clever (*adj.*) (1) Performing with skill and address. In 1776 *The Battle of Brooklyn* referred to:
"clever horses."
(2) Good natured (limited to New England). A 1758 journal described
"a very clever family."

cleverly (*adv.*) (1) In good health. Describing one who had been ill, Abigail Adams in 1784 noted,
"She is cleverly now."
(2) Completely. Jefferson wrote in 1788 that:
"revolution . . . is cleverly under way."

climate struck Lazy. In 1724 Hugh Jones described Virginia,
"the Heat of the Summer makes some very lazy, who are then said to be Climate-struck."

clip (*v.*) (1) To pare the edge of a coin for the purpose of stealing some metal. To prevent this, coins were milled or had inscriptions on their edges. A 1705 Boston newspaper reported:
"a Proclamation, Prohibiting the Importation of any clipt Money."
(2) To cut off as a punishment. In 1729 in Rhode Island, J. Comer recorded that:
"Nicholas Octis stood in ye pillory, and had his ears clipt for making money."

clog (*n.*) Any device put upon an animal to hinder motion. A 1776 Connecticut newspaper reported,
"A horse was galled on the off side of her neck with a clog."

close (*n.*) An enclosed place, an enclosed field or piece of land. A 1638 description in the Charlestown, Mass., land records mentions a place:
"bounded on the west by Bakers close."

closet (*n.*) (1) A small room for privacy. In 1710 William Byrd wrote that he:
"set things in order in my closet."
(2) A large case for curiosities or valuables.
"A closet full of pieces of rock crystal." [1756]

cloth colored Undyed. Samuel Sewall in 1725 described:
"One full Suit of Striped Satin lined with Cloth-colour Lutestring."

clothier (*n.*) One who fulled and dressed cloth, not a maker of clothes. A 1714 Boston newspaper referred to:
"Jeremiah Jackson Cloathier and Stuffe Weaver."

clout (1) (*n.*) A cleat; an iron plate on an axle tree to prevent wear.
(2) A patch; a piece of cloth.
(3) (*v.*) To patch clothing. *Forefathers' Song* in 1630 complained,
"our other in-garments are clout upon clout . . . they need to be clouted soon after they're worn."

clove (*n.*) A ravine. From Dutch *klove* 'a rocky cleft or fissure.' In 1779 Jared Sparks described:
"a clove which runs round that ridge on which the forts are situated."

clover (*n.*) In some contexts, refers to sweet clover added to medicinal plasters to give them a green color.

club (*v.*) To unite for a common purpose. Franklin in 1771 recorded:
"clubbing our books."

clunce (*v.*) To stop up. Possibly from *clunch*, 'a type of clay.' A 1781 Maryland document included,
"We never clunced the ceiling, that is stopped the cracks."

clyster (*n.*) An enema. From Latin *clyster* 'syringe.' As a treatment for fever William Byrd in 1710:
"put on blisters and gave her a clyster which work very well."

coach (*n.*) A large, ornate, four-wheeled vehicle with doors and an elevated driver's seat, drawn by four, six, or eight horses.

coachee (*n.*) A carriage longer and lighter than a coach, open in front, and with only two horses.

coal (*n.*) Charcoal as well as coal as we know it.

coal dish A charcoal container. The word appears in a 1640 Connecticut inventory.

coaler (*n.*) A dealer in coal. In 1710 William Byrd referred to one.

coal wood Wood for charcoal. In 1788 Washington wrote,
"The Men were cutting the Tops of the Trees which had fallen for Rails into Coal-wood."

coast commission A commission agent's fee. A 1754 letter of instructions to a sea captain offered,
"You are to have four out of 104 for your coast commission."

coaster (*n.*) **(1)** One who coasts; an idler.
(2) A vessel carrying cargo between ports on the coast. A 1739 Boston document warned,
"Our Fishery and Coasters . . . will be exposed."

coatee (*n.*) A short close-fitting military tunic. *Harper's Magazine* in 1775 reported,
"Every officer to provide himself with a blue cloath Coatie faced and cuffed with scarlet cloath."

coat money The money given a soldier to buy a coat. A 1775 New Hampshire document referred to:
"their wages, exclusive of Coat Money."

cobbler (*n.*) One who mended shoes; a cordwainer made them.
"It is never well, when the cobbler looketh above the ankle."

cob house A toy house of twigs or corn cobs in imitation of a log cabin. In 1776 John Adams wrote,
"They are erecting governments as fast as children build cob-houses."

cob money Pieces of eight. From Spanish *cabo de barra* 'end of a bar.' A bar of metal was sliced and then die struck to make coins.

cock (*n.*) The part of a musket to which the flint is attached. The cock was drawn back and triggered to create a spark. (Guns occasionally went off half-cocked.) In 1646, during Bacon's Rebellion,
"[fusiliers] who with their cocks bent presented their fusils at a window."

cockarouse (*n.*) *Algonquian.* Chief.

cocket (*n.*) A document given by the officer of a custom house certifying that the merchandise has been entered. From French *cachet* 'seal.' A 1756 invoice included:
"duty and cocket £ 5."

cockscomb (*n.*) Short for *cockscomb oyster*. In 1710 William Byrd wrote,
"We drank coffee and cockscomb for breakfast."

codille (*n.*) In the card game omber, the loss of the game by the challenger. From Spanish *codillo* 'angle.' A 1725 song cheered,
"The King is forced to lose codille."

codling (*n.*) An apple suitable for coddling, parboiling. *See* **caudle.**

coetus (*n.*) The body governing the Dutch and German Reformed Church from 1747 to 1793.

cog (*v.*) To cheat. A slang word from Swedish *kugga* 'cheat.' A song *Newgate's Garland*, date unknown, was about:
"Ye gallants of Newgate whose fingers are nice/ In diving in pockets, or cogging of Dice."

cohoes (*n.*) A waterfall.

cohonk (*n.*) Virginia Indian. **(1)** A winter or year.
(2) A wild goose. In 1724 Hugh Jones writing about Virginia,
"They reckon the Years by the Winters, or *Cohonks*, as they call them; which is a Name taken from the Note of the Wild Geese."

coif (*n.*) A cap worn by sergeants at law and clerics.
"A close fitting white coif under the hood."

colewort (*n.*) A species of cabbage. The word has now evolved into *collard*.

colica pituitosa A phlegmy colic. The term was used figuratively by Henry Muhlenberg in 1764,
"a strange republic which has caught a fever or rather a suffering from colica pituitosa."

colin (*n.*) A quail. Adopted from Mexican.

collate (*v.*) To institute a clergyman. In 1683 James II wrote to Gov. Dongan of New York,
"And we do by these presents authorize and empower you to collate any person or persons to any churches."

collect (*n.*) The pond at Pearl and Franklin Streets in New York. An English corruption of its Dutch name *Kalch-hook* 'Shell point.'

college Indian An Indian who has gone to school. Hugh Jones used the phrase in 1724 writing about Virginia.

collier (*n.*) A coal miner or a coal merchant.

colloct (*v.*) A misreading of *collect*: to infer.

collop (*n.*) A thin slice of meat. From Middle English *scalop* 'scallop.' A 1787 cookbook instructed,
"Cut a stale leg of mutton into as thin collops as you can."

colluvies (*n.*) An accumulation of filth or dregs. From Latin *colluvio* 'a collection of dregs.' Nathaniel Ward in 1647 wrote,
"We have been reputed a colluvies of wild opinionists."

colony (*n.*) **(1)** A plantation or settlement. In 1624 The West India Company adressed itself to:
"All such as shall plant any colonies in New Netherlands."
(2) A government in which the governor is elected by the inhabitants under a charter of incorporation by the king, in contrast to one in which the governor is appointed.

colour (*n.*) A superficial cover, palliation, excuse. In 1765 Cadwalader Colden wrote,
"[The leaders of the mob] wanted some colour for desisting from their designs and save their credit from the deluded people."

comb fry A lady's miscellaneous toilet articles. *Fry* is a collective term for insignificant things, e.g. small fry. In 1740 William Byrd wrote,
"She threw her comb frey with all its furniture."

come in (*v.*) To cause to enter; import. In 1710 William Byrd and his wife had a:
"quarrel about the things she had come in."

comfit (*n.*) A piece of dried fruit preserved with sugar. From Latin *confectum* 'something prepared.' In 1722 Samuel Sewall reported that:
"Madame W[inthrop] served comfits to us."

comfrey (*n.*) A plant whose mashed roots were used to treat wounds. In 1775 Philip Fithian said that:
"the Hostler . . . fill[ed] it with Comfrey Roots pounded Soft."

command (*n.*) **(1)** A request to get or do something. In 1718 William Byrd:
"Went to know if Lord Boyle had any command to his father."
(2) An order for goods.
"I desire to be favored with her commands for London."

commencer (*n.*) A candidate for a bachelor's degree. Commencement takes place when the degree is granted.

commerce (*n.*) A card game in which cards were exchanged. William Byrd played it in 1718.

commissary (*n.*) **(1)** A church officer representing a Bishop of the Church of England. From Latin *commissarius* 'one to whom a duty is committed.'
(2) A Vice-Admiralty judge. In 1753 a commission read,
"We do by these Presents make . . . James Michie Esquire to be our Commissary."

commission of the peace The authority to act as a Justice of the Peace. In 1718 William Byrd:

"could get no commission of the peace for our country."

commissioners for collecting evidence An appointed body that took depositions for use in other jurisdictions. The phrase appeared in a 1780 New York document.

commit (*v.*) To incarcerate pending trial. After the Boston Massacre in 1770 a newspaper reported that:

"Capt. Preston was committed as were the soldiers who fired a few hours after him."

Committee of Correspondence A committee created by the Colonial legislatures in the 1760s and 1770s. The Virginia House of Burgesses created one:

"whose business it shall be to obtain most early and authentic intelligence of all such acts and resolutions of the British Parliament or proceedings of administration as may relate to or affect the British Colonies in America and to keep up and maintain correspondence and communication with our sister colonies respecting those important considerations."

Committee of the States A committee that acted as an executive committee when the Continental Congress was not in session.

commode (*n.*) **(1)** A kind of headdress. A 1787 advertisement in *Harper's Magazine* proposed:

"to furnish ladies with braids, commodes, cushions."

(2) A bureau. The use of the word to apply to a piece of furniture holding a chamber pot did not appear until 1851. In 1773 "[Joseph Cox] makes commodes, dressers and toilet-tables."

commodious (*adj.*) Convenient, suitable. In 1608 Capt. John Smith described Virginia as:

"pleasing and commodious."

commodity (*n.*) An advantage. In 1630 Francis Higginson promised:

"to tell the truth and tell the discommodities as well as the commodities."

common (*n.*) Any land owned by the public. It might be land held for timber or pasture, either outlying or in the center of town, as the Boston Common.

commonage (*n.*) The right of pasturage on a common. A 1734 Eastchester, New York, deed transferred:

"the right of commonage within Eastchester olde Patent."

commonality (*n.*) The common people. In 1676 Nathaniel Bacon rebelled against,

"unjust taxes on the commonality for the advancement of private favorites."

commonplace (*n.*) Short for *commonplace book*, a notebook. William Byrd:

"read a little in my commonplace" in 1710.

commons (*n.*) The common people. In 1676 Nathaniel Bacon, speaking for his peers stated:

"This we, the commons of Virginia, do declare . . . "

commonwealth (*n.*) A free state, a popular or representative government. The term legally applied to all, but only Massachusetts, Pennsylvania, and Virginia used it as such.

communibus annis *Latin* 'in average years.' A 1697 report on Virginia mentioned

that tobacco:
"sold communibus annis at five shillings."

company keeper It could be a prostitute, but doesn't have to be. Jonathan Edwards was prone to exaggerate in 1737:
"a young woman who had been one of the greatest company keepers in the whole town [Northampton, Mass.]."

compotier (*n.*) A fruit dish. [From French]

compound (*v.*) To settle amicably. In 1710 William Byrd wrote that:
"A man came . . . to compound for land escheated to the Queen."

compromit (*v.*) To put in danger by some previous act. In 1787 Jefferson wrote,
"The public reputation is, every moment, in danger of being compromitted with him."

conceit (*n.*) **(1)** A favorable opinion. In 1784 Franklin wrote,
"This was enough to put us out of conceit of such defenders."
(2) A conception, thought, idea. In 1619 minutes of the Virginia Assembly contained,
"such as may issue out of every man's private conceits."

concern (*n.*) **(1)** A motivation toward religious activity. In 1772 future minister Philip Fithian referred to:
"some under concern."
(2) An interest. Gouverneur Morris:
"proposed to him the supplying of the marine with provisions and offerd him a concern."

concert (*v.*) To arrange by agreement with someone, to form plans. A 1676 report on Bacon's Rebellion stated,
"300 men, taking Mr. Bacon for their commander, met and concerted together."

concession (*n.*) The 1664 grant to the inhabitants of New Jersey by the proprietors Berkeley and Carteret.

concourse (*n.*) A meeting; an assembly. A 1715 bulletin to The Board of Trade referred to:
"these concourses of people."

condition (*v.*) To make terms. In 1760 Washington wrote,
"Mr. Clifton came here and we conditioned for his land."

Conestoga wagon The covered wagon of western fame, first made in 1716 in the town of Conestoga, Lancaster County, Pennsylvania. It was named for a local Indian tribe whose name meant:
"at the place of the immersed pole."

conf. (*n.*) An abbreviation of *confection*; a mixture.

congee (*n.*) **(1)** Departing with customary civilities. Philip Fithian in 1775 wrote,
"after the ceremony of introduction, and our congees were over."
(2) Formal permission to leave. When Jefferson was ambassador to France,
"I have not yet received my conge." [From French *congé* 'permission, leave']

congo (*n.*) A black Chinese tea. A corruption of *kung-fu* 'work.' A 1783 newspaper advertised,
"Teas: Tonkay, Congo, Bohea."

Congregational Church The established church in Connecticut and Massachusetts. All were taxed to support it.

conner (*n.*) A variant of *cunner*, the blue perch. Samuel Sewall in 1685:
"Supped with a new sort of Fish called conner."

conquedle (*n.*) The bobolink. Etymology unknown. In 1783 John Latham wrote,
"This species is known in the country by the names of Bob-Lincoln and Conquedle."

construe (*v.*) To translate. In 1745 Yale Regulations required students to be:
"able extempore to read, construe and parse Tully, Vergil."

contain (*v.*) To abide; be contained in. In 1637 John Winthrop wrote a word used chiefly in Scotland and northern England,
"Two so opposite parties could not contain in the same body."

contemn (*v.*) To despise, to scorn. In 1732 William Smith wrote,
"Pretending himself to be a Protestant, dissenting minister, contemning and endeavoring to subvert the Queen's ecclesiastical supremacy."

continental (*n.*) **(1)** A soldier in the Continental Army as contrasted to one in the militia of one of the various states.
(2) Currency or securities issued by the Continental Congress after 1774.

contrive (*v.*) John Witherspoon used an obvious ellipsis when in 1781 he wrote,
"I wish we could contrive [to transport] it to Philadelphia."

convent (*v.*) To call before. In 1619:
"Capt. Spellman was convented before the [Virginia] General Assembly."

conventicle (*n.*) A secret assembly. New Netherland Regulations in 1641 said that,
"conventicles and meetings have been held here."

conveyancer (*n.*) One whose occupation is to draw deeds and leases for the conveying of property. In 1771 Franklin wrote about:
"two who were clerks to an eminent scrivener or conveyancer in the town."

convict servant A man sentenced to being an indentured servant. A 1751 newspaper advertisement appealed,
"Ran away from the Subscriber, last night, a Convict Servant Man, Named Edward Sutton."

conyfish (*n.*) One of several fish. Possibly named because it hides in holes of river banks as a rabbit does on land. Capt. John Smith in 1612 wrote,
"We were best acquainted with Conyfish, Rockfish, Eeles, Lampreyes, Catfish."

cooper (*n.*) One who makes casks. In 1610 the Virginia Colony had need of:
"good artificers as shipwrights, sturgeon dressers, turners, coopers, salt makers, iron men for furnaces and hammer, mineral men, gun founders, plow wrights, brewers, sawyers, fowlers, vine dresser."

copalm (*n.*) A tree which produces an amber-like exudation. In 1775 Bernard Romans wrote,
"Live oak abound here, intermixed with copalm and other timber."

copivi (*n.*) Short for *Balsam of Copivi*, a resin from several species of *Copiafera*; it was prescribed as a cure for gonorrhea, leucorrhea, and lung ailments.

copperas (*n.*) A green vitriol; used as a dye, as an ink base, and in tanning.

coppers (*n.*) A game, probably another name for *faro*, in which one places a copper on

or against his card. Caleb Rea in 1758, during the campaign against Ft. Ticonderoga, wrote,
"No officer nor Soldier shou'd play at Cards or Coppers."

copyhold estate A tenure of land in which the only evidence of title is in the copy of the rolls kept by the steward of a manor.

copy money The cost of copyright. In 1771 Franklin wrote that it:
"cost him nothing for copy money."

coral (*n.*) The ground up coral used in medical preparations for its alkaline and absorbent qualities.

coram (*adj.*) *Latin* 'before, in the presence of.' A 1713 document, when he was Judge of the Court of Common Pleas in New York, was signed,
"Coram, Caleb Heathcote."

cord (*n.*) **(1)** The hanging noose. A 1779 New York newspaper wrote about:
"four men of the Provincial corps, who had been made prisoners on the North River, tried and destined to the cords."
(2) A bedcord, a rope strung on a bed frame to support the mattress. A 1653 Massachusetts document referred to:
"one bedsteed and cord."

corder (*n.*) One who saw to it that wood for sale was in full cords. In 1654 two men in Boston were:
"chosen for corders of wood."

cordial (*n.*) **(1)** Anything that comforts, gladdens, or exhilarates. In 1775 Charles Lee wrote to a friend,
"The New England delegates I am told have lately received so many ribs that they want a Cordial."
(2) A stimulating drink for medicinal purposes. William Byrd in 1710 wrote that:
"Mr. Anderson advised me to give my people cordials since other physics failed."

cordwainer (*n.*) A shoemaker. From French *cordouan* 'leather from Cordoba.'

corfish (*n.*) A salted fish. In 1616 Capt. John Smith wrote,
"They take nothing but small Cod, whereof the greatest they make Cor-fish, and the rest is hard dried, which we call Poore-John."

corlear (*n.*) The Indian appellation for the Governor of New York. William Smith's 1757 *History of the Province of New York* explained,
"All Governors of New York were called corlear by the Indians in honor of a dutchman called Corlear who in 1665 saved Indians at Schenectady from the French." The Corlears Hook section of Manhattan, at the end of Grand Street, on the East River, is named for him.

cornet (*n.*) **(1)** The officer in a cavalry troop who carried the flag. In 1707 in Braintree, Massachusetts,
"Cornet Jos Allin was chosen Town Treasurer."
(2) A woman's headdress, originally Dutch, with two horn-like lace points.

corporation (*n.*) Cooperation was purposely misspelled in a 1780 song *A Pastoral Elegy* to rhyme with *oration.*
"They forc'd our Troops to ground their arms and eke their corporation."

correspondency (*n.*) A relationship. In 1619 The Virginia House of Burgesses tried to:
"keep them in such good respect of correspondency."

corruption (*n.*) Any putrid matter, pus. In 1692 Cotton Mather, describing one bewitched in Salem, Massachusetts, who had a sore lanced, wrote,
"several gallons of corruption ran out of it."

corslet (*n.*) A piece of body armor. In 1644, Southampton, New York, decreed that:
"Euery man within this towne that beareth armes shall haue a sufficient coslet of clabboard or other wood."

cosmographer (*n.*) One who describes the world. Charles Wolley in 1678 reported that:
"The City of *New York* by Dr. *Heylin* and other cosmographers is call'd *New Amsterdam.*"

cossas (*n.*) Plain Indian muslins. From Hindu *khassah* 'special.' A 1790 Pennsylvania newspaper advertised,
"Two yard Pullicat Cossacs."

cottrel (*n.*) A variant of *cotterel*, a pot hook. A 1651 Massachusetts document referred to:
"an iron pot, tongs, cottler & pothookes."

coulter (*n.*) The fore-iron of a plow that cuts the earth. A 1664 Connecticut inventory included:
"a share & culter."

Council of Estate A council created for the governance of Virginia under the instructions of the Virginia Council to Gov. Gates in 1609. It consisted of Philip, Earl of Montgomery, William, Lord Paget, and Sir John Starrington.

Council of Trade A council made up of the Lord High Chancellor, the Lord Treasurer, and ninety-nine others was committed with the care of the trade with the plantations in America by Charles II in 1660. It was superseded by the Board of Trade and Plantations in 1696.

countenance (*v.*) To favor; encourage. In 1749 Franklin wrote of the need to:
"encourage and countenance the youth."

counter bond A bond or security posted to indemnify another. A 1729 Philadelphia newspaper offered them for sale.

country custom Business from the surrounding countryside. In 1771 Washington had
"country custom coming in" to his mill at Piney Branch.

country mark A distinctive tribal scar on a slave's face. A 1754 South Carolina newspaper wrote of a slave:
"with several of his country marks down each side of his face."

couranteer (*n.*) A newspaper publisher. From Dutch *krant* from *korant* 'newspaper.' *The New England Courant* in 1722 reported:
"A full Meeting of the Couranteers, Gazetteers, &c."

coureur de bois French. 'a runner of the woods.' A Canadian hunter, trapper, or trader. A 1700 New York document referred to:
"severall of the French Coureurs de Bois or hunters."

course (*v.*) To place in orderly rows. A 1685 Maryland bill was:
"For the carpenter for pulling down the dormant windows of the court house and coursing the same with good boards."

court baron A court conducted by the lord of a manor to punish offenses of tenants and to settle disputes involving less than 40 shillings. From Latin *curia baronis* 'court of the baron, (or lord).'

courtier (*n.*) A supporter of the royal court, a Tory. Philip Fithian in 1774 surmised, "I conclude he is a courtier."

court leet A sheriff's court for criminal offenses below the degree of treason. *Leet* is from an Old English word, 'coming together, meeting.'

court messenger The official messenger of a civil jurisdiction. Claes van Elslant was the court messenger whom Van Tienhoven, the fiscal of New Amsterdam, sent in 1654 to chase the men from West Chester.

Court of Assistants The court in Massachusetts, organized in 1630, consisting of the Governor, Deputy Governor, and elected Assistants. It exercised both legislative and judicial power.

Court of Chancery A court of equity.

Court of Common Pleas A civil court.

Court of Exchequer A court of record in Virginia, administrating justice in questions of law and revenue. In 1771 the Governor of Virginia was instructed to:
"take care that a court of exchequer be called."

Court of General Sessions. A criminal court.

court of guard Not a court at all, but a guardhouse. A corruption of the French phrase *corps de garde* 'guard-house.'

Court of Judicature A court of appeals.

Court of Ordinary (*n.*) The probate or surrogate's court in New Jersey, Georgia, and South Carolina.

Court of Oyer and Terminer A court in New York and Virginia (1683–1691) with civil, criminal, and appellate jurisdiction. Directly from Old French meaning 'to hear and determine.'

Court of Quarter Sessions A criminal court, meeting quarterly. In 1732 *Poor Richard's Almanac* reported,
"Courts of Quarter Sessions are held at Philadelphia."

Court of Vice-Admiralty A court for marine cases.

cousin-german (*adj.*) Closely related. The word is related to *germane* 'akin,' rather than to Germany. Gouverneur Morris described an expression as:
"cousin-german to contempt."

cover (*v.*) To cause (animals) to breed. Washington once wrote that he:
"had a mare covered."

coving (*n.*) An arched projection supporting an upper story of a house. In 1713 Samuel Sewall:
"observed the water to run trickling down a great pace from the Coving."

covenous (*adj.*) Collusive, deceitful. The 1641 Massachusetts Body of Liberties referred to,
"all covenous or fraudulent alienations or conveyances of land."

cowboy (*n.*) An outlaw with Loyalist sympathies who ravished The Neutral Ground, southern Westchester County, New York, from the Battle of White Plains in October 1776 until government was reestablished in 1783. *See* **skinner.**

cowkeep (*n.*) One who tended the town cattle. In 1643 the citizens of Plymouth, Massachusetts, voted that:
"John Smythe shal be the Cowe Keep for this yeare to keep the Townes Cowes."

cowl (*n.*) A large tub. A 1640 Connecticut inventory included,
"4 brueing vessells, 1 cowl, 2 firkins."

cow lease (1) A pasture.
(2) The right to pasture in common, commonage. In 1642 in Massachusetts a man bequeathed his farm:
"reserving a peece of land called the cowleas."

cowpen (*v.*) To fertilize land by penning cattle on it. In 1760 John Clayton wrote that:
"a fresh piece of Ground . . . will not bear Tobacco past two or three years, unless Cow-penn'd."

cowskin (*n.*) A rawhide whip. In 1738 Franklin suggested that:
"A good cowskin, crabtree, or Bulls pizzle may be plentifully bestowe'd on your outward man."

cow walk Common pasture land. In 1652 a man bequeathed,
"My three divisions in the Cow walke of Dorchester [Mass.]."

coxcomb (*n.*) A superficial pretender to knowledge. Gouverneur Morris in 1774 wrote that:
"The troubles in America during Grenville's administration . . . stimulated some coxcombs to rouse the mob."

cozen (*v.*) To cheat. The etymology is debatable, but it may be from cousin 'kinsman, to cheat under pretext of kinship.' In 1620 William Bradford wrote,
"the rogue would cozen him."

crabs' eyes A concretion on the head of a fresh-water crawfish. It was prescribed to treat acid stomach and as a laxative.

crackling (*n.*) (1) Fat after rendering. A cookbook called for:
"1 qt. sifted corn meal and a teacup of cracklin."
(2) Corn bread containing crackling.

cracknell (*n.*) A hard, brittle cake. A 1701 dictionary defines it as:
"A sort of cakes made in shape of Dish and bak'd hard, so as to crackle under the Teeth."

cradler (*n.*) A workman who had rods attached to his scythe to catch the flax when he mowed it. In 1766 Washington recorded,
"pulling flax . . . and two cradlers hired."

crail (*n.*) A variant of *creel,* a wicker fish trap. Today it applies to the basket in which fish are placed after being caught on a line. In 1775 James Adair wrote,
"Indians . . . catching fish in long crails made with canes and hiccory splinters, tapering to a point."

crank[1] (*adj.*) Liable to capsize. From Dutch *krengen* 'careen.' John Harris' 1704 Lexicon defined it as,
"the Sea Term for a Ship that Cannot bear her Sails . . . for fear of oversetting."

crank[2] (*adj.*) Bent. A 1701 document referred:
"to a tree called the crank tree."

crape (*v.*) To curl hair, to form into ringlets. From French *crèpe* 'curled.' In 1774

Philip Fithian described one of the Carter girls' hair,
"It was crap'd up with two Rolls at each side."

credence, letter of A letter commending the bearer. In 1666 the Maryland legislature instructed The Lieutenant General to:
"draw the letters of Credence for Mr. Charles Brooke."

credit (*n.*) The capacity of being trusted. In 1766 Gov. Bernard of Massachusetts wrote of something:
"proved by the oaths of two gentlemen of credit."

creeper (*n.*) A pair of small andirons set between a larger pair to hold shorter logs, etc. Someone in 1655 in Massachusetts bequeathed:
"a p[air] of creepers & p[air] of toungs."

crib (*n.*) A small wooden raft. In 1776 Charles Carroll wrote,
"The smaller rafts are called *cribs*."

cricket (*n.*) An early form of bat and ball game with as few as two on a side. From Old French *criquet* 'hooked stick.' William Byrd played it in 1710 with two on a side on one occasion, with four on another.

crimp (*n.*) **(1)** An unscrupulous recruiter for ships' companies. In 1758 John Blake wrote,
"a crimp . . . who makes it his business to seduce the men belonging to another ship."
(2) An agent for a shipping company. In Franklin's *Autobiography*, first published in 1791, he reported that:
"a crimp's bill was put into his hand."

cripple (*n.*) A swamp. A 1647 deed described land as:
"extending along a meadow to a cripple or brushwood."

crisping pin A curling iron. In 1790 Mercy Warren in a poem referred to:
"wimples, mantles, curls and crisping pins."

croaker (*n.*) A predictor of misfortune. In his *Autobiography* Franklin wrote in 1771,
"There are croakers in every country, always boding its ruin."

crock (*v.*) To black with soot. In 1781 Thomas Hutchinson wrote,
"The thunder cloud gathered black enough to crock charcoal."

croes (*n.*) A variant of *croze*.

cronocko (*n.*) Virginia Indian, advisor. In 1618 William Strachey writing about Virginia mentioned:
"his cronoccoes, that is councellours."

croop (*n.*) Probably a Scottish pronunciation and spelling of *crop*. John Harrower (who was born in Scotland) recorded in his diary:
"spinning [his] croop of cotton at night."

crooper (*n.*) A variant of *crupper*, a horse's rump. In 1705 Samuel Sewell confessed,
"My horse fell with me this Journey, broke my crooper."

crop (1) (*n.*) A distinctive cut to indicate ownership. The 1699 Mamaroneck, N.Y., town records state,
"The mark of Capt Jeams mott a half Crop on the uper side of the Left ear."
(2) (*v.*) To cut off one or both ears as a punishment. In 1773 in Connecticut a man was:
"punished by branding, cropping and imprisonment."

cross cloth A head band.

cross dollar A Peruvian coin depicting a cross on one side, worth, in 1704, four shillings, four pence, three farthings.

cross garnet A door hinge. A 1653 Massachusetts document referred to:
"two payer of cross garnet & a payer of esses for doores." (You can almost hear the down-east accent.)

cross or pile The gambling game of flipping a coin. A corruption of the French *croix* 'the obverse of a coin' *ou* 'or' *pile* 'the reverse of a coin.'

croup (*n.*) Diphtheria, not merely the respiratory ailment and cough, although the word is of imitative origin. The cure prescribed was the juice of roasted onions.

crowd (*n.*) A descendant of an ancient Celtic six-stringed instrument. From Middle English *croude* 'belly.' In 1774 Dr. Alexander Hamilton reported that:
"the miller, I found, professed music and would have tuned his crowd to us."

crowdy (*n.*) A thick oatmeal.

crown (*n.*) A scalp. In 1687 in New York it was reported that:
"the Indians have taken 8 men 1 woman and 8 crowns or scalpes."

crowner (*n.*) A variant spelling of *coroner*. Roger Williams in 1656 referred to:
"the Crowners Inquest."

crown glass The finest English window glass; later superseded by cylinder glass. An advertisement in a 1725 Boston newspaper offered,
"the best Sort of London Crown Glass to put over prints."

croze (*n.*) The groove at the end of a barrel stave which admits the head. The 1730 Virginia Tobacco Law governed:
"hogsheads, which exceed eight and forty inches in the length of the stave, or thirty inches at the head, within the croes."

crud (*adj.*) Unripe, unrefined, unprepared. A shortening of the Latin *crudis* 'crude, raw.'

crump (*adj.*) Crunchy. A 17th-century cookbook described vegetables as:
"crump and green."

crupper (*n.*) A horse's rump. Sometimes used to apply to humans as in:
"jigg her crupper at dancing school." To *come a cropper* is to fall on one's backside, especially by being thrown over a horse's croup.

crusado (*n.*) This Portuguese silver coin had a cross on it because Alfonso I (1112–1185) had been a crusader.

cry (*v.*) To auction. In 1644 in New Haven,
"The marshall is to cry all lost things."

cucking stool. A chair into which a scold or a dishonest tradesman was fastened. Passersby could throw objects or insults at the victim. Occasionally the chair would be taken to water and the victim ducked. The word comes from Old Norse *kuka* 'dung,' from the resemblance of the stool to that which held a chamber pot. In 1665 the court in Maine ordered that:
"every town shall take care that there be a pair of stocks, a cage and couking stool."

cuckold (*n.*) A variant of *cockle*, burdock, a plant having small barbed fruits.

cucumber tree The magnolia tree, whose fruit looks like a small cucumber.

cuddy (*n.*) A small, ship's cabin under the poop deck; sometimes a cook room. In 1649 John Winthrop recorded that:
"he threw himself in at the door of the cuddy."

cuffee (*n.*) A word used for a Negro. From Tshi (the language of the Gold Coast) *Kofi* 'the name given to boys born on Friday.'

culheag (*n.*) A type of trap. Probably an Indian word. In 1784 Jeremy Belknap in New Hampshire recorded that:
"we saw the culheags or log-traps, which the hunters set for sables."

culler (*n.*) An inspector who selects, or culls, merchantable hoops and staves for market.

culliver (*n.*) A variant of *caliver*, a kind of hand gun, musket. In Connecticut in 1676 it was required that each man have:
"one good and seruiceable firelock gunn, viz a musket, culliver or curbine."

cully (*n.*) One easily tricked, culled, or imposed on. William Byrd in 1740 referred to:
"so many cullys at the other end of town."

culm (*n.*) A species of coal, difficult to ignite and yielding a smell. A 1703 law imposed:
"duties upon Coles, Culm and Cynders."

culverin (*n.*) A long, slender field piece with long range. An adaptation of the French *culevrin*, from Latin *colubra* 'snake.'

cup (*v.*) To employ a method for raising blood or other fluid to the surface of the skin. Heated cups were placed on the skin; as they cooled a vacuum was created causing a welt or wheal. In 1757 Franklin reported that:
"they cupped me on the back of the head."

curricle (*n.*) A chaise with two wheels drawn by two horses abreast. In 1775 Andrew Burnaby wrote,
"At colonel Washington's I disposed of my horses, and, having borrowed his curricle and servant I took leave of Mount-Vernon."

currier (*n.*) One who dressed and colored leather after it was tanned. Edward Peggy was a "curryer" in Boston in 1685.

curry. (*n.*) A shortening of *currency*. In 1760 Washington referred to:
"£1700 curry."

curtain (*n.*) The rampart of a fortified place between two bastions. A 1741 South Carolina document described:
"a square Fort . . . with four Bastions; the Curtain about sixty yards in length."

curtalax (*n.*) A variant of *cutlass*, a broad, curving sword. In 1685 a Boston man bequeathed:
"to my son Daniel Gookin . . . my curtelax."

cusk (*n.*) A burbot. In 1624 Capt. John Smith noted:
"cuske or small Ling, Sharke, Mackarell."

customer (*n.*) A customs Collector. In Massachusetts in 1649,
"Edward Bendall . . . chosen customer for the yeare ensuing."

cut (1) (*n.*) Something less than a full meal. In 1770 Washington:
"would not stay for dinner, taking a cut before it."

(2) (*v.*) To castrate. In 1710 William Byrd recorded that:
"Mr. Mumford cut my young horse."

cutler (*n.*) One who makes cutlery, knives, or other cutting instruments. In 1771 Franklin wrote,
"My father at last fixed upon the cutler's trade."

cut money Fractions of the Spanish dollar, which was frequently cut into halves, quarters, and eighths, and the pieces circulated as coins.

cut off To kill, probably by cutting off one's head. In 1710 William Byrd hired Tuscarora Indians:
"to cut off those Indians that committed the murder in Carolina."

cut work Lace, open work.

cuttoe (*n.*) A large knife. In 1654 land was bought on Long Island, they had to:
"pay to the afore said Ratiocan, Sagamore, three coats, three shirts, two cuttos."

cylinder glass Glass made into a cylinder after which it was cut and flattened. This process, introduced in 1752, eliminated the knob found in crown glass.

cymling (*n.*) A squash. A 1779 New Jersey document recorded,
"We . . . destroyed a large country of corn, pumpkins, cymlings, cucumbers."

cyttle (*n.*) A variant of *kettle*. In 1634 in Maine John Wynter wrote,
"The chimney is large . . . we can brew and bake and boyl our cyttle all at once."

dabble (*v.*) To tamper, meddle. In 1744 John Harrower referred to:
"seeing so many dabling wives at Johnsmiss."

daggle (*v.*) To run through mud and water. William Byrd went:
"daggling through the rain after him."

d—n (*v.*) John Leacock used the word in a 1776 play. It seems that it was all right to say it, but not to print it, although it appears spelled out in Webster's 1806 *Dictionary*.

damascene (*n.*) A damson plum. The tree was introduced into Greece and Italy from Damascus, Syria. In 1693 Increase Mather wrote about:
"choice Damascen Plumbs."

Damien and Ravillac The former suffered martyrdom in the third century for which he was sainted. The latter was François Ravillac, murderer of Henry IV of France (1553–1610). An anonymous writer in 1774 said,
"the tortures of Damien and Ravillac would be rendered abortive." This is an example of the literary allusions which complicate the reading of documents of an earlier age when education and referents were much different from ours.

damnify (*v.*) To damage. In 1775, a book on animal husbandry instructed to:
"condemn and burn that which appears damnified or insufficient."

dangerous (*adj.*) In a perilous condition. In 1776 a woman wrote,
"My husband was wounded . . . he is very dangerous."

dart (*v.*) To shoot. In 1774 Philip Fithian admitted that Princeton students:
"dart sunbeams upon the townspeople" with mirrors.

date (*n.*) Dog feces. Pomet's *Compleat History of Drugs* (1712) recommends,
"Take the powder of the white date of a dog . . . to take the stayns out of linnen."

daub (*n.*) The mud and plaster with which to fill the open spaces of a log house.

deaden (*v.*) To kill. James Adair in 1775 wrote that the Indians:
"deadened the trees by cutting through the bark."

dead men's caps A growth found at the base of certain trees. In 1675 John Josselyn recorded,
"There is an excrescence growing out of the body of the tree called spunck or dead men's caps."

dead shout In 1758 Robert Eastburn as a former captive of the Indians reported,
"They frequently every Day gave the dead Shout, which was repeated as many Times, as there were Captives and Scalps taken!"

deal (*n.*) A division of a piece of timber, a board or plank. In 1724 Hugh Jones wrote,
"may be found good Clapboards, Pipe Staves, Deals, Masts."

death head A skull or a design resembling one. A 1776 Boston newspaper advertised,
"death head buttons."

decline (*n.*) A deterioration caused by disease. In 1778 Jonathan Carver thought that rock liverwort:
"is esteemed as an excellent remedy against declines."

decreation (*n.*) A dialectal rendition of *recreation*. Robert Mumford in a 1776 play wrote,
"Why might not their servants have a little decreation."

decretal (*adj.*) Pertaining to a decree. A 1689 Pennsylvania document was:
"persuant to a Decretall order."

decumbent (*n.*) One lying down. In 1722 Dr. William Douglas wrote about:
"more decumbents, the infection [smallpox] was the more intense . . . October . . . was the time of the greatest decumbiture and mortality."

de die in diem *Latin.* 'From day to day.' In 1771 George III instructed the Governor of Virginia:
"You are not to allow them [the legislature] to adjourn themselves otherwise than *de die in diem* except Sundays and Holidays."

dedimus (n.) *Latin.* 'We have given.' Authorization as a judge. In 1711 Samuel Sewall recorded,
"By a dedimus, Col. Phillips . . . and my self."

deed poll A deed not indented, made by one party only. So called as it is cut straight across, polled, rather than indented as it would be were two parties to sign.

defensif (*n.*) A covering for a wound to keep air out.

delenda est Carthago *Latin.* 'Carthage must be destroyed.' In a 1775 speech before the Second Continental Congress rejecting Lord North's motion of reconciliation, a delegate used the exhortation immortalized by Cato the Elder (234-149 B.C.):
"An avowed partisan of ministry has more lately announced against us the dreadful sentence, 'delenda est Carthago.'"

delve (*v.*) To dig, to open the ground with a spade. A Scots immigrant returned home in 1774 because:
"he could not raise so much corn by delving as would maintain his family."

demicastor (*n.*) A hat made of beaver fur and some additive. *See* **castor.** A 1654 Massachusetts will bequeathed,
"1 Tafetie Scarfe, 6s; 1 demycaster."

demur (*n.*) **(1)** In law, a demurrer. A pleading in an action that the opponent's claim is insufficient and the action should be stopped.
(2) In ordinary speech, an objection. In 1775 John Rowe wrote,

"I bought them . . . and twill be a great hardship to have . . . a demur about them."

denizen (*n.*) A citizen. In New York in 1664 the law provided,
"That whoever shall take the Oathes is from that time a free Denizen."

deodand (*n.*) A personal chattel which caused the death of a person. It was forfeited to the king and sold for the benefit of the needy. In the patent for the Manor of Scarsdale, N.Y., from William III to Caleb Heathcote in 1701, it said,
"enjoying the premises, & every parte & parcell of the same, & all waifes, estrays, deodands, & goods of fellons, happening, or to happen, being or to be, forfeited within the s[ai]d Lordship or Mannour of Scarsdale."

derange (*v.*) To throw into confusion physically. In 1771 Franklin wrote,
"He deranged all our mercantile operations."

descant (*v.*) To comment, to discourse. In 1749 Franklin advocated teaching:
"morality, by descanting and making continual observations on the causes of the rise or fall of any man's character."

desobligeant (*n.*) *French.* 'A chaise for only one person;' also, 'unobliging.' One cannot, with room for only one, be very obliging. In 1770 Franklin:
"Got into my desobligeant to go home."

despot (*adj.*) A dialectal spelling of *desperate*, meaning 'great or very.' A character in a 1781 play commented in rather foppish, affected speech:
"This is despot good tea."

detinue (*n.*) An action to recover personal property retained unlawfully (if you couldn't get the culprit for piracy). In 1742 William Bollan, King's Advocate in Boston, wrote to the Board of Trade,
"As a cure of this mischievous trade is that actions of detinue be brought against some of the principal offenders."

devil's weed The hawkweed. In 1731 J. Seccomb advocated,
"Some Devil's Weed, And Burdock Seed to season well your porridge."

devoirs (*n.*) An act of civility or respect. In 1775 Philip Fithian wrote,
"After the ceremony of introduction and our devoirs were over."

devotion (*n.*) The state of being dedicated; ardent love or affection. In 1722 William Byrd wrote,
"If her daughter had been but one year older, she should have been at his devotion."

diabetis (*n.*) An emission of a long, continued, increased quantity of urine. In 1739 William Byrd discreetly wrote,
"Goblins scare a maid and her mistress into a diabetis."

diachylon (*n.*) A soothing medicinal plaster that contained several juices. The word comes from the Greek for 'very juicy, succulent.'

dialth *See* **marshmallow.**

diapalm (*n.*) An irritating medicinal lead plaster. It originally included palm oil.

diaper (*n.*) A linen fabric originally came *d'Ypres*, 'from Ypres,' Belgium. A 1686 inventory included:
"four diaper table cloths."

diascordium (*n.*) The dried leaves of the water germander, or scordium, were mixed with honey to stimulate stomach action.

diaseterion (*n.*) A powder of the herb satyrion mixed with honey; used as an aphrodisiac. A 17th-century cookbook prescribed,
"3 drams of diaseterion."

dicker (*n.*) A group of ten. From Latin *decem* 'ten.' It was used as a unit of trade of hides or skins.

diet (*v.*) **(1)** To feed; to board. In 1771 Franklin wrote,
"and there I lodged and dieted."
(2) To provide food. A 1782 Virginia document reported,
"two shillings for dieting a soldier."

diet drink A medicinal drink. Jonathan Carver in 1778 noted that wintergreen can be used:
"as a diet-drink for cleaning the blood."

dimity (*n.*) A stout, ribbed linen cloth resembling corduroy. A 1778 Boston newspaper offered:
"India Dimothy, Buttons and Twist, Snail Trimmings" for sale.

dingeely (*adv.*) Painfully as a result of bouncing. An adaptation from the verb *ding*, 'to strike or bounce.' In 1704 Sarah Knight wrote,
"This bare mare hurts me Dingeely."

dingle (*n.*) A narrow dale or valley. A 1660 Massachusetts document stated,
"Land lyes betweene two dingles."

dip (*v.*) To baptize by immersion. In 1782 Lucinda Dalrymple referred to:
"six people to be dipt."

Director General and Council of New Netherland The Director General was appointed by the Assembly of XIX and was tantamount to Governor of the province. The Council consisted of five men, the Provincial Secretary, and the Schout.

discommodity (*n.*) A disadvantage. *See also* **commodity.**

discover (*v.*) To uncover, disclose. In 1771 Franklin wrote,
"He would not discover the author."

dismal (*n.*) A swamp. In 1763 Washington wrote,
"5 miles from the aforesaid mills, near to which the Dismal runs."

disoppilate (*v.*) To clear obstruction.
"Sassafrass comforteth the liver and stomach and doth disopilate."

disordered (*adj.*) Disorderly. William Byrd in 1717 wrote that:
"my cousin Braye had been disordered, for which I gave him a good scolding."

disrest (*v.*) To disturb. Benjamin Church in 1696 hoped:
"to disrest and remove the Enemy from that Post."

disseize (*v.*) To dispossess wrongfully from freehold land. The Federation of Rhode Island in 1647 provided,
"No person in this Colony shall be taken or imprisoned or be disseized of his land."

dissuetude (*n.*) The failure to exercise or assert a privilege. In the 1640 *Freedoms and Exemptions* of the West India Company appears,
"in case of privilege, innovation, dissuetude, customs, laws."

distaff (*n.*) The staff of a spinning wheel to which a bunch of flax or tow was tied and from which the thread was drawn.

distemper (1) (*n.*) A political disorder, tumult. John Winthrop in 1645 wrote about:
"such distempers as have arisen."
(2) A disease. A 1750 Pennsylvania law referred to:
"mortal and contageous distempers."
(3) (*v.*) To make drunk. In 1656 William Bradford wrote,
"About 80. lustie men . . . did so distemper them selves with drinke as they became like madd-men."

distress (*v.*) To harass. In 1771 Franklin wrote of interferences with business that:
"distress't our trade."

dittany (*n.*) Pennyroyal; also, sometimes, snakeroot. It was brewed as a drink to counter nausea and it had a strong smell. Charles Wolley in 1678 wrote,
"Penny-royal or Ditany, whose leaves bruised are very hot and biting upon the Tongue, which being tied in a clift of a long stick, and held to the nose of a Rattle Snake, will soon kill it by the smell and scent thereof."

divident (*n.*) A share or division of land. A 1624 Virginia statute provided:
"that every privatt planters devident shall be surveyed."

division (*n.*) **(1)** A share or allottment of land; a divident. In Providence in 1721 a man received:
"Eleven acres of Land . . . upon the forty acre devision."
(2) A discord, variance, difference. In 1774 Gouverneur Morris wrote to John Penn,
"I was present at a grand division of the city."

dock (*n.*) A sheltered area, as a cove, where ships anchor. A 1648 Boston document recorded,
"The accounts of Mr. Hill . . . Edward Bendall about the cove or dock."

dog dollar A Dutch silver dollar depicted a lion on the obverse, jokingly described as a dog. A 1697 Virginia document referred to
"52 Dollers, commonly called Lyon or Dog Dollers."

dog fox A male fox. A female is a bitch. Washington often hunted foxes; in 1769 he noted,
"Started and killed a Dog fox."

dog whipper One hired to chase dogs out of church. In 1662 in Massachusetts,
"The owner of the dogs shall pay sixpence for every time they come to meeting, that doth not pay for the dog whipper."

dogwood (*n.*) A brew from the flowers, fruit, and outer bark of the dogwood tree prescribed to counteract fever and malaria; a brew from the inner bark, taken for dysentery. In 1717 William Byrd
"took a dogwood which made me sleep pretty well."

don (*n.*) An important person, or maybe one who just thinks he is. From the Spanish title of respect. In 1744 Dr. Alexander Hamilton wrote of the Hungarian Club in New York,
"To talk bawdy and to have a knack att punning passes among some there for good sterling wit. Govr. Clinton himself is a jolly toaper and . . . is esteemed among these dons."

dool (*n.*) A variant of *dole*, a boundary. A 1653 Massachusetts law provided,
"In Cace That any neglect to set up Dools by stacks or fences They shall paie 5s."

dopping stool A cucking or ducking stool. In 1654 in Portsmouth,
"It is ordered that a dopping stool shalbe made in this toowne and sett at the side of the po[n]de."

dormant (*adj.*) Neglected, unused. A 1662 Plymouth law referred to:
"both meddow lands improved lands or dormand lands."

dornick (*n.*) A coarse fabric used for curtains; it originally came from Doornick, Belgium (French *Tournai*). A 1648 Massachusetts will bequeathed,
"a payre of darnicle Curtaines & Vallens."

dorp (*n.*) The Dutch word for 'village,' used in New Netherland and later in New York.

dorseteen (*n.*) A dorset cloth; a low grade, plain-woven cotton or wool fabric. It was advertised for sale in a 1774 Philadelphia newspaper.

double bowl A punch bowl that held two quarts. A tavern in Newburyport, Maine rendered a bill for:
"A double bowl punch."

double house A house with rooms duplicated on each side of the entrance. A 1726 Boston newspaper offered,
"To be Sold, A well built brick double House, in good repair."

doublet (*n.*) A double-thick garment fastened in front, generally without sleeves, worn by women or, usually, men. In 1675 Benjamin Tomson rhymed,
"Deep-skirted doublets, puritan capes/ Which now would render men like upright apes."

doubloon (*n.*) A Spanish gold coin worth sixteen silver dollars. Originally double the value of a *pistole*. In 1757 Richard Haddon, commander of the privateer *Peggy*, testified,
"Having on Board ten Doubleloons."

dowd (*n.*) A nightcap. William Byrd in 1740 wrote,
"Tho she put on nothing but the dowd she lay in."

dower (*n.*) Property owned by a bride at the time of her marriage. Washington's diary in 1760 refers to:
"3 Dower Negroes" and a "dower plantation," and in 1769 he:
"Rid over [his] dower Land."

dowlas (*n.*) A coarse linen cloth originally from Daoulas, Brittany. A 1780 Philadelphia newspaper offered:
"check dowlas."

dowry (*n.*) The share of a man's estate which a widow holds for her lifetime. *See also* **dower**. A 1708 deed provided,
"free of intails, joynters, dowries, extents."

doxy (*n.*) A prostitute. A character in a 1776 play said,
"I'll go and inform his Lordship and his pair of doxies; I suppose by this time they have trimmed their sails, and he's done heaving the log."

dozens (*n.*) A coarse woolen cloth, Devonshire kersey. In 1629 a man ordered a:
"suit of Northern Dussens."

drab (*n.*) A heavy, woolen cloth used for overcoats. Undyed it was a drab color. A 1713 Massachusetts document stated,
"He is making a Coate of extraordinary good drab."

draft (*n.*) (**1**) An upper branch of a stream. A 1742 report in Maryland stated,
"We follow the Greatest Longest Branches & Drafts."
(**2**) A drawing. A 1778 letter to Gen. Gates spoke of:
"orders for our having an equal draft for our clothing."
(**3**) An allowance for error made in weighing. In 1757 William Thompson wrote,
"To put his Foot into the Scale to weigh it down to make the Draft good."

drag (**1**) (*n.*) A kind of harrow.
(**2**) The trail of scent left by a fox. In 1772 Washington wrote,
"Touched the Drag where we found the last, but did not move the fox."
(**3**) (*v.*) To hunt a fox with dogs. In 1773 Washington:
"dragged a fox for an hour."

dragee (*n.*) A sugar-coated nut or fruit; also, a sugar-coated medicinal pill. In 1774 Monsieur Lenzi offered:
"All sorts of sugar plums, dragees, barley sugar, white and brown sugar candy . . . for sale."

draggle tail A skirt dirtied by dragging on the ground. A song sang of:
"Girls with their milking pails, who trudge up and down with their draggle tails."

dragon beam A short horizontal beam in a hip roof of a house. There are also a *dragon summer* and a *dragon tie.*

dragon's blood The rhizome of *draconis calamis.* It was ground, and, in different mixtures, prescribed for diarrhea, catharsis, and syphilis.

dragoon (*n.*) A mounted infantryman. Whereas cavalry fought on horseback, dragoons scouted, pursued, and moved on horseback, but dismounted to fight. The word is derived from a firearm called a *dragon,* which spit fire from its mouth. Benedict Arnold's 1780 estimate of the strength of the garrison at West Point included:
"Colonel Sheldon's Dragoons."

drail (*n.*) A fishhook used for trolling. An adaptation of *trail,* which one does when one trolls. In 1634 William Wood wrote,
"These Macrills are taken with drails."

drake (*n.*) A small piece of artillery. From Latin *draco* 'dragon.' *See* **dragoon.** In 1649 John Winthrop recorded,
"at their landing the Captain entertained them with a guard and divers vollies of shot and three drakes."

dram (**1**) (*n.*) A drink of whiskey, taken in one gulp. Technically it is ⅛ fluid ounce. The word comes from the Greek coin *drachma* which weighed, in apothecaries' weight, ⅛ ounce. By extension there are *dram bottle, dram cup*, and *dram shop.* John Rowe's 1774 diary refers to:
"my leather dram bottle."
(**2**) (*v.*) To drink drams. In 1771 Franklin recorded,
"They discovered his dramming by his breath."

draper (*n.*) A dealer in cloth.

draught (*n.*) A piece of land to be acquired by drawing lots. A 1673 Connecticut law provided,
"Every man hence forward shall have their draughts of land." *See also* **draft** with which it was often interchangeably used.

draw (*v.*) (**1**) To take from an oven or kiln. In 1760 Washington:
"began drawing bricks, burning lime."

(2) To eviscerate. A 17th-century cookbook instructed,
"Take a fat capon & pull & draw it."

drawback (*n.*) **(1)** A deduction from profit. A 1775 letter regarding a cargo said,
"However considerable you may consider this drawback I assure you it is much less than I apprehended would have been the case from the miserable situation of the cargo."
(2) A remission of duty upon the export of imported goods. In 1771 Gov. Dunmore of Virginia was instructed to enact:
"An Act to prevent Frauds in the Drawback of the Duties on Liquor imported into that Colony."

drawboy (*n.*) Originally, a boy who drew a loom's harness cords; later the mechanism that did it; also, the kind of cotton cloth so made. A 1776 Boston newspaper advertised,
"124 pieces hairbines, 32 pieces draw-boys, 150 dozen cuttoe knives."

drawers (*n.*) In addition to the undergarment which one draws on one's legs, Franklin called a pajama-like lounging garment which he wore in hot weather his:
"long drawers."

drawing plaster A poultice that promoted the formation of pus.

drawn way A road for hauling or drawing wood. A 1640 Dedham, Mass., law referred to:
"who so euer hereafter shall annoy any high way or drawen way."

draw window A window opened by drawing inward.

drench (*n.*) Any medicine forcibly given. In 1750 Thomas Walker wrote,
"I rub'd the wounds with Bears oil, and gave him a drench of the same."

Dresden work A lace made by removing some threads and drawing others together to form patterns.

dress (*v.*) **(1)** To put in good order. In 1643 Roger Williams wrote,
"They plant it, dresse it, gather it." Also, The Pennsylvania Flour Inspection Act of 1725 referred to:
"ill dressed or unmerchantable wheat."
(2) To search thoroughly. A 1676 Connecticut document recorded,
"We girt the s[ai]d swamp and with English & Indian souldrs drest it, and within 3 hours slew and tooke prisoners 171."

dresser (*n.*) One employed in preparing or trimming anything. A *sturgeon dresser* prepares fish for cooking. A *leather dresser* finishes leather after tanning.

dressing glass A mirror over a dressing table. A 1732 South Carolina newspaper offered for sale,
"Sconces, and dressing Glasses."

drift (*n.*) A driving. Hence, *drift highway*, *driftway*, a common road for driving cattle. A 1751 deed in Mamaroneck, N.Y., states,
"Beginning at a heap of Stones which is the South east Corner of Underhill Budds Land and the Northwesterly Side of a Drift way left by the proprietors of Mamaroneck between the Great lots and lower lots."

drill (*n.*) A cotton material with a diagonal design. From German *Drillich* 'triple-twilled (thread).' The 1792 Congress felt:
"It would . . . be good policy to raise the duty . . . on . . . drillings, osnaburgs, ticklenburgs."

drink (*v.*) To smoke, to inhale. In 1638 Roger Williams wrote,
"Arthur called him to drink tobacco."

drisk (*n.*) A drizzly fog. Samuel Sewall in 1717 recorded that:
"my calash defended me well from the Cold Drisk."

driver (*n.*) **(1)** One who impounded cattle and swine. In 1686 Charlestown, Mass.,
townspeople:
"Chose . . . drivers of the sd pasture."
(2) A slave acting as a slave driver. In 1772 Col. Joseph Habersham had:
"A most valuable Negro . . . . The fellow is my Driver at Dean Forest [Georgia]."

droger (*n.*) A cargo vessel. In 1781:
"a droger, laden with tobacco" was seen off Maryland.

drop shot The firearm shot made by dropping molten lead in a shot tower to get it
perfectly round. A 1638 Maryland document referred to:
"a rondlett of drop-shot, 2 gunnes."

drove (*n.*) A group of Negro slaves. They were treated so impersonally that a group
was sometimes referred to as one would refer to a *drove* of horses or cattle. Robert
Rogers did so in 1765,
"Their droves of negroes are employed round the year."

drover (*n.*) One who dealt in cattle and sheep; also, one who drove them. In 1774 a
writer reported that:
"The factor was also a drover."

drugget (*n.*) A wool cloth for wearing apparel. It was one of the products mentioned
in the Woollen Act of 1699.

drum (*n.*) A noisy gathering at a private home. John Andrews in a 1773 letter wrote
of:
"a drum or rout given by the admiral last Saturday evening."

dry bones A skinny person. In 1737 Jonathan Edwards reported,
"The noise amongst the dry bones waxed louder."

dry salter A dealer in salted or dry meats, pickles, etc. It was one of the trades which
in 1681 William Penn said depended on navigation.

ducape (*n.*) A stout silk cloth. Origin uncertain. Widow Hendly offered:
"Ducapes and castor hats" for sale in a 1783 Philadelphia newspaper.

ducatoon (*n.*) A silver coin, Italian or Flemish, first struck in 1598. A little ducat. A
1671 Maryland document referred to:
"Sterling duccatones att Seaven Shillings."

ducid (*adj.*) Phonetic spelling for *deuced*, 'devilish.' One line of *Yankee Doodle* goes,
"Upon a ducid little cart."

ducking stool *See* **cucking stool.** In 1663 Maryland passed:
"An Act for the Erecting a Pillory Stocks and Ducking stoole in every county."

duffel (*n.*) A coarse but soft woolen cloth widely used for trading with the Indians. It
was originally made in Duffel, near Antwerp, Belgium. Among other things
Stephanus Van Cortlandt gave:
"14 fathoms of Duffels" to the Indians for land in 1677.

Duke's Laws When the British took over New Netherland from the Dutch, the

Duke of York convened delegates from all the towns in the province. They enacted a code of laws for the governance of the province of New York on June 24, 1665.

dumb betty A mechanical device such as a dumb waiter or a washing machine. A 1766 Boston newspaper wrote of:
"The utility of Tubs, Cags, and Dumb-Bettys."

dum latet in herba. Latin. 'While hiding in the grass.' In 1679 Charles Wolley chose to say it in Latin.

Dumpler *See* **Dunker.**

dun (*n.*) A mayfly. William Byrd in 1740 wrote,
"If a dun happens to ruffle his temper."

Duncard *See* **Dunker.**

dunfish (*n.*) A dunned codfish. Twice salted, the fish became dun colored. A 1776 Boston newspaper advertised,
"Choice Dumb-Fish."

dung (*v.*) To manure with dung. A 1775 book said,
"The raising of hemp required rich land and dunging." *See* **manure.**

dunghill fowl An ordinary chicken. In 1689 Samuel Sewall recorded that:
"Mr. Mather, Son and I sup'd on two Dunghill fowls."

Dunker (*n.*) A member of the German Baptist Brethren. So called because they dipped three times in the ceremony of baptism. From German *tunker* 'to dip.' Also *Dumpler, Duncard.*

durance (*n.*) A glazed woolen stuff called by some 'everlasting.' In 1744 James MacSparran recorded,
"My wife put her red Durance Petticoat in the Frame."

durante placito Latin. 'During pleasure.' The 1767 South Carolina *Remonstrance* deplored:
"marriages that are only temporary or *durante placito.*

durham boat A large, shallow-draft boat. It was used on the Delaware River, could carry 50 to 60 casks of flour, and was named for its designer.

duroy (*n.*) A coarse woolen fabric like tammy; not the same as corduroy. A 1715 Boston newspaper advertised,
"Winter Goods, Shallouns, Duroys."

Dutch (*adj.*) German. Probably in confusion with German *Deutsch* 'German.' The word survives in *Pennsylvania Dutch.*

Dutch gold An alloy of 11 parts of copper and 2 of zinc; used as a substitute for gold leaf. In 1749 Franklin wrote,
"Take leaf gold, leaf silver, or leaf gilt copper, commonly called leaf brass or Dutch gold."

Dutch oven There were two types: a covered cast-iron pan to hold burning coals, and a brick oven in which a fire was built, then removed. Both were used for baking.

Dutch pound In 1678 Charles Wolley wrote that in New York:
"a Dutch pound contains eighteen ounces."

Dutch quill A pen from Holland, hardened by heating. A 1778 Boston newspaper

advertised:
"Dutch Quills, Spinnet Hammers, Japan'd Waiters."

Dutch stove A German stove. It was stoked from a room other than the one heated.
In 1744 Franklin commented,
"You do not lose the pleasing Sight nor Use of the Fire, as in the Dutch stove."

ear mark A cut on the ear of an animal to indicate ownership. In 1738 W. Stephens in Georgia wrote,

"He swore that his Hogs were all marked with the same Ear-Mark."

earning (*n.*) A curdled milk or rennet. From Middle English *erne* 'to curdle.' A 17th-century cookbook instructed to:

"Put in a little mild earning in a gallon of new milk."

earwig (*n.*) An insect reputed to crawl into people's ears; hence, a sycophant or whispering busybody who metaphorically crawls into people's ears. In 1778 *Lady's Magazine* wrote,

"Instigated by some of those dirty earwigs, who will for ever insinuate themselves near persons in high office."

Eastland merchants Those traders from countries bordering on the Baltic Sea. In 1681 William Penn listed them as ones benefiting from navigation.

easy (*adj.*) Not burdensome, moderate. Samuel Sewall in 1700 commented,

"Though they might have it at easy rates."

ebenezer (*n.*) A song of praise to God. Cotton Mather in 1693 said,

"Many an Ebenezer has been erected unto the Praise of God."

Ebo (*n.*) A slave from the African Ibo tribe. A 1732 South Carolina newspaper advertised,

"Stolen . . . an old Ebo Negro Man."

ebullition (*n.*) The operation of boiling. In 1721 Cotton Mather wrote,

"I must mightily take heed unto my own Spirit, and watch against all Ebullitions of Wrath, lest being provoked, I speak unadvisedly with my Lips."

ebulum (*n.*) The juice of elder and juniper berries, spiced and sweetened.

economist (*n.*) One who manages domestic concerns frugally. Philip Fithian in 1775 described the wife of his employer,

"Mrs. Carter . . . a remarkable economist."

écu (*n.*) A French silver coin. It was about the size of an English crown and depicted an *écu* 'shield.'

eddo (*n.*) A variety of arum. An African word from the Gold Coast. In 1775 Bernard Romans wrote that it:
"is good food for negroes."

edging (*n.*) The land bordering a shore. In 1783 a Long Island, N.Y., man bequeathed:
"my edgings from the beach to the beach channel."

eelpout (*n.*) A delicate fish resembling an eel. In 1775 Bernard Romans wrote,
"Besides these there are three Species of Eel Pouts."

effulgent (*adj.*) Shining, bright. In 1774 John Trumbull rejoiced,
"The morning dawns, the effulgent star is nigh."

elaboratory (*n.*) A laboratory, a munitions factory. In 1776 Congress authorized:
"at Carlisle, Pennsylvania, a magazine . . . and also . . . an elaboratory adjacent."

elbow chair An armchair. Samuel Sewall in 1696 wrote,
"I reach'd the elbow chair to him and with my Arms crowded him into it."

Election Court In Plymouth and Massachusetts Bay, the General Assembly which elected the colony's officers. William Bradford in 1656 spoke of:
"ye spring of ye year, about ye time of their Election Court."

electuary (*n.*) A confection of powders and honey. A 1756 medical book noted that:
"the antiscorbutic Electuary . . . is very efficacious in this disease."

elixir (*n.*) In medicine and in general use, a liquid with more than one component. Sometimes intoxicating.

ell (*n.*) A measure of length. In the Colonies the English *ell* of 45 inches was used. In other countries it designated other lengths. Originally it was the distance from the elbow to the tip of one's fingers. William Bradford in 1630 wrote of:
"125 yards of kersey, 127 ellons of linen."

embassage (*n.*) The sending of an ambassador. Thomas Morton in 1632 wrote of undertaking:
"an embassage to treat with foreign princes."

embody (*v.*) To form or collect into a body. In 1675 Connecticut:
"Ordered, that each county doe speedily rayse . . . sixty soulders . . . who shall be imbodyed."

emolument (*n.*) Profit. The 1668 royal patent to John Richbell for Mamaroneck and Scarsdale, N. Y., entitled him to:
"all other profits, immunities and emoluments to the said parcel or tract."

emulous (*adj.*) Desirous or eager to imitate. William Eddis in 1792 wrote,
"Attracted by the moderation and equity of his government [they] were emulous to obtain settlements."

en cavalier *French.* Arrogantly. In 1739 William Byrd used the phrase to describe the way Mrs. Spotswood's sister, Miss Theys, greeted the Governor.

enfeoff (*v.*) To grant a freehold estate. A 1683 Indian deed to Stephanus Van Cortlandt in New York provided,
"to bargain, sell, alein enfeof and confirm."

enfranchise (*v.*) To make a freehold, a land lease in perpetuity. In 1687 the royal grant to John Pell in New York involved:

"land . . . held, deemed . . . be an intire infranchised townshipp, manner and place . . . [to] have, hold and enjoy."

engage (*v.*) To promise. *See* **gage.** In 1760 Washington recorded,
"Call'd at Mr. Possy's . . . after he had engaged to let me have it at 20/."

engine (*n.*) A trap or snare; often abbreviated to *gin.* In 1616 Capt. John Smith wrote of young Indians,
"He is very idle who is past twelve years of age and cannot do very much; and she is very old who cannot spin a thread to make an engine to catch them."

enginery (*n.*) A machination. In 1766 Robert Rogers mentioned:
"all the engin'ry of love at work."

English corn Any cereal except Indian corn; maize. In 1698 Samuel Sewall reported:
"a plentifull Harvest both English and Indian."

English grass Bluegrass. In 1785 Washington complained,
"The little rain which fell prevented my continuing to pull the seeds of the bleu or English grass."

Englishman's fly A bee. In 1778 Thomas Anburey wrote,
"The Indians . . . have no word for a bee, and therefore they call them . . . the Englishman's fly."

Englishman's foot A plantain. In 1687 botanist John Clayton wrote,
"As to our Plantain, they [Indians in Virginia] call it the Englishman's foot."

English potato An Irish potato. In 1750 James Birket remarked,
"They have . . . English or whats commonly called Irish Potatoes."

English school An elementary school. A 1780 New Jersey document stated that:
"an English School is kept contiguous to the Academy, where Reading, Writing, Arithmetic and several Branches of the Mathematics are taught."

engross (*v.*) **(1)** To copy in a large hand. Statutes were engrossed when they were ready for final action. The Declaration of Independence was engrossed on July 3, 1776.
(2) To purchase large quantities with a view to sell again. In 1771 instructions to the Governor of Virginia stated,
"large tracts of land have been engrossed by particular persons." Also, in 1710 a Boston newspaper reported,
"Our Governour has Issued a Proclamation, prohibiting all persons to engross any large quantities of all sorts of provisions."

enjoy (*v.*) To get pleasure from. When in 1710 William Byrd wrote,
"In the afternoon I enjoyed my wife," he meant 'physically.'

enlist (*v.*) To enter on a list. In 1768 Washington:
"began to enlist my Corn Ground at the mill."

ensign (*n.*) The lowest commissioned officer in the infantry; he carried the ensign or flag. In 1756 Washington wrote,
"I can instance several cases where a captain, lieutenant, and . . . ensign . . . will go on duty at a time."

entail (*n.*) The limiting of the settlement of a landed estate to issue or certain classes of issue. A 1708 deed to part of Ridgefield, Ct., mentioned,
"will, intails, joynters, dowries . . . extents."

enter (*v.*) To file a claim to land by entering, or recording it in a land office.

entertain (*v.*) To keep in service. William Byrd in 1710 wrote of:
"getting evidence against the men who entertained my negroes."

entertainment (*n.*)   **(1)** Provisions and lodging. The 1767 South Carolina *Remonstrance* referred to:
"a tavern . . . [to] provide entertainment for man and horse."
(2) Provision for the table. In 1675 Mary Rowlandson complained,
"We were feeble with our poor and coarse entertainment."

entry (*n.*) The act of entering. Also, the land obtained in this way. In 1733 William Byrd:
"rode with my Overseer to a new Entry I had made on Blue Stone Creek."

environ (*v.*) To surround. Capt. John Smith described Indians hunting,
"Having found the deer, they environed them with many fires."

epispastic (*adj.*) Blistering.

equivote (*n.*) A tie vote. The 1641 Massachusetts Body of Liberties provided that:
"the Governor shall have a casting voice whensoever an Equi vote shall fall out."

erf (*n.*) *Dutch.* 'A land measure about one-half acre.' A 1675 New York deed (eleven years after Dutch withdrawal) still mentioned:
"making over ye said erve or parcell of land."

erminet (*n.*) A material spotted to look like ermine. A 1754 South Carolina newspaper advertised,
"cotton gowns, fine striped hollands, erminets, blue and white printed handkerchiefs."

eryngo (*n.*) The sea holly. A 17th-century cookbook instructed,
"take a pound of fayre oryngo roots yt are not knotty."

escheat (*n.*) The land forfeited to the state because a man died intestate or for want of an heir or claimant; also, the forfeiting thereof. The 1771 instructions to the Governor of Virginia included:
"You do not dispose of any forfeitures or escheats to any person . . . ."

espontoon (*n.*) A spontoon or half-pike; a spear with a crossbar. The 1792 Congress provided that:
"the commissioned officers shall Severally be armed with a sword or hanger, and espontoon."

Esquire The title given to any owner of a large tract of land. It was also the title given to a Justice of the Peace, but as nearly every lawyer in colonial America at one time became a J.P., the title ultimately devolved on all lawyers. The word was originally *squire* from Latin *scutarius* 'shield-bearer.'

essoin (*n.*) An excuse for neglecting to appear in court. The 1660 Navigation Act provided,
"Wherein no essoin, protection or wager of law shall be allowed."

estate (*n.*) A condition. In 1608 Capt. John Smith wrote,
"[We] greatly refreshed our weak estates."

estrange (*v.*) To pass ownership. A 1661 deed in Mamaroneck, N.Y.:
"[I] doe this day alienate and estrange from mee, my heires and assignes."

estray (*n.*) A beast that has strayed from its owner. The 1701 grant to Caleb Heathcote for Scarsdale, N. Y., read,

"William The Third . . . doe . . . grant . . . all waifs, estrays, deodands & goods of fellons.''

Ethiopian (*n.*) A Negro. A 1722 Boston newspaper reported:
"Having in his Garden a plentiful Crop of Rare Ripes, he agreed with an Ethiopian Market Man.''

euphorbium (*n.*) The sap of the spotted spurge was a strong emetic and laxative; in a plaster it was used for palsy. The plant, originally from Africa, was named for Euphorbus, a Greek physician to Juba, King of Mauritania.

Evangelical (*adj.*) Anglican.

Evangelists of Almighty God The four gospels. A 1717 document mentioned:
"being sworn on the holy Evangelists.''

even (*n.*) A shortening of *evening*. In 1692 Samuel Sewell referred to,
"last sabath day sennight at even.''

everlasting (*n.*) A wool or wool-cotton cloth for clothing. *See* **durance**. It was advertised for sale in a 1783 Philadelphia newspaper.

excite (*v.*) To call into action. The 1767 South Carolina Remonstrance hoped that:
"learned and goodly men may be excited to come over to us.''

execution (*n.*) The carrying into effect of a court sentence. In the 1677 charter of West New Jersey:
"And if he . . . [is] condemned by legal trial . . . [to] lie in execution till satisfaction of the debt.''

exequatur (*n.*) A written recognition issued to a consul or commercial agent. An adopted Latin word meaning 'he may perform.'

exercise (*v.*) To conduct a religious service. In 1633 John Winthrop wrote,
"Refusing to leave either the place or his exercisings he was disenfranchised and banished.''

exhibit (*v.*) **(1)** To pay for maintenance. In 1722 a grant was given at Harvard,
"The yearly interest [is] to be exhibited to such members of the College as need it.''
(2) To present to a court. A 1704 Boston newspaper reported,
"[Men] were brought to the Barr, and the articles exhibited against them read.''

expin (*n.*) A linchpin; a pin through an axle to keep the wheel from slipping off. A 1648 inventory included,
"waine, wheels, expinns.''

expostulation (*n.*) Reasoning with a person in opposition. The 1643 New England Articles of Confederation said,
"without any further meeting or expostulation.''

ex supra abundatandi *Latin* 'generously from above [The States General].' In 1634 the patroons of New Netherland wrote to The States General,
"The Patroons Colonies were *ex supra abundatandi* confirmed.''

extent (*n.*) A writ commanding a sheriff to value the land of a debtor. A 1708 deed in Connecticut provided,
"free of . . . will, intails, joynters, dowries . . . extents.''

eye servant A servant one had to keep his eye on. In 1717 William Byrd described one who:

"Would make an admirable overseer where servant will do as they are bid, but eye-servants who want an abundance of overlooking are not so proper to be committed to his care."

fabian (*adj.*) Delaying, dilatory. In imitation of the Roman general Quintus Fabius Maximus who conducted operations against Hannibal in 202 B.C. by harassing him but declining decisive battles, thus living to fight another day. A 1777 Philadelphia newspaper said,
"Washington persisted in his Fabian system of defense."

facetious (*adj.*) Merry, jocular. From Latin *facetus* 'well made, choice, elegant.' In 1775 Philip Fithian wrote,
"He calls the Doctor facetious, sensible and prudent."

facit (*adj.*) Artificial. Derived from Latin *facit,* the third person singular, present tense of *facere* 'make.'

factor (*n.*) An agent. From Latin. A 1742 letter from New York to the Board of Trade said,
"Trade from Holland is carried on by factors here for the sake of their commission."

faculty (*n.*) A personal quality. A 1623 document referred to:
"trades, professions and faculties of all the pass[enger]s."

fag end The useless, untwisted end of a piece of rope. The phrase was often used metaphorically. Thomas Morton in 1632 wrote,
"The fag end of it he passes away, as a superfluous remnant."

faggot (*n.*) **(1)** A bundle of sticks used for fuel. In 1780 Benedict Arnold described the defenses of West Point as:
"easily fired with faggots dipped in pitch."
(2) A bundle of pieces of iron or steel ready to be heated and rolled out into bars. A 1714 Boston newspaper advertised,
"To be sold . . . best English Steel, in Fagotts."

fain (*adj.*) Glad, pleased. In 1646 William Bradford recorded,
"This fellow was so desperate a quarreler, as the captain was fain many times to chain him under hatches from hurting his fellows."

fair chance A card game. William Byrd played it in 1717.

faith (*adj.*) Faithful. In 1679 Charles Wolley recorded,

"[Indians] are faith guides in the woods in times of peace and dangerous enemies in times of war."

falchion (*n.*) A short, curved sword. From Latin *falx* 'sickle.' A 1783 song referred to:
"her patriot faulchion sheaths."

fall (*n.*) A wide, unstarched collar. A 1673 inventory included,
"12 pa[ir] fr[ench] falls."

fall back Designating a type of chaise whose top could fall back. A 1776 Boston newspaper advertised,
"A Fall Back Chaise with harness compleat."

fall down To sail toward. A nautical term. In 1649 John Winthrop wrote,
"The *White Angel* fell down for Plymouth."

falling sickness Epilepsy.

falling weather (*n.*) Any bad weather when rain or snow was falling. In 1760 Washington recorded,
"In the Evening it . . . promisd falling weather but no appearance of a thaw."

fall out To happen; to occur. The 1641 Massachusetts Body of Liberties provided that:
"the Governor shall have a casting voice whensoever an Equivote shall fall out."

fallowed (*adj.*) Plowed and harrowed for sowing at some future date; allowed to lie fallow. In 1769 Washington wrote,
"The Fallowed Ground . . . contain abt. 40 Acres."

false conception A conception in which no fetus is produced; the placenta undergoes deterioration and is discharged. William Byrd in 1710 wrote,
"She was delivered of a false conception."

famed (*adj.*) Much talked of; renowned. In 1756 Dr. Thomas Lloyd claimed,
"I am sensibly famed."

familist (*n.*) One of the religious sect called the Family of Love, an Antinomian sect created in Holland by Hendrik Niclaes. Cotton Mather in 1702 wrote,
"There was a generation of Familists in our town and other towns who . . . did secretly vent sundry and dangerous errors and heresies."

family (*n.*) **(1)** A religious unit. In 1772 John Woolman:
"visited Joseph White's family."
(2) The staff of an army officer. In 1780 Robert Harrison deposed that Col. Richard Varick was:
"in and one of the late Major General Arnold's family."

fancy goods Any novelties to strike one's fancy. A 1772 Boston newspaper advertised,
"A large and extensive assortment of staple and fancy Goods."

fandango (*n.*) A dance, a ball. An adopted Spanish word. A 1780 New Jersey document recorded,
"They were found at a *fandango* or merry-meeting, with a party of lasses."

fanega (*n.*) A Spanish measure which varied in size from one to one and a half bushels. 1774 orders to a sea captain referred to:
"20 fanegas of almonds."

fantastical (*adj.*) Unsteady; irregular. William Byrd deplored:
"the man so tame as to be governed by an unprofitable and fantastical wife."

farcy (*n.*) A disease of horses and mules, sometimes of oxen, akin to scabies or mange.

A 1706 document referred to:
"curing your horse of Cold & farsey."

fardel (*n.*) A bundle or pack. Jeremy Taylor (1613–1667) instructed,
"A woman should be the fardel of friendly toleration."

farina (*n.*) A pollen. In 1770 Washington wondered:
"whether the corn for want of the Farina will ever fill."

farm (*v.*) To lease the right to collect taxes on an area. In 1698 Lord Bellomont reported to the Lords of Trade that:
"Brooks . . . has gon and farmed the Excise of the county of West Chester to Col. Heathcote for seaven pounds."

farmer (*n.*) The owner of the right to farm. *See* **farm.** In 1643 a Massachusetts document referred to:
"customers, farmers & collectors of customs."

far nations Those Indians living west of the seaboard as far as the Mississippi. So referred to by William Smith in 1757.

farrier (*n.*) A smith who shoes horses and professes to treat their diseases. A 1723 Boston newspaper asked,
"Why take you no Notice of Sow-gelders & Farriers that take the title of *Doctor?*"

farthingale (*n.*) The framework, usually whalebone, that makes a hoop skirt hoop. A corruption of old Spanish *verdugado*, same meaning.

fascine (*n.*) A long, bound bundle of brushwood. Used both to make military defenses and in the assault on them. In 1780 Benedict Arnold, describing the defenses at West Point, wrote,
"Fort Arnold is built of Dry Fascines and Wood."

fast (*n.*) That which fastens, a hawser by which a ship is made fast. In 1720 Samuel Sewall recorded,
"In the . . . Storm . . . several Ships were driven from their fasts at the Wharf."

fast land The upland. *Fast* in the sense of 'firm or secure; safe from flooding.' A 1681 Delaware deed referred to:
"724 acres of fast Land."

fault (*n.*) Having lost a scent while hunting. In 1786 Washington complained,
"I came home and left the Dogs at fault."

Fayal (*n.*) A wine made on Fayal, one of the Azores. A 1776 Boston newspaper advertised,
"Sale on John Hancock wharf . . . Fayal wines."

fearnaught (*n.*) A very thick woolen cloth for clothing. A 1775 Philadelphia newspaper wrote of a:
"fearnaught jacket" on a runaway.

feather, rise at a To lose one's temper easily. In 1794 Jefferson reflected,
"Being so patient of the kicks and scoffs of our enemies and rising at a feather against our friends."

featheredge (*n.*) Clapboard. One edge is thinner than the other. John Harrower in 1774 wrote of:
"new weather board on the house with featherage plank."

feather merchant A loafer or slacker; a person of questionable honesty. A 1784 Bos-

ton newspaper reported,
"A couple of feather merchants were taken up here last week for passing counterfeit French Guineas."

fee (1) (*n.*) A feudal legal term. According to Sir William Blackstone in his 1767 *Commentaries on the Laws of England*:
"Feodum, or fee, is that which is held of some superior, on condition of rendering him service."
(2) (*v.*) To pay a fee to. In West New Jersey, according to its 1677 Charter:
"No person shall be compelled to fee an attorney"

feedings (*n.*) A rich pasture. The 1697 Cortlandt [N.Y.] Manor grant included:
"fields, feedings, woods."

fee-farm lease A lease in perpetuity; a freehold subject to a fixed yearly rent.

fee simple A fee without limitation; an interest in land in one or more persons exclusive of anyone else. A 1655 Massachusetts deed said,
"A good perfect and Absolute estate of inherytance in fee simple."

feetail (*n.*) An interest in land limited to lineal descendants. An Act of the 1769 New York Assembly included:
"a freehold in lands, messuages, or tenements, or rents, in fee, feetail or for life."

feeze (1) (*n.*) A state of fretful excitement or alarm. From Middle English *fesen* 'to drive away.' A 1647 Rhode Island document included:
"Without making any assault upon his person or putting him in a fease."
(2) (*v.*) To drive away. In 1689 Cotton Mather wrote,
"A Devil would . . . make her laugh to see how he feaz'd 'em about."

feign (*v.*) To cover up. From Latin *fingere* 'to form, mold, feign.' Franklin in 1771 wrote,
"His proselytes would be left at liberty to feign for him."

feist (*n.*) A small dog. In parts of England a *feist* was a puff ball. Hence a small dog from its appearance. Washington in 1770 referred to:
"a small foist looking yellow cur."

felicity (*n.*) The prosperity. In 1754 the records of Princeton College referred to:
"several gentlemen . . . [from] New Jersey who were well wishers to the felicity of their country."

fellmonger (*n.*) A dealer in skins *fells* or hides.
"Glovers, Fellmungers, and Furriers are orderly turned to their trades," wrote Edward Johnson in 1654.

felloe A variant of **felly**.

fellowship (*n.*) The arithmetic method of computing a partner's proportionate profit or loss. In 1775 Philip Fithian recorded that,
"Harry began at reduction and is now working Fellowship."

felly (*n.*) A two-spoke, wooden section of the rim of a wheel. Also *felloe*. Franklin in 1773 referred to:
"the new Art of making Carriage wheels, the Fellies of one piece."

felon de se A suicide; felo-de-se. In 1659 in Massachusetts,
"these persons . . . become felons de se and the sovereign law salus populi been preserved."

female hemp *See* **karl**.

fence viewer One who saw to it that fences were erected and maintained. In 1791 on Long Island,
"The fence viewers shall have halef a croun a day for viewing fences."

fennel (*n.*) An herb. A brew of fennel seeds was taken to counteract nausea.

fenugreek (*n.*) An Asiatic plant whose seeds were an ingredient of curry. From Latin *foenum Graecum* 'Greek hay.' Washington sowed some in 1765.

feoffee (*n.*) A trustee holding land for a minor, or a trustee of a school for the public use. 1653 Harvard records show,
"I am willing to refer it to the President and Feoffees & Overseers."

ferret (*n.*) A narrow tape, usually of cotton or silk, used to tie leather breeches at the knee or to tie up documents. *Green ferret* had the meaning that *red tape* does today. From Italian *fioretti* 'floss silk,' literally 'little flower.' A 1765 Boston newspaper advertised,
"Tammy, Paduasoy, Shalloons, Camblets, Alopeen, Bombazeen, Silk Ferrets, Ticks."

feudatory (*n.*) A land holder under obligation of military service. The 1629 charter of the West India Company referred to:
"all Patroons and feudatories."

feu de joie *French* 'fire of joy.' A joyous firing of guns timed to effect a continuous noise to mark a celebration. In his 1778 orderly book Maj. Fishbourne referred to a:
"joie de feu."

feverbush (*n.*) One of several bushes from which remedies for fever were made. Jonathan Carver in 1778 wrote,
"The Fever Bush grows about five or six feet high."

fief (*n.*) An inheritable right to land with a mutual obligation of protection by the lord on one hand and a duty of homage and service to him on the other. The 1640 Freedoms and Exemptions in New Netherland referred to:
"matters pertaining to possession of benefices, fiefs."

field carriage The wheels with which to move a cannon. In 1628 the Virginia House of Burgesses pleaded,
"Wee doe intreat you to send us . . . 11 field carriages for demi Culverin."

field day A day for military exercise. A 1775 Boston newspaper wrote of:
"the method generally practised at Review, Field-day, etc." The slang *to have a field day* 'to engage in uncontrolled activity, revelry, etc.' did not come into use until after the Civil War.

field driver One who kept stray cattle from roads and highways. In 1736 in Boston:
"Mr. Nathanael Tuttle be Haward or field driver."

fifth day Thursday, among Quakers. In 1698 Samuel Sewall recorded,
"Am going to keep Court at Springfield, next Fifth day."

filature (*n.*) A place where silk yarn is put on reels. A 1759 book said,
"The Silk-Balls . . . are then to be carried to the Filature, or Silk House, where the Money is to be paid."

file (*n.*) A mispronunciation of *foil*, as:
"bile" is sometimes said for *boil*. The 1745 rules at Yale College provided,
"And if any scholar shall play at swords, files or cudgels, he shall be fined not exceeding 1 s."

fill (*n.*) A variant of *thill* 'the shaft of a cart or carriage.' A 1795 South Carolina document stated,
"The young horse was not able to get on in the fills."

fillet (*n.*) An obstetrical device, a loop, for extracting a fetus. A 1721 Boston newspaper wrote,
"That they be completely armed with Incision, Lancet, Pandora's Box, Nut Shell and Fillet."

fimble (*n.*) The male hemp plant. *See also* **karl.**

final (*n.*) The interest-bearing paper finally issued in 1780 by the Continental Congress in exchange for continental currency at its depreciated value of forty to one. A 1788 Baltimore newspaper advertised,
"Wanted at said office, Finals, Depreciation Certificates and every other kind of Paper."

find (*v.*) To supply, provide, furnish. In 1661 in Bedford, N.Y.,
"Joshua Webb doth bind himself to finde the town at hop-ground with good meale." In Scarsdale, N.Y., an indenture provided,
"Said master shall and will find and allow unto his said servant meat, drink, washing and lodging."

fine (*v.*) To bring to an end. In 1677 in South Carolina they complained,
"Compelled to buy ourselves guns . . . and keep ourselves from fining."

fine, in In the end, in conclusion. In 1751 Franklin wrote,
"In fine, a nation well regulated."

finery (*n.*) A hearth where cast iron is made malleable. In 1748 an advertisement in a Philadelphia newspaper offered,
"To be sold . . . a good Forge, or iron-work, having three fires, viz. two finerys and one chasery."

finesse (*n.*) Ingenuity, subtlety. An adopted French word. In 1774 Gouverneur Morris wrote,
"The troubles in America . . . put our gentry upon their finesse."

finical (*adj.*) Fastidious; overly concerned with trivial details. In 1744 Dr. Alexander Hamilton:
"was shaved by a little finicall humpbacked old barber."

fire (*n.*) An Indian household, family; or nation. Apparently an anglicization of an Indian word.

fire and candle (*n.*) The home. In 1696 part of the verdict in the case of Ann Richbell against the people of Rye, N.Y., stated,
"The Pattent with the rest of Papers needful Given to the Jury, and the Sheriffe sworn to Keepe them from fire & candles &c untill they bringe in their verdict."

fire and candle, keep To stay at one's home. A 1683 New York petition for a new charter stated,
"And if any ffreeman should bee absent out of the Citty a space of Twelve moneths and not keep fire and candle and pay Scott and lott should lose his ffreedom."

fire brig A vessel filled with combustibles used to set fire to enemy ships. There were also *fire boats, fire rafts, fire ships,* and *fire sloops.*

fire lock A flintlock gun. A 1770 Boston newspaper reported,
"They would club their fire-locks and return home."

fireplace (*n.*) A place on a coast for a fire as a beacon. A 1666 Long Island, N.Y., deed described pieces of land,

"one at the landing place one at the humuck [hummock] & one at the fire place."

fire room A room with a fireplace. A 1708 Boston newspaper offered for rent:

"a good Dwelling House, three Fire Rooms on a Floor."

fire slice A long-handled tool for removing baked goods from an oven; a peel. In 1665 in Massachusetts a:

"Drawing shave . . . fire slice" was bequeathed.

fire stick In the singular, a poker; in the plural, tongs.

fire ward One who directed fire fighting. A 1711 Massachusetts law appointed:

"firewards . . . to command and require assistance for the extinguishing and putting out the fire."

firkin (*n.*) A measure: 56 pounds of butter; eight gallons of ale, soap, or herring; nine gallons of beer.

first cost The cost of the raw material before adding overhead, handling, etc. William Byrd in 1710 recorded that he:

"brought my goods for Williamsburg to the value of 2,000 first cost."

first day Sunday, among Quakers.

first rate Of the largest size, not (necessarily) of the highest excellence. In 1775 Washington referred to:

"all vessels except Ships of the first Rate."

first table One of the Puritan arrangements of the Ten Commandments. The Massachusetts *Body of Liberties* (1641) alludes to:

"punishing all such crimes (being breaches of the First or Second Table) as are committed against the peace of our sovereign lord."

fiscal (*n.*) **(1)** In New Amsterdam, the fiscal, van Tienhoven, was public prosecutor, treasurer, and sheriff.

(2) In Massachusetts, a revenue officer. A 1705 Boston newspaper reported,

"And then it Shall be free for the Governour, Fiskal or Receiver to accept of the sale of the said Goods at the price they set on them."

fish (*v.*) **(1)** To fertilize with fish. A process taught at Plymouth by the Indians. In 1651 Samuel Hartlib wrote,

"In New-England they fish their ground."

(2) In Harvard College slang, to seek approval. Thomas Hutchinson in 1774 recorded,

"He courts me a good deal and fishes [for compliments]."

(3) To strengthen a mast with a piece of timber. Probably from French *ficher* 'to fix.' The journal of the sloop *Revenge* in 1741 recorded,

"Wednesday 22. Fish Our Mast and made him as Strong as Ever."

fish pot A bag net for catching fish; a fyke. In 1785 Washington complained,

"The Fish pots, of which there are many in the River, serve to clog the Navigation."

fish stake A stake to which a net may be fastened, still used in the Hudson River for shad fishing. In 1754 a Massachusetts newspaper advertised,

"To be sold . . . a Farm . . . very convenient for carrying on a fishery and has Fish Stakes already erected."

fishy (*adj.*) Drunk. Bleary eyes and turned-down mouth corners make a drunk resemble a fish. A 1737 Philadelphia newspaper described a man as:
"fishy."

fistul (*adj.*) Hollow. From Latin *fistula* 'pipe.'

fitch (*n.*) Short for *fitchew*, the European polecat, similar to a ferret. In 1616 Capt. John Smith wrote of seeing:
"17 Fitches, Musquassus, and diuerse sorts of vermine, whose names I know not."

five and forty A card game, forty-five, in which the object is to score forty-five points. In 1775 Philip Fithian recorded,
"In our dining room companies at cards, Five & forty, Whist, Alfours, Callico-Betty etc."

Five Nations The Indian alliance comprising the Cayugas, Mohawks, Oneidas, Onondagas, and the Senecas. *See also* **nation; Six Nations.**

fives (*n.*) A game of handball, for two or four people, still played in England. In 1775 Philip Fithian wrote:
"Newark reminded me of my old days at Princeton . . . playing at fives."

fizgig (*n.*) A harpoon with barbed prongs. From Spanish *fisga* 'harpoon.' The 1673 inventory of the ship *Providence* included:
"1 fiz gigg."

flag (*n.*) An aquatic plant with long, broad leaves used for mats, roofing, and chair seats. Hence, *flag bottom* and *flag chair*. In 1634 William Wood wrote,
"In Summer they gather flagges, of which they make Matts for houses."

flagitious (*adj.*) Grossly wicked, scandalous. A 1768 circular letter exhorted,
"Exert your utmost influence to defeat their flagitious attempt to disturb the public peace."

flake (*n.*) A platform for drying fish. In 1635 in Massachusetts,
"Granted unto Mr. John Holgrave fisherman three quarters of an acre . . . for flakes, &c."

flam (*n.*) A falsehood. A 1776 song referred to:
"puffs and flam and gasconade." Short for *flim-flam*.

flanker (*n.*) A projecting fortification designed to flank an attacking force. In 1630 William Bradford recommended,
"Make flankers in convenient places with gates to shut."

flanking mare A horse which tended to move sidewise, shying, and generally being tedious to ride. An actor in a 1770 play complained of being obliged:
"to ride a flanking mare about camp (which was no small mortification)."

flappet (*n.*) A little flap; an appendage to a woman's cap. A 1754 New York newspaper inveighed on European fashions,
"These foreign invaders first made their attack upon the stays, so as to diminish them half down the waist exposing the breast and shoulders. Next to the caps; cut off the flappets and tabs."

flare (*n.*) A variant of *flair*, a flat fish; a ray or skate. Charles Wolley in 1679 wrote,
"I mean the shark . . . mouth . . . in shape like a skate or flare as we call them in *Cambridge*."

flasket (*n.*) A flat basket. A 1651 will in Massachusetts bequeathed:
"a flasket & a paile."

flat (*n.*) A broad flat-bottom boat. In 1710 William Byrd recorded,
"Came with several flats to fetch 36 hogsheads of tobacco."

flatting (*n.*) A kind of apple. In 1709 John Lawson wrote that in Carolina:
"we have . . . the long apple . . . Flattings, Grigsons."

flaw (*v.*) To flay; to skin. A 17th-century cookbook instructed,
"Take 2 chickens, kill and flaw them hot."

fleche (*n.*) A fortification with two faces and an open rear, in the shape of an arrowhead. From a French word meaning 'arrow.' In 1776 Jared Sparks wrote,
"It was my intention . . . to throw up a great number of large fleches or redans."

fleer (*v.*) To mock. From an anonymous song, "Cobler's End," from 1728 or earlier:
"She would flounce and she would fleer."

fletcher (*n.*) One who makes or deals in arrows. *See* **fleche.**

flight (*n.*) A light fall of snow. From Old English *fliht* 'flake.' A 1670 Massachusetts document recorded,
"This day was the first flight of snow this winter."

flight shot The distance that an arrow, or flight, flies. A 1676 description of Bacon's Rebellion said,
"Not a flight shot from the end of the state house."

flint corn One variety of Indian corn usually having hard kernels. Robert Beverley in 1705 said in Virginia,
"One looks as smooth, and as full as the early ripe Corn, and this they call *Flint-Corn.*"

flip (*n.*) A drink of hot, spiced wine whipped up with egg. In 1763 John Adams wrote,
"they drink flip" in the caucus room.

flirt (*v.*) To throw with a jerk. Franklin, in a 1770 letter regarding soap making wrote of:
"flirting the froth with a skimmer."

fliting (*v.*) Scolding, brawling. A word used in Scotland. John Harrower in 1774 described:
"some shiting, some farting, some flyting, some daming."

float (1) (*n.*) A sluice for irrigating or draining. A 1650 Massachusetts document referred to:
"a floate or sluce to preuent damage by floods."
(2) A timber or lumber raft. In 1749 William Douglass wrote,
"All the other falls are passable for floats of timber and for canoes."
(3) A scow or small boat. A 1734 Massachusetts document referred to:
"a float or small Boat of about sixteen or eighteen feet Keel."
(4) (*v.*) To flood, to inundate. In 1683 Topsfield, Connecticut, authorized,
"Float soe much of the Towne Common as is for ye good and Vese of ye Mille."

flor (*n.*) Flowers.

Florence flask A round-bottomed bottle encased in straw often used for a superior kind of Italian olive oil. In 1744 Franklin recommended,
"A Florence Flask stript of the straw is best." In 1765 in a Boston newspaper Benjamin Faneuil, Jr. offered:
"Ravens Duck, Oznabrigs, Florence Oil."

flourish (*n.*) An act of hasty sexual intercourse. Possibly from the flourishing of a weapon. In 1709, 1710, and 1711 William Byrd entered in his diary,
"I gave my wife a flourish this morning." (Once was on the billiard table.)

flow (*v.*) To flood, to inundate. A 1685 Massachusetts document recorded:
"Granted to John Hanchet, ten acres of Land . . . provided he make a dam & flow it."

flower-de-luce (*n.*) An iris. An anglicization of French *fleur de lis.*

fluke (*n.*) A double plow. From the shape of the tail of a whale. In 1775 Washington ordered,
"Get 2 light fluke Plows."

flummery (*n.*) **(1)** A sort of jelly thickened with cornstarch. A 1769 cookbook instructed,
"When you make a hen's or bird's nest, let part of your jelly be set in your bowl before you put in your flummery."
(2) By transfer from the above, flattery, nonsense, empty trifling.

flushing (*n.*) A coarse cloth from Flushing, Netherlands. A 1790 Boston newspaper offered:
"Goods suited to the season . . . flushing and common Duffils."

flux (*n.*) Almost any flow, bleeding, purging, or abortion. William Byrd in 1717 wrote,
"I gave her ten Guineas to flux."

flux and reflux of the sea, within High tide; between the flow and the ebb of the sea. In Boston in 1717:
"7 convicted and 6 hanged for piracy within flux and reflux of the sea."

fly (*n.*) A lowland. From Dutch *vly* 'valley.' In 1695 a New York document described:
"a valley begginning att the head of a flye or Marshe."

fly-blow (*n., v.*) A fly egg deposited in the flesh of an animal, hence, used in reference to something tainted or contaminated, as a noun or a verb. In 1645 Nathanael Ward wrote,
"yet that Beelzebub can fly-blow their intellectuals miserably."

fly boat A large, flat-bottomed vessel for bulk transport. First used on the Vlie, the channel between the North Sea and the Zuider Zee. A 1707 Boston newspaper reported from New York,
"A Fly Boat arrived here from Boston." *See also* **fly.**

flying (*adj.*) Mobile, as applied to a military installation. There were *flying artillery, flying camps, flying hospitals,* and *flying sappers.* In 1776 the Continental Congress:
"Resolved that the flying camp be under the command . . . general officers."

flying machine A fast stagecoach. A 1770 Philadelphia newspaper carried an advertisement,
"The Flying Machine kept by John Barnhill in Elm-street sets out for New-York, on Mondays and Thursdays, and performs the Journey in Two Days."

flying seal A seal attached to, but not sealing, a letter so that it may be read by the person forwarding. A 1780 letter read,
"I inclose you mail to Wilson under flying seal."

foenicl. (*n.*) Fennel. An abbreviation of *Foeniculum vulgare,* its botanical name.

fog dram A drink taken as protection against fog, like one taken as protection from snakebite.

fogrum (*n.*) One who is behind the times, a fogey. In 1760 John Rowe deprecated: "some of these old fogrums."

fol. (*n.*) Leaves. An abbreviation of Latin *folia*.

folly[1] (*n.*) A sin. When William Byrd went to Williamsburg to attend meetings of the House of Burgesses he frequently recorded, "I committed folly with F——, God forgive me."

folly[2] (*n.*) A variant of **felly**.

foment (*v.*) To bathe with warm medicated liquids. William Byrd in 1710 recorded, "Jack had a bad knee so I sent John to foment it."

fontanel (*n.*) A puncture or incision, made by a heated instrument, for the discharge of pus or other fluid.

fool (*n.*) A puree of gooseberries, scalded and pounded, with cream.

foot causey A foot causeway. *See* **causey**. A 1649 Connecticut document provided, "There shall bee a foot Causey made from ye Dwelling howse of George Steele."

foot lock A locked leg iron. A 1763 Massachusetts document regarding an escaped prisoner reported, "[He] had on when he went away, Part of a Chain and Foot Lock."

foot post A mail carrier on foot; also, the service he performs. In 1790 Congress said: "If any person . . . shall be concerned in setting up any foot or horse post."

forbear (*v.*) To delay. In 1648 a New Hampshire document recorded: "The petition of the inhabitants of Exeter for their rate and head money to be foreborne."

fore bay A reservoir above a water wheel. In 1770 Washington recorded, "Began to Grind Sand in my Mill, the Water being let in upon the Fore Bay."

forehanded (*adj.*) Prudent; thrifty; free from debt. In 1777 John Adams observed, "Here and there [one finds] a farmer and a tradesman, who is forehanded and frugal enough to make more money than he has occasion to spend."

foreign (*adj.*) Coming from another area. In 1660 Plymouth, Mass., passed a law, "Noe strange or forraigne Indians shal be permitted to come into any parte of this jurisdiction."

foremastman (*n.*) An ordinary seaman. Officers slept aft; seamen slept before the mast. John Josselyn in 1674 wrote, "To every Shallop belongs four fishermen, a Master or Steersman, a midship-man, and a Foremast-man, and a shore man who washes it out of the salt."

foreroom (*n.*) The main room of a house, the parlor. In 1745 a man in New Hampshire bequeathed: "to my beloved wife . . . The following part of my dwelling house Namely: the fore Room Next to the Street."

forestall (*v.*) To intercept one or obstruct on a highway. A 1757 New York document referred to: "oppressions, extentions, forestallings, regratings, trespasses."

forestaller (*n.*) One who buys a commodity secretly in anticipation of a price increase.

Gouverneur Morris wrote,
"There is enough wheat in the Kingdom, but it is bought up by forestallers."

forest cloth A type of cloth. A 1776 New Jersey newspaper offered:
"common coatings, hunters, forest cloth."

forfeit (*n.*) A penalty paid, generally playfully, for having made a mistake. In 1774 Philip Fithian admitted that he:
"had a forfeit for kneeding biscuit."

forlorn (*n.*) A soldier member of a vanguard. Short for *forlorn hope* From Dutch *verloren hoop* 'lost troop.'

form[1] (*n.*) A backless bench. A 1640 Connecticut inventory included:
"sixe cushions and one little forme." The origin of this use of the word lies in French *s'asseoir en forme* 'to sit in a row,' as applied to the bench in a choir stall.

form[2] (*n.*) Type arranged and ready for printing. In 1771 Franklin referred to:
"having imposed my forms."

forsado (*n.*) A person forced into service. From Spanish *forzado* 'a galley slave.' Daniel Coxe, describing Carolina in 1722 wrote,
"The Majority of the Inhabitants, are Forc'adoes or forc'd people, having been Malefactors in some Parts of Mexico." (Carolina was not divided into North and South until 1729.)

fort (*adj.*) Strong. Also used in medical terms. Gouverneur Morris in 1789 wrote a truism,
"Each individual has his peculiarities of fort and feeble."

fort major The deputy commander of a fort. A 1711 Boston newspaper reported,
"Panabicot [Penobscot] Indians . . . wounded Fort-Major William Elliot."

fortune biter A sharper, a swindler. Partridge attributes the phrase to coinage by Thomas D'Urfey in his 1698 *Mr. Lane's Magot.*

fortune le garde John Winthrop probably meant "Good fortune guard him" when he wrote,
"Signed underneath fortuune le garde and no more to it."

forwardness (*n.*) An advanced state beyond the usual degree. Richard Corbin in 1759 exhorted,
"Animate the overseers to great dilligence that their work may be in proper forwardness."

found (*v.*) To be supplied, furnished. An apprentice or an indentured servant was *found* with food and clothing; a ship was *found* with food and stores. *See* **find.**

founder (*v.*) Of a ship, to sink; of a horse, to trip and fall. In 1710 William Byrd reported,
"The Doctor's horse was foundered so that he could not go."

fourfold (*n.*) A quadruple assessment. A 1779 Vermont document instructs,
"The listers shall add the sum total of such additions and four-folds, to the sum total before mentioned."

fourpence (*n.*) The Spanish silver half-*real*, worth five to six cents. A 1759 Massachusetts document reported,
"A Sailor coming from a vessel in the Harbor was nigh as a four pence to a groat of being drowned."

fourpenny (*n.*) A type of ale, sold at four pence a quart. In 1729 Franklin wrote,
 "Let him give notice where any dull stupid rogue may get a quart of four-penny for being laughed at."

fourth day Wednesday, among Quakers.

fowler (*n.*) One who hunts wild birds, generally with nets. It was one of the trades or occupations listed as needed in the Virginia colony in 1610.

fowl meadow grass *Poa trivialis.* So called for its resemblance to a bird's foot.

foxwood (*n.*) A fox fire; phosphorescent decayed wood. In 1775 Silas Deane wrote,
 "He always depended on fox-wood, which gives light in the dark, to fix on the points of the needle of his compass."

fraise (*n.*) A pancake with bacon in it. From French *fraise* 'a ruffle.' In 1710 William Byrd recorded,
 "I ate some bacon fraise for dinner."

franchise (*n.*) A privilege specifically given by the crown appended to letters patent, such as fowling, hawking, advowsons, deodands, etc.

frankincense pine The loblolly pine, whose exudation may be used for incense. Humphrey Marshall in 1785 referred to:
 "Virginia Swamp, or Frankincense Pine."

frank-pledge (*n.*) A pledge or surety for good behavior. From a Norman mistranslation of Old English *frith-borh* 'peace pledge.' The 1632 Maryland Charter included:
 "to have and to keep a view of frank-pledge, for the conservation of the peace and better government."

freak (*n.*) A whim, a capricious prank, a sudden turn. From Old English *frek* 'quick.' On March 16, 1770 John Rowe recorded in his diary,
 "Mr. [Samuel] Otis got into a mad freak tonight and broke a great many windows in the Town House."

freedom of the city The rights of a citizen. In 1683 in New York one had to pay a tax and be admitted by a magistrate in order to sell merchandise or ply a trade.

Freedoms and Exemptions The special privileges, powers, and exemptions granted by the Assembly of XIX (which see) to members of the West India Company who would establish plantations in "Nieuw Netherlandt."

freehold (*n.*) A lease in perpetuity.

freeman of the commons The term used in Boston for one with the rights of a citizen. John Winthrop reported, ca. 1640, that:
 "all the freemen of the commons were sworn to the government."

free stone Any stone, especially sandstone or limestone, that may be cut easily. In 1629 Francis Higginson listed stone available near Boston,
 "limestone, freestone, and smoothstone, and ironstone and marblestone."

free thinker An unbeliever. It was included in Gottfried Mittleberger's list of religions represented in Pennsylvania in 1750.

free willer An indentured servant who of his free will sold his services, generally for five years, in exchange for his passage from Europe.

French bean The kidney bean. William Byrd said he ate them in 1740.

French crown An *écu.*

"1 french Crown" appears in the 1741 account of the crew of the *Revenge* to her owners.

French fall shoes The shoes of a French style worn by both men and women. Referred to in Boston newspapers in 1705, 1710, and 1714.

French heel A heel for women's shoes, sometimes as high as three and a half inches. In 1760 *Universal Magazine* ridiculed fashion change with,
"Now high in French heels, now low in your pumps."

French Indian An Indian allied with the French. In 1711 a Boston newspaper reported,
"They wrote from Albany that several Cannoo's with French Indians and their Families are come thither."

frenchman (*n.*) A tobacco plant which grows tall rather than bushy. P. A. Bruce explained in 1896 that the Virginian mind associated tallness with Frenchmen.

French prophet One of a fanatical Protestant sect in the south of France which claimed the gift of prophecy. In 1771 Franklin wrote,
"He had been one of the French prophets and could act their enthusiastic agitations."

French roll A roll resembling French bread in texture. In 1763 an advertisement in a New York newspaper stated,
"Spring Gardens, near the college . . . Tea in the afternoon from 3 till 6. The best of Green tea etc. Hot French rolls will be provided."

French wheat Buckwheat. A 1658 cookbook instructed,
"Take . . . a pint of French wheat flower."

fresh (*n.*) Short for *freshet*; a stream of fresh water. In 1760 Washington:
"took a view of the ruins the fresh had caused."

fresh marsh A fresh-water marsh as contrasted to a salt marsh. A 1698 New Hampshire will bequeathed,
"I give to my Eldest Son John Cutt . . . all my Fresh Marsh at the head of the Creek."

fresh meadow The land a little higher than a fresh marsh. A 1635 Cambridge, Mass., deed conveyed,
"All the right title and Intrest which he hath in the ffresh Meaddows and the Ox pastuer."

fret (*n.*) The agitation of the surface of a fluid by fermentation. Ebenezer Cook's 1704 *The Sotweed Factor* included,
"Who found them drinking for a whet, / A cask of cider on the fret."

fribble (*n.*) A trifle. Possibly a variant of *frivol*. In 1774 Philip Fithian referred to:
"many womanish fribbles."

frieze[1] (*n.*) A coarse woolen cloth with a nap on one side. From French *friser* 'to curl.' It is one of the fabrics covered by the Woollen Act of 1699.

frieze[2] (*n.*) Short for *cheval-de-frise*. In 1781 Washington recorded,
"There is an abatis around the Work, but no friezing."

frigate (*n.*) A swift naval craft, usually with three masts, raised quarterdeck and forecastle, and more than 20 guns.

frippery (*n.*) A place where old clothes were sold. From French *friperie* 'rags, old

clothes.' In 1740 William Byrd wrote,
"Ransack the fripperies of Long Lane for finery." Long Lane in London, ¾ mi. north of St. Paul's Cathedral, was noted for its dealers in second-hand clothes.

frock (*n.*) A man's short, loose hunting shirt worn over his other clothes. Ebenezer Denny's 1781 *Journal* said that Lafayette's men were:
"chiefly all light infantry, dressed in frocks and overalls of linen."

froe (*n.*) A tool for splitting shingles. In 1775 Bernard Romans wrote,
"A river or splitter . . . rives them with the fro."

frolic (*n.*) A party. From Dutch *vrolijk* 'merry.' In 1737 Jonathan Edwards deplored,
"It was their manner to frequently get together in conventions of both sexes for mirth and jollity which they called frolics."

frost (*n.*) A shoe with calks, or frost nails. Samuel Sewall in 1718 wrote,
"Great Rain, and very slippery: was fain to wear Frosts."

frost fish The tomcod, because it appears in the winter. William Wood in 1634 mentioned:
"Th' Frost fish and the Smelt."

frumenty (*n.*) A dish made of wheat boiled in milk with sugar, raisins, and egg yolk added. From Latin *frumentum* 'corn.' In 1717 William Byrd:
"ate some frumenty."

fry (*n.*) The offspring. Applied to children as well as fish. In 1584 Richard Hakluyt in recommending colonization wrote,
"The fry of the wandering beggars of England, that grow up idly, and hurtful and burdensome to this realm, may there be unladen."

full (*v.*) To clean and thicken cloth.

fuller (*n.*) One who fulls cloth.

fulling mill A mill where fulling is done. In 1670 Plymouth, Mass.,
"Sett up a ffulling mill soe as it annoy not the Corn Mill."

fundament (*n.*) Either buttocks or rectum. In 1710 William Byrd recorded,
"I had eight stools and my fundament was swelled with a sharp humour and very sore."

fundor (*n.*) One with credit in a fund. In the Massachusetts Colony a 1682 document said,
"If one Fundor passeth Credit to another."

furbelow (*n.*) The edge of an overskirt or the hemline of a petticoat. From French *falbela* 'flounce.'

furnace (*n.*). A cooking kettle. A 1644 Connecticut document included:
"An Inuentory . . . iron spitts, pot hangers . . . a Fornace."

furniture (*n.*) That with which anything is furnished. For the person, it was body armor. In 1644 in Rhode Island a document referred to:
"Furniture for their bodies in time of war." For a gun, it was powder, shot, match, etc. In 1639 a Rhode Island document read,
"It is ordered, that Eight Gunns and their furniture . . . be taken off." For a horse, saddle or harness. In 1682 Mary Rowlandson complained,
"There being no furniture upon the horse's back." For a ship, masts, sails, rigging, and stores. In 1699 Duncan Campbell deposed,
"The said ship being disabled from comeing for want of furniture."

furniture check An upholstery fabric with a checked pattern. In a 1762 Boston newspaper advertisement:
"Nathaniel Williams [offered] furniture Check, Cambricks."

fusee (*n.*) A fusil.

fusil (*n.*) A light flintlock gun. From French. Originally developed for artillery guards, it was later carried by light infantry and officers.

fusilier (*n.*) A soldier armed with a fusil; a light infantryman. In a 1705 Boston newspaper:
"That a Sum may be provided sufficient to pay One Hundred Fusileers."

fustian (*n.*) A coarse, stout, twilled cotton. A 1797 Boston newspaper mentioned,
"Caleb Johnson's Variety Store [offered] Kerseymeres, Fustians, Janes, Moreens."

fustic (*n.*) A West Indian tree from which a light-yellow dye was produced. A 1776 Boston newspaper advertised,
"14 tons of lignum vitae and fustick."

fuzee (*n.*) A fusil.

fyke (*n.*) A bag-net. A 1775 New York colonial law empowered two men to build a bridge to what is now City Island which would:
"moreover afford a convenient and proper station for taking great quantities of fish with nets and fikes."

gabion (*n.*) A wicker basket, cylindrical in form, filled with earth as a field fortification. Ebenezer Denny recorded,
"One third of the army on fatigue every day, engaged in various duties, making gabions, fascines."

gad (*n.*) A cut on an ear of cattle as a sign of ownership. It might be a *fore gad* or a *rear* [*hind*] *gad*, depending on what part of the ear was cut. A possible derivation is that the mark kept the cattle from gadding, rambling, about. In 1704 in Portsmouth, N.H., one was recorded:
"The Eare marke . . . a hind gad on the Right Ear."

gage (*v.*) To pledge. In 1770 Samuel Sewall wrote,
"And God gaged His blessing in lieu of any loss."

Gagite (*n.*) A soldier serving under British General Thomas Gage. In 1775 H. P. Johnston wrote,
"The number of those Slain in the Battle between Putnam and the Gagites is uncertain."

galebury (*n.*) *See* **gallberry**. In 1763 Washington described land as:
"abounding in Pine and Galebury bushes."

gal-knipper (*n.*) *See* **gallinipper**.

gall (*v.*) To wound by rubbing. William Byrd in 1711 wrote,
"I threatened . . . for galling the harrow horse."

gallberry (*n.*) A holly.

galleon (*n.*) A large ship with three or four decks. The Spanish used them to carry treasure from South America. John Rowe in 1760 recorded that:
"Admiral Sanders has taken a Galloon worth half a million."

galley (*n.*) A ship of war with oars and two lateen (triangular) sails. Those that Benedict Arnold built in 1776 on Lake Champlain were 72 feet long, 20 ½ feet wide, and 6 feet, 2 inches high; they held 80 men.

gallinipper (*n.*) A biting insect; a gally (bold) nipper. A 1701 document bewailed,

"Poor brother Jenkins was baited to death with musquitoes and blood thirsty Gal-Knippers."

gallio (*n.*) A detatched, unconcerned person. After Gallio, the Proconsul who refused to try Saint Paul. Edward Johnson in 1654 wrote facetiously,
"Be sure to make choice of the most atheistical person they can find to govern, such as are right galios."

galliot (*n.*) A small galley with one mast and 16 to 20 seats for rowers. An anonymous pirate in 1680 wrote,
"Capt. Cooke in his way to us meetes with a Spanish galliote."

gallipot (*n.*) A small jar used by apothecaries. Wyndham Blanton wrote about:
"salvatory bottles and gallipots."

galloon (*n.*) A narrow lace of gold, silver or silk thread used in trimming. From French *galonner* 'to adorn the hair with ribbons.' The 1673 inventory of the ship *Providence* included:
"4 pieces of Galloune."

gallows and wheel customer A candidate for hanging or torture. *See* **wheel.** In 1750 Gottfried Mittleberger wrote:
"Pennsylvania is an ideal country for gallows and wheel customers."

gallows balk A beam in a chimney with hooks for pots. It looks like a gallows beam.

gallows crook A pothook for the gallows balk.

gamb. (*n.*) An abbreviation of *gamboge*. The powdered gum resin of an eastern tree exported from Singapore and Canton was used as a drastic cathartic and as a yellow dye. The word is a corruption of *Cambodia.*

gambrel (*n.*) A crooked stick used by butchers to hang up a hog by its hind leg. A 1764 Massachusetts document said,
"He first knock'd her down with a Gammerill, then run a fork into her neck."

gammon (*n.*) A smoked ham. By extension, buttocks, as in a 1776 play,
"I'll stick your knife in your gammons."

gander pulling A sport. A goose with a greased neck was hung by the feet. A man, riding quickly on horseback, tried to pull the goose's head off.

ganymede (*n.*) A serving boy, after the cupbearer of the Greek gods; a catamite. In 1710 William Byrd wrote,
"Went away by himself except his little ganymede that was with him." From other entries in Byrd's diary regarding Mr. Gee it is believed he meant a serving boy.

gaol (*n.*) A jail. The old British spelling was used in the colonies. Noah Webster's 1806 *Compendious Dictionary* lists both spellings.

garlix (*n.*) A sort of linen fabric originally from Gorlitz, Silesia. In 1765 in Boston, Briggs Hallowell advertised,
"cestor hats, durants, dowlass, ⅞ & ¾ garlix, thicksets."

garron (*n.*) A horse; a hack; a jade. From Gaelic *gearran*, same meaning. In 1696 Farmer Glover complained,
"Ten pounds for a Garran not worth Forty shillings."

garter (*n.*) A band wrapped around the leg below the knee to hold up stockings. Utilitarian, but also often very fancy. Snakeskin garters warded off leg cramps. In 1608

Capt. John Smith wrote of another use,
"Whom he bound to his arm with his garters and used him as a buckler."

Gascoign Powder A medicine. Bezoar, white amber, hartshorn, pearls, crabs' eyes, coral, and the black tops of crabs' claws were ground up and made into balls as large as walnuts. Who Gascoign was is unknown. William Byrd took the medicine in 1715.

gasconade (*n.*) A boast; boasting; bravado. The natives of Gascony, France, have a reputation for boastfulness. A 1776 song referred to:
"puffs and flam and gasconade."

gate (*n.*) A right of pasturage. In 1648 Rowley, Mass., legislated,
"Euery half Two Acre lott shall haue two gates and a quarter."

gauger (*n.*) **(1)** An exciseman whose business it was to ascertain the contents of casks. The 1693 Civil List included:
"Wm Shaw gauger att Albany."
(2) One who examined weights and measures used in commerce. In Springfield, Mass., in 1793,
"Symon Smith was Chosen Gager & Packer for the year ensuing."

gavel (*n.*) A variant of *gable*, the end of a house. John Harrower in 1775 wrote,
"It blowed in the gavel of a brick house."

gavelkind (*n.*) A custom for dividing a deceased man's property whereby:
"The Lands of the Father were equally divided among all his Sons," according to the definition given in 1701 by Charles Wolley.

gay (1) (*n.*) Any gaiety, merriment. A 1765 song went,
"Behold a man whose heart was set on gai."
(2) (*adj.*) False. William Byrd in 1730 wrote,
"He had been a Romish priest . . . quit that gay religion."

Gayhead (*n.*) Gay Head Indians from Martha's Vineyard were in great demand as boat steerers in the whaling fleets. It was the boat steerer who cast the harpoon and the Gay Head Indians were judged to be the most skillful and courageous. In 1782 in a Hartford, Ct., newspaper, Younglove Cutler advertised,
"Gayhead wanted."

gazetteer (*n.*) A newspaperman. From Italian *gazzetta*, first published in Venice (c. 1550), so called for a small coin paid for the newssheet. In a 1776 play Hugh H. Brackenridge wrote:
"of gibing wits and paltry gazetteers."

gehazi (*n.*) See **ghazi.**

general (1) (*n.*) A particular beat of a drum as a signal to assemble. According to a 1757 set of General Orders:
"Upon Hearing ye Genll. in Camp they Are to repair to ye Plais Appointed."
(2) (*adj.*) Public or common. Hence, *general fence, general field, general muster.* In 1638 in Rhode Island it was:
"ordered that a General fence be made." In Derby, Ct., in 1692,
"The Town have voted & Agreed to fence in a general field." In 1624 Edward Winslow reported,
"Captain Standish diuided our strength . . . And at a general Muster or Trayning, appointed each his place."

general assistant A town official or clerk. In 1666 in Portsmouth, New Hampshire,
"The Towne Counsell Chose for yt yeare Mr. William Baulston Genrill assistant."

General Court The governing body in most of the colonies; a legislative as well as a judicial body.

generality (*n.*) The majority. In 1792 William Eddis referred to:
"the generality of the inhabitants."

general recorder The official in Rhode Island who was in charge of its records. In a 1662 document,
"The Lawes, and orders which Come from the Gennerall Recorder."

General sergeant In Rhode Island, a sheriff. A 1747 document said,
"He that is chosen Generall Sargant shall be an able man of estate, for so ought a Sheriff to be."

geneva of mint A gin flavored with mint.
"It relieved me," wrote John Rowe in 1773.

Genoa velvet A richly patterned velvet. A 1759 Newport, R.I., newspaper advertised,
"To be sold by Simon Pease . . . Cotton velvet, Best Genoa ditto, Double Allapeens."

gentian (*n.*) A tonic brewed from the rhizome and roots of yellow gentian. The plant's genus is *Gentiana* named after the Illyrian king Gentius (fl. 180–168 B. C.), who first discovered its properties.

gentile (*n.*) A pagan; a heathen. In 1711 William Byrd predicted:
"that before the year 1790 the Jews and Gentiles would be converted to the Christianity."

gentleman (*n.*) Originally, one who, without a title, was entitled to a coat of arms; later, anyone above the status of a yeoman. The 1641 Massachusetts Body of Liberties decreed,
"Nor shall any true gentleman nor any man equal to a gentleman be punished by whipping."

gentleman of fortune An adventurer. In 1775 Philip Fithian called:
"Mr. Billy Booth a young gentleman of fortune."

gentry (*n.*) Any people of education and good breeding. In 1774 Gouverneur Morris wrote,
"The troubles in America . . . put our gentry upon their finesse."

get in To collect. In 1715 William Byrd took steps to:
"get in a debt."

ghazi (*n.*) A Moslem warrior; a champion against infidels. In 1679 Charles Wolley wrote,
"To take a fee a reward or gratuity from a Naaman or a person able to employ the proper faculty, is to act the Gehazi, and not the Prophet Elisha."

gibbet (*n.*) A gallows from which condemned criminals were suspended in chains after hanging and left slowly turning in the wind as a warning. Pirates were gibbeted on Nix's Mate and Bird Island in Boston Harbor after being hanged at dockside.

gigg (*n.*) A variant spelling of *jig*. In 1775 Philip Fithian wrote,
"Ladies and Gentlemen began to dance . . . first Minuets . . . then giggs . . . third reels."

gilder (*n.*) One who does gilding, applies gold leaf. The 1796 Boston Directory listed,
"M'Donald, William, gilder and carver."

gilefate (*n.*) A vat for brewing ale or beer. A 17th-century cookbook instructed,
"Put in a gilefat with yeast."

gilly flower A carnation, pink, or sweet william.

gilt (*n.*) Any gold-plated dishes. In 1716 William Byrd:
"lent Mrs. Harrison on this occasion my knives and gilt."

gim (*adj.*) Spruce, neat. In 1710 William Byrd wrote of:
"a wench that was gimm and tidy."

gimp (*n.*) Silk, wool, or cotton tape used for edging. In 1774 Alexander Bartram
advertised in a Philadelphia newspaper,
"pinchbeck, hand stilliards, gimp, & glover's needles."

gin (*n.*) **(1)** A snare or trap for game. Short for Middle English *engin* 'contrivance.' It
was illegal:
"to take or kill or destroy partridges, pheasants or quails with nets, snares, gins or
any other engines or devices in the Manor of Philipseburgh."
(2) A traplike opening between the end of a fence and a body of water. A 1665
Long Island, New York, document complained,
"There is damage done upon the plaine by the neglect of those that keepe the gin."

ging (*n.*) A gang. From an Old Norse word meaning 'going together.' In the 1619
Virginia General Assembly they referred to:
"Capt. Martin and the ging of his shallop."

girdle (1) (*n.*) A wampum belt, in addition to other types of belts. A 1666 Massachusetts document referred to:
"having sent a Girdle of Wampum to the Mowhawkes."
(2) (*v.*) To kill a tree by cutting the bark completely around. Girdle Ridge in
Bedford, N.Y., is so named because the French soldiers stationed there before going
to the Battle of Yorktown tied their horses to the trees and damaged the bark.

gittern (*n.*) A guitar. One was included in an early Virginia inventory.

give an air To put on airs. In 1710 William Byrd complained,
"Mrs. Russel had told him I only gave myself an air in pretending to wait on the
Governor."

give joy To express empathy. In 1711 William Byrd wrote:
"Came the Doctor and I gave him joy for his wife's arrival in this country."

give out To give up; to quit. In 1760 Washington admitted,
"After several efforts to make a plow . . . [I] was feign [fain] to give it out."

glacis (*n.*) A sloping bank in front of a fortification. It exposed the attacker to fire
from the defender. Ft. Lafayette at Verplanck, N.Y., had one, but that didn't prevent its capture.

glass (*n.*) The length of time which an hour glass runs. On shipboard the glass ran a
half-hour. In 1699 in testimony about Capt. Kidd a man said,
"It required eight men every two glasses to keep her [the ship] free."

glasshouse (*n.*) A glass factory. In 1700 Francis Pastorius said there were:
"already established several good mills, a glasshouse, pottery" in Frankfort, Pa.

glebe (*n.*) The land set aside for a parish minister. Occasionally used to apply to any
cultivated land. Parsonage Point was set aside in 1662 by the citizens of Rye, N.Y.,
for their minister. In 1772 Joseph Warren wrote,

"With one hand they broke the stubborn glebe, with the other they grasped their weapons."

gleet (*n.*) In general, an ooze; in particular, gonorrhea. In 1715 William Byrd confessed,
"My gleet was much better."

gloss (*n.*) **(1)** An interpretation, an explanation. The 1647 Massachusetts School Law included,
"Meaning of the original might be clouded by false glosses."
(2) A specious interpretation. In 1637 Thomas Morton wrote,
"They charged him (because they would seem to have some reasonable cause against him to set a gloss upon their malice) with criminal things."

glotted (*adj.*) Surprised, startled. Mercy Warren in a 1775 play *The Group* wrote,
"Could laugh to see her glotted sons expire."

glutton (*n.*) A wolverine, from its appetite. Jefferson in 1781 said in Virginia,
"There remains then the buffalo, red deer, fallow deer, wolf, roe glutton."

glykyrhig (*n.*) Licorice. Utimately from Greek *glykys* 'sweet,' *rhiza* 'root.'

Goddard's Drops, Dr. Dr. C. Goddard received a patent in 1673 for this medicine, which he sold to Charles II for £1500. It was made by mixing oil extracted by heating human bones with spirits of niter and spirits of wine. For vertigo or migraine, bones from the skull were used; for gout, it was brewed from the bones of the limb affected. Try 20 to 60 drops in a glass of canary. William Byrd did.

Godfrey's Cordial A patent medicine containing opium and sassafrass, patented by Ambroise Godfrey in 1660.

goffer **(1)** (*v.*) To crimp or flute.
(2) (*n.*) on who puts a crimp into something. A *goffer* used a *goffering iron* to iron ruffles.

Gold Coast The area of Africa, now Ghana, whose principal city was Accra. Named for the grains of gold mixed with the sand of its rivers. In 1756 Capt. Lindsey wrote from Cape Coast Road, a minor city,
"There is not one Hogshead rum on the Gold Coast to sell." (But there were plenty of slaves to buy.)

gondola (*n.*) A gundalow.

Goodman (*n.*) An appellation of civility; equivalent to *Mister*. A 1685 Massachusetts deed described land,
"By said road easterly to the land of Goodman Simons."

Goodwife (*n.*) The feminine of *Goodman*. In 1712 Joshua Hempstead in Connecticut recorded,
"Goodwife Morgan Died Suddenly."

Goodwin Sands The shoals in the Straits of Dover. In 1754 Franklin wondered,
"Could the Goodwin Sands be laid dry by banks?"

Goody (*n.*) Informal for *Goodwife*. A 1682 document recorded,
"He was present when Goody Jones and Geo. Walton were talking together, and he heard the said Goody Jones call the said Walton a wizard."

go off the stage A euphemism for *to die*. Philip Fithian used the expression in 1775.

goose (*n.*) A tailor's smoothing iron. From the resemblance of the handle to a goose's

neck. In 1782 John Trumbull used it metaphorically,
"Chang'd tailor's goose for guns and ball."

gorget (*n.*) **(1)** Something for the throat. A piece of armor or a symbolic badge. A 1757 letter to Washington commented,
"To see Sash & Gorget with a genteel uniform."
(2) A ruff worn at the neck by a woman. In 1658 a Dr. Smith wrote,
"A stomacher upon her breast so bare,/ For stripes and gorget were not then the wear."

gossip (*n.*) **(1)** A sponsor, a godparent. From Anglo-Saxon *god sib* 'God related.' In 1714 William Byrd recorded,
"There came abundance of company and I and Dick Kennon with Jenny Bolling were gossips."
(2) A partner. In 1675 Mary Rowlandson while a captive of Indians wrote,
"I . . . invited my master and mistress to dinner, but the proud gossip, because I served them both in one dish, would eat nothing."

gourd (*n.*) **(1)** A shell of the dried fruit used as a container.
(2) A bottle of any material resembling a gourd. A 1776 Boston newspaper offered "160 gourds of aloes."

gown (*n.*) An investiture or ordination of one who wears a gown, a judge or a clergyman. In 1774 Philip Fithian wrote,
"He . . . is going in the Spring for the Gown to England." He was going to take clerical orders.

gracht (*n.*) A ditch, moat, or canal. A word left over from the Dutch occupation of New Amsterdam. In a 1673 New York document it says,
"In this Citty to the east of the moate or Ditch, commonly called the prince Graght."

graft (*v.*) To join one thing to another, to repair. A 1749 New York newspaper advertised,
"Elizabeth Boyd is removed to Bayard's Street . . . where she follows as usual new grafting and footing all sorts of stockings."

granadilla (*n.*) **(1)** The fruit of passionflower. In 1751 Washington recorded,
"After Dinner was the greatest Collection of Fruits I have yet seen on the table there was Granadello the Sappadilla Pomgranate. . .."
(2) The wood of the green ebony. William Browne's 1664 deposition included,
"There was Aboarde the Shipe when shee was taken from Ro't Cooke bowt 48 hogsheads of Sugar, Some Cocco, Ebbony, Granadilla." From Spanish *granadilla* diminutive of *granada* 'pomegranate.'

granado (*n.*) A grenade. In 1721:
"some unknown Hands, threw a fired Granado into the chamber" of Cotton Mather.

grand committee A committee of the whole. A 1775 report stated,
"The Congress resolved itself into a Grand Com[mitt]ee . . . to order the General to storm or bombard Boston."

granny (*n.*) A nurse. In 1794 Washington recorded,
"Kate at Muddy hole . . . to serve the negro women (as a Granny) on my estate."

grasier (*n.*) *See* **grazier.**

grassum (*n.*) A fine paid on transfer of a copyhold estate. A variant of *gersum*, from Anglo-Saxon *gaersum* 'treasure.' A report on Scottish immigration in 1774 commented,

"William Sutherland . . . left his own country because the rents were raised . . . and larger fines or grassums."

gravamen (*n.*) A remonstrance. From Latin *gravamen* 'a physical inconvenience.' In 1764 in his account of the Paxton Boys, Henry Muhlenberg wrote,

"They had repeatedly sent their gravamina to the government in Philadelphia."

grave (*v.*) To clean a ship's bottom and coat it with tar. In 1775 Capt. Zachariah Burchmore reported,

"I have cleared out for Gibraltar and shall grave the vessel."

gravel (*n.*) A variant of *gable*, the upper side wall of a house. In 1744 Dr. Alexander Hamilton wrote of:

"houses . . . with their gravel ends facing the street."

graver (*n.*) An engraver. The 1796 Boston Directory included:

"Blackburn John, Graver Sea street."

grazett (*n.*) A cheap, gray woolen cloth. A corruption of French *grizette*, same meaning. A 1774 Philadelphia newspaper advertised many fabrics including,

"hairbines, brilliants, grazetts, striped Bengals."

grazier (*n.*) One who grazed cattle. In a 1705 Boston election:

"Mr. John Briggs grasier to serve as Constable."

great (*n.*) A variant of *groats*, hulled and crushed oats. A 17th-century cookbook instructed,

"Put in two quarts of great oatmeal."

Great and General Court The name of the governing body of the Virginia Company and the Massachusetts Bay Colony, according to their charters in 1612 and 1629, respectively.

Greek Testament The New Testament in Greek. One of the requirements for graduation by Yale in 1745 was to be:

"able . . . to read . . . Greek Testament."

green scalp A fresh scalp. Robert Eastburne in 1758 reported,

"An Indian . . . had a large Bunch of green Scalps."

green seed cotton A variety of cotton. Bernard Romans in 1775 said it was:

"also known by the name of green seeded cotton."

Gregorian Calendar Although Pope Gregory XII decreed a revised calendar in 1582, it was not until 1752 that it was adopted by England and her colonies. The beginning of the year was changed from March 25 to January 1. Before that, January, February, and the first 24 days of March were at the end of the calendar year. Also, the year 1752 lost 11 days to adjust the calendar properly to the solar-based cycle of seasons; hence, the day after September 2 was September 14. If you read that George Washington was born on February 22, 1731/32, it means that he was born on February 11, 1731 Old Style, or February 22, 1732 New Style.

grenadier (*n.*) A member of an elite troop that usually served as one of the flank companies of each regiment. They were originally large, powerful men who could throw hand bombs (grenades). In 1776 Gen. Charles Lee reported,

"I have formed two companies of grenadiers to each regiment."

griskin (*n.*) The spine of a hog. From Middle English *gris* 'pig.' In 1739 William

Byrd:
"ate pork griskins."

groat (*n.*) An English silver coin worth about four pence. From *great*, because before this coin there was no silver coin larger than a penny. In 1748 Franklin observed, "Six pounds a year is but a groat a day."

groats (*n.*) Hulled oats. From Middle English *grotes*, same meaning. Now, *grits*.

grogram (*n.*) A silk and mohair cloth. From French *gros grain* 'large grain.' A 1732 Charleston, S.C. newspaper offered:
"lately imported . . . Dowlasses, Dantzick, Grograms with Trimming."

ground brief A license from the Governor in New Amsterdam which permitted the holder to buy land from the Indians. An anglicization of Dutch *grondbrief* 'land letter.'

ground leaves The leaves of a tobacco plant nearest the ground, which were not satisfactory. A 1640 Maryland document read,
"Bad tobacco shall be judged ground leafes."

ground nut (1) In New England, the root of the wild bean. In 1675 Mary Rowlandson in Massachusetts reported,
"that day . . . the Indians . . . gleaning what they could find . . . some found groundnuts."
(2) In the South, the peanut. Bernard Romans in 1775 mentioned,
"the *ground nut* also introduced by the Blacks from Guinea."

grum (*adj.*) Morose, surly, glum. In 1771 Franklin deplored:
"my brother, still grum and sullen."

grunt (*n.*) A dessert made of dough filled with berries steamed for an hour and a half.

grutch (*v.*) To begrudge. Describing Virginia in 1705 Robert Beverley wrote,
"They spunge upon the Blessings of a warm sun, and a fruitful Soil, and almost grutch the Pains of gathering in the Bounties of the Earth."

guaiacum (*n.*) A brew made from the hardwood tree *lignum vitae* which increased perspiration, a treatment for venereal disease. A Haitian word. *Also* **guejac.**

gudgeon (*n.*) The socket in which a fireplace crane was seated. In 1762 Franklin explained,
"The spindle, which is of hard iron . . . is made to turn on brass gudgeons at each end."

guejac (*n.*) *See* **guaiacum.**

guest house An infirmary. Capt. John Smith in 1609 wrote,
"On the other side of the river, is Mount Malado (a guest house for sick people)."

guilder (*n.*) A corruption of Dutch *gulden* 'gold coin.' In 1704 the three guilder piece was worth five shillings, two pence, one farthing.

guinea (*n.*) A British gold coin, issued between 1663 and 1813, worth 21 shillings. So named because it was first struck from gold from Guinea on the Gold Coast.

guinea corn The durra or millet. In 1743 Mark Catesby wrote,
"Bunched Guinea Corn . . . It was at first introduced from Africa by the negroes."

gum elemi A gum resin used for varnish and as an ointment. In 1729 Mark Catesby wrote,

"The Gum-elimy Tree . . . produces a large quantity of Gum . . . the consistency of Turpentine."

gunboat (*n.*) A small boat with one or two cannon. Propelled by oars, it may or may not also be moved by a sail. The 1777 Continental Congress:
"Resolved . . . That General Gates be empowered to order such a number of gallies, gunboats, fire-rafts."

gundalow (*n.*) A double-ended, flat-bottomed, one-masted boat with one heavy gun mounted on a forecastle deck foreward and two or four guns broadside. A 1777 document reported,
"Colonel Brown has taken Ticonderoga . . . a number of gundeloes, one armed sloop."

gunstick (*n.*) A ramrod.

Gunter Reference to Edmund Gunter (1581–1626), an English mathematician.
"Gauging by Gunter" or "according to Gunter" meant to measure by the most precise method. *Also* **gunter**.

gurry (*n.*) What is left of a whale after the oil is tried out; the offal of any animal, especially a fish. Etymology unknown. A 1776 Connecticut newspaper advertised:
"Oil and Gurry to be sold by the barrel."

gusset (*n.*) The clock on a stocking. A 1754 newspaper editorial deplored recent fashions which:
"lately shortened the rear, so that the heels and ancles are exposed, even for the very gusset and clock."

gust (*n.*) A sudden squall and blast of wind. In 1731 Joshua Hempstead recorded,
"Sund[ay] 7 hot a Thunder gust & shower."

gut (*n.*) Short for *gutter*, a channel worn by a current of water. In 1770 Washington recorded,
"I also marked at the Mouth of another Gut lower down."

gut scraper A fiddler. The strings of a fiddle are made of catgut. A 1698 song exhorted,
"Strike up drowsie Gut-Scrapers."

gynecandrical (*adj.*) Men and women together. In 1684 Increase Mather deplored,
"There are questions regarding gynecandrical dancing or that which is commonly called mixed promiscuously dancing viz men and women together. Now this we affirm to be utterly unlawful and it cannot be tolerated in such a place as New England without great sin."

habit (*n.*) Dress, garb. In addition to nuns, it applied to others. In 1749 Franklin wrote,
"They have peculiar habits to distinguish them from other youths."

hack (1) (*n.*) A shortening of *hackney coach*. A 1733 Benjamin Lynde diary entry read,
"Fair and hot . . . Barbacue; hack overset."
(2) (*adj.*) Short for *hackneyed*, 'much used; common, trite.' In 1771 Franklin referred to:
"employment as a hack writer."

hack hammer A hatchet, for cutting hacks or notches. From Dutch *hakken* 'to chop.' In 1646,
"1 brass lampe, 1 little hackhamer" was bequeathed in Massachusetts.

hackle (1) (*n.*) A comb for dressing flax or hemp. A 1770 Baltimore newspaper offered:
"one set of the Best Flax Hackles, three to a set."
(2) (*v.*) Samuel Johnson's 1755 *Dictionary* defined it,
"To dress flax."

hackney coach A four-wheeled coach, drawn by two horses, and kept for hire.

ha-ha (*n.*) A ditch, with or without a fence, as a barrier which one would not see in looking straight across a field. From the expression of surprise. In 1785 Washington wrote of:
"The Post and Rail fences running from the Kitchen to the South Haw ha!"

hairbine (*n.*) A head band, to bind the hair. A 1774 Philadelphia newspaper advertised,
"hairbines, brilliants, grazetts."

hair line A fishing line made of hair. In 1646 in Massachusetts a man bequeathed,
"two haire lines & 3 sives."

hair plush A cloth made of mohair with a pile more than one eighth of an inch long. In a 1776 Boston newspaper, Johnson & Phillips offered:
"wilton, velverets, hair plush, Kilmarnock caps."

hake (*n.*) A pot hook. From an anonymous poem of the 17th century:
"On went the boilers till the hake had much ado to bear 'em."

halberd (*n.*) A military weapon; a cross between a spear and a battle axe. From Old French *halebarde*, same meaning. At the time of the American Revolution, Gen. William Heath commented that he:
"took a halbert, a musket and two bayonets . . . ''

hale (*n.*) A pot hook. In 1647 a Massachusetts man bequeathed,
"one postiron, a hale & a how.''

half (*n.*) The share of a tenant farmer. In 1733 William Byrd rode:
"as far as Major Mumford's Quarter, where Master Hogen was Tenant upon Halves.''

half joe Slang for a Portuguese coin, the *johannes*. In 1722 Frederick Chase recorded that one had:
"let Mr. Ripley have a guinea, half a jo and 9 coppers.''

halfthick (*n.*) A kind of coarse, woolen cloth. A 1774 Philadelphia newspaper advertised,
"wiltons, baizes, halfthicks, rattinets.''

halfway covenant A form of partial membership in the Congregational Church of New England.

halter (*n.*) The noose for hanging. The 1767 South Carolina *Remonstrance* stated,
"Save rogues from the halter.''

hammerman (*n.*) A smith; one who works with a hammer. A 1776 Philadelphia newspaper offered for sale,
"sundry negroes, viz. one a hammerman, one a refiner and one a stack taker.''

hammock (*n.*) (1) A small hill. In 1709 John Lawson instructed,
"Steer W.N.W. the East-point of Bluff-Land at Hatteras bearing E.N.E. the Southermost large Hammock toward Ocacock.''
(2) A piece of land suitable for hardwoods. In 1765 John Bartram wrote,
"The hammocks of live-oaks and palmettos are generally surrounded either with swamp or marsh.''

hand (*n.*) A standard measure of wampum, tobacco, herring, bananas, plantain, or ginger root. The size depended on the quantity measured. In 1723,
"the Cagnawagos sent seven hands of wampum'' to Deerfield, Mass.

handbarrow (*n.*) A frame on which something might be carried with handles at both ends. In 1760 Washington:
"was making wheel and hand barrows.''

hand horse The left or near horse of a team. Washington's 1760 diary referred to:
"Postillion and hand Horse.''

hand iron An andiron. A 1649 Massachusetts will bequeathed,
"one paire Handle Irons.''

handler (*n.*) A trader with the Indians. From Dutch *handlaar* 'trader.' A 1754 Massachusetts document began,
"We, the traders (or handlers) to Oswego.''

hands (*n. pl.*) A scoop formed by cupping two hands together. An English description of a Dutch measure, a *geest* 'shoe buckle.' Among other trading goods paid by John Richbell in 1661 to the Indians for land at Mamaroneck, New York, was:
"twenty hands of powder.''

handy (*adj.*) Ingenious or, in an ironic sense, underhand. In 1710 William Byrd read:

"a letter from Mrs. Dunn directed to my wife by which I found out some handy dealings which put me out of humour."

hanger (*n.*) A short, broad sword used by seamen, originally hung from the belt. A 1758 deposition reported,
"fourteen Hangers which was all the Arms on board."

hard marsh A firm, barren sand. In 1737 John Wesley described it as:
"A firm but barren sand bearing only sour rushes."

harmonica (*n.*) A musical instrument, invented by Benjamin Franklin, made of a collection of musical glasses. In 1774 Philip Fithian boasted,
"Mr. Carter . . . has here at Home a Harpsichord, Forte-Piano, Harmonica, Guittar, Violin & German Flutes."

harquebus (*n.*) An arquebus, the ancestor of the musket. From Dutch *haakbus* 'hook gun.' Early models were so heavy that they were supported by a permanently affixed hook.

harrateen (*n.*) A curtain fabric. A 1744 Maryland document recorded,
"4 Pair of Green Harrateen Windsor Curtains."

hartshorn (*n.*) The horn of a stag. Shave it; add water; boil until a jelly is formed; serve the jelly as a nourishing diet. In 1774 Philip Fithian took:
"spirits of hartshorn for my head."

haslet (*n.*) The edible organs; heart, liver, etc., of a hog. In 1710 William Byrd:
"ate hog's haslet."

haste (*v.*) To move rapidly; hasten. William Bradford said,
"and were hasted ashore" in 1630.

hastener (*n.*) A metal reflector placed in front of a fireplace to hasten the cooking.

hasty pudding (*n.*) A concoction of oatmeal or cornmeal boiled with water or milk. In 1717 Samuel Sewall recorded,
"Sat awhile in the wigwam . . . eat roste alewife and very good hasty pudding."

hatchel (*n.*) A variant of **hackle**.

haw (*n.*) A hawthorn berry. From Middle English *hawe* 'an enclosure or yard,' for which purpose hawthorne trees were used. Francis Higginson thought,
"haws of Whitethorne [are] neere as good as our Cherries in England."

hayward (*n.*) One whose job it was to keep stray cattle and swine from breaking into enclosed fields. Also *haward*. He warded, or guarded the hay. Connecticut enacted a law in 1674:
"There shall be a Hayward or Haywards chosen in each plantation in this Colony."

hazard (*n.*) A simplified form of and a forerunner to the game of craps. In 1710 William Byrd:
"played at hazard and lost 7 pounds and returned home very peaceful."

haze (*v.*) To roam aimlessly. Instructions for the square dance *Innocent Maid* included,
"First three couples haze, then lead down the middle and back again."

head (*n.*) **(1)** The topic under discussion. In 1742 Cadwallader Colden wrote,
"As we have never heard from you on this head, we want to know what you have done on it."
(2) The most remote part of a stream, a town, or a frontier. A 1704 Boston newspaper reported,

"The Enemy was beaten off with loss but are yet hovering on the head of those towns."

(3) A person. The 1701 records of Bedford, N. Y., read,

"The town by major vote doth agree that ye land westward of ye first purchase shall be paid by heads, and every head that payeth ye Indians for it shall have every one of them an equal [right] according to what they pay."

head line The base line for a survey. A 1656 Connecticut document stated,

"From the said head lyne we measured for the length . . . 6 miles & a halfe."

head money A poll tax. In 1648 a New Hampshire document recorded,

"The petition of the inhabitants of Exceter for their rate & head money to be forborne."

head right **(1)** A share. In 1708 the town of Bedford, N. Y., recorded,

"A copy of ye account of ye proprietors of ye aforesd new Purchase in s[ai]d Bedford . . . of Expressing their Rights in ye same by head Rights are, viz: Zachariah Roberts, 2 Head Rights . . . the number of Rights, 36."

(2) A right to land granted to the head of a family of settlers. In 1798 O.A. Rothert referred to:

"Colonel William Campbell's headright on Caney."

head souse A head cheese. Odd pig's parts, cut up fine, boiled, seasoned and pressed. From Middle English *souse* 'to soak in brine.' In 1704 Sarah Knight recorded,

"My guide said it smelt strong of head sause."

heart, in Fertile. In 1774 Philip Fithian deplored,

"Without any regard to continue their Land in heart, for future crops."

heat (*n.*) An agitation of mind. In 1722 Dr. William Douglas in discussing smallpox vaccination said,

"However, many of our clergy had got into it and they scorn to retract; I had them to appease, which occasioned great heats."

heater (*n.*) A triangular piece of heated iron placed into a smoothing iron. A 1684 Massachusetts inventory included:

"a box smoothing iron with 2 heaters."

heathen (*n.*) A common way of referring to an Indian. In 1667 John Winthrop observed,

"We are surrounded by great nations of the heathen."

heave out To elevate. A 1774 New York colonial law for collecting quitrents defined,

"The first and south division to extend so far north til it comes to the hove out lands."

hecatomb (*n.*) A sacrifice of one hundred oxen, hence a slaughter. An adopted Greek word. Regarding the Battle of Bunker Hill, Hugh Brackenridge wrote,

"And offer up, this band, a hecatomb to Britain's glory."

heckle (*v.*) A variant of *hackle*, to comb flax. In 1774 John Harrower wrote,

"Break swingle and heckle flax."

hen (*n.*) A hen clam. In 1623 Richard Whitbourne wrote of:

"Lobsters, Crafish, Muskels, Hens, and other varieties of Shelfish."

herba (*n.*) A grass cloth, originally imported from Persia, China, and India, called *panni d'herba* 'cloth of grass' by Venetian merchant Cesare Federici in 1563. It is one of the fabrics listed in the Revenue Act of 1764.

herb of grace The herb rue. In 1679 Charles Wolley wrote,
"Every Country family understood the vertue of Rue or Herb-a-grace, which is held as a preservative against infectious Disease."

heriot (*n.*) A tribute paid to a lord on the death of a tenant. From Old English *heregeatu* 'military equipment.' Under the laws of Canute the payment was made in military equipment. The 1641 Massachusetts Body of Liberties said,
"All our lands and heritages shall be free . . . from all heriots."

Herrnhuter (*n.*) A Moravian. The sect was founded in Herrnhut, Germany, around 1722. It was one of the religions in Pennsylvania listed by Gottfried Mittleberger in 1750.

Hessian (*n.*) A mercenary from the principality of Hesse. Although all the German mercenary troops during the Revolutionary War were generally referred to as Hessians, men were also hired from Brunswick, Anspach-Bayreuth, Waldeck, and Anhalt-Zerbst. Of the almost 30,000 who arrived here 7,754 died and 5,000 deserted.

hewer (*n.*) One who hews wood or stone. It was one of the occupations that William Penn said was needed in 1681 in Pennsylvania.

high church That part of the Anglican or Protestant Episcopal Church which stressed ritual. A 1728 Massachusetts document referred to:
"the high church party (being but a few though very noisy)."

High German An immigrant from south Germany. It was applied to one who spoke High German, a particular dialect and not a term of approval. *See* **Low Dutch.** In 1706 in Pennsylvania there was:
"a petition of . . . about 150 high and low Germans."

highlone (*adv.*) An alteration of *alone*, apparently to express intensity. In 1760 Washington wrote of:
"mares . . . so much abused . . . they were scarce able to go highlone, much less to assist."

High Mightinesses The States General. The Supreme Parliament of the Republic of The Netherlands was made up of representatives of the seven provinces. The 1627 *Freedoms and Exemptions* of the West India Company were:
"under the supreme jurisdiction of their High Mightinesses the States-General."

Hilary (*n.*) Hilarymas, the mass of St. Hilary, January 13; one of the quarter days. The Charter for Virginia specified,
"They should hold four assemblies a year on the next to last Wednesday of Hilary term, Easter, Trinity and Michaelmas terms."

hip[1] (*n.*) A depression of spirits, the blues. A variant of *hyp*, a shortening of *hypochondria*. In 1775 Philip Fithian reported that:
"Mrs. Green is better, but Miss Beatty says she has the hipp."

hip[2] (*n.*) The fruit of the dog rose. A 17th-century cookbook explained how:
"to make a tart of hipps."

hiperion tea A labrador tea. No connection can be found between this tea and the Greek sun god, Hyperion. A 1767 Rhode Island newspaper commented,
"The Hiperion or Labradoe tea is much esteemed, and by great numbers vastly preferred to the poisonous Bohea."

hippocras (*n.*) A wine with cloves, ginger, cinnamon, and nutmeg added. From Latin *vinum Hippocraticum* 'wine of Hippocrates,' as it was filtered through a flannel hip-

pocrates bag. In 1709,
"After the christening were brought wafers, comfits . . . and hipocras and muscadine wine."

hips (*n.*) Once women wore "falsies" on their hips. A 1770 New Hampshire newspaper advertised:
"stays . . . french hips."

hive[1] (*n.*) A conical, straw headdress. A 1757 New York newspaper advertisement offered:
"Shades lorrain, bonnets and hives."

hive[2] (*v.*) To sequester. In 1774 a friend asked Philip Fithian,
"What do you mean by keeping hived up sweating in your room?"

hobbing iron A grass-cutting tool. From *hub*, 'an uneven piece of ground or sod.' A 1643 Connecticut document included,
"A Inuentory . . . 1 spade, 1 hobing iron, 5 siues."

hoe cake A cornmeal cake originally cooked on a hoe, or fire rake.

hog corn (*n.*) A poor quality corn, fit only for hogs. Washington's 1787 diary recorded,
"30 Barrls sound and 11 Hog Corn."

hog howard A variant of *hog hayward*. The clerk in the town of Mamaroneck, N.Y., described his duties:
"Upon due notice being given him of any hog running at large in the town without being rung, to ring the same forthwith."

hog mane A horse's mane cut short like a hog's bristles. Someone advertised in 1767 in a Boston newspaper,
"Strayed or Stolen, a large Brown Horse, Hogg Mein, bob Tail."

hogreeve (*n.*) A town official who impounded stray hogs. This title was used in Braintree, Mass., in 1766.

hogshead (*n.*) A cask varying in size from 63 to 140 gallons depending on the contents and the then current usage. The derivation of the word, from *hog's head*, has not been explained.

holland (*n.*) A fine, linen fabric, first made in Holland, widely used for curtains, garments, and upholstery. A 1774 Philadelphia newspaper advertised,
"Kenting and lawn aprons, brown Hollands, Marseilles quilting."

Hollands acre 2.1 acres; a morgen. A 1645 New York document referred to:
"Gardens or Orchards not exceeding one Hollands acre being excepted."

homespun (*n.*) A rough, loosely woven wool fabric one might make at home. Isaac Coutant wrote in New Rochelle, N. Y.,
"Elderly women wore the old style short-gowns and petticoats of homespun or linsey-woolsey."

hominy (*n.*) A ground, parched corn. From *rokahominy*, an Algonquian word of the same meaning.

hone (*v.*) To long; to pine. In 1710 William Byrd recorded,
"The Doctor was much better, but honed after strong drink very much."

honey (*n.*) A sweetening agent. Used medicinally to hide the unpleasant taste of some medicines.

hood (*n.*) **(1)** A head covering deeper than a bonnet. In 1711 a New York publication ordered,
"All ladies who come to church in the new fashioned hoods, are desired to be there before divine service begins, lest they divert the attention of the congregation."
(2) A bald scalp that resembled a hood. Used jokingly or facetiously. In 1732 Samuel Sewall wrote,
"Col. Townsend spake to me of my hood, should get a wig. I said 'twas my chief ornament."

hoof (*n.*) An animal. In 1683 Plymouth, Mass., decreed,
"Which bridge shalbe for hoof and foot." For man and beast.

hoopwood (*n.*) Black ash. It was suitable for making barrel hoops. In 1770 Washington:
"also marked . . . an Ash and hoopwood."

hopple (*n.*) A variant of *hobble*, a fetter for horses. The Mamaroneck, N. Y., town clerk spelled it this way in 1759.

hordealed (*adj.*) With barley. From Latin *hordeum* 'barley.'

hore (*n.*) Fuzz. Related to *hoar frost*. A 17th-century cookbook instructed,
"peaches . . . wipe off theyr white hore."

horner (*n.*) One who works horn to make spoons, combs, etc.

horns, to wear To be cuckolded. Cuckolds were reputed to have horns. The origin lies in the taking over a herd of does from an older stag by a younger one. *Poor Richard's Almanac* warned,
"You cannot pluck roses/ Without fear of thorns,/ Nor enjoy a fair wife/ Without danger of horns."

horse (*v.*) To put someone on another's back in order to flog; hence, to flog. In 1775 Philip Fithian reported,
"You published in Mr. Washington's Family that Mr. Fithian horsed me for Staying out all night."

horse hoe A horse-drawn cultivator. In 1775 the anonymous author of *Animal Husbandry* referred to:
"the inventor of horse-hoeing husbandry."

horse leech A veterinarian. An anonymous 1689 writer regarding the administration of Gov. Andros referred to:
"The illegalities done by these horse leeches in the two or three years that they have been sucking of us."

horse litter A carriage on poles borne between two horses, one behind the other. In 1715 Samuel Sewall reported that Capt. Warren was:
"carried on a Horselitter."

hortage (*n.*) Garden vegetables. From Latin *hortus* 'a garden.' A 1634 letter from Maryland reported,
"sugar cane of our own planting, beside hortage coming up very finely."

hosiery (*n.*) Knitted articles of apparel. *Fleecy hosiery*, that with a fleece-like nap. In 1794 John Jay wrote from London to his wife Sally regarding his rheumatism,
"Having been advised to wear vests of fleecy Hosiery under my shirt, I had some made."

hospital (*n.*) A shelter for paupers. An Old French word designating a place of recep-

tion for guests. Cotton Mather in 1713 wrote of:
"setting up a Christian hospital for the good education of poor children."

hotspur peas A kind of early pea. Like a hotspur it is impetuous and comes out early. An April 1765 Boston newspaper advertised,
"Golden hotspur peas, early charlton peas, marrow-fat peas, Leadman's dwarf peas, Windsor beans."

house (*n.*) A college in a university. The rules at Harvard in 1646 warned scholars not to:
"transgresse any of the Lawes of God or the House." Harvard still has "houses."

house burn The damage to tobacco while curing in a tobacco house. In 1640 Maryland decreed,
"Bad tobacco shall be judged ground leafs Second crop leafs notably bruised or worm eaten or leaves house burnt sun burnt."

house joiner A craftsman who did the finished woodwork of a house after the carpenter had framed it. In 1785 Washington noted:
"one Richd Boulton a House joiner and undertaker, recommended to me."

housen (*n.*) A plural of *house*. In 1740 George Whitefield wrote,
"We went round by the upper housen parish."

House of Burgesses The legislative body in Maryland and Virginia.

house of easement A privy. In 1658 Boston legislated,
"That there bee two houses of easement sett upp about the dock for the accommodation of strangers."

house of entertainment An inn for travelers. *See* **entertainment** (1). In 1738 Providence, Rhode Island, enacted a law that:
"Will. Balston shall erect and sett up a howese of entertainment."

house of office A privy. A definition of *office* is the action of discharging feces. In 1652 Boston passed a law:
"It is ordered that noe house of Office . . . shall stand within twentie foot of any hie way."

housewife (*n.*) A pocket or bag for sewing materials.

housewifery (*n.*) The business of the mistress of a family. In 1740 William Byrd wrote,
"I gave Fanny twenty-four pounds cotton for her and her sister to encourage housewifery."

hoy (*n.*) A sloop-rigged ship used for conveying passengers and goods. An adaptation of a Dutch word, *hoei*, same meaning.

hubbub (*n.*) An Indian game played with bones and a tray and much shouting, "hub hub." In 1764 Thomas Hutchinson described,
"Another game they call hubbub, the same the French call jeu de plat the game of the dish among the Hurons."

huckaback (*n.*) A kind of linen cloth with a raised figure for toweling. Now just *huck*. A 1729 Philadelphia newspaper advertised,
"huckabags and Russia linen."

hue and cry A "wanted" notice; a person ignoring the notice and not apprehending the person wanted was guilty of a misdemeanor. The redundancy is from French

huer 'to shout' and *crier* 'to scream.' The 1687 grant to John Pell in New York required,
"Send fforwards to the next townes all publick packquetts and letters, or hew and cryes coming to New Yorke or going from thence."

huggermugger (*n.*) Privacy; secrecy. Origin uncertain. In 1654 Edward Johnson wrote about those who do not conform to his Puritan principles,
"and not deluded any by keeping their profession in huggermug but print and proclaim to all."

humbles (*n.*) A variant of *numbles*, the heart, liver and kidneys of a deer. A 17th-century recipe directed,
"take ye humbles of a deer." Made into a potpie, it was *humble pie*.

humhum (*n.*) A kind of plain, coarse, cotton cloth from India. From Arabic *hammam* 'turkish bath,' as it was used in baths. A 1745 Philadelphia newspaper advertised,
"Quilted humhums, grassetts, single allopeens."

hummock (*n.*) A small hill. A 1666 Long Island, N. Y., deed described pieces of land,
"one at the landing place one at the humuck."

humor (*n.*) The disposition, temper, mood. Because the temper of the mind is supposed to depend on the humor of the body. William Byrd in 1728 observed,
"The inhabitants of North Carolina devour so much swine's flesh that it fills them full of gross humors."

hundred (*n.*) A division of a county. The term was used in Maryland, Pennsylvania, and Virginia and is still used in Delaware. A 1683 Pennsylvania document had,
"Power to Divide the said Countrey and Islands, into Townes, Hundreds and Counties." Originally, a *hundred* was the settlement of one hundred free families of Saxon colonists.

hundredweight (*n.*) 112 pounds. Probably originally 100 pounds, hence the name. The Navigation Act of 1673 said,
"There shall be answered and paid . . . these following rates of duties: for sugar white the hundredweight, containing one hundred and twelve pounds, five shillings."

hungary water A distilled water made with the tops of rosemary. It was first concocted for a queen of Hungary. In 1740 William Byrd:
"sent Captain Hardyman some Hungary water." The family must have liked it for his father in 1689 had bought 12 quarts.

hurdle (*n.*) **(1)** A sled upon which criminals were transported to the gallows. William Byrd in 1739 wrote,
"Upon Tyburn Road in a cart or a hurdle."
(2) A pallet, woven of sticks by the Indians for roasting meat. Capt. John Smith in 1620 wrote that they:
"roast their fish and flesh upon hurdles."
(3) A pallet for sleeping. William Byrd in 1722 recorded,
"The Indians have no standing furniture in their cabins, but hurdles to repose their persons on."

husband (*v.*) To use sparingly, as any good master of a household would. In 1715 William Byrd referred to:
"a bottle of wine husbanded very carefully."

husbandman (*n.*) A farmer; also, the head of a family. In 1751 Franklin wrote,
"The husbandman subsisting on much less the gardener on still less."

hush (*v.*) A variant or misspelling of *hash*, to mince. In 1710 William Byrd:
"ate hushed pork."

huskanaw (v.) *Algonquian* To initiate a Virginia Indian boy at puberty through imposed fasting and the use of narcotics. In 1733 William Byrd wrote,
"And the Joy of meeting my Family in Health made me in a moment forget all the Fatigues of the Journey, as much as if I had been husquenawed."

hussy (*n.*) A shortened form of *housewife*, both the person and the container.

hutch (*n.*) A table having a box below a hinged top.

hyacynth (*n.*) A confection of hyacinth was prescribed to cure jaundice.

hydra (*n.*) An evil; any monstrous thing; by extension from the snake in Greek mythology, killed by Hercules, which grew two heads for each one cut off. In 1774 a Newport, R. I., handbill referred to:
"that hydra, the Stamp Act."

hyperic (*n.*) St. John's wort.

hyson (*n.*) A green Chinese tea. From Chinese *Hsi-ch'un* 'blooming spring.' David Sears advertised in a 1783 Philadelphia newspaper:
"Teas: Tonkay, Congo, Bohea, Hyson, Soatchoun."

hyssop (*n.*) An extract of this herb was used as tonic.
"Teas: Tonkay, Congo, Bohea, Hyson, Soatchoun."

ignoramus (*n.*) The refusal of a grand jury to prosecute an indictment. Latin 'we ignore.' The word appears in the indictment of Benjamin Blackledge in 1694.

imbrue (*v.*) To drench or stain, especially with blood. A 1690 New York letter said, "Leisler's advocates mortally hated them; not only because they had imbrued their hands in the blood of the principal men of their party."

immature (*adj.*) Too early, untimely. A 1682 Massachusetts broadside: "mentioned the immature death."

immunity (*n.*) An exemption from a duty which a feudal lord usually required. The 1668 royal patent to John Richbell for Mamaroneck, N. Y., entitled him to: "all other profits, immunities and emoluments to the said parcel or tract."

impale (*v.*) **(1)** To enclose with pales, stakes, posts, or palisades. The 1648 instructions to the Governor of Virginia ordered residents to: "apply themselves to the impaling of orchards and gardens." **(2)** By extension of the above, to take jurisdiction over. John Winthrop wrote in a letter, "Without order of the court he had impaled at Newton above one thousand acres and had assigned lands to some there."

imparlance (*n.*) A delay or continuance before appearing in court. The 1739 Hat Act provided, "No essoin protection or wages of law or more than one imparlance shall be admitted or allowed for the defendant."

imperial A fine Chinese tea, allegedly drunk by the Imperial household. Advertised in a 1741 Philadelphia newspaper.

impertinent (*adj.*) Rude. In 1727 William Byrd recorded, "A bear diet makes him so vigorous that he grows exceedingly impertinent to his poor wife."

import (*v.*) To state or allege. From Middle French *importer* (to signify). In 1773 Franklin wrote, "Make your arbitrary tax more grievous . . . by public declarations importing that your power of taxing them has no limit."

impost master A customs officer. A 1775 Watertown, Mass., document referred to:
"Honorable James Russel, Esq. Impost Master."

impostume (*n.*) An abscess. In 1710 William Byrd recorded,
"Cape Doyley died yesterday . . . of an imposthume in his head."

imprest (*v.*) To advance (money). A 1782 document signed by George III referred to:
"any money in your hands that may be applied to this service or that may be imprested to you for the same."

improve (*v.*) To use for advantage. In 1700 Springfield, Mass., legislated,
"No stranger . . . shal box any tree or Improve the sam for turpentine."

improver (*n.*) **(1)** One who cultivates. A 1687 New York document stated,
"The Dutch are great improvers of land."
(2) A refiner of lead. A 1734 Maryland list included,
"shoemakers, taylors, improvers, dressers."

inaccommodate (*adj.*) Unfit; unsuitable. William Bradford wrote in 1620,
"This long voyage and their inacomodate conditions."

incommode (*v.*) To inconvenience; to annoy. In 1751 Franklin wrote,
"The Dutch underlive and are thereby enabled to underwork and undersell the English; who are thereby extremely incommoded."

incontinency (*n.*) Lewdness. The 1619 Virginia Assembly recorded,
"Evidence or suspicion of incontinency or of the commission of any other enormous sins."

increase (*n.*) Any progeny. In 1768 Washington listed,
"two Milch Cows (one half of whose Increase I am to have)."

Ind. (*n.*) An abbreviation of *Indies*, either East or West. In 1774 John Trumbull wrote regarding Boston,
"From either Ind thy cheerful stores were filled."

indent (*v.*) To bind, by contract, a person to work for another. The colonial population included many indentured servants who agreed to work, generally for four or five years, in exchange for their passage from Europe. Young people were apprenticed, generally for seven years, to learn a trade or craft. Orphans were bound until they were 21 to learn a trade or craft in exchange for food, shelter, and clothing.

indenture (*n.*) A document executed in duplicate. The two parts were laid together and notched (indented) so that the parts corresponded. From Latin *indentatus* 'notched,' related to *dentatus* 'toothed.' The 1619 Virginia Assembly referred to a person who might:
"contract himself . . . by indenture or otherwise."

Indess (*n.*) A female Indian. John Josselyn in 1674 observed,
"The *Indesses* that are young, are some of them very comely."

indiaman (*n.*) A large, well-built, armed sailing vessel used in the trade to India; specifically, one owned by the East India Company.

Indian gift A gift given with the expectation of an equivalent return. Thomas Hutchinson in 1764 remarked:
"An Indian gift is a proverbial expression, signifying a present for which an equivalent return is expected." Today it is often taken to mean a gift that one expects to be taken away by the donor.

Indian physic A concoction of gillenia was used as an emetic. William Byrd wrote,

"I agreed with her [Mrs. Fleming] that those remedies might be very good, but would be more effectual after a dose or two of Indian physic."

Indian weed Tobacco. In 1708 Ebenezer Cook wrote,
"Leaving behind, to raise up Seed,/ And tend a stinking Indian Weed."

indite (*v.*) To compose. In 1774 Deborah Cushing wrote of:
"a friend who I know will excuse all errors in righting and endighting."

in eternitatem pingo *Latin.* Literally, 'I paint into eternity.' That which I paint will last forever. A 1774 newspaper editor used the expression while exhorting separation from Great Britain.

infantry (*n.*) Infants. In 1679 Charles Wolley referred to:
"the minors and the infantry of the best families."

infantry, light Troops made up of hardy, quick, and better marksmen. Armed with musket, bayonet, and tomahawk, they served as flank guards and made forays against the enemy.

in forma pauperis *Latin.* 'in the manner of a pauper.' A poor person could sue without liability for costs.

information (*n.*) A prosecution for an offense against the government on the basis of the accusation of an individual, not of a grand jury. In 1735 Andrew Hamilton, the Philadelphia lawyer who defended John Peter Zenger, stated,
"The practice of informations for libels is a sword."

infra fluxum et refluxum maris *Latin.* 'between the flow and the ebb of the sea.' High tide; the hour at which pirates were hanged. The order for the execution of Captain William Kidd in 1701 specified this time.

inkle (*n.*) A kind of narrow tape, usually of linen and often used for trimming. Father Andrew White, in a 1635 list of items one should bring with one to Maryland, suggested:
"inkle for garters."

in minori propositione *Latin.* 'in the lesser proposal.' In Henry Muhlenberg's 1764 account of the Paxton Boys he said,
"He expressed the hearty desire and hope that these characteristics might be found among them *in minori propositione* and that they might become known by their fruits."

inquisition (*n.*) **(1)** A judicial inquiry. The 1774 Administration of Justice Act provided,
"Governor . . . to direct . . . that the inquisitions, indictments or appeal shall be tried."
(2) A place of detention, by transfer from imprisonment for an inquisition. A 1776 play referred to:
"Houses of our God converted into . . . inquisitions, barracks and jails."

instance (*v.*) To give an example. In 1756 Washington wrote,
"I can instance several cases where a captain, lieutenant, and . . . ensign will go on duty at a time."

intendant (*n.*) A superintendent. In 1776 in Rhode Island,
"There shall be two persons annually appointed by this General Assembly, as intendants of trade."

interest (*n.*) A farm. A 1663 document in Massachusetts referred to:
"fencing stuffe from our wood interest."

interval (*n.*) A low ground beside a river. Sometimes spelled *intervale* 'the valley between' two hills. A 1647 Massachusetts document deeded,
"Fifty acres of Interval."

intestine (*adj.*) Internal. "N" in a 1775 New York newspaper wrote:
"that by causing intestine broils at home it would force her to recall her troops from America."

intra praesidia *Latin* 'within the defenses; in a place of safety.' The judge's verdict in a 1742 trial said,
"She not being carried intra praesidia, but only plundered and let go."

Invalid Corps A group of wounded veterans of the Revolution. They served in hospitals, magazines, and garrisons. In 1778 Maj. Fishbourne referred to:
"The Invalid Corps at Philadelphia."

inveterate (*adj.*) Obstinate, deep-roooted. In 1769 William Shepherd complained,
"Everybody [was] inveterate against me."

ipecacuanha Ipecac. The dried roots of *cephaelis ipecacuanha* produced an expectorant and emetic useful in treating amoebic dysentery. In a 1776 Providence, Rhode Island, newspaper,
"John Chace, Druggist [offered] Cantharides, Opium, jalap, ipecacuana, jesuits bark."

iron man One who works in an ironworks. One of the trades, according to Capt. John Smith, needed in the Virginia colony in 1610.

iron ring A ring worn for its alleged curative properties. In 1769 Washington,
"Put an iron ring upon Patcy [his step-daughter] (for fits)."

iron ruffles Handcuffs. A character in a 1776 play threatened,
"I'll make each of them a present of a pair of iron ruffles."

ironstone (*n.*) Iron ore. In 1634 in Maryland,
"We have sent over a good quantity of ironstone for a trial."

irrefragable (*adj.*) Irrefutable. In 1760 Joseph Galloway wrote,
"Conduct of the great Lord Bacon exhibits an irrefragable proof."

isinglass (*n.*) A gelatin made from the bladder of a sturgeon-like fish. A corruption of Dutch *huisenblas* 'sturgeon's bladder.' A 17th-century recipe instructed,
"Let it boyle with four ounces of Ising glass."

island (*n.*) (1) A hill surrounded by level ground, or a clump of trees surrounded by a plain. A 1703 Providence, Rhode Island, document referred to:
"a little island of upland in s[ai]d meadow." Also, in 1770 Washington described:
"Large Planes 30 Miles in length without a Tree except little Islands of Wood."
(2) An isolated place. A 1659 Maryland indenture involved,

jack (*n.*) A waxed leather mug or pitcher. A 1633 New Haven, Conn., inventory included:
"1 jack of leather to drink in."
(2) An engine for turning a spit, etc. An operation formerly done by a small boy, and small boys are often called Jack, according to Isaac Watts in his 1724 *Logick*.
(3) A tiny bit. A 17th-century cookbook directed,
"Add ye second time a Jack of water."

jackanapes (*n.*) A coxcomb. A *jackanapes* suit was a very fancy suit.

jack boot A high, stout boot that serves as armor for the leg. Possibly showing the use of *jack* in the sense 'coat of mail.'

Jack Cade The man who in 1450 led an unsuccessful rebellion against Henry VI. In 1774 Gouverneur Morris deplored,
"These fellows became the Jack Cades of the day."

jack pudding A buffoon. A translation of German *Hanswurst*, the comic buffoon in old German pantomime. Dr. Alexander Hamilton in 1744 related,
"Our landlord Todd entertained us as he stood waiting with quaint old saws and jack pudding speeches."

jaconet (*n.*) A kind of coarse muslin, first made in Jagannath, India, used for dresses and infants' clothes. A 1790 Boston newspaper offered,
"Black Modes . . . Jackonet Muslins . . . Castor Hats."

jaculate (*n.*) A variant spelling of *chocolate*. In 1774 John Harrower wrote,
"For breakfast either coffee or jaculate."

jade (*n.*) A mean or poor horse. A 1779 New York newspaper reported,
"The Rebel officers and men quitted their Jades."

jadish (*adj.*) Mean. In 1647 Nathaniel Ward wrote,
"Be they [consciences] never so dirty or jadish."

Jagers (*n.*) 600 green-clad mercenaries under General von Wurmb during the Revolutionary war. The German word for 'huntsmen.'

jagg (*n.*) A shortening of *jagging iron*, a tool for cutting notches. A 17th-century cookbook directed,
"Cut ye superflous paste with a jagg."

jakes (*n.*) A privy or john. The word dates to about 1530 and the origin is uncertain. In 1679 Charles Wolley foresaw pollution in New York,
"The longer and the more any Country is peopled, the more unhealthful it may prove by reason of Jaques, Dunghills and other excrementitious stagnations."

jalap (*n.*) The powdered root of a plant from Jalapa, Mexico; used as a strong laxative. A 1776 Providence, Rhode Island, newspaper advertised:
"Cantharides, Opium, jalap, ipecacuana."

James's Powder A fever powder, made by dissolving antimony in nitric acid, patented in 1743 by Dr. Robert James, a friend of Samuel Johnson's and who wrote a *Dictionary of Medicine* in the same year. It was still being made and sold as recently as 1910. In 1775 Philip Fithian wrote,
"If his disorder does not abate tonight . . . a dose of James's Powder."

Jamestown weed Jimson weed, an extremely poisonous plant from whose leaves the drug stramonium is produced. In 1687 botanist John Clayton wrote,
"The Soldiers . . . lighting in great Quantities upon an Herb called James-town weed, they gathered it; and by eating thereof in plenty, were rendered apish and foolish."

jane (*n.*) A variant of *jean*, a kind of fustian. From *Genoa fustian*. Cf. **jeans**. A 1797 Boston newspaper advertised,
"Kerseymeres, Fustians, Janes, Moreens."

Jannes and Jambres Two Egyptian magicians who imitated Moses' miracles. In 1647 Nathaniel Ward wrote,
"The persecution of true religion and toleration of false are the jannes and jambres to the Kingdom of Christ."

japanner (*n.*) One who applied japan, a very hard lacquer, in the manner of the Japanese. In 1712 Samuel Sewall referred to:
"Pendleton, The Japanner."

jaques *See* **jakes**.

jeans (*n.*) A kind of fustian originally from *Gênes*, French for 'Genoa.' A 1775 Boston newspaper advertised:
"Fustians and Jeans."

Jehu (*n.*) A King of Israel (843–816 B.C.) who led a furious attack. In 1675 Mary Rowlandson describing some Indians wrote,
"Then like Jehu they marched on furiously."

jerkin (*n.*) A sleeveless pullover with a slit at the neck. Origin unknown.

Jerusalem oak seed A wormseed from which an oil was distilled that was effective against intestinal worms. In 1759 Richard Corbin reported,
"The children of slaves were given Jerusalem oak seed twice a year."

Jesuit (*n.*) One who is designing, cunning, deceitful. Applied to Tories during the Revolution. In 1774 John Adams wrote,
"I admire the Jesuits! Bowing . . . to persons whom . . . they would gladly butcher."

Jesuit's bark Quinine. The bark was known to Jesuits in Lima, Peru, around 1630, and it is alleged that Father de Lugo was the first to bring cinchona (quinine) to Rome.

jetty (*n.*) The part of a building that juts out over a lower. In Boston in 1677 it was recorded:
"the widdow Walker hath set up 4 posts upon the towne land to support the Gettie of her house."

jiggin iron A hook for large pots. A 1776 New York inventory included,
"1 hang iron, 2 toasters, 2 jiggin irons, 1 baking pot."

jilt (*n.*) A woman who trifles with her lover. In 1723 William Byrd, regarding poor advance planning, said it:
"was leaving too much to that jilt, hazard."

jireh (*v.*) *Hebrew*. 'will see.' In 1720 Samuel Sewell said,
"I wrote Mr. Eyre his name in his book . . . it cost me 8 shillings. Jehovah jireh [the Lord will see if it was worth it]!"

jobbing (*n.*) The buying and selling of goods in order to profit. Thomas Paine in 1777 wrote,
"The savage obstinacy of the King and the jobbing gambling spirit of the court."

jockey (*n.*) **(1)** A horse dealer. In 1774 Philip Fithian recorded,
"My horse seems (as jockeys say) in good Flesh."
(2) A cap like a jockey cap. A 1759 Boston newspaper advertised:
"Sattin Jockeys with Feathers for Boys."
(3) A cheat. In a 1770 play Robert Mumford alluded to:
"coxcombs and jockies."

joe (*n.*) Slang for a *double johannes*. Cf. **johannes.** Capt. Zachariah Burchmore in 1775 wrote,
"He has advanced me about 460 half-joes and given me a bill for £80 sterling."

johannes (*n.*) A Portuguese coin issued from 1722 to 1835 and named for the figure of John V on the obverse. A 1741 account of the crew of the *Revenge* mentioned the sum of:
"2½ Johannes."

johnny cake A corn bread. May have derived from **journey cake** or **jonakin**, which see. In 1765 Silas Deane:
"breakfasted on tea and johnny cake."

Johnsmas (*n.*) St. John's Mass, Midsummer Day, June 24, one of the quarter days.

joiner (*n.*) The craftsman who did the finish woodwork of a house; also, a cabinet-maker. In 1626 Plymouth records say,
"No handy craftsman . . . as taylors, shoemakers, carpenters, joyners."

joint stool A stool made of parts fitted together with mortised joints. In 1771 Franklin put something:
"within the cover of a joint stool."

jointure (*n.*) Provision for a widow to get property on the death of her husband, usually made before marriage. One 1708 deed was:
"free of will, intails, joynters, dowries extents."

jolly boat A small boat of a large ship, like a dinghy. Possibly from Danish *jolle* 'yawl, small boat.'

jonakin (*n.*) A corn bread. Possibly an Algonquian word, the forefather of **johnny**

cake, which see. Benjamin Tompson in 1675 referred to:
"other fare than jonakin and mush."

joseph (*n.*) A woman's riding coat. Buttoned down the front, it had a short cape. Ostensibly named after the coat Joseph left behind.

journey cake A corn bread. *See also* **johnny cake, jonakin.** In 1754 John Fries wrote,
"Today I bak'd Journey Cakes."

journeyman (*n.*) A worker, having served his apprenticeship, who could hire out or go into business for himself, but was not yet qualified as a foreman or master. One meaning of the word *journey* is 'a day's work.' In 1771 Franklin related,
"I was to serve as an apprentice till I was twenty-one years of age, only I was to be allowed journeyman's wages during the last year."

Jovis, Die Latin. 'Jove's Day,' i.e., Thursday. From the Roman god *Jove*; equivalent to the Scandinavian god Thor, for whom Thursday was named. The New York Provincial Congress dated its minutes in Latin.

jud. (*n.*) An abbreviation of Latin *judicamentum* 'judgment.' A 1713 document signed by Caleb Heathcote is headed,
"Jud. duodecimo die Dec."

Judicat ex mento non mente puella maritum Latin. 'A woman judges a husband by his chin and not by his mind.' In 1678 Charles Wolley, describing Indians, wrote,
"They be very curious about the Hair of their Heads, yet they will not endure any upon their Chins, where it no sooner grows but they take it out by the Roots . . . so that I leave to the other Sex: *Judicat ex mento non mente puella maritum.*"

juggler (*n.*) A trickish fellow; hence, an Indian medicine man. William Smith in 1735 referred to:
"Coarse imagery in wooden trinkets in the hands of their jugglers."

jumbal (*n.*) A small sugar cake. Possibly because the ingredients are jumbled, mixed. Mrs. E. Smith had a recipe for *jumbals* in 1742.

jump (*n.*) A woman's loose stays or waistcoat. In a 1764 New York newspaper, Joseph Beck, Staymaker, advertised,
"Mecklenburg Stays and Jumps."

juniper (*n.*) The oil of juniper berries, used as a diuretic, to reduce flatulence, and to control menstrual discharge.

junk (*n.*) (**1**) A pipe for tobacco. Sarah Knight wrote in her 1704 *Journal*,
"John made no answer . . . fumbled out his black junk, and saluted that instead."
(**2**) Scrap iron. In 1781 John Sheafe wrote in a letter,
"200 weight of junck to make plum[b] for the publick boats."

Junto (*n.*) (**1**) The name of a club formed by Benjamin Franklin. In 1730 he wrote,
"By the help of my friends in the Junto."
(**2**) A cabal, a faction. From Spanish *junta* 'meeting.' Gov. Francis Bernard of Massachusetts, in a letter to the Earl of Shelburne in 1766, referred to:
"a weekly paper conducted by Otis and his junto."

jurat (*adj.*) Sworn. A shortening of Latin *juratus*. A 1752 certificate of ownership of a ship was headed,
"Jurat: William Johnson."

juratus coram me *Latin.* 'sworn before me.' Samuel Perkins' 1698 deposition was sworn before Ralph Marshall and used this expression.

jure primae occupationis *Latin.* 'by right of first occupation.' A 1622 New York document included,

"Now His Majesty having incontestably the right to the said country *jure primae occupationis.*"

karl (*n.*) The female hemp plant; misspelling of *carl*, carl hemp. It was so named because the female hemp plant grows bigger and tougher than the male and was first thought to be male. A 1732 South Carolina newspaper erroneously said:
"Hemp is of two kinds; male, popularly called Karl; the female Fimble."

keeler (*n.*) A shallow pan; a cooler. One meaning of *keel* is 'to cool.' In 1754 Franklin advised,
"A shallow tray, or keeler, should be under the frame."

keep (*n.*) **(1)** A keeper, one who takes care of a herd. A 1641 Boston law told what to do:
"if any goates shall be found without a keep."
(2) (*v.*) To board. Boston records in 1710 said,
"At present She keeps at ye House of Solomon Townsend."

keeping room The parlor. In 1771 John Copley:
"forgot weither or not there was to be a Clossit in the Keeping Room."

Kendal cotton A green, napped, woolen fabric made in Kendal, England. A 1732 South Carolina newspaper advertised,
"Welsh plains and Kendall cotton."

kennel[1] (*n.*) A facetious use of the place for dogs applied to human quarters. In 1739 William Byrd:
"discoursed til ten and then retired into our kennel."

kennel[2] (*n.*) The watercourse of a street; a canal or channel; a gutter. From Middle English *canel*, same meaning. In 1777 Franklin wrote,
"The pavement and even the kennel were perfectly clean."

kental (*n.*) A spelling of *quintal*, a hundred pounds. A 1645 Massachusetts document referred to:
"One thousand Kintall of dry Cod fish."

kenting (*n.*) A type of linen made in Kent, England. A 1774 Philadelphia newspaper advertised,
"kenting and lawn aprons."

kersey (*n.*) A coarse, ribbed, narrow woolen cloth originally from Kersey, England. A 1732 South Carolina newspaper offered:
"Yorkshire kerseys." It was one of the fabrics covered by The Woollen Act of 1699.

kerseymere (*n.*) A variant of *cassimere*, a woolen fabric. A 1797 Boston newspaper advertised:
"Kerseymeres, Fustians, Janes."

kickshaw (*n.*) Something uncommon or something that has no particular name. From French *quelque chose* 'something.' A 1777 song referred to:
"mitts, hose and a thousand kickshaws."

kid (*n.*) In Virginia, an indentured servant. Derived from *kidnap*, the word applied to both those who were kidnapped and to free willers.

kiddle (*n.*) A fish trap. A 1724 law was passed in Pennsylvania:
"for demolishing . . . Fishing Dams, Wears & Kedles set across the River."

kidney (*n.*) A temperament; kind, class. In 1744 Dr. Alexander Hamilton described:
"one of the best behaved of that kidney I had ever met with."

kilderkin (*n.*) A small barrel, varying in size from a quarter to a half barrel, generally two firkins. In 1687 in Connecticut it was decreed,
"Every barrel . . . shall contain thirty-two gallons, every kilderkin sixteen gallons."

kill devil West Indian rum. Edward Ward in 1699 said,
"Rum, alias Kill Devil, is as much ador'd by the American English, as a dram of brandy is by an old Billingsgate."

killick, to come to a To come to anchor. In 1649 John Winthrop reported,
"The wind overblew so much at N.W. as they were forced to come to a killock at twenty fathoms."

kilmarnock (*n.*) A broad-topped, plaid, woolen cap, originally from that city in Scotland. A 1776 Boston newspaper advertised:
"hair plush, Kilmarnock caps, death head buttons."

kilter (*v.*) To condition. In 1712 Joshua Hempstead:
"was kiltering my saw."

kimnel (*n.*) A large tub used around the house. Probably from the diminutive of Anglo-Saxon *cumb* a liquid measure.

king and queen A card game; possibly the one better known as *royalty*. In 1715 William Byrd:
"played basset . . . then we drew king and queen."

king's evil Scrofula, a tubercular disease. So called as it was thought that it could be cured by the touch of a king. In 1630 Francis Higginson praising New England weather said,
"One of my children that was formerly . . . of the king's evil, but since he came hither he is very well over . . . by the very wholesomeness of the air."

kiskatom (*n.*). A nut of a hickory tree. From Abnaki *nese kouskadamen* 'I crack with my teeth.' A 1750 newspaper advertised:
"Kisky Thomas."

kit (*n.*) A wooden vessel made with hooped staves. From Dutch *kitte*, same meaning.

In 1679 Charles Wolley:
"ordered him to fetch a kit full of water."

kittereen (*n.*) A one-horse, two-wheeled chaise. Possibly after Kit Treen who once ran a carriage between Penzance and Truro in England. In New York in 1745 a newspaper offered,
"Several very good Riding Chairs and Kittereens to be sold."

kittle-pins *See* **logget.**

knee timber Some timber in the shape of a bent knee, as that used in ship building to connect the beams with the sides. John Richbell's 1660 instructions included,
"Save all your principal timber for pipe stands and clap board and knee timber."

knight's service The military service for the king done as one of the feudal conditions of holding land. It was abolished in 1660. The 1697 patent for Bedford, N. Y., was:
"Given and Granted . . . in Free and Common Lonage and not in . . . Knight's Service."

knop (*n.*) A bud. A 17th-century cookbook instructed:
"Put into it 2 handfulls of lavendar knops."

Korah (*n.*) A man who rebelled against Moses. The earth opened and swallowed him and 250 others. In 1701 Cotton Mather inveighed,
"Man, be zealous, lest the fate of Korah's company be thy fate."

Labadist (*n.*) A member of a religious sect founded in Holland by Jean de Labadie (1610–1679).

labor (*v.*) To prosecute with effort, to urge. In 1756 John Woolman wrote,
"I found myself under a necessity in a friendly way, to labor them on that subject."

laboratory (*n.*) An arms and ammunition factory. In 1776 the Continental Congress resolved:
"that ye Board of War be directed to prepare a plan for establishing a continental Laboratory, and a military Academy."

labour (1) (*n.*) Any land, title to which was earned by working on it. A 1694 North Carolina document stated,
"The dividing line . . . shall begin about the length of a chaine up the swamp from a little house built upon Alexander Speeds labour." The "u" was not dropped until 1828 when Noah Webster published his *American Dictionary of the English Language*.
(2) (*v.*) To urge; to argue. In 1756 John Woolman wrote,
"I found myself under a necessity in a friendly way to labour with them on that subject."

labouring oar The most burdensome duty. In 1776 Gen. William Smallwood of Maryland complained,
"We have generally acted in Brigade under Northern Brigadiers General, who have seldom failed to favor their own & put the laboring oar on our Regiment."

Labrador tea A brew from the leaves of an evergreen bush, *Ledum Groenlandicum*. A 1767 Boston newspaper reported,
"There is a certain herb, lately favoured in this province, which begins already to take Place in the Room of Green tea and Bohea tea . . . It is called Labrador."

lack (*interj.*) Short for *alack*. Regret. A character in a 1770 play said,
"Good lack, why didn't you tell me?"

Lady Day March 25, the Feast of the Annunciation, one of the quarter days. Until 1752 the first day of the year. *See* **Gregorian Calendar.**

lagan (*n.*) Any goods thrown overboard at sea with a line and buoy attached for later recovery. A 1753 commission of a Vice-Admiralty judge empowered, "Concerning all Casualties at Sea, Goods wrecked, Flotson and Jetzan, Lagan."

lampoon (*n.*) A personal satire in writing; abuse. In 1710 William Byrd: "directed a letter to Nat Burdwell with a lampoon in it."

lanctie loo A variant of *lanterloo*, a card game now shortened to *loo*. In 1708 Ebenezer Cook wrote, "A jolly female crew/ Were deeply engaged in lanctie loo."

landau (*n.*) A four-wheeled closed coach whose top might be opened. From Landau, Germany. A 1759 Philadelphia newspaper advertisement listed "Coaches, chariots, landaus, phaetons, two and four wheeled chaises."

landaulet (*n.*) A small landau. Also spelled *landarett*. In 1761 a Boston newspaper advertised: "a new landeritt Chaise . . . to be sold."

landgrave (*n.*) A county nobleman in the Colony of Carolina. In 1738 William Byrd wrote, "Neither land-graves nor Cassicks can procure one drop for their wives."

land jobber A land speculator. The 1777 Constitution of Vermont referred to: "certain favorite land jobbers in the government of New York."

land layer One who laid out lots; a surveyor. A 1673 Salem, Mass., document provided that: "any two of those aforesayd land layers may act according to order from the town."

landlooper (*n.*) A landlubber; a land man as contrasted to a seaman. In 1679 Charles Wolley wrote, "The materials of this Journal have laid by me several years expecting that some Landlooper or other in these parts would have done it more methodically."

land tacks on board, to take To go by land. A 1776 Massachusetts document recorded, "Maj'r Meigs & I agreed to take our Land-Tacks on board and quit the boat."

landwaiter (*n.*) A customs officer who attended, or waited, on the landing of goods. A 1696 examination of John Dann referred to: "the Land Waiter of that Port, one Maurice Cuttle."

language (*n.*) Talk, conversation. In 1775 Philip Fithian wrote, "I suppose you join in the general language and assert your liberties and oppose oppression."

lansquenet (*n.*) A card game; any number played against the banker. From German *landsknecht* 'footsoldier.' German footsoldiers invented the game. William Byrd reported playing it in 1710.

lantern (*n.*) A fried tart, shaped like a half moon. One line of *Yankee Doodle* went, "Punk-in pye is very good and so is apple lantern."

lanthorne (*n.*) A lantern, in its usual sense.

lap (*n.*) A shortening of Latin *lapis* 'stone.'

lap[1] (*n.*) A rabbit. In 1679 Charles Wolley listed: "beavers, the lapps, minks, grey foxes, otters, rackoons." Another plural was *lappen*.

lap² (*n.*) **(1)** A bundle of hides. The word comes from its use in the sense of *fold*. A lap of deer hides was 20. A 1673 New Jersey document stated,
"They presented about 20 deer skins . . . 3 laps of Beaver, and 1 string of Wampum."
(2) The area enclosed by a bend of a rail fence. In 1787 Washington noted in his diary:
"In the laps of the fence Inclosg. it 139 pumpkin hills were Planted."

lasses (*n.*) A shortening of *molasses*. A 1730 song went,
"There'll be some a drinking round and some a lapping lasses."

last (*n.*) **(1)** A measure of capacity of a ship, two tons. From Old English *hlaest* 'a burden.' In 1650 Adrien Van der Donck had a contract:
"to charter a suitable fly boat of two hundred lasts."
(2) A standard of measurement equivalent to 12 barrels of fish, 24 barrels of gunpowder, 80 bushels of corn, 12 dozen hides, 20 dickers of leather, 12 sacks of wool, or 12 sacks of feathers.

lasting (*n.*) A shortening of *everlasting*. A 1790 Philadelphia newspaper advertised:
"Public vendue . . . Lastings, Durants, Camblets."

last money Tonnage tax. A document referred to:
"the last money paid Apr. 13th, 1739." *See* **last (1)** .

latitudinarian (*adj.*) Moderate in one's views; giving latitude to one's doctrine. In 1744 Mrs. Cume of Philadelphia deplored the clergy of Maryland who:
"take orders from some latitudinarian bishop and return learned preachers."

lavend (*n.*) A shortening of *lavendula spica*, the herb lavender. Its oil was used as a stimulant and tonic.

lax (*n.*) Diarrhea. From Old French *lasche* 'loosening.' An 18th-century doctor in Virginia:
"gave a vomit to Davy this Morning . . . he had complained of a lax for several days."

lay (*n.*) A rate of pay. In 1772 Washington
"agreed with . . . Powell . . . to continue another year on the same lay as the last."

lay a great belly To deliver a child. In 1712 William Byrd speculated,
"Mrs. Russel was going to Pennsylvania for her recovery which some think is to lay a great belly there, but this is a malicious idea."

lay in (*v.*) To make provisions for. In 1771 H.P. Johnston wrote,
"[I] have Laid in with Mr. Strong for his horse."

lie together (*v.*) To stay, in the sense of 'lay over' or 'lay up.' William Byrd in 1709 recorded,
"The Doctor and I lay together."

lie with (*v.*) To stay; lay together. Later that year Byrd wrote,
"Frank Eppes lay with me."

leach¹ (*n.*) A quantity of wood ashes through which water passed to leach out the lye. In a 1770 letter Franklin instructed,
"Sett a leach or leaches that will contain 18 bu. of Ashes."

leach² (*n.*) A jellied dish with meat, eggs, fruit, or nuts. A 17th-century cookbook

suggested,
"To make the best Leech take Ising-glass . . . then take almonds."

lead (*n.*) Lead acetate was used medicinally for ulcers.

leaded (*adj.*) Glazed, when lead was an important ingredient of the glaze. A 17th-century cookbook advised,
"A earthen pot, well leaded."

leading strings Strings by which children were supported while learning to walk. In 1794 Noah Webster said,
"Americans are still in their leading strings."

lead water A dilute solution of lead acetate *See also* **lead.** In a 1780 letter to Franklin, his sister wrote about her grandson,
"A severe Humer came in His forehead . . . we have constantly washed it with Lead-water which I remember you used when you came from Canady and had a breaking out on your skin."

leap (*n.*) The act of copulation. A 1775 Baltimore newspaper reported,
"The noted horse Smiling Tom stands in high perfection for covering mares . . . at 20 shillings the leap."

learned languages Greek, Latin, and Hebrew. In 1754 Samuel Johnson, its first president, in writing about King's College, New York, (now Columbia University) said that they had:
"set up a course of tuition in the learned languages."

leasing (*adj.*) Lying. In 1773 Franklin wrote,
"Encourage and reward these leasing men, secrete their lying accusations."

lese majesty, lesa majestas An act of high treason. From Latin *laesa majestas;* pl. *laesae maisetates,* 'injured greatness.' The 1640 Freedoms and Exemptions in New Netherland dealt with:
"matters pertaining to possession of benefices, fiefs, lesae majestates."

let (*n.*) A hindrance, an obstacle. From Old English *lettan* 'to hinder.' In 1702 Caleb Heathcote made an agreement in Scarsdale, N. Y.,
"without any Lett, trouble, denyall or interruption." The word survives in tennis for a served ball partly obstructed by the net.

letter founder A type founder. In 1771 Franklin wrote,
"Our printing-house often wanted sorts, and there was no letter-founder in America."

lettre de cachet *French.* An arbitrary warrant for imprisonment. The 1767 South Carolina *Remonstrance* complained of acts in:
"as arbitrary a manner as in France by a *lettre de cachet* or in Spain by a warrant from the Inquisition."

level (1) (*v.*) To make a contour map by using a surveyor's level. In 1770 Washington:
"went to level the ground."
(2) (*adj.*) Even. In 1775 Philip Fithian wrote,
"I am level with her." The British still use the term.

levy (*n.*) One of a body levied, or conscripted for military service. The troops raised in the Revolution by the states were known as *levies.* They were paid by Congress, but were not part of the Continental Army.

libel (*n.*) A written charge, particularly against a ship in Admiralty cases. From Latin *libellum* 'little book.' A 1777 Boston newspaper announced,
"Notice is hereby given that Libels are filed before me against the following vessels . . . all which Vessels and Cargoes, so libelled."

liberty (*n.*) (1) The area over which a person's jurisdiction extends. A 1668 deed in Yonkers, New York, stated,
"Beginning at the boggy swamp within the Liberty of said Patent." And a 1717 document enjoined:
"Demand you to make dilligent search and inquiry within your several counties and liberties for the said Caverley." And in 1769 wagons were prohibited:
"within the said city of Philadelphia, or within the Northern Liberties thereof."
(2) A permission. The 1701 patent for the West Patent of North Castle, N. Y., said,
"The persons named have liberty to enter thereon."
(3) A privilege. The same document as above granted,
"all the other profits, benefits, liberties, privileges, advantages."

liberty tea The stalk and leaves of the four-leaved loosestrife. It was brewed to avoid drinking imported tea.

Liberty Tree An elm tree planted in 1646 near a tavern of the same name on Hanover Square, now Washington Street, in Boston. Those out of favor with the mob were hanged in effigy from it. It yielded 14 cords of firewood when the British soldiers cut it down. Gov. Francis Bernard wrote in 1768,
"The effigies of Mr. Paxton & Mr. Williams were hanging upon the Liberty Tree."

licorice (*n.*) The dried root had several medicinal uses, mainly as a sweetener, as it is said that it is the only sweet that quenches thirst.

lie common To be neglected. In 1774 Philip Fithian saw some cattle and hogs rooting and bewailed:
"the neglect of the people in suffering their graveyards to lie common."

light (*n.*) A pane of window glass, or, in this case, a paper one. From Latin. In 1698 R. Chamberlin referred to:
"stones . . . breaking the Glass Windows, and a Paper-Light."

lighterman (*n.*) A person who manages a lighter, or barge. The Navigation Act of 1696 addressed:
"all the wharfingers, and owners of quays and wharfs, or any lighterman, bargeman, waterman . . . shall be subject to the pains and penalties."

light horse Lightly armed cavalry. In 1776 Philip Fithian recorded,
"The militia . . . have taken already a number of their Light-Horse."

light infantry *See* **infantry, light.**

light money A tax on ships to pay for maintaining lighthouses.

lightwood (*n.*) The pine used for kindling. *See* **candlewood.** In 1705 Robert Beverley wrote that the Indians in Virginia:
"generally burn Pine or Lightwood."

likely (*adj.*) Handsome, well-formed. A 1779 New Jersey newspaper advertised:
"A likely mare with a sucking colt."

limeburner (*n.*) One who burns limestone into lime. In 1783 Timothy Pickering

wrote that:
"money is due to the artificers and limeburners."

limonum (*n.*) Lemon juice, used for counteracting nausea, vomiting, and fevers.

line (*v.*) To impregnate. In the sense of 'to put on the inside.' In 1768 Washington recorded,
"Hound bitch . . . shut up chiefly with a black dog who lined her several times."

lini (*n.*) Flax. Linseed oil, from crushed flax seed, was taken internally as a laxative and used externally as a poultice.

link (*n.*) A linear measure; ⅟₁₀₀ of a chain, or 7.92 inches. The first road laid out after Scarsdale, New York, became a town, The Crossway, in 1792 began:
"two chains and fourteen links south of an apple tree."

linsey-woolsey (*n.*) A homespun cloth in which the warp is linen and the woof is wool. From Lindsey, Suffolk, England. Isaac Coutant in New Rochelle, N. Y., wrote,
"The ordinary dress worn by elderly women was the old style short-gown and petticoat of homespun or linsey-woolsey."

linter (*n.*) A slurring of *lean-to*, an addition to a house. A 1779 New Jersey newspaper advertised,
"To be sold, A very good house . . . with a linter to the house for a shop fit for any business."

lion dollar A Dutch silver coin which depicted a rampant lion; the dog dollar. A 1723 New York document reported,
"The Current Cash being wholly in the Paper Bills of this Province and a few Lyon dollars."

list¹ (*n.*) A ridge of soil thrown up by a plow. In 1768 Washington wrote of:
"having run only a single furrow for a list."

list² (*v.*) To desire. In 1645 John Winthrop wrote,
"He has liberty to do as he lists."

list³ (*v.*) A shortened form of *enlist*.

litharge (*n.*) A lead monoxide; used in making flint glass, glazes, and drying oils. A 1776 Boston newspaper advertised:
"1200 gallons of train oil, 5 barrels litharge, 6 tons braziletto."

litharge of gold A ground red lead. It was combined with camphor to make an unguent. A 1782 Hartford, Conn., newspaper advertised,
"Quill, Jesuits Bark, Opium, Litharge of gold, Verdigrise."

lively (*adj.*) Fertile. In 1770 Washington wrote of:
"a pretty lively kind of Land grown up with Hick[or]y."

liverwort (*n.*) A plant similar to moss. A brew made from it was used against dizziness and cough. In 1791 G. Motherby's *A New Medical Dictionary* declared it to have "no medical virtue." In 1670 Francis Higginson referred to:
"pennyroyal, winter savory, sorrel, brooklime, liverwort, caruell, and watercresses."

livery (*n.*) **(1)** The delivery of legal possession of lands or tenements. The Massachusetts Body of Liberties said,
"All our lands and heritages shall be free from all fines and license upon alienations,

and from all heriots, liveries, primer seisens, year day and waste.''

(2) Maintenance for a servant. A *livery cupboard* was one in which food and drink were kept.

livre (*n.*) A French coin. It was worth a pound of silver in Charlemagne's time. In 1754 a ship's captain was instructed to:
"proceed without loss of time to St. Vincent, there dispose of your slaves if they will fetch 900 livres round in money.''

lock (*n.*) An iron ring to hold a prisoner. A 1638 Massachusetts document recorded, "The Court Judged him to be severly whipped & a lock vpon his ffoote.''

lockram (*n.*) A linen fabric from Locronan, France. A 1673 ship inventory included: "1 halfe p'ce lockram.''

loft (*v.*) To provide with an upper story. A 1646 Virginia law regarding schoolhouses required:
"that they be lofted with sawn boards.''

loggerhead (*n.*) A long-handled, iron tool with a spherical container on the end, used for heating liquids. Alice Morse Earle in *Colonial Dames* quoted,
"Where dozed a fire . . . And nursed the loggerhead, whose hissing dip,/ Timed by nice instinct, creamed the bowl of flip.'' Formerly, a similar but larger tool was used to heat tar. When sailors threw tar at each other, they were at *loggerheads*.

logget (*n.*) A variant of *loggat*. A game, later called *kittle-pins*, like quoits or horseshoes. In 1686 playing it was prohibited at *The Anchor* in Lynn, Mass.

logwood (*n.*) A tree from Mexico the red heartwood of which contained haematoxylon, used in dyeing. In 1696 Samuel Sewall wrote,
"Inclosed is a Bill of Lading for Two Tuns and fifteen hundred of Logwood.''

lonage (*n.*) This word, found in the 1697 patent for Bedford, N. Y., is obviously an error in transcription. From comparison with other patents, *socage* is the word intended.
"Given and Granted . . . in Free and Common Lonage.''

long arm A carbine or musket. A 1696 Connecticut law addressed:
"such Troopers as shall neglect to prouide themselues with long armes, viz. a carbin or muskett.''

long bullet The competitive sport of tossing an iron weight as far as one can. Probably the same as pitching the bar. *See* **bar.** In 1775 Philip Fithian observed:
"some throwing long bullets.''

Long Knife The Indian name for a Virginian. In 1871 John L. Peyton telling of his grandfather's experiences wrote,
"The Indians . . . deliberately prepared to crush the force of 'Long Knives' as they called the Virginians under Lewis.''

loo (*n.*) An abbreviation of *lanterloo*, a card game. The characters in a 1771 play decided to:
"try our luck at loo.''

looby (*n.*) A fool, a lubber, a booby. A 1698 song referred to:
"Twittenham loobies.'' *Twittenham* is a pun on Twickenham (near London) and *twit* 'fool.'

loop (*n.*) A doubling of a cord through which another loop might be passed for closing garments. In an old play a man threatens a country lad,

"I'll make your buttons fly." The lad replies,
"All my buttons is loops."

loot (*n.*) A misspelling of *lot*. In 1681 the General Court in Hartford, Conn., gave permission to settle Bedford, N. Y., with the admonition,
"They ear to tacke care yt there be a suitable loot laid out for the first minister."

lord of a manor In America, simply the owner. *Lord* was never a noble title in America.

Lord of Misrule The director of Christmas-time jollity. In 1637 William Bradford wrote,
"And Morton became Lord of Misrule, and maintained (as it were) a School of Atheism."

Lord Proprietary The title held by Cecil Calvert, Lord Baltimore, who was granted the land between the Chesapeake and Delaware Bays.

lorimer (*n.*) One who makes bits for horse's bridles.

lose one's voyage (Of a pirate) to gamble away one's share of a privateer's plunder. An anonymous 1680 writer attested,
"Everyone tooke his way, onely seven men abord that had lost their Voyage."

lot layer One who laid out lots, a surveyor. In 1636 Ipswich, Mass.,
"Granted to Serjent French, ten acres of upland . . . to be laid out by the lott layers."

lottery ticket (*n.*) A card game in which prizes are won by holding cards the same as those set aside. In 1715 William Byrd:
"played at lottery ticket and I won."

loup-cervier A Canada lynx. A word adopted from Canadian French. From Latin *lupus cervarius* 'wolf that hunts deer.' In 1744 Arthur Dobbs wrote,
"The Loup-Cervier, or Lynx, is of the Cat Kind, but as large as a great Dog."

louring (*adj.*) A variant of *lowering*, cloudy, gloomy. In a 1774 poem John Trumbull wrote,
"Will shrink unnerved before a despot's face/ Nor meet thy louring insolence with scorn."

love (*n.*) A thin, silk fabric. Etymology unknown. A 1685 New York clothing inventory of Mrs. De Lange included:
"3 black love-hoods."

love feast A gathering, especially among Methodists, mixing food and religion. In 1754 John Fries wrote,
"We kept a Lovefeast with the Journey Cakes, and afterward a blessed Communion."

Low Dutch The language spoken by immigrants from Holland. It describes a variety of Germanic spoken in the lowlands and is not a term of opprobrium. *See* **High German**. A 1759 Boston newspaper wrote of:
"A White Girl . . . who talks good English, high and low Dutch."

Low Dutch Congregations German-speaking congregations. The words *Dutch* and *German* were used interchangeably. In 1753 William Smith referred to:
"Low Dutch Congregations."

lower counties The three counties of Pennsylvania which now constitute Delaware.

The Duke of York gave them to his friend William Penn in 1682. After 1703 the Delaware electorate chose its own assembly.

lower party Loyalists. In Westchester County, N. Y., during the Revolution, many of the loyalists fled to the lower part of the county seeking the protection of the troops there. When Major André was stopped by three militiamen he said,
"My lads, I hope you belong to our party." John Paulding asked,
"What party" Then André fatally answered,
"The lower."

low room A room on the ground floor. A 1708 Boston newspaper offered:
"a Convenient Dwelling House, having a Cellar, Low Room, Chamber and Garret."

lubber (*n.*) A clown. In 1777 Tory Nicholas Cresswell deplored,
"General Howe, a man brought up to war from his youth, to be puzzled and plagued for two years together, with a Virginia tobacco planter. O! Britain how thy laurels tarnish in the hands of such a lubber!"

lucina (*n.*) A midwife, after the Roman goddess of childbirth. In 1679 Charles Wolley wrote about Indian women,
"Their hardiness and facility in bringing forth is generally such as neither requires the nice attendance of Nursekeepers, nor the art of a dexterous *Lucina*."

luffee (*n.*) A sweetheart. From Dutch *liefje*, 'sweetheart'. Apparently local usage in Albany, New York. Dr. Alexander Hamilton in 1744 noted,
"The young men here at Albany call their sweethearts luffee and a young fellow of eighteen is reckoned a simpleton if he has not a luffee."

lug the wrong sow by the ear To capture the wrong person. John Leacock in a 1776 play had Dick, a shepherd, say:
"He sent his dogs to a wrong place, and lugg'd the wrong sow by the ear."

lugger (*n.*) A vessel carrying three masts and a lug sail, a square sail bent on a yard that hangs obliquely. It could have one, two, or three masts and be with or without jibs, topsails, or both.

lug pole The pole of green wood (therefore not as likely to burn) in a fireplace from which to hang a kettle. It was supported by stones projecting from the fireplace.

lumber (*n.*) Any miscellaneous odds and ends around the house. In 1775 Philip Fithian described,
"Stuffing rags and other lumber under their gowns." Still used in this sense in Britain.

lumber room A room for odds and ends and unused things. A 1773 Virginia document recorded,
"A Dairy Sixteen by Ten to be built and one end to fitted up Close for a Lumber Room."

Lunae, Die *Latin.* Monday. From *Luna*, the moon goddess.

lunation (*n.*) The time between two new moons; a lunar month. The title page of *Ames' Almanac* for 1726 said,
"Wherein is contained the lunations."

lungee (*n.*) An Indian cloth. A variant of Hindi *lungi*, same meaning. A 1759 Rhode Island newspaper advertised,
"Worsted Damask, Lungee, Romals."

lupine (*n.*) A spikey, white plant *Lupinus albus*. The seed was eaten. In 1633 Andrew White describing the food in Maryland wrote,
"What shall I say of the lupines, the most excellent beans, roots and other things of this kind?"

lusory (*adj.*) Playful. In 1679 Charles Wolley described Indians as:
"being naturally uninclin'd to any but lusory pastimes and exercises."

lustration (*n.*) A ritual cleansing or purification by water. In 1772 Benjamin Trumbull wrote,
"At every shrine perform'd lustrations."

lustring (*n.*) A glossy silk cloth. Also *lustrine*. A 1783 Philadelphia newspaper offered,
"Jerseys, Bengals, Court Plaster, Lutestrings, Rotten Stone."

luted (*adj.*) Sealed. *Luting* is a moldable substance used for sealing. A 17th-century cookbook instructed,
"Let it stand all night in ye still close luted."

luzern (*n.*) A variant of *lucern* 'lynx.' In 1602 John Brereton described animals in Virginia:
"We saw in the country . . . Beares . . . Luzernes, Blacke Foxes."

lymbic (*adj.*) The limbic lode, a part of the brain; hence, mental. The anonymous author of Nathaniel Bacon's 1676 epitaph wrote,
"Souls replete with dull chilled cold, he'd animate with heat Drawn forth of reasons lymbic."

Lynch's Law A law enforced by self-appointed individuals. Authorities differ as to which Lynch was the progenitor, but *A Dictionary of American English* makes a strong case for Captain William Lynch (1742–1820) of Pittsylvania, Virginia, in 1780 .

macaroni (*n.*) A fop. From the Macaroni Club for young dandies in London. It in turn was named by those fashionable travelers for the pasta from Italy. In the famous song:
"Yankee Doodle . . . put a feather in his cap and called it macaroni."

maccarib (*n.*) A Quinnipiac word for caribou. In 1672 John Josselyn wrote,
"The Maccarib, Caribo, or Pohanc, a kind of Deer."

maccuba (*n.*) Snuff ground in Macouba, Martinique. In 1780 Baron Friedrich Wilhelm Ludolf Gerhard Augustin von Steuben wrote to a friend,
"Send me three containers of good Maccuba tobacco or three pounds of good Rappe tobacco."

macock (*n.*) A kind of melon. From *Mahcawq*, an Algonquian word. In 1612 Capt. John Smith described:
"A fruit like unto a muske millen, but lesse and worse."

macquerett (*n.*) A coiled ornamental braid. A 1779 Boston newspaper advertised,
"Drugget, Mecklenburghs, Maqueretts."

madder (*n.*) *Rubia tinctorum*, a red vegetable dye. The root was also used medicinally. A 1774 Philadelphia newspaper advertised,
"Copperas, Madder."

magazine (*n.*) A storehouse. From French *magasin*, same meaning. In 1619 John Pory, Speaker of the Virginia House of Burgesses, wrote,
"Ab[raha]m. Percy the cape merchant said they had not yet rec'd any such order from the adventurers of the magazine in England."

magistery (*n.*) Authority. Lt. Gov. William Bull in 1765 wrote from Boston to the Board of Trade,
"I had none but the civil magistery to enforce my orders."

magistracy (*n.*) The body of magistrates. A 1646 Massachusetts law protected:
"the ordinance of magistracy or their lawful authority."

mago (*adj.*) Magical. A 1658 doctor's bill charged 100 pounds of tobacco for:
"1 cordiall mago." The word *mago* was used in a chemical sense as pertaining to

magic and chemistry. The cordial must have been thought magical to have cost 100 pounds of tobacco.

magot (*n.*) A musical impromptu. The word was used in the name of many dance tunes, such as *Mr. Lane's Magot* (1698).

mail pillion A pad behind a saddle for baggage, not mail. One meaning of *mail* is a sack, bag, or traveling bag; from Middle English *male* 'a bag.' In 1711 Thomas Buckingham:
"brought from home . . . A mail pillion, Snapsack."

main[1] (*n.*) The mainland. The 1666 patent in Westchester County, New York, to Thomas Pell was for land:
"either upon the Main or upon Long Island."

main[2] (*n.*) The point in the game of hazard. From French *main* 'hand.' In a 1664 song some sailors sang,
"To pass our tedious hours away, we throw a merry main."

mainprize (*n.*) The release of a prisoner in someone's custody. From French *main* 'hand' and *prise*, from *prendre* 'to take.' A 1772 New York law provided:
"that offenders be fined or committed to jail for the space of three months without bail or main-prize."

maize thief A bird which steals corn. In 1770 Peter Kalm reported,
"The laws of Pennsylvania . . . have settled a premium of three-pence a dozen for dead Maize thieves."

make (1) (*n.*) The shape, form. Dr. Alexander Hamilton in 1744 in Seabrook, Connecticut, recorded,
"My landlady goes here by the name of Madam Lay. I cannot tell for what, for she is the homliest piece both as to mien, make and dress that I ever saw."
(2) (*v.*) To cure. In 1679 a Massachusetts document described:
"One [house] on Damariscove an Island to make Fish on."
(3) (*v.*) To mature. In 1763 Washington recorded,
"Observed that my y[oun]g Corn was just beginning to show . . . Quere, has it time to make or Ripen"

make interest for To indicate an interest in. In 1710 William Byrd:
"wrote a letter to England to make interest for the Government of Maryland." He applied for the Governorship.

malkin (*n.*) A baker's mop. From *Moll*, a diminutive of the given name *Mary*.

malmsey (*n.*) A species of grape, also a wine. Originally from Monemvasia, Greece.

malster (*n.*) One who makes malt; a maltster. A 1657 deed was:
"between John March, Planter and Thomas Lynde, malster."

Malvasia (*n.*) A wine from Monemvasia (Malvasia), a town on the southeast coast of Greece. A 1740 letter instructed a ship agent to:
"procure the sale of his 45 pipes of Malvasia."

Manchester check A cloth with a square pattern. A 1781 Boston newspaper advertised,
"Marseilles Quilting, Manchester check, Chip Hats."

manchet (*n.*) A small loaf of bread made from the finest of flour. Etymology obscure. In 1660:
"Ralph Burdsell [was punished] for making manchettes too light."

mandillion (*n.*) A soldier's coat, a loose garment. From Italian *mandiglione* 'soldier's coat.' In 1629 Washburne, the secretary of the Plymouth Colony, recorded the importation of:
"small hooks and eyes for mandillions."

Manito (*n.*) The Algonquian Great Spirit. Also *manitou, manitu.* In 1790 Charles Wolley wrote,
"They are of opinion that when they have ill success in their hunting, fishing, &c. their *Menitto* is the cause of it."

mankind (*n.*) Males, not including females. The 1641 Massachusetts *Body of Liberties* addressed itself to:
"If any man lies with mankind as he lies with a woman."

manna (*n.*) The juice of the flowering ash. An adopted Aramaic word. It was taken medicinally as a mild laxative. In 1693 Samuel Sewall wrote:
"By Dr. Oakes advice, I give her a little Manna."

manor (*n.*) In the Province of New York, a tract of land granted by the king in return for a payment of rent, generally nominal. The rights and duties of the landholder were spelled out in a patent or in a confirmation of a grant from the Dutch. John Nanfan, Lieutenant Governor, in the name of William III, granted to Caleb Heathcote the patent that established the:
"Lordship and Manor of Scarsdale" on March 21, 1701.

Manor of East Greenwich East Greenwich and Kent were never subjugated by the Normans, hence land held there was subject only to fealty and allegiance, not to the other feudal obligations. In 1664 Charles II granted New York to his brother the Duke of York,
"To be holden of us our Heirs and Successors, as of our Manor of East Greenwich and our County of Kent, in free and common soccage and not in Capite, nor by Knight Service."

man stealer One who steals and sells men. The 1647 Federation of Rhode Island Towns specified,
"Under the law for men stealers . . . comes theft, larceny, trespass, etc."

manteca de porco *Spanish.* 'pork fat.' Nathaniel Butler recorded in his 1639 diary that a Spanish frigate:
"was laden with mantega de Porco, Hides and Tallowe."

mantelet (*n.*) A small, woman's cloak. A 1742 Maryland document lists:
"One blew Velvet manteelet lined with silk."

mantle (*n.*) An outer cloak; a baby's christening gown.

mantua (*n.*) A loose-fitting woman's gown, generally with a train. A corruption of French *manteau* 'cloak.'

mantua maker A dressmaker in general, not limited to mantuas. In a 1743 Boston newspaper Henrietta East advertised,
"Ladies may have their Pellerines made at her mantua-making shop."

manumission (*n.*) The act of freeing a slave. To accomplish this, the owner filed a simple statement with his Town Clerk, after obtaining a certificate from the Overseers of the Poor, that the person freed could fend for himself and would not become a public charge.

manure (*v.*) To cultivate. Originally from French *main oeuvre* 'hand work.' Washington recorded that he:

"manured the field and then I spread dung on it." Also, John Richbell included in a 1684 petition,
"And manureing the same and to Settle thereon with themselves and families."

maqua (*n.*) An Indian, probably a Mohawk. Samuel Sewall in 1709 wrote,
"Col. Hobbey's Regiment musters, and the gov[erno]r orders the Maquas to be there and see them."

maracock (*n.*) The maypop, the fruit of the 'passiflora, passion flower.' From Algonquian. In 1612 Capt. John Smith wrote that:
"a fruit that the Inhabitants call Maracocks . . . is a pleasant fruit much like a lemond."

margin (*n.*) A variant of *morgen*, the Dutch land measure. The 1697 grant for the Manor of Morrisania described a plot:
"containing 250 margin or 800 acres of land."

marjoram (*n.*) A mint of the genus *Majorana*. It was believed that marjoram was useful in the treatment of disorders of the head and nerves, catarrhs, and asthma.

mark (*n.*) A Scottish silver coin worth 13s 4d, or its equivalent. The Massachusetts Bay records for 1631 state:
"The constable of Rocksbury returned the receipt of Mr. Shepheards ffine of 5 marks."

marker (*n.*) One who marks trees for a surveyor. A 1743 New Jersey document instructed,
"You are to employ . . . an assistant surveyor . . . also proper chainbearers & markers."

market (*n.*) Short for *market basket*. In 1679 Charles Wolley enjoyed the sights of New York:
"And upon the Ice its admirable to see Men and Women as it were flying upon their Skates from place to place, with Markets upon their Heads and Backs."

marl (*n.*) A soil mainly clay and calcium carbonate, used as a fertilizer. Washington experimented as a farmer and in 1760 he tried:
"to have 600 Tobo. Hills Marld at Williamson's Quarter" and also,
"sewd 500 hills of the Same ground without marl."

maroon (*n.*) Camping out. In the manner of West Indian Maroons, originally runaway slaves, living in the hills. From Spanish *cimarron* 'wild.' Israel Angell's 1779 diary recorded,
"Lt. Cook . . . Come from the Meroon frolick last night."

marque, commission of/letter of An authorization to fit out and operate a privateer against an enemy. In 1771 George III instructed Lord Dunmore of Virginia:
"not to grant commissions of marque or reprisal . . . without our especial command."

marquee (*n.*) A large, officer's field tent. From French *marquise* 'a large tent.' In 1776 A. R. Robbins noted: "Treated with great civility by Capt. Walker; supped and lodged well in our markee."

marrow fat A kind of rich pea. A reference to the fatty marrow found in bones. A 1765 Boston newspaper advertised:
"golden hotspur peas, early charlton peas, marrow-fat peas."

marseilles (*n.*) A two-layer cotton quilting used for petticoats. In 1787 Edward A.

Holyoke:
"Bought Marseilles Quilting."

marshmallow (*n.*) An unguent from the marshmallow root, which provided protection of the mucous membrane, especially in treating hemorrhoids as William Byrd did; a brew was used for kidney complaints.

Martis, Die *Latin*. Tuesday. From the Latin *'day of Mars'*.

mask (*n.*) **(1)** A screen which hides an artillery battery from enemy view.
"[It] has been made a mask for a battery, a stalking horse."
(2) A face covering, not for masquerades or trick-or-treat, but for protection against wind and cold or even for privacy (as in a public place). Women wore black velvet or white or green silk masks held by hand, by a portion in the mouth, or by templets. A 1729 Philadelphia newspaper offered:
"Masks for women."

Mason and Dixon Line The disputed boundary line between Pennsylvania and Maryland was run by English surveyors Charles Mason and Jeremiah Dixon in 1767.

masquerade (*n.*) A shimmery material for dresses. A 1774 Philadelphia newspaper advertised:
"Cambletees, sagathies, masquerades, hair bines, brilliants."

masquered (*adj.*) Shimmery in appearance. A 1775 Boston newspaper offered:
"Plain or Masquered Bengals."

mast (*n.*) Acorns and beechnuts, generally any nut. In 1670 Daniel Denton in describing New York wrote,
"The Greatest part of the Island is very full of Timber . . . Chestnut-trees, which yield store of Mast for Swine."

mast ship A ship that was specially designed to carry masts for the British Navy. Doors in the stern permitted tree trunks one hundred feet long to be slid into the holds. In 1740 William Douglas wrote,
"The mast ships built peculiarly for that use . . . carry from forty-five to fifty masts per voyage."

match (*n.*) A rope or cord used to fire artillery, etc. A *slow-match* was hemp impregnated with saltpeter which burned at the rate of a foot an hour. A *quick-match* was cotton coated with gunpowder. William Smith in 1757 described soldiers:
"with their arms, drums beating, and colours flying and lighted matches."

match coat A coarse, woolen, Indian coat imitating one of matched fur pelts. In 1722 William Byrd described:
"Indian ladies wrapped in their red and blue match coats."

mathematical instrument An instrument using mathematics, as a theodolite. In 1754 Washington described:
"The plan . . . exact as could be done without mathematical instruments."

mathematician (*n.*) An astrologer. In 1722 William Byrd wrote,
"That indeed he was rightly served for committing his affairs to the care of a mathematician whose thoughts were always among the stars."

mathook (*n.*) A reaping tool. In 1775 Bernard Romans wrote,
"I would advise the introduction of the short scythe and hook, called in New York government segt and mat hook."

matross (*n.*) A private in the artillery who assisted a gunner in loading, firing, and

sponging the guns. In 1771 the Governor of Virginia was instructed,
"Paid out of our said revenues . . . clerk of assembly, gunners and matrosses the usual salaries and allowances."

matter (*n.*) The type already set up. In 1771 Franklin reminisced,
"Mixing my sorts, breaking my matter."

maugre (*prep.*) In spite of. From French *malgré*, 'in spite of.' In 1662 Michael Wigglesworth said,
"Cheer on, sweet soul, my heart is with you all,/ And shall be with you, maugre Satan's might."

mawkin (*n.*) A variant of *malkin*, a baker's mop.
"The oven, the mawkin, the bavin, the peel."

mazarine (*n.*) A little dish set in a larger one, used for draining water from boiled food. An 18th-century cookbook said to:
"place them on your mazarine."

mazer (*n.*) A maple cup. In 1635 Thomas Heywood wrote of:
"carouseing . . . bowles of wood . . . mazers, noggins, whiskins."

mazy (*adj.*) Winding, as in a maze. In 1774 John Trumbull described:
"Where the clear rivers pour their mazy tide."

mead[1] (*n.*) A fermented liquor made of honey and water sometimes enriched with spices. In 1710 William Byrd recorded,
"At night we drank some mead of my wife's making."

mead[2] (*n.*) A meadow. In a 1766 play, Robert Rogers wrote of:
"ye flowery meads and banks and bending trees."

mean (*adj.*) **(1)** Low minded. In 1730 William Bradford wrote,
"The aged and graver men to be ranked and equalized in labors and victuals, clothes, etc. The meaner and younger sort thought it some indignity and disrespect unto them."
(2) Of little value. In 1723 Massachusetts Gov. Shute wrote,
"This House [of Representatives] consists of about one hundred [men] . . . the greatest part of them are of small fortunes and mean education."

measurer (*n.*) **(1)** One who measured land, a surveyor. In 1636 Dedham, Massachusetts, decreed,
"We doe order yt all highways . . . be orderly set out by our Measurer."
(2) One who measured commodities. In 1659:
"Francis Hudson is chosen a measurer of salt" in Boston.

mechanic stone Stone cut by hand by a mechanic or stone cutter. *Ames' Almanac* (1758) described:
"Vast quarries that teem with mechanic stone."

mechlenburg (*n.*) Mechlin lace, from Mechlin, Belgium. All Flemish lace, except Brussels and double point, was known as Mechlin lace. A 1779 Boston newspaper advertised,
"Drugget, Mecklenburghs, Macqueretts."

mechoacán (*n.*) A root, white jalap, used medicinally to induce vomiting. From the state of Michoacán in Mexico.

medium (*n.*) Short for *medium of exchange*; paper money. The 1784 *History of Dartmouth College* says, "difficulties . . . attend the education of youth in this Province, by reason of . . . the discredit of our medium."

medlar (*n.*) A European tree similar to a wild crab apple. A 1666 anonymous description of Carolina said,
"There are many sorts of fruit trees, as vines, medlars, peach, wild cherries."

meer (*adj.*) A variant of *mere*, on one's own initiative. The 1701 Patent for the Manor of Scarsdale read,
"Know yee that of our special grace, certain knowledge, & meer motion, wee have given . . ."

mel (*n.*) Honey. From Latin.

melilot (*n.*) Clover. From its genus name; originally from Greek *meli* 'honey,' *lotos* 'lotus.'

melocoton (*n.*) A peach tree grafted onto a quince tree. In 1634 one of the adventurers in Maryland wrote,
"We also have English pease, and French beans, cotton, oranges, lemons, melocotons, apples, pears."

member (*n.*) A subordinate part of a manor. In 1701 William III granted to Caleb Heathcote:
"all the rights, members, libertys, priviledges" in the Manor of Scarsdale, New York.

memorial (*n.*) A written representation of facts accompanied by a petition. In 1759 the Virginia Committee of Correspondence wrote,
"It is to be hoped gentlemen in the trade [British merchants] will be satisfied that there is no necessity to solicit their memorial."

mend (*v.*) To improve. In a 1766 play Robert Rogers wrote,
"Die both together then, 'twill mend the sport."

mensalia (*n.*) Table talk. From Latin *mensa* 'table.' In 1679 Charles Wolley recorded,
"We continued our mensalias the whole meeting in Latin."

menstruum (*n.*) Any fluid that dissolves a solid body. From Latin *menstruus* 'monthly.' Thomas Paine in 1776 wrote,
"Nothing but the sharpest essence of villainy . . . could have produced a menstruum that would have affected a separation."

merchant (*n.*) A supercargo. In 1697 Benjamin Franks deposed,
"The Owner and the Merchant dyed on board [died on the ship]."

merchant mill A mill which ground grain for a fee. Philip Fithian reported in 1774 that:
"Mr. Carter's merchant mill begins to run today."

Mercurii, Die *Latin.* Wednesday. From the Roman deity *Mercury* identified with the Germanic *Woden*, after whom the day was named.

mercury (*n.*) Mercury was used in many medicinal applications, especially for the treatment of syphilis.

mere (*n.*) A boundary. *See* **merestone**. Originally cognate with Latin *murus* 'wall.'

mere office The act of a judge proceeding in a case when there is no one corresponding to a plaintiff. The phrase appears in a 1753 commission of a Vice Admiralty judge.

merestead (*n.*) A farm. *See* **mere.** In 1620 a Plymouth, Massachusetts, document read,
"The meresteads & garden plotes of which came first layed out 1620."

merestone (*n.*) A boundary marker. *See* **mere.** In 1687 a Hartford, Connecticut, document said,
"One percell . . . Bounded with meer Stones."

merk (*n.*) A variant of *mark*, the Scottish silver coin. A report on Scottish immigration in 1774 said,
"My grandfather paid only eight merks Scots."

merlon (*n.*) The part of a parapet between two embrasures of a fortification. In 1771 Franklin recorded,
"The battery was soon errected, the merlons being framed of logs."

messenger (*n.*) An officer in the Plymouth Colony who was both policeman and town crier. In 1637:
"Josua Pratt was sworne the Messenger for the whole government."

messuage (*n.*) A dwelling house and the adjoining land and buildings. The 1701 patent to Caleb Heathcote for Scarsdale, New York, included:
"together with all & every ye messuages, tenem[en]ts, buildings, barnes, houses, out-houses."

metheglin (*n.*) Spiced mead. The Quartering Act of 1765 referred to:
"all houses of persons selling of rum, brandy, strong water, cider or metheglin by retail."

metump (*n.*) A tumpline. Jonathan Carver in 1778 wrote,
"The Indians draw their carriages with great ease . . . by means of a string which passes round the breast. This collar is called a Metump."

meums and tuums Mine and yours. An adapted Latin phrase. Thomas Paine used this popular phrase expressing the rights of property.

Michaelmas (*n.*) September 29, the mass of St. Michael, the archangel. One of the quarter days.

mickle (*n.*) A great quantity. *Poor Richard's Almanac* observed,
"Every little makes a mickle."

mico (*n.*) A chief. From Muskogee. In 1737 John Wesley wrote,
"Nor have they any kings or princes . . . their meikos, or headmen, having no power."

middling (1) (*n.*) A middle-sized piece of ground grain. A 1766 Rhode Island document stated,
"I shall send you the 30 Bbs. Middlings agreeable to your Order."
(2) (*adj.*) Moderate, neither high nor low class. In 1744 Dr. Alexander Hamilton referred to:
"the middling sort of people here" in Boston.

miffy (*adj.*) Apt to take slight offense; easily miffed. In 1789 Franklin wrote,
"Our Nantucket family were always subject to being a little miffy."

mile (*n.*) A Dutch mile was equal to four English miles. In 1627 the West India Company provided that:

"the Patroons . . . shall and may be permitted . . . to extend their limits four miles along the river."

military chest The money available to an army commander. In 1776 the Continental Congress:
"Resolved That General Washington be directed to order . . . the payment out of the military chest."

militia (*n.*) A body of soldiers enrolled for training, but not engaged in service except in emergencies. The state militias during the Revolution were in theory to serve short periods of time, without pay, operating solely within their own states. In practice, they served for long periods, were paid by Congress, and traveled all over.

milk (*v.*) To tap a tree for sap. In 1746 a Massachusetts law referred to:
"cutting off any timber, wood, hay, milking pine trees."

milk, in Full of a white fluid, almost ripe. John Habersham in 1772 commented,
"The Rice come up rather unequal, so that a good deal of those Fields were in Milk."

milk-and-water Watered down. In 1783 in the Continental Congress one participant said,
"Change the milk-and-water style of your last memorial [and] assume a bolder tone."

milky (*adj.*) Having a sap resembling milk. In 1765 Washington recorded,
"Note, the [mulberry] Stocks were very Milkey."

milled (*adj.*) (Of cloth), fulled.

milo (*n.*) A grain similar to durra. From Bantu *maili*, same meaning. In 1715 William Byrd:
"Had milk and milo for breakfast."

milter (*n.*) A male fish, one capable of producing milt. A 17th-century cookbook said,
"Take a well grown carp yt is a melter."

mimbo (*n.*) A drink composed of rum, loaf sugar, and a splash of water. A tavern in York, Pennsylvania, in 1752 charged,
"1 Quart Mimbo made best W[est]. I[ndies]. Rum and [sugar] Loaf . . . 10 d."

miner (*n.*) A soldier who digs passages under a fort. Benjamin Fishbourne in 1778 referred to:
"companies of sappers and miners."

mineral man One who is versed in minerals and their extraction. It was one of the occupations listed in 1610 as needed in the Virginia Colony.

mingo (*n.*) A chamber pot. From Latin *mingo* 'I urinate.' A 1775 Massachusetts inventory included:
"5 Mingos and a Bed pan."

minion (*n.*) A small cannon that could fire a three-inch ball about 100 yards. A 1642 New Haven, Connecticut, document recorded,
"[He] doth promise to lend the Country two peeces of Ordnance Sakers or Minions."

minister (*n.*) A chief servant, an agent. In 1617 William Byrd:
"took my first minister, Harry Morris, up the hill."

ministerial (*adj.*) Supporting the body of ministers of state, hence British. Adjutant

General of the Continental Army, Horatio Gates, in 1775 directed,
"You are not to enlist any deserter from the ministerial army."

minument (*n.*) A variant of *muniment*, a document by which one can defend one's
right to an estate or privilege. The Stamp Act in 1765 covered:
"memorandum, letter, or other minument or writing."

miscarriage (*n.*) Ill conduct. In 1630 William Bradford wrote,
"He had often been punished for miscarriages before."

misprision (*n.*) Misconduct. *Misprision of treason* is concealing or neglecting to report
treason. The 1771 instructions to the Governor of Virginia noted,
"persons indicted of high treason or misprision of treason."

missinet (*n.*) Mission net, a coarse curtain material. A 1775 Boston newspaper advertised,
"Alamodes, Persians, Missinets, Peniascoes, Shalloons."

Mississippi nut Probably the pecan. In 1765 Washington wrote,
"some think like the Pignut—but longer, thinner shell'd and fuller of meat."

mob cap A loose, baggy woman's hat of cotton or other soft material, generally worn
informally around the house.

mobby (*n.*) A distilled drink. From Carib *mabi* 'drink made from sweet potatoes.' In
1705 Robert Beverley wrote,
"Others make a Drink of them [peaches], which they call Mobby."

mobility (*n.*) The mob. From Latin *mobile vulgus* 'movable or excitable crowd.' In
1775 Gouverneur Morris wrote,
"The heads of the mobility grow dangerous to the gentry."

mode (*n.*) A shortening of *alamode* 'a light, glossy silk material.' A 1780 New Jersey
newspaper offered,
"Rich modes of the best kind."

model (*v.*) To make into a formation. In 1711 William Byrd recorded,
"The Governor modelled the horse and put commanders at the head of them."

moidore (*n.*) A Portuguese gold coin, minted from 1640 to 1732, worth six pieces of
eight. A corruption of Portuguese *moeda d'ouro* 'gold coin.' In the 1741 account of
the crew of the *Revenge* are listed,
"Gold—54¾ Moidrs."

moiety (*n.*) A half. The manor grant in 1793 to Vredrick Vlypsen included,
"the said moiety or equal half part of the meadow."

moldboard (*n.*) The part of a plow that cuts and turns the soil.

monack (*n.*) A woodchuck. A variant of Virginia Indian *moonack* 'digger.' In 1666
George Alsop wrote," The Monack, the Musk-Rat, and several others . . . inhabit
here in Mary Land."

money maker A counterfeiter. In 1729 John Comer recorded,
"This day came up ye case of ye money makers to trial."

monmouth cap A knitted cap ending in a tassel; opinions differ as to whether it was
flat or long. In 1629 Washburn suggested that immigrants to the Plymouth Colony
bring:
"2 Monmouth Caps, about 2s apiece."

monteith (*n.*) A punch bowl with a scalloped edge, said to have been named for a man of that name who wore a coat with a scalloped hem. William King in his *Art of Cookery* (1701) said,

"New things produce new names, and thus Monteith/ Has by one vessel saved his name from death."

Moravian (*n.*) One of a religious sect called the United Brethren, which was formed in 1772 in Herrnhut in Saxony.

Morea (*n.*) The Peloponnesus peninsula of Greece. In 1705 Robert Beverley extolled,

"The Pleasantest of all Clymates. As for example, *Canaan, Syria* . . . the *Morea, Spain, Portugal.*"

moreen (*n.*) A heavy stuff of wool or wool and cotton, used for curtains. A 1797 Boston newspaper advertised,

"Kerseymeres, Fustians, Janes, Moreens."

morfew (*n.*) A variant of *morphew*, a scruffy skin eruption. A 17th-century cookbook said:

"Pummatum, It is good to take away morfew, freckls & to clear ye scin."

morgen (*n.*) A land measure equal to 2.1 acres; a Holland's acre. An adopted Dutch word. Originally it was the amount of land a man could plow in one *morgen* 'morning.' A 1626 report to the States-General said,

"The Island of Manhattan . . . contains 11000 morgens of land."

morrow (*n.*) Morning. From Middle English *morwen*, same meaning. In 1675 Benjamin Tompson asked,

"Good morrow, brother, is there aught you want?"

mortification (*n.*) Gangrene. In 1741 William Byrd recorded,

"The operation [to cut her nails and corns] gave her such a Gash an the little Toe, that she was forct to live a whole month upon water-gruel to keep it from a mortification."

mortify (*v.*) To tenderize meat by beating. A 17th-century-cookbook instructed,

"Then beat ye flesh to mortifie it."

mortling (*n.*) Wool plucked from a dead sheep. The Woolen Act of 1699 applied to:

"Wool, wool-fells, shortlings, mortlings, woolflocks, worsted, bay, or woolen yarn, cloth, serge, bays, Kerseys, says, friezes, drugget, cloth-serges, shalloons [etc.]."

Moscovado (*n.*) Russia. In 1675 Benjamin Tompson wrote of:

"vines from France and Moscovadoe."

moses boat A ship's boat. Named for Moses Lowell, who built them in Salisbury, Massachusetts. A 1776 Boston newspaper announced,

"To be sold in Salem 40 Chaldrons of Sea Coal [and] 1 Moses boat."

mother (*n.*) A madam. In 1715 William Byrd:

"paid my mistress a guinea and my mother another."

mother-in-law (*n.*) A stepmother. William Byrd, Henry Fielding, and William Thackeray used it that way.

mount (*n.*) A tower on which a soldier could mount guard. In 1724 Northfield, Massachusetts, allowed:

"1 days warding for a soldier which did work at the mount."

mountebank (*v.*) To cheat by boastful and false pretenses. From Italian *montambanco* 'to mount a bench' (from which a quack could sell his nostrums). In

1647 Nathaniel Ward wrote regarding Satan,
"For such are fittest to mountebank his chemistry into sick churches and weak judgements."

mounting (*adj.*) Designating the left side of a horse, the side on which one mounts. A 1732 South Carolina newspaper described:
"A bay Horse . . . branded with H on the mounting buttock."

mourning (*n.*) The dress worn by mourners. The Charlestown, Massachusetts, *Non-Importation Agreement* of 1769 said,
"That we will use the utmost economy . . . in our persons . . . we will give no mourning or gloves or scarves at funerals."

mowhake (*n.*) Dark wampum beads, worth twice the light-colored ones. From a Narragansett word. In 1632 William Wood wrote,
"The Narragansetts . . . are the most curious minters of their Wampompeagues and Mowhakes which they forme out of the inmost wreaths of Periwinkle-shel."

moy (*n.*) A salt measure, 15 bushels. From French *mui* 'bushel.' In 1775 Zachariah Burchmore wrote,
"I shall take in 100 moys of salt," and,
"commonly turning out 15 bu. to the moy."

muche (*n.*) A measure for rum, about one fifth of a pint. Adopted from Dutch *mutsji*. In 1673 in Hempstead, New York, it was legislated,
"If any man shall Refuse to go [to run the bounds of the town] . . . he shall pay six muches of Rume to them that goes."

muckle (*v.*) To mix lightly.

mudsill (*n.*) In bridge, building the footplate that is laid at the bottom of the river. A 1718 Pennsylvania document recorded,
"Ye Neck Bridge . . . Down into yee Mudsells."

muftee (*n.*) A little muff. A New York newspaper in 1745 announced,
"Elizabeth Boyd is removed to Bayard's Street . . . where she follows as usual . . . making and mending of silk gloves, mittens, muftees."

mulatto (*adj.*) Light brown in color. From Spanish *mulato* 'young mule.' In 1788 Jefferson described:
"The Soil a barren mulatto clay."

mulct (*n.*) A fine imposed on a person guilty of some offense; also the act of imposing one. In 1635 a town in Massachusetts was empowered:
"also to lay mulcts and penalties for the breach of these orders."

mullein (*n.*) An herb, thought to have curative powers. In 1709 William Byrd recorded,
"Old Ben had his leg bathed in milk and mullein."

mum (*n.*) A German malt liquor brewed of wheat, oats, and beans. In 1685 Thomas Budd referred to:
"Beer, ale and Mum."

mumbudget (*adj.*) A silent sack or pouch. Jeremy Taylor (1613–1667) wrote, "A woman should be . . . the mumbudget of silence."

murderer (*n.*) A small piece of ordinance generally used at sea to repel boarders. In 1634 one of the Maryland adventurers recorded,

"We have built a good strong fort or palisado, and have mounted upon it one good piece of ordnance and four murderers."

muscovado (*n.*) Unrefined sugar. From Portuguese (*açucar*) *mascavado* 'raw or unrefined sugar.' The 1663 Navigation Act referred to:
"brown sugar and muscovadoes."

Muscovy (*n.*) Russia. Grand Duke Ivan IV of Muscovy assumed the title of Czar of Russia in 1547. In 1733 William Byrd referred to:
"The Czar of Muscovy."

musket (*n.*) A smooth-bore gun, originally fired by means of a lighted match, later by a fire lock. Capt. John Smith in 1608 wrote,
"At whom they shot with their ordnances and muskets."

musketoon (*n.*) A short, thick musket, the shortest kind of blunderbus. In 1729 in a Boston newspaper the following appeared:
"To be Sold by John Osborne & Company, choice Musquets and Musquetoons for Shipping."

muslin (*n.*) A fine cotton cloth originally from Mosul in what is now Iraq, used for all kinds of clothing. A 1732 South Carolina newspaper advertised,
"suits of Diaper, Muslins, Cambricks."

muslinet (*n.*) A coarse kind of muslin. In 1768 Philip M. Freneau, "the Poet of the American Revolution," rhymed,
"All that would suit man, woman, girl or boy;/ Muslins and muslinets, jeans, grogram, corduroy."

musquash (*n.*) The muskrat. An Algonquian word. In 1637 Thomas Morton wrote,
"The Muskewashe, is a beast that frequenteth the ponds."

mustard (*n.*) Medicinally, a preparation of mustard seed was used as a diuretic and to help digestion.

mustee (*n.*) An octoroon; loosely, any person of mixed breed. A shortening of Spanish *mestizo* 'octoroon.' The New York law of 1817 decreed that:
"every negro, mulatto or mustee . . . born before the fourth day of July, 1799 shall, from and after the fourth day of July 1827 be free."

muster master One who takes account of troops and their equipment. The 1642 instructions to the Governor of Virginia said,
"We ordain that there be one muster master general . . . for the colony."

mux (*n.*) A tool the Indians used for drilling shells. Apparently a Shinnecock (Algonquian) word, as it was used in Indian deeds on Long Island, New York.

myrmidon (*n.*) A civil servant who follows orders diligently. The Myrmidions went to the Siege of Troy with Achilles and were noted for their diligence and blind devotion. In 1776 John Adams complained,
"Our petitions . . . are to be answered with myrmidons from abroad."

myrrh (*n.*) A gum resin, the gum of the *Commiphora myrrha*. In Biblical times and today, a perfume base. In Colonial days it was used medicinally as a soothing restorative to wounds and taken internally to clear obstructions, stimulate the stomach, and promote appetite and digestion. In 1779 a New Jersey newspaper advertised,
"Jesuits bark, Brimstone, Gum assafoetida, Tartar emetic, Bateman's drops, British oil, Godfrey's cordial, Turlington's balsom, gum myrrh."

N

nailer (*n.*) A nail maker. A 1643 deed in Massachusetts was:
 "granted unto Edward Jackson of Cambridge nayler."

nankeen (*n.*) A firm-textured, brownish-yellow, cotton cloth originally from Nanking, China. In 1781 Abigail Adams wrote,
 "There are some articles, which come from India . . . Bengals, nankeens, Persian silk."

nanquitoche (*n.*) A sort of Floridian tobacco. Apparently an Indian word. Bernard Romans in 1775 wrote,
 "There are present but two sorts produced viz. *Nanquitoche* and *Pointe coupee*, the first infinitely superior to the second."

nanticoke (*n.*) A kind of bean. From the name of a Maryland Algonquian Indian tribe. In 1737 John Brickell wrote,
 "The Nanticoaks are another kind of Pulse."

nants (*n.*) A brandy from Nantes, France. In 1678 Charles Wolley wrote,
 "Their quaffing liquors are Rum-Punch and Brandy-punch, not compounded and adulterated as in *England*, but pure water and pure *Nants*."

nap (*n.*) A flannel-like cloth. A 1760 Newport, Rhode Island, newspaper advertised,
 "To be Sold . . . Naps of different colours."

napkin (*n.*) A handkerchief. John Harrower, a Scottish immigrant, wrote in 1774,
 "I bought 1 cotton napkin for three biscuits."

nappy (*n.*) A frothy ale. Probably because its head was nappy, frothy. A 1728 song extolled:
 "a jug of brown Nappy."

narrow ax An ax used for chopping as contrasted to a broad ax used for hewing. A 1641 Connecticut document included,
 "A broad axe, 2 narrow axes, 1 wimbell [wimble] & chessells [chisels]."

nasaump (*n.*) Samp, coarsely ground corn or porridge made from it. A Narragansett word. In 1643 Roger Williams wrote,

"Nasaump, a kind of meale **pottage**, unparch'd. From this the English call their Samp."

nation (*n.*) A tribe of Indians. On October 14, 1726, Gov. William Burnet of New York made:
"an Account of my late Transactions with the Six Nations at Albany" to the Lords of Trade.

natural philosophy The study of nature, hence physics. In 1749 Franklin wrote of:
"experiments in natural philosophy."

nature, in a state of Natural, undeveloped, unordered. In 1776 John Adams said,
"There will be an immediate dissolution of every kind of authority; the people will be instantly in a state of nature."

nave wood A hardwood strong enough for wheel naves, hubs. In 1685 it was recorded in Springfield, Massachusetts,
"We marked . . . A Nave Wood Tree O.O. in a Swamp."

navy (*n.*) A naval sword, probably the same as a *hanger*. In 1777 Brig. Gen. Anthony Wayne reported,
"Lieutenant Henry . . . dangerously wounding two of the Indians with his navy."

N. C. D. An abbreviation of Latin *nemine contra dicente,* 'unanimous; none dissenting.'

neat[1] (*n.*) A bovine animal, as distinguished from horses, sheep, or goats. Enacted in 1772 in New York:
"An act for returning neat cattle and sheep to their owners."

neat[2] (*adj.*) Net. In 1678 Charles Wolley wrote,
"Tobacco is two pence halfpenny a pound, a merchantable Hogshead contains four hundred pound neat, i.e. without the Cask."

necessary (*n.*) A privy. In 1769 Philadelphia customs collector William Shepherd wrote,
"I found in the necessary house belonging to my lodgings the following abusive letter directed 'To the infamous Scoundrel Sheppard.'" Also, in 1778 Maj. Benjamin Fishbourne recorded,
"The Regimental Quarter Master is to be pointedly exact in haveing vaults sunk for necessaries; & see they are regularly covered every morning."

necklet (*n.*) A neck cloth. In 1719 in New York an apprentice at 21 received:
"a new suit, four shirts and two neckletts."

negro cloth A plain cloth for slaves' clothing. The 1769 Boston Non-Importation Agreement included:
"negro cloth commonly called white and colored plains."

negus (*n.*) A wine drink with hot water, sugar, nutmeg, and lemon juice, first popularized by Col. Francis Negus (d. 1732).

nem. con. An abbreviation of Latin *nemine contra dicente* 'unanimous; none dissenting.'

nemine contra dicente *Latin.* 'unanimous; none dissenting.'

ne plus ultra *Latin.* 'nothing more; further; the furthest one can go.' In 1669 John Lederer complained,
"The coldness of the Air and Earth together, seizing my Hands and Feet with numbness put me to a *ne plus ultra.*"

nets (*n.*) A netting to protect horses' ears from flies. In 1760 John Rowe ordered:
"a pair of nets for horses. Let them be large."

netop (*n.*) A partner. A word adopted from the Narragansett Indians. A 1662 New Haven document recorded,
"The Indian shooke her . . . by ye hand, and asked her where her netop was."

new found Lately reclaimed, as from swampy ground. In 1763 Washington wrote,
"The Inhabitants of what they call new found land, which is thick settled, very rich Land."

New Hampshire grants The land west of the Connecticut River, in what is now Vermont, was granted by the Royal Governor of New Hampshire from 1749 to 1764. New York claimed the area, and King George III in 1764 agreed. Some of the settlers, notably Ethan Allen, and his Green Mountain Boys, forcibly defended their New Hampshire grants. In 1793 Gen. William Heath in his *Memoirs* referred to:
"Col. Ethan Allen of the New Hampshire Grants."

New Jersey tea A shrub from whose leaves a tea was brewed during the Revolution. In 1785 botanist Humphry Marshall wrote,
"American Ceanothus, or New-Jersey Tea-tree, is a low shrub, growing common in most parts of North America."

new land Land lately brought under cultivation. In 1763 Washington wrote of:
"The arm of Dismal, which we passed through to get to this new land (as it is called)."

new Light (1) One of the Calvinist Methodists influenced by George Whitefield (1714–1770); one who accepted new enlightenment.
(2) One of the Presbyterians who left the Philadelphia synod in 1741.
(3) One of the New England Congregationalists who formed a revival movement in 1740.

new negro A slave newly arrived from Africa. In 1701 Charles Wolley recorded,
"In Barbados new Negro's (i. e. such as cannot speak English) are bought for twelve or fourteen pound a head."

new rate bill The legislation establishing a rate of exchange of currency. John Adams referred to this legislation in a letter to his wife, Abigail, in 1778. The colonies were continually revising the rate of exchange of their currencies to keep pace with inflation. *See* **new tenor.**

new tenor The paper currency issued first in 1737 in Massachusetts and in 1740 in Rhode Island stating that it had a new value equivalent to a certain amount of silver or gold coin. An adaptation of *tender.*

nick (1) (*n.*) A false-bottomed glass. From *kick*, the indentation in the bottom of a glass. In 1632 Thomas Morton wrote,
"And he handled the matter as if he dealt by the pint and the quart with nick and froth."
(2) (*v.*) To make a winning throw at dice. In a 1738 song we find,
"Pray give me a ticket./ Main seven I nick it."

nicknackery (*n.*) A petty contrivance, a trick. A variant of *knickknackery.* In 1771 Franklin described a man as:
"very ingenious in many little nicknackeries."

night gown A gown for lounging, not sleeping. In a 1741 letter John Webb wrote that the ship's:
"Comp'y Gave the Capt. a Night Gown."

night walking Dictionaries define the word to mean prowling or prostitution. In this quotation by Jonathan Edwards in Northampton, Massachusetts, in 1737, merely walking at night is probably meant:

"Licentiousness for some years greatly prevailed among the youth of the town; they were very much of them addicted to night walking, and frequenting the tavern, and lewd practices, wherein some, by their example, exceedingly corrupted others."

nimis bibendo appotus *Latin.* 'drunk from drinking too much.' In 1774 Philip Fithian wrote,

"Among the first of these Vociferators was a young Scotch-Man, Mr. Jack Cunningham, he was nimis bibendo appotus; noisy, droll, waggish, yet civil in his way wholly inoffensive."

noble (*n.*) A gold coin, named for the superior quality of its gold. First issued by Edward III (1327–1377); the George noble of Henry VIII depicted the English patron saint, St. George. In 1646 a Massachusetts will provided that:

"Abigail and Israell have 20 nobles each, when twenty-one."

nocake (*n.*) Parched Indian corn. From an Algonquian word. In 1634 William Wood observed,

"*Nocake* (as they call it) . . . is nothing but Indian Corne parched in the hot ashes."

noggin (*n.*) A small mug or wooden cup; a unit of measure equal to a gill. A man in 1745 was described as drinking:

"about a quart a day, a noggin at a time."

nolle prosequi *Latin.* 'unwilling to pursue.' A statement that the matter will be pursued no further. In South Carolina in 1767 they petitioned:

"that no *nolle prosequis* or *traverses* be filed against informations made against transgressors of the local or penal laws."

nominate (*v.*) To call. In a warning to a ship captain in 1723 The Philadelphia Committee for Tarring and Feathering wrote,

"We are nominated to a very disagreable but very necessary service."

none-so-pretty (*n.*) An ornamental braid. A 1754 South Carolina newspaper advertised:

"Just imported . . . silk watch strings, none-so-pretties, star and scarlet gartering."

nonsuch (*adj.*) a thing that has no equal. A variant of *nonesuch*. In 1778 Christopher Marshall noted,

"She was a nonsuch gardener."

nonsuit (*v.*) To determine that a plaintiff drops his suit on the default of his appearance. In South Carolina in 1749 in a law regarding the assize of bread the phrase appeared:

"and if the plaintiff be nonsuited or discontinue his action."

non sum informatus nil dicet *Latin.* 'I have no information or belief about this matter [and consequently] cannot answer.' A 1763 New Jersey document regarding a suit for trespass used the phrase.

noodle (*n.*) A silly, naive person. Thomas Paine wrote about a Tory in Philadelphia,

"A friendly noodle who is now in this city."

nook (*n.*) A narrow piece of land between two bodies of water. In 1638 a Massachusetts document said,

"Henry Bayly desires a little nooke of land next [to] Mr. Conants howse at Catt Cove."

Norris's Drops A patent medicine with an antimony base. In 1772 Washington bought:
"two bottles of Norris's Drops for Miss Custis £1." for her epilepsy. She died seven months later.

North Britain Scotland after its union with Great Britain in 1707.

notorious (*adj.*) Publicly known. Gen. William Heath recorded,
"I am determined that all my conduct respecting the Convention be notorious."

notting (*v.*) Remaining after deductions. A variant of *netting*. A 1754 bill of lading to the slaver *Sierra Leone* provided,
"Said goods notting with primage and average accustomed."

novanglian (*adj.*) Applying to New England. From Latin *nova Anglia* 'New England.' In 1757 James MacSparran referred to:
"The Novanglian clergy of our Church."

novelty (*n.*) Something new; an innovation. In 1652 Roger Williams wrote of:
"The odiousness of sects, heresies, blasphemies, novelties, seducers and their infections." He was apparently opposed to any change.

nubbin (*n.*) An undersized ear of corn. In a 1692 Maryland document one finds,
"Jones saw him buy one beaver skin . . . for thirty ears and nubbins of corn."

numb palsy A paralysis with no tactile sensitivity. In 1766 Jane Mecom wrote to her brother, Benjamin Franklin,
"I am greeved to hear poor Mrs. Smith has the numb palsy."

nunnery (*n.*) A brothel. William Byrd in his *London Diary* referred to:
"nuns of Drury Lane . . . the poor jades." In 1776 John Leacock wrote of:
"houses of our God converted into nunneries."

nun's holland A very fine linen cloth. In 1745 J. F. Watson wrote of:
"nuns, bag and gulix."

nun's thread A fine, linen thread suitable for lace making. In 1691 Samuel Sewall directed,
"Send me . . . a pound of very fine Nuns Thred."

nurse keeper A nurse. In 1679 Charles Wolley, writing about Indians said,
"Neither requires the nice attendance of nurse-keepers."

nut shell Nut shells were used in cupping. *See* **cup.** A 1721 Boston newspaper said that doctors should:
"be completely armed with Incision, Lancet, Pandora's Box, Nut Shells and Fillet."

Oath of Allegiance and Supremacy The oath required of all public officials when William and Mary became rulers of England in 1689. In 1715 Mayor John Johnson of New York signed a document which stated,
"Daniel Bonnet of New Rochelle appeared in Open Court, did take the Oaths, by Law appointed to be taken, instead of the Oaths of Allegiance and Supremacy."

object (*v.*) To present, point out. In 1789 Gouverneur Morris wrote,
"He objects his office to which I replied that he need not appear in it."

obligans et renuncians a bona fide *Latin.* 'obliging and rejecting in good faith.' The phrase was used in the transport from the Director of New Netherland to Kiliaen Van Renssallaer in 1630.

occamy (*n.*) An alloy imitating silver. An adaptation of *alchemy*. In 1696 Samuel Sewall wrote,
"30 Dozen of Ockimy Spoons."

occasionally (*adj.*) By chance. Franklin used the word this way in 1771.

off wheel The farthest, right, wheel of a vehicle, as contrasted to the *near*, left.

Ohio Company A land company of Virginian adventurers which received a patent for land south of the Ohio River from George III in 1749. Ohio is from Iroquoian *oheo* 'beautiful.'

oidonia (*n.*) A wine. In 1750 James Birket wrote,
"The wine . . . is from the Canaries & Western Islands, called Oidonia, tis of pale collr. tasts harsh and inclined to look thick."

oil nut A butternut. In 1778 Jonathan Carver wrote,
"The Butter or Oilnut . . . The tree grows in meadows where the soil is rich and warm."

oil spring A seep of natural petroleum. In 1765 Robert Rogers reported,
"Those remarkable springs, greatly esteemed by the Indians as a remedy for almost everything, they are called oil-springs."

old field A field long cultivated by the Indians. In 1761 a South Carolina document said,

"There are dispersed up and down the Country several large Indian old fields."

old ground A field that has been long cultivated. In 1769 Washington wrote,

"Got over the old ground Corn."

Old Light A member of the Philadelphia Presbyterian Synod after 1741.

old money Paper money before revaluation. A 1780 Virginia document stated,

"Fix my pay in the first footing of ten shillings old money, or fifty pounds of Tobacco pr: day."

old style Describing a date according to the Julian Calendar. On November 16, 1767, John Rowe wrote in his diary,

"This is my birthday O.S."

old tenor The paper currency issued in Massachusetts before 1737. *See* **new tenor.** A 1738 Massachusetts document read,

"We enjoin you . . . That the Funds be laid in Paper Bills of the Old Tenor, and not in Bills of the New Tenor."

Old Virginia Eastern Virginia, the long settled area. In 1624 Capt. John Smith described:

"a Map of the old Virginia."

old wife An old prating woman. As in *old wives' tale.*

oleum olivarum *Latin.* 'olive oil.' It was taken internally as a laxative, used externally as a dressing for burns.

ombre (*n.*) A card game, generally for three, played with a Spanish pack: forty cards; no tens, nines, or eights. From Spanish *juego del hombre* 'game of the man.' In a 1664 song we hear of:

"serious ombre play."

on liking On trial. In 1771 Franklin wrote,

"I was sent to be with him some time on liking."

on the high rope Excited; very angry. In 1711 William Byrd wrote,

"I met Mr. Holloway and reasoned with him about his account, but he was on the high rope and gave me back my papers."

onus probandi *Latin.* 'burden of proof.' In 1735 James Alexander wrote,

"But we will save Mr. Attorney the trouble of proving a negative, and take the onus probandi upon ourselves."

ooze (*n.*) A tanning liquid. In 1656 a Connecticut law provided,

"Nor shall [any person] put any leather into any hott or warm oozes w[ha]tsoever."

oppilation (*n.*) An obstruction, generally of the lower intestines. Nicholas Monardes said of sassafrass,

"It healeth opilations."

orderly book A book for every company in which the sergeants write general and regimental orders. A 1775 letter to Washington complained,

"Orderly Books, being lost I could not gett an authentick copy."

ordinary (*n.*) (1) A clergyman who said prayers for a condemned man. William Byrd was being facetious when in 1710 he wrote,

"Mr. Commissary got £5 as ordinary by his teaching us."

(2) A tavern, plainer than an inn. In Virginia in 1774 Philip Fithian recorded,
"All Taverns they call 'Ordinarys.'"

ore tenus *Latin.* 'by word of mouth, orally.' John Winthrop wrote,
"Ratlif being convict ore tenus of most foul scandalous invectives."

orgeat (*n.*) A liquor from barley water and sweet almonds. A borrowing from French.
It was mentioned in an 18th-century cookbook.

orignal (*n.*) See quotation. An adopted Canadian French word, originally from Basque
oregna 'stag.' In 1775 J. Anderson wrote,
"In North America they have a species of deer, called by the natives Orignial or
Aurignial . . . probably the Moose-deer."

oringo (*n.*) A variant of *eryngo*.

oronoco (*n.*) A tobacco from Venezuela (where the Oronoco River flows). A 1660
Virginia document read,
"Two thousand five hundred pounds of good, sound, bright and large Arronoca
Tobacco."

orris (*n.*) A gold or silver lace. It can be traced back to Latin *auriphrygium* 'embroidery,' literally, 'Phrygian gold.' In 1774 a newly arrived weaver advertised in a
Philadelphia newspaper,
"girth webs and orris."

ortolan (*n.*) A bird about the size of a lark and delicious eating. In 1730 William Byrd
described a triskaidekaphobic woman,
"Yet she once refus'd to taste a Pye, because it had 13 ortolans in it."

O. S. An abbreviation of *Old Style*; according to the Julian Calendar. *See also* **Gregorian calendar.** In 1767 John Rowe said,
"This is my birthday O. S."

osnaburg (*n.*) A coarse linen originally from Osnaburg, Germany. Benjamin Faneuil,
Jr., advertised,
"Ravens Duck, Ticklinburg, Oznabrigs" in a 1765 Boston newspaper.

outbreaking (*n.*) An outburst. In 1771 Franklin wrote,
"He . . . seemed ready for an outbreaking."

outcry (*n.*) A sale at public auction. In 1657 a court in North Castle, New York,
ordered:
"The estate of John Finch sold at a outcry at a townes meeting."

outdrift (*n.*) An easement over which to drive cattle. In 1697 in Albany it was
recorded,
"They will give him 50 acres . . . with free outdrift for his cattle."

outhouse (*n.*) Any building at a little distance from a main house. Cambridge land
records in 1635 listed:
"One Dwellinge House with other out houses."

outlandish (*adj.*) Foreign. The author of a 17th-century cookbook acknowledged that:
"This receipt was sent to him by an outlandish man."

outlet (*n.*) A place where anything is let out; a grazing area. In 1752 James MacSparran
commented,
"The Climate is benign, and their Outlets or Commonages large."

outliver (*n.*) One who lives in a sparsely inhabited area of a town. A 1675 New York

document recorded,
"The Towne paying double to what the Outlivers.''

outlot (*n.*) A lot of ground outside the control of a town. A 1774 document referred to:
"An out-lot of ten acres, contiguous to the town.''

outlying (*adj.*) **(1)** Pertaining to those living in the woods as scouts. During the expedition to Ft. Duquesne an officer reported to Washington,
"In our way Discover'd two outlying men one of which was taken.''
(2) Pertaining to animals which have escaped from their pens. In 1676 a Delaware document recorded,
"They fetch in their old out Lying hoghs.''

out party A scouting party. In 1756 Robert Rogers reported,
"A party of 220 French and Indians were preparing to invest the outparties at Fort Edward.''

outport (*n.*) A facility used for the transfer of cargo from larger to smaller ships. Such places were especially useful for smuggling. A 1742 letter to the Board of Trade from William Ballan said,
"The country which abounds with outports where vessels employed in their trade unlade their cargoes into small vessels.''

outpublish (*v.*) To have the marriage banns published for the last time. In 1719 Samuel Sewall wrote,
"I was Out-published on the Thanksgiving-Day.''

outward (*adj.*) Foreign. In 1756 John Woolman wrote,
"He had a view of some outward affairs.''

outwharf (*n.*) A jetty and wharf. One was built in 1673 in Boston Harbor; so much has been filled in that Atlantic Avenue is there now. In 1710 the records show,
"The proposalls . . . will be a means to have the Out wharves brought into good repair.''

overcast (*n.*) A cast, or computation, at too high a rate. In the Connecticut records appears,
"There was an overcast made by the listers upon the grand levy of the year 1761.''

overcut (*n.*) A short cut. A 1636 Boston document reads,
"All the ground lying betweene the two brooks . . . and soe to the other end unto shortest overcut beyond the hill.''

overkeel (*n.*) A mark made with keel 'red ocher' to indicate ownership. A 1677 Delaware document records,
"In the right eare a overkeel.''

overlooker (*n.*) One who superintends. In 1792 Washington observed,
"All the articles in the world would not enforce the measure longer than he himself was under the observation of an overlooker.''

overnight (*n.*) The night before. In 1770 Washington wrote,
"After much Counselling the overnight, they all came to my fire.''

overplus (*n.*) A surplus. A 1765 Massachusetts law commanded,
"the offender to return double the overplus.''

overset (*v.*) To turn bottom up, as a chair or coach. In 1711 William Byrd wrote,
"Mr. G—. had overset himself and was lame.''

overslaugh (*n.*) A sand bar in the Hudson River. An adaptation of a Dutch word *overslag* 'to pass over.' In 1776 Charles Carroll of Carrollton wrote,
"Having passed the overslaw, had a distinct view of Albany."

oxgate (*n.*) An ox pasture. *See* **gate.** In 1660 on Long Island, New York,
"There is this Day Leet to Edward Titus the Towene Oxe Gatts for the sume of A Leavene [eleven] Shillings."

oxycroceum (*n.*) A mixture of saffron and vinegar used to form a healing plaster.

oxymel (*n.*) A mixture of honey and vinegar. Boiled to a syrup, it was used to give body to medicines.

oyster basket The female vagina; a place for depositing oysters, gobs of semen. A version of *Yankee Doodle* ran,
"Heigh for our Cape Cod/ Heigh ho Nantasket/ Do not let the Boston wags/ Feel your Oyster Basket."

paced (*adj.*) Thoroughgoing; out-and-out. In 1760 Washington described a man as:
"nothing less than a thorough pac'd rascall."

pachad and **chesed** *Hebrew.* 'dread' and 'loving kindness.' In 1679 Charles Wolley wrote,
"*Adam* . . . had marks imprinted upon [him] by the finger of God, which marks were, *pachad* and *chesed*."

packet (*n.*) A fast schooner or brigantine which carried dispatches, mail, or diplomatic agents.

paduasoy (*n.*) A corded silk fabric. From French *peau de soie* 'skin of silk.' In 1765 a Boston newspaper advertised,
"Tammy, corded Paduasoy, Shalloons, Camblets."

painfulness (*n.*) Diligence. A 1643 description of Harvard commented on a teacher,
"Approved himselfe for his abilities, dexterity and painfulnesse in teaching."

Palatine (*n.*) **(1)** One from the German state, the Palatinate, now part of Bavaria. In 1710 a Boston newspaper reported,
"The three Transports that are arrived with Palatines are the Fame, Baltimore and Town Frigor."
(2) The senior of a system of nobility planned for the Carolinas from 1669 to 1693. The word means to have royal or palace privileges. A 1682 document was addressed:
"To the Right Honorable William Earl of Craven Pallatine, and the rest of the true and absolute Lords and Proprietors of the Province of Carolina."

pale (*n.*) **(1)** A pointed stake. A 1634 letter from Maryland reported,
"The Captain's men which were employed in felling trees and cleaning pales for the palisado."
(2) A fence of pales.
(3) An enclosure, actual or implied. In 1611 Capt. John Smith described land:
"With a pale of two miles cut over from river to river."
(4) Bounds; limits. In 1628 Jonas Michaelius wrote,
"Within the pale of my calling."

pan (*n.*) A square, wood frame, filled with bricks or plaster, on which to anchor a

building. In 1773 Philip Fithian wrote,
"The Colonel shewed me and explain'd the Pan of his Mill."

panada (*n.*) a food made by boiling bread to a pulp, then sweetened. An adopted Spanish word.

pandemonium (*n.*) A tumult. From the capital of Hell, the place of all demons. In a 1776 play a character said,
"To give their attendance at my pandemonium."

pandor (*n.*) A bestial Croatian soldier. The 1767 South Carolina *Remonstrance* complained of:
"incursions of hussars and pandors."

Pandora's Box A doctor's box of miscellaneous supplies and equipment. Probably local jargon. A 1721 Boston newspaper said,
"That they be completely armed with Incision, Lancet, Pandora's Box, Nut Shells and Fillet."

panegyric (*n.*) Eulogistic talk; praise. In 1744 Dr. Alexander Hamilton commented,
"He bestowed much panegyric upon his own behavior and conduct."

panela (*n.*) An unrefined brown sugar. An adopted Spanish word. The Molasses Act of 1733 covered:
"all sugars and paneles of such foreign growth."

pantile (*n.*) An S-shaped roof tile. Dr. Alexander Hamilton in 1744 described roofs:
"covered with pan tile."

pantry (*n.*) A closet where bread and dry provisions were kept. A 1710 New Jersey document referred to:
"a pantry with dressers and shelves."

pap (*n.*) An apple pulp. Ebenezer Cook in 1708 referred to:
"hominy and cider-pap."

papaver (*n.*) *Latin.* 'the white poppy, a narcotic.'

paper light An oiled-paper window pane. In 1698 R. Chamberlain wrote,
"I also found many Stones . . . to fly in, breaking the Glass Windows, and a Paper-Light."

papist (*n.*) A Roman Catholic. In 1629 a Virginian wrote,
"No Papists have been suffered to settle their aboade amongst us."

paracelcian (*adj.*) According to the practice of Theophrastus Bombastus von Hohenheim (1493–1541), Swiss physician and philosopher, who wrote under the name of Philippus Aureolus Paracelsus. In 1676 an epitaph said that Nathaniel Bacon:
"corrupted death by parasscellcian art."

parade (*n.*) A show, ostentation. In 1776 Col. William Smallwood reported,
"The enemy might be checked in their career. For this you may relye on however their parade may indicate the contrary."

paragon (*n.*) A double camlet, an angora fabric. The 1673 inventory of the ship *Providence* included:
"2 scarlett parragon coates."

parallel (*n.*) A trench parallel to the place under attack. In 1781 Washington wrote that:

"a deserter . . . gave notice of his approaching his parallel."

parcel (*n.*) A number of persons. In 1722 Dr. William Douglas regarding a smallpox epidemic wrote,
"Of this first parcel very few died."

parish (*n.*) **(1)** In Georgia and Virginia, a political division. A 1641 Virginia document read,
"Resolved, that the county of Upper Norfolk be divided into three distinct parishes."
(2) In New England, an ecclesiastical jurisdiction. In 1684 Increase Mather recorded,
"Four other parishes were very much endamaged."

park (*n.*) A place for encamping the artillery and all its attendant troops and equipment. In 1775 Washington reported,
"The remaining companies of the Provincial troops, and the whole park of artillery, were ordered to hold themselves in readiness to march."

parley (*n.*) A conference with an enemy. In 1781 Gen. William Heath reported to Gov. Hancock,
"On the 17th they [British] beat a parley—the 19th surrendered."

parlor (*n.*) The room in a house used for conversation which the family usually occupies, as distinguished from a drawing room intended for the reception of company.

paroch (*n.*) A parish clergyman. From Latin *parochus*, same meaning. In 1760 James Reed wrote,
"I have now sent you, according to promise, my No. I Paroch."

parole (*n.*) **(1)** A watchword given only to officers of the guard. The countersign was given to all members. Maj. Benjamin Fishbourne's 1778 orderly book referred to:
"parole and countersign."
(2) A promise given by a prisoner of war when he was released with restrictions, principally not to bear arms. Shortened form of French *parole d'honneur* 'word of honor.'

parts (*n. pl.*) Qualities, powers, faculties. In 1777 Nicholas Cresswell described Washington:
"His education is not very great nor his parts shining; his disposition is rather heavy."

pasquinade (*n.*) A satirical writing, sometimes publicly posted. A character in a 1776 play complained,
"Scandalous verses, lampoons and pasquinades be made upon us."

pasty (*n.*) A pie made of paste (dough made with shortening) and baked without a dish. In 1739 William Byrd:
"ate fried venison pasty."

patent (*n.*) A right, granted by a sovereign not only to an invention, but also to a territory, district, or piece of land. Also, the property so granted.

pateraro (*n.*) A variant of Spanish *pedrero* 'small cannon for throwing stones.' In 1675 Sir Edmund Andros wrote,
"If I can will gett and fitt up a Petrara for Capt. Chambers, having none in the fort ready."

patrociny (*n.*) Patronage. A 1741 protest from a Philadelphia synod referred to:

"poor, credulous people, who in imitation of their example, under their patrociny, judge their ministers to be graceless."

patroned land The land belonging to a church parish. In 1755 Thomas Chalkley wrote,
"Subscribers have processioned all the *Patroned* land within the bounds of Cap. Wm. Christian's Company."

patroon (*n.*) The owner of a tract of land with manorial privileges granted by the West India Company in New Netherland. A word adopted from the Dutch. The 1627 *Freedoms and Exemptions* of the company referred to:
"acknowledged Patroons."

patten (*n.*) A foot clog with a thick wooden sole, further elevated by an iron ring.

pattern (*n.*) Enough material for a dress. In 1695 Samuel Sewall ordered:
"Send my wife a pattern of silk for a gown."

patty (*n.*) A little pie. A 1776 inventory in New York included:
"47 pattee pans."

Pavonia (*n.*) A short-lived Dutch colony on the west side of the Hudson River.

pawawe (*n.*) A variant of *powwow*, an Indian medicine man. John Winthrop wrote,
"One of their pawawes told us that there was a conspiracy."

Paxton Boys A group of men living near Paxton, Pennsylvania, which was politically active in the 1760s.

pay (*v.*) **(1)** To beat. Using a play on the meaning of the next definition, Delaware River pilots in 1773 were warned,
"See that his bottom be well fired, scrubbed and paid."
(2) To cover a ship's bottom with tallow, sulfur, and tar. In 1768 Washington:
"began to Cork [caulk] and pay the bottom of my schooner."

peace maker A Justice of the Peace. A 1683 Pennsylvania document speculated,
"The Question was asked in Councill whether Peace Makers should sitt once a month."

peace officer A sheriff or constable. A 1747 Georgia document stated,
"There would be an absolute Necessity of a Peace Officer living in the said [Creek] Nation, to preserve the Peace as well among the White Men as Indians."

peachy (*n.*) A drink made from peaches. Samuel Peters in 1781 wrote that in Connecticut:
"They make peachy and perry; grape, cherry, and currant wines."

peague (*n.*) *Narragansett.* Wampum, shell money. *Ames' Almanac* for 1741 says,
"Other names for sewant, or shell currency: peague, pompeague or wompompeague."

peak[1] (*n.*) A variant of *peague*. In 1738 William Byrd wrote,
"That species of conque shell which the Indian peak is made of."

peak[2] (*n.*) A child's pointed cap. A 1736 Boston newspaper advertised,
"Children's Silver Peaks & Flowers, Dutch Prettys."

pearl (*n.*) Barley with the husk removed; after hulling it resembled a pearl. In 1740 William Byrd drank:
"hordealed cinnamon water with prepared pearl."

pearlash (*n.*) A purified, white potash used in baking, from its pearly color. In New

Netherland an old recipe for *doed-koecks* 'dead cakes' called for:
"two teaspoonsfls of pearlash."

pease (*n.*) Peas.

peculiar (*n.*) **(1)** A piece of land not in the jurisdiction of any town.
(2) One who owns or occupies a peculiar. A 1720 Connecticut record reads,
"Mr. John Reed, who dwells between Fairfield and Danbury [shall] be likewise annually listed as a peculiar to Danbury."

pedrero (*n.*) A small cannon used for throwing stones. An adopted Spanish word. In 1680 an anonymous pirate wrote of:
"fiering off their Paderroro's to frighten us."

peeling (*n.*) A variant of *pelang*, a thin, Chinese silk, dress fabric. In 1775 a New York newspaper advertised:
"A great variety of ribbons, persians, modes, sarsinets, peelong."

pejorate (*v.*) To derogate. In 1751 Franklin wrote,
"Slaves also pejorate the families that use them; the white children become proud, disgusted with labor, being educated in idleness, are rendered unfit to get a living by industry."

pele fish A paddlefish, from the description. In a 1609 book by Richard Hakluyt appears:
"There was another fish called a pele fish: it had a snout of a cubit long, and at the upper lip it was made like a peele."

pelerine (*n.*) A woman's fur cape. In a 1743 Boston newspaper Henrietta Maria East advertised that:
"Ladies may have their Pellerines made at her mantua-making shop."

pellitory (*n.*) A medicinal root, the *Parietaria pennsylvanica*. John Lawson in 1709 reported,
"Pelletory grows on the Sand-Banks and Islands. It is used to cure the Tooth-ach."

peltry (*n.*) Pelts, skin, furs. In 1770 Washington wrote,
"To enrich the Adventurers with the peltry for which there is a . . . good Market."

Pemaquid (*n.*) A 1626 settlement in Maine near the mouth of the Damariscotta River. In 1675 Thomas Mitchell said,
"And when he came back from Pemequid."

pencil work A kind of needlework with pendants resembling pencils. In a 1751 newspaper,
"Martha Gazley . . . makes and teaches the following curious works, viz. . . . Pencil-work."

pendle (*n.*) Any projection from a building. In 1701 Boston enacted:
"No person shall Erect or set up any Pentice [penthouse], jetty or Pendal over any of the Streets, lanes or highwayes of this town."

penetrate (*v.*) To affect the mind. In 1789 Gouverneur Morris described a lady who:
"is penetrated with gratitude at this slight attempt to serve her."

peniascoe (*n.*) An anglicization of Spanish *penasco*, a strong silk material. In a 1775 Boston newspaper,
"Nathaniel Sparhawk sells: Silk & worsted Sagathees . . . Missinets, Peniascoes, Shalloons."

penistone (*n.*) A coarse woolen stuff, originally from Penistone, England. In 1667 Thomas Mayhew listing a ship's cargo stolen by Indians included:
"Red cloth 6 yards, 3 or 4 yards pemistone."

pennyroyal (*n.*) An herb from which a brew was made that was taken to counteract nausea. From Latin *puleium regium* 'flea bane' for the effectiveness of the European plant against fleas. In 1630 Francis Higginson wrote,
"Diuers excellent Pot-herbs grow abundantly among the Grass, as Pennyroyal."

pennyworth (*n.*) A good bargain. In 1727 William Byrd wrote,
"They send them better goods and better penny worths than the traders of Carolina."

penthouse (*n.*) Any subsidiary structure, usually with a sloping roof, appended to a building. *See* **pendle.**

people (*n.*) Slaves. Common usage in Virginia. In 1739 William Byrd:
"talked with my people and prayed."

pepperidge (*n.*) The black gum tree. In 1743 Joshua Hempstead:
"sawed of a p[ai]r Peperage wheels for my Stone Cart."

perambulate (*v.*) To walk around the borders of a town to renew its boundaries. In 1708 Samuel Sewall wrote,
"Capt. Culliver and others perambulating for Baintrey and Milton went with us."

perboyle (*v.*) To boil slowly; not to parboil (part boil). A 17th-century cookbook warned,
"You must first perboyle yr meat."

perch (*n.*) A unit of land measurement, a square rod. Part of the 1693 grant to Vredrick Vlypsen was for:
"six acres, three rods and eight perches."

perdu, lay To perform dangerous military duty, as acting as an outpost. An adopted French word meaning 'lost, hidden.'

periauger (*n.*) **(1)** A dugout canoe. An adaptation of Carib, *piragua*, same meaning. A 1696 South Carolina statute applied to:
"any person [who] shall steal, take away, or let loose any boat, perriaguer or canoe."
(2) A two-masted ship. The foremast raked sharply forward and the main sharply aft. This eliminated a jib and bowsprit, a feature desirable in working around ships and wharfs. Jan Dobbs used one to ferry people across the Hudson in the first half of the 18th century.

perizomata (*n.*) An item of Indian apparel worn about the waist. In 1634 one of the Maryland adventurers wrote,
"About their middle all women and men . . . wear perizomata (or round aprons) of skins."

Perogative Court A misspelling of *Prerogative Court.* A 1712 legal document read,
"Exhibited into the registry of the Perogative Court of the Province of New York."

perpetuana (*n.*) A durable, woolen fabric made in England. A fabricated name like *Durance* and *Everlasting.* In 1696 John Dann testified,
"In those Shipps they tooke some Small Armes, Chestes of Lynnen and perpetuenes."

perry (*n.*) A fermented juice of pears. In 1705 Robert Beverley wrote,
"Perhaps too it may come by new and unfine Cyder, Perry, or Peach-drink, which the People are impatient to Drink before they are ready."

persian (*n.*) A thin, silk cloth, primarily for linings. Originally from Persia, it was later imitated in France and England. A 1775 Philadelphia newspaper advertised, "White, blue and pink Persians."

Persicaria (*n.*) The buckwheat family of plants. In 1766 John Bartram complained, "We were nearly stopped by the pistia and persicaria growing all in a matt."

persico (*n.*) A cordial prepared by mashing peaches in alcohol. In 1711 William Byrd: "went to Will Randolph's where I drank more persico."

peru (*n.*) The peruvian balsam. It came from Central America, not Peru. It was brewed and used to counteract asthma and colic.

peseta (*n.*) A Spanish silver coin, equal to one quarter of a Spanish dollar.

pest house A hospital for those with contagious diseases. In 1767 John Rowe referred to smallpox and the:
"pest house" in Boston.

pestilence (*n.*) Smallpox. The first inoculation against the disease was given by Zabdiel Boylston to his son in Boston in 1721.

petchamin (*n.*) A persimmon. An Indian word. In 1607 Capt. John Smith wrote, "We daily feasted with good bread, Virginia Peas, pumpions and putchamins."

petticoat (*n.*) Depending on the time and place, it may be a skirt showing beneath a draped overskirt, the skirt of a dress, or just a skirt. Sometimes worn alone, sometimes in many layers. Both boys and girls up to the age of six wore them.

petticoat trousers Men's wide, baggy trousers. A 1753 New Jersey document stated, "He took with him . . . two Pair of Petticoat Trowsers."

pettifogger (*n.*) An inferior lawyer employed in mean or small business. From French *petit vogue* 'little credit.' In 1646 William Bradford commented,
"But this Morton abovesaid, having more craft than honesty (who had been a kind of pettifogger of Furnival's Inn)."

petulant (*adj.*) Wanton. In 1684 Increase Mather questioned,
"Shall the Gentiles condemn petulant dancing?"

phaeton (*n.*) An open carriage like a chaise, with four wheels, drawn by two horses. After Phaethon, son of Helios, driver of the sun chariot in Greek mythology. In 1759 a Philadelphia newspaper advertised,
"Landaus, phaetons, two and four wheeled chaises."

phalanx (*n.*) A body of soldiers in close array. Hugh Brackenridge in a 1776 play said,
"These are the men, who in firm phalanx, threaten us with war."

philosophy (*n.*) All study was divided into theology, physics, logic, and ethics. In 1679 Charles Wolley wrote,
"By the Latitude above observ'd, *New-York* lieth 10 Degrees more to the Southward than Old *England*; which difference according to Philosophy it should be the hotter Climate, but . . . "

phizz (*n.*) Slang for *physiognomy.* In 1744 Dr. Alexander Hamilton:
"observed several comical grotesque phizzes in the inn."

phocina (*n.*) A porpoise. From *Phocaena,* the genus of harbor porpoises. In 1633

Andrew White recorded,
"Of the fishes, those that follow have already come into notice . . . sturgeons, herrings, phocinae."

phylaselle (*n.*) A variant of *filoselle*, a silk thread like floss. A 1647 Massachusetts will bequeathed:
"1 phylaselle cloake lined with plush."

physic (*n.*) **(1)** The art of healing disease, medicine. In 1749 Franklin recommended that:
"all intended for divinity should be taught the Latin and Greek; for physic, the Latin, Greek and French."
(2) Medicines, not limited to a cathartic. *Ames' Almanac* for 1758 wrote of:
"rich soil capable of producing food and physic."

physic dance A spring Indian dance in which medicines were involved. In 1765 Henry Timberlake reported,
"There was to be a physic-dance at night."

picaroon (*n.*) A pirate, either the man or the ship. In 1679 Charles Wolley wrote,
"The Ship may founder by springing a Leak, be wreckt by a Storm or taken by a Pickeroon."

picket (*n.*) A guard posted in front of an army. In 1776 a Maryland soldier:
"march'd with a Piquet by way of New Ark to one Peck's."

pided (*adj.*) A variant of *pied* 'variegated, spotted.' A 1757 South Carolina newspaper reported lost:
"a black and white pided cow."

piece of eight The Spanish peso of eight *reals*. A 1775 letter to Capt. Burchmore instructed,
"It [cocoa] must be the dark black shell and should it be as low as 10 or 11 pieces of eight, would have you take largely of it."

pier glass A mirror placed on the pier, the area between two windows. William Byrd wrote,
"I was carried into a room elegantly set off with pier glasses."

Pietist (*n.*) A member of a religious sect founded in Germany in the 17th century. They despised ceremony. Gottlieb Mittleberger reported them to be in Pennsylvania in 1750.

pig (*v.*) To squeeze together like pigs. In 1727 William Byrd:
"lodged with a family where reckoning women and children we mustered in no less than nine persons all pigged lovingly together."

piggin (*n.*) A small, wooden pail with an erect handle, used as a dipper. In 1681 Increase Mather related,
"The man tried to save the milk, by holding a piggin side-wayes under the cowes belly."

pig nut This name was used for many plants. In 1760 Washington referred to:
"Pignut Ridge."

pigtail (*adj.*) Twisted into a small roll. In a 1776 Boston newspaper appeared,
"Public sale on John Hancock Wharf: Fayal wines, Pig-tail tobacco."

pilate (*n.*) A variant of *pilot*, a guide not only of a ship but also through any unknown area. Thomas Lloyd in 1756 wrote,

"We had 500 miles to go and having a bad pilate out of 200 horses we brought in but 4 or 5."

pillar (*n.*) A Spanish dollar. It depicted the Pillars of Hercules. A 1683 Connecticut law provided,
"All pieces of eight, Mexicoe, pillor and Civill pieces shall pass at six shillings apeice."

pillion (*n.*) A cushion for a woman to sit on behind a person on horseback. A 1648 Connecticut document included,
"An Inuentory of Tho: Dewys Estate . . . A saddell & pillion."

pillow bere A pillow bier, the case which contains the feathers. In 1682 Mary Rowlandson had to:
"make a shirt for his papoose, of a Holland-laced pillowbere."

pimp (*n.*) A thoroughly evil person. A 1774 Connecticut document about the Boston Port Act referred to:
"pimps and parasites."

pinch (*n.*) A steep portion of a road. In 1754 Washington said,
"Wagons may travel . . . by doubling the teams at one or two pinches only."

pinchbeck (*n.*) An alloy of four parts of copper to one part of zinc, used to imitate gold in cheap watchcases, invented by Christopher Pinchbeck, a London watchmaker (1670–1732). A 1754 South Carolina newspaper advertised:
"An assortment of gold, silver and Pinchbeck watches."

pinder (*n.*) An impounder. From *pin*, in its sense of enclose. In 1642 in New Haven, Connecticut, the law fined:
"A peny a head for goates and kids, half to the bringer in of the cattell & half to the pound, or if the pinder take all the pains he is to have all."

pinfold (*n.*) A pound. *See* **pinder**. A 1654 Massachusetts law provided:
"fourpence to the keeper of the pinnefold."

pink (*n.*) A small ship with a flattish bottom, bulging sides, and a narrow, rounded stern. A word adopted from the Dutch. In a 1700 deposition William Fletcher told of:
"a pink of about 100 tons bound from Barbadoes."

pinkaninny (*n.*) A variant of *pinkeny*, a term of endearment, a darling. From *pink* 'small' + *eye*. A 1694 song went,
"Dear Pinck-a-ninny,/ if half a Guin-ney,/ To love will win ye." Not related to *pickaninny*, a colored child, which comes from the diminutive of Spanish *pequeño* 'little, young.'

pinking iron A sharp instrument used to cut fabric with a pinked, or scalloped, edge. In 1761 Sally Tippet wrote,
"I first began to image taste . . . and have ever since been so scrupulous an observer of it that I never was the mark of a pinking iron behind it."

pinkroot (*n.*) Wormroot, used medicinally to kill worms. In 1764 a document reported,
"Produce of South Carolina . . . Pink-root 1 cask."

Pinkster Day Pentecost or Whitsunday or Whitsuntide, the seventh Sunday after Easter, a day for celebrations. An adopted Dutch word. The translation of the title of a 1667 book written in Dutch by Adrian Fischer is, *The Story of the Descent of the Holy Ghost on the Apostles on Pinkster Day.*

pinnace (*n.*) A small sailing vessel with oars and sails, generally with two masts and schooner-rigged. In 1619 the Virginia House of Burgesses decreed,
"No man shall trade into the Baye either in Shallop, pinnace or ship with out the Governours License."

pinner (*n.*) An apron with a bib. Probably a shortening of *pinafore*. A 1750 letter said,
"Mary is most wise with her child . . . She has little David in what she wore herself, a pudding and pinner."

pin up the basket To end, to finish. In 1776 Gen. William Smallwood wrote,
"If the British cut off the retreat to New Jersey it will pin up the basket."

pintado (*n.*) A painted cotton fabric, chintz. An adopted Portuguese word meaning 'painted.' A 1633 Connecticut inventory included:
"3 ruggs, 2 blanketts, 1 pentadoe."

pioneer (*n.*) A soldier who repaired roads, dug trenches, and undermined fortifications. Gen. William Heath wrote of:
"opportunities for the pioneers to open avenues."

pipe[1] (*n.*) A cask of two hogsheads; 126 gallons. An adopted French word. In 1678 Charles Wolley wrote,
"Pipe staves are fifty shillings or three pound a thousand, they are sent from *New-York* to the *Madera* Islands and *Barbados*, the best is made of White Oak."

pipe[2] (*n.*) A penis. A 1727 song *The Milkmaid* ends,
"My pipe has done its best,/ Maria smiles no more."

pipe stand A stand for a pipe. John Richbell's 1660 instructions from his partners included,
"Save all your principal timber for pipe stands and clap board and knee timber."

pipe tomahawk A combined tomahawk and pipe used as a peace pipe. A 1757 letter to Washington said,
"Wm. Grymes 2 lbs. Butter & a pipe Tomahawk."

pipkin (*n.*) A small clay boiling pot. In 1770 John S. Copley advised,
"Take a Glaz'd pipkin."

pippin water Water in which apples have been boiled. From the variety of apple. A 17th-century cookbook instructed,
"Put them in pippin water as fast as you pare them."

pique (*v.*) To take pride in. In 1789 Gouverneur Morris wrote,
"The French who pique themselves on possessing the graces."

piquet (*n.*) A two-handed card game played with 32 cards. In 1710 William Byrd:
"played a pool at piquet."

pirogue (*n.*) A dugout canoe. A corruption of Carib *piragua*. In 1728 William Byrd recorded,
"They passed over it in the pirogue and landed in Gibb's marsh."

pistareen (*n.*) A silver coin, a *peseta*. In 1757 Richard Haddon said that on a French schooner there were:
"one hundred fine pistareens and some small silver."

pistia (*n.*) Water lettuce. In 1766 John Bartram complained of:
"pistia and persicaria growing all in a matt."

pistole (*n.*) A Spanish coin, worth four pieces of eight. In 1741 the crew of *The*

Revenge reported:
"38 pistoles" to the owner.

pitch[1] (*n.*) The result of distilling coal tar or petroleum; also, the latter in its natural state. In 1610 Thomas Morton wrote,
"The country yieldeth abundance . . . of pitch and tarre."

pitch[2] (1) (*n.*) The land assigned to a settler. Probably so called because he made a pitch (choice) for it. A 1699 Connecticut document described,
"the laying out of John Pringle's pitch upon the good hill," and there is:
"Pitch Swamp" in Bedford, New York.
(2) The tip of a cape. In 1677 William Hubbard described:
"the Sea coast from the Pitch of Cape Cod to the Mouth of the Connecticut River."
(3) (*v.*) To marshal or arrange in order for a battle. In 1608 Capt. John Smith recorded,
"Having thus pitched the fields."
(4) To plant. A 1772 Maryland document said,
"We have pitched above 9 tenths of our Crop."

pit coal Mined coal. In 1744 Franklin wrote,
"If Pit Coal should not be here discovered."

pit saw A two-man saw for cutting large timbers. One man stood on the timber, the other in a pit. A 1678 Maryland document included,
"an iron sledge and a hand saw Iron—and Pit Saw."

place (*n.*) Employment in public service. Franklin wrote,
"You offer us hope, the hope of place, pensions and peerages."

placeman (*n.*) One employed in public service. A word used sneeringly to imply incompetence. A 1768 song referred to:
"swarms of placemen and pensioners."

plague of the back Empyema, pus in the chest cavity. John Josselyn in 1672 wrote of:
"that sad Disease called there Plague of the Back, but with us empiema."

plaguey (*adj.*) *Slang.* Exceedingly. A character in a 1781 play exclaimed,
"This is plaguey good bread."

plain (*n.*) A plain cloth. The 1769 Charlestown, Massachusetts, Non-Importation Agreement referred to:
"white and coloured plains."

planetarium (*n.*) A device which shows the motions and orbits of planets; an orrery. In 1774 John Adams recorded,
"Here we saw . . . an orrery or planetarium, constructed by Mr. Rittenhouse, of Philadelphia."

plantain (*n.*) A weed with broad, flat leaves. In 1676 T. Glover wrote,
"There grow wild in the woods plantain of all sorts."

plantation (*n.*) (1) A British colony in America. The colonies were supervised by:
"The Board of Trade and Plantations."
(2) A settlement. In 1682 Mary Rowlandson wrote,
"There was, as I said, about six miles from us, a small Plantation of Indians."
(3) A farm or cultivated estate. A 1773 Pennsylvania newspaper offered,
"A Plantation containing Two Hundred and odd Acres." Generally, from Maryland north, they were farms; to the south, plantations.

planter (*n.*) One of those who settled new and uncultivated territory. In 1659 a Dedham, Massachusetts, document stated,
"The first planters agreed that they would entertain only sixty persons to the priveledge of house lotts."

plant patch A piece of ground in which young plants are started; a nursery. In 1764 Washington:
"visited my Quarters and saw a plant patch burnt at the Mill."

platan (*n.*) The plane tree, *Platanus orientalis.* In 1698 Samuel Sewall:
"set . . . the Poplar to the street and the Platan at the upper corner."

plate (*n.*) **(1)** Silver bullion or bars. From Spanish *plata* 'silver.' In 1721 the Westchester County, New York, Supervisors passed:
"An Act for collecting arrears . . . 10,000 oz. of plate or 14,545 Lion dollars."
(2) Silver dishes, platters, cups, etc. In 1715 William Byrd:
"gave the Major's five daughters each £20 for a piece of plate."
(3) A sloop-rigged vessel with shallow draft. It was mentioned in the 1558 Navigation Act.

plater (*n.*) One who plates metal. In 1719:
"Richard Hanford & Joseph Watts Platers" were expelled from Boston.

platform (*n.*) A plan for the government of churches. *See* **Cambridge Platform.**

platilla (*n.*) A sort of linen from Silesia. A 1783 Philadelphia newspaper offered,
"Platillas and Brittanias."

plating forge A forge where metal was beaten into thin, flat pieces. A 1750 Maryland document referred to:
"One Plateing forge with two Tilt Hammers."

platman (*n.*) One who draws plats, maps. A 1683 Pennsylvania letter said,
"I shall observe what thee writes as to the platman."

play the fool (*v.*) To act foolishly. In 1739 when William Byrd went to Williamsburg he recorded,
"I played the fool with Sally, God forgive me."

plebe in consulto *Latin.* 'Having consulted the people.' John Winthrop wrote,
"For a peace only, the magistrates might conclude *plebe in consulto.*"

plint (*n.*) A chip. In 1608 Capt. John Smith wrote,
"His arrowhead he quickly maketh with a little bone which he ever weareth at his braces of any plint of a stone or glass in the form of a heart."

pluck (*n.*) The heart, liver, etc., of an animal plucked out and used for food. Anna Winslow in 1772 wrote:
"One contained three calves heads (skin off) with their appurtinences anciently called pluck."

plumb (*n.*) Ballast. From Latin *plumbum* 'lead.' In 1781 James Sheathe wrote of:
"junck for to make plum for the publick boats."

plump (*adv.*) Without reservation; directly. An onomatopoeic word, from the sound of a body falling into water. In 1776 John Adams wrote,
"Our delegates in Congress, on the first of July, will vote plump."

plumping house A barn where animals were fattened. In 1740 William Byrd wrote,
"Taken out of the plumping house . . . nourishing diet."

plurality (*n.*) The possession of more than one ecclesiastical office at a time by one per-

son. In 1775 William Eddis wrote that:
"pluralities have never been admitted."

pocket (*n.*) A bag attached to a tape tied around the waist. They were usually worn in pairs so there was a pocket on each hip. They weren't sewn into garments until about 1840.

pockily (*adv.*) Probably a corruption of *particularly*. *Yankee Doodle* went,
"The flaming ribbons in his hat/ They looked so taring fine ah,/ I wanted pockily to get,/ To give to my Jemimah."

pocoson (*n.*) A swamp. Also spelled *pocosin, pocosen.* An adopted Algonquian word. In 1728 William Byrd wrote,
"But this firm land lasted not long before they came upon the dreadful pocoson they had been threatened with."

point (1) (*n.*) A character used to mark the division of writing: comma, semicolon, colon, period. Franklin used the term.
(2) (*v.*) To plow. In 1760 Washington recorded,
"as did the other plow, abt five oclock after Pointing."

pointe coupee A kind of Floridian tobacco. Bernard Romans in 1775 wrote:
"There are present but two sorts produced viz. *Nanquitoche* and *Pointe coupee*, the first infinitely superior to the second."

points (*n.*) Short strings for fastening parts of a garment, such as the hose to a doublet or for lacing a bodice. They survived on garments as decorations, sometimes with metal tips, after the need was gone.

poisoned field Land where the vegetation was considered harmful to cattle. In 1724 Hugh Jones describing Virginia wrote,
"The whole Country is a perfect Forest, except where . . . poisoned Fields and Meadows."

poke[1] (*n.*) A plant whose leaves were used by the Indians as tobacco; Indiana tobacco. A 1634 letter from Maryland said,
"He takes out the pipe and divides the poke from one to one."

poke[2] (*n.*) A shortening of *poke bonnet*, a bonnet with a brim in front poking forward. In 1740 William Byrd wrote,
"Tis impossible even for Miss Tidy . . . either the plaits will lie uneven or the Poke Stand quite ascue [askew]."

polacre (*n.*) A three-masted, square-rigged vessel. Also, *polacca, polacra.* Etymology debatable. In 1775 the Georgia General Assembly enacted,
"All Masters of Vessells . . . shall pay . . . for every Snow Brig Polacre or Sactia."

poldavy (*n.*) A coarse cloth used for sailcloth. Originally from Poldavide, near Brest, France. In 1665 on Long Island, New York,
"Jeremiah Meacham iunior and James Diament findinge a peece of pole Davice Containing nere Sixty yards."

pole (*n.*) Both a linear and a square measure, a rod. 16 ½ feet or 30 ¼ square yards. In 1659 a Providence, Rhode Island, document stated,
"His House share . . . containeth . . . in breadth on the wes[t] parte Eight poles." And a 1638 Massachusetts deed concerned:
"one pole of ground lying before his house."

pole end horse A wheel horse as distinguished from a leader. A *pole* is the shaft from

the axle of a vehicle between the horses. In 1760 Washington:
"put the poll end horse into the plow in the morning."

poleziton (*n.*) A misspelling of *pollicitation*, a promise or a document containing one. This misspelling appears in a purchase money mortgage in 1763 for Minneford's (now City) Island, New York.

policy (*n.*) A stratagem; dexterity of management. Gen. William Heath wrote,
"The British proceeded on to Concord where they destroyed a part of the stores, while others were saved by the vigilance, activity or policy of the inhabitants."

polity (*n.*) The form or constitution of the government of a colony. The 1641 Massachusetts Body of Liberties stated,
"We conceive that the patent (under God) to be the first and the main foundation of our civil polity here."

poll (*n.*) **(1)** The head. In 1766 John Adams stated,
"I shall know the polls and estates, real and personal, of all the inhabitants." He would know them by sight.
(2) An election. In 1770 Robert Mumford in the play *The Candidate* wrote,
"I was thinking you did not intend to stand a poll [run for election]."

polonaise (*n.*) A woman's loose dress. In 1771 Mercy Warren wrote,
"Yet Clara quits the more dressed neglige/ And substitutes the careless polane."

poltroon (*n.*) A coward. In 1776 Gen. William Smallwood related,
"We have twice stripped from these poltroons several of our soldiers' coats."

pomace (*n.*) Crushed apples, the residue of making cider. In 1786 Washington:
"beat about one Bushel of the Wild Crab into pumice."

pomander (*n.*) An aromatic ball carried to ward off infection. From French *pomme ambré* 'amber apple.'

pomatum (*n.*) An unguent used mainly for hair dressing; pomade. In 1657 W. Coles said,
"Pomatum, which is of much use to soften and supple the roughness of the skin."

pompion (*n.*) A pumpkin. The word *pumpkin* is derived from *pompion*, from French *pompon*, same meaning. In 1608 Capt. John Smith wrote,
"We daily feasted with good bread, Virginia Peas, pompions and petchamins."

pon (*n.*) Probably a shortening of *puncheon*, a cask in which sugar was commonly shipped. Washington noted in his diary,
"Canes is from 40 to 70 pons of sugar, each pon valued at 20/."

pone (*n.*) Corn bread. From Algonquian, *oppone*. In 1612 Capt. John Smith related,
"Eating the broth with the bread they call Ponap."

pool (*n.*) A collection of wagers. From French *poule* 'stakes.' In 1710 William Byrd:
"played a pool at piquet."

poor John Dried and salted cod. Origin unknown. In 1616 Capt. John Smith wrote,
"You have cod again to make corfish or Poor John."

poor Robin's plantain Rattlesnake weed. A 1789 tract stated,
"The *Hieracium venosum* . . . grows from the north to Virginia inclusively; is called poor Robins plantain; and is said to frustrate the bite . . . of the rattle snake."

Pope (*n.*) An effigy of the Pope, on Guy Fawkes' Day. In 1764 John Rowe recorded,
"The wheel of the carriage that the Pope was on run over a boy's head."

Pope Day Guy Fawkes' Day, commemorating the gunpowder plot to blow up the Houses of Parliament on November 5, 1605, in revenge for the penal laws against Catholics. In 1769 John Rowe commented,
"The People have behaved Well, [despite it] being Pope Day."

popery (*n.*) The religion of the church of Rome. In 1760 Joseph Galloway wrote,
"In order to introduce popery your former governors have dispensed with the laws."

Pope weather A wet, rainy day. Always blaming something one doesn't like on another person. In 1767 John Rowe noted,
"A wet rainy day. Pope weather."

poppet (*n.*) A small, humanoid figure used in witchcraft. A 1692 document stated,
"They are their own Image without any Poppits of wax or otherwise."

populeon (*n.*) An ointment made from black poplar buds. It was used to treat burns and scalds.

portage-bill (*n.*) A list of the crew of a vessel with their claims for wages and allowances. A 1776 Rhode Island document recorded,
"To amount of cargo, outfit and portage bill of the schooner Eagle."

porterhouse (*n.*) A house where porter, ale, beer, are sold. The word *porter* is short for *porter's ale*, as it was originally chiefly drunk by porters and the lower class of laborers. In 1786 Norris Rich kept a porterhouse in New York City at 3 Broadway.

port fire A way of firing cannons similar to using a match. From French *porte feu* 'carry fire.' A 1775 New Hampshire resident stated,
"My whole time has been taken up . . . making Cartridges, Cannisters and Port Fires for the field pieces."

porthen (*n.*) A portion. In 1773 Philip Fithian wrote,
"Securing the several porthens to the children."

portledge (*n.*) A variant of *portage-bill*. In 1673 a Boston court decided in favor of:
"the six seamen according to their Portlidge bills."

portmanteau (*n.*) A bag for carrying apparel on a journey, especially on horseback. In 1782 Lt. Col. Olney wrote,
"Permission granted . . . Capt. John Greene with his letter and portmanteau."

posh (*v.*) A variant of *pash* 'to mash.' An onomatopoeic word. A 17th-century cookbook directed,
"Take all ye pease & posh ym with a spoone."

posnet (*n.*) A little basin, porringer, skillet, or saucepan. From French *pocenet*, the diminutive of *pocon* 'pot.' In 1642 a Salem, Massachusetts, man bequeathed:
"unto my wife . . . a great brasse posnett and a chafing dish."

posse comitatus *Latin.* 'To avail of an attending multitude; all the citizens a sheriff can call on for help; a posse.' Lt. Gov. William Bull of Massachusetts in 1765 wrote to the Board of Trade,
"The civil magistery . . . supported by the posse comitatus."

possession house A building to support a claim to land in the New Hampshire grants. A 1772 New York document referred to:
"hutts hastily Built on small Spotts of Ground which they Term possession Houses."

posset (*n.*) Milk curdled with wine. An 18th-century cookbook told how:
"to make a custard posset."

post (*n.*) One who carries mail and, by extension, the mail itself. Mail was originally carried by soldiers from one military post to the next. Also used in combination with things or people connected with the post: *post day* 'the day mail arrives or leaves'; *post horn* 'a horn used by mail coachmen'; *post house* 'a post office'; *postman* 'a mail carrier'; *post road* 'a road on which the post was carried'; *post town* 'town with a post office.'

post chaise A closed four-wheeled carriage seating two or four, especially one hired from one stage (post) to another. A 1765 Boston newspaper offered:
"chariots, post chaises, phaetons."

post-fine (*n.*) A fine paid for the right to levy fines. The 1697 Cortlandt, New York, Manor grant wrote of:
"sums of money to be paid as a Post fine."

postillion (*n.*) One who rides the left horse and guides the first, or only, pair of horses drawing a coach. Also spelled *postilion*. A *postillion horse* is the near or left horse of a team. When the team is guided by a postillion there is no coachman. In 1774 Philip Fithian recorded,
"The postillion keeps a fox in the stable."

postliminium (*n.*) The right which restores rights to property after the property, which had been captured, is returned to the control of the government; postliminy. An anglicization of the Latin *jus post liminium* 'law after threshold.'

posture master One who practices artificial postures of the body; a contortionist. A 1752 New York newspaper announced,
"Richard Brickell, with the famous Posture-Master lately arrived here, has taken the Theatre in Nassau-Street."

pot halyard A rope for raising a pot. Used in the slang phrase *throw up pot halyards* 'to give up drinking.' A character in a 1776 play said,
"Throw up your commission, throw up the pot-halliards, you mean, old piss-to-windward."

potherb (*n.*) Any herb that is boiled in a pot, such as spinach. In 1630 Francis Higginson observed:
"Diuers excellent Pot-herbs grow abundantly among the Grass."

potoso (*n.*) A variant of French *peau de soie* 'paduasoy.' A 1662 inventory included
"one black silk potoso-a-samare, with lace." *See* **samare.**

pottage (*n.*) A broth, soup. A 1630 song went,
"Instead of pottage and puddings and custards and pies,/ Our pumpkins and parsnips are common supplies."

pottle (*n.*) Two quarts in either liquid or dry measure. In 1630 William Bradford wrote,
"Small things, by the quart, pottle, and peck."

pottofoo (*adj.*) An informal anglicization of French *pot au feu* 'pot on the fire.' It implied 'homey; something used about the house,' as in a 1685 clothing inventory that included:
"one black pottofoo petticoat."

pot valiant Brave only when stimulated by drink. In 1696 Gurdon Saltonstall wrote,
"Foolish if not pot-valiant firing and shooting off guns."

poulterer (*n.*) One who deals in poultry; which included not only domesticated fowl but also hares and game. In 1763 in New York,
"Hyam Myers at the Sign of the Poulterers in Broad Street, near the City Hall . . . intends to keep a poulterer's shop in the same manner as they are kept in London.''

pound (*n.*) An enclosure, erected by authority, for impounding stray cattle or swine. Hence, an *impounder* or *pounder* was employed by a town to do *poundage* in a *pound*.

powder (*v.*) To salt; to corn, as meat. In 1609 Capt. John Smith recorded that:
"one among the rest did kill his wife, powdered her, and had eaten part of her before it was known.''

powdering tub A tub in which a person infected with syphilis was treated by sweating. Named from its resemblance to a tub for powdering, or pickling in brine. In 1789 Gouverneur Morris described a man:
"as complete a skeleton as ever came out of the powdering tub.''

powwow (*n.*) An Indian medicine man. An adopted Narragansett word. In 1697 Cotton Mather wrote,
"The Indians employed their *sorcerers*, whom they call *powas*, like Balaam, to curse them.''

pray (*v.*) To ask with earnestness. In 1734 in Boston:
"The Application . . . Praying for Liberty to Entertain the Town . . . [was] disallow'd.''

praying Indian An Indian converted to Christianity. In 1682 Mary Rowlandson wrote,
"She was about ten years old, and taken from the door at first by a Praying Indian and afterwards sold for a gun.''

precept (*n.*) An order in writing from some authority to an officer to perform some act. The 1702 instructions to the Governor of Virginia included:
"Precepts and warrants are drawn upon the receiver-general.''

precinct (*n.*) **(1)** In the Carolinas, a political subdivision. The 1619 Constitution of Carolina ordered,
"Each county shall consist of eight signories, eight baronies, and four precincts; each precinct shall consist of six colonies.''
(2) In New England, the area covered by a clergyman. In 1708 in Braintree, Massachusetts,
"It was then voted that there should be two distinct precincts or societies, in this town.''

pre-eminence (*n.*) Superiority in rank, a granted privilege. In 1697 in New York Stephanus van Cortlandt was granted:
"priviledges, jurisdictions, prehemmenences, emoluments.''

pre-emption (*n.*) The right of purchasing before others. In 1779 in Kentucky:
"Michael Stoner . . . claimed a right to a settlement and preemption to a tract of land lying on Stoner's fork.''

premium (*n.*) A bounty. In 1734 Massachusetts:
"Voted, That for the further encouraging the raising of Hemp and Flax within this Province, the Premiums be doubled.'' In 1711 a Boston newspaper reported,
"On Monday last Lieut. Hilton brought here three Indian Scalps for which the Government paid him the premium.''

prerogative court A court for probating wills. In 1711 in Connecticut,

"Mary Wakeman, an orphan, has made application to this Assembly for liberty to appeal from an act or sentence of the prerogative court of Fairfield."

press (*v.*) To pay press money for or to. A variant of *prest.* In 1776 the Continental Congress:
"Resolved that the quarter masters in every department be ordered to avoid pressing horses and carriages as much as possible."

press money Money paid to army and navy recruits to induce them to serve and to bind them to the service agreement.

pretense (*n.*) A claim, either true or false. In 1710 William Byrd:
"read Mrs. W's pretense against me."

pretty (1) (*n.*) A well-crafted ornament. A 1736 Boston newspaper offered:
"Children's Silver Peaks & Flowers, Dutch Prettys."
(2) (*adj.*) Sly, crafty. In 1760 a character in a play described another,
"He's such a pretty fellow."

prevalence (*n.*) Influence; ability to prevail over. In 1760 John Rowe wondered,
"Who has any prevalence with my uncle?"

prick (*v.*) To tamp powder into a touch hole of a cannon. A 1775 Massachusetts document read,
"I order'd my men . . . to prick dry Powder into the Touchholes."

pricked (*adj.*) Acid or pungent to the taste. In 1701 there were on Capt. Kidd's boat:
"3 barrels of pricked cider."

primage (*n.*) A small duty paid to the master of a ship. A 1754 bill of lading read,
"Said goods notting with primage and average accustomed."

primer seisin Under feudal law, the right of the king to one year's profits of the land from the heir of a tenant. The 1641 Massachusetts Body of Liberties provided,
"All our lands and heritages shall be free from all . . . primer-seisins."

priming (*n.*) The tastiest part. In 1717 William Byrd wrote,
"The primings of a young doe . . . were slighted among these dainties."

princes stuff Princess stuff, an English dress material of goat's hair and silk. In a 1775 Boston newspaper we find,
"Nathan Spearhawk sells: Silk and worsted sagathees . . . Princes Stuff."

prising (*n.*) A misspelling of *prizing* 'pressing tobacco into a cask.' *See* **prize**[1]. The 1730 Virginia Tobacco Law made:
"reasonable allowance for prising."

privilege (*n.*) **(1)** The right of commonage, or to the use of common land.
(2) The land used in the exercise of the above right. A 1724 New York deed included,
"also a five pound privilege in the patent of Eastchester."
(3) A small duty paid to the master of a ship; primage. A 1754 letter offered,
"You are to have five slaves privilege, your chief mate two."

privity (*n.*) The knowledge of a private matter along with another person. A 1702 Virginia memorandum mentioned:
"subsequent privity and knowledge of the Council."

prize[1] (*v.*) To compress tobacco into a hogshead. Hugh Jones in 1724 described,
"[They] by Degrees *prize* or press it with proper Engines into great Hogsheads."

prize² (*v.*) To appraise. In 1760 Washington:
"got a promise of him to Prize and Inspect his tob[acc]o at the Warehouse."

prizer (*n.*) One that estimates the value of a thing, an appraiser. *See* **prize²**. A 1652 Massachusetts document stated,
"Hee left a smale house . . . which was vallued by the prissers of his said estate."

probation (*n.*) An examination. A 1643 description of Harvard students referred to:
"the probation of their growth in Learning."

process (*n.*) The means taken to compel a defendant to appear in court. A 1635 Massachusetts document stated,
"Mr Allerton shalbe sent for, by processe, to the nexte Court **of** Assistants."

procession (*n.*) A formal march. *See* **perambulation.** A 1662 Virginia statute required,
"The time for processioning lands hereafter [shall] be between the last day of 7ber [September] and the last day of March."

proclamation money The British equivalent value of the various foreign coins circulating in the colonies; established by a proclamation of Queen Anne on June 18, 1704. In 1720 Abraham De Peyster acknowledged receipt of money,
"On account of His Exc. Brigadier Robt. Harris being for a warrant for 37 pounds proclamation Money."

proctor (*n.*) A person employed to manage another's case in court. In 1773 Franklin alluded to:
"wrangling proctors and pettyfogging lawyers."

procul a bulmine A mistaking of Latin *procul a fulmine*. The whole expression was *Procul a Jove, procul a fulmine* 'Far from Jove is far from his thunder.' In 1631 Thomas Dudley wrote,
"Very unlike is it that now (being procul a bulmine) we should be so unlike ourselves." Being far from the throne has its compensation: one may escape the royal anger.

prodigy (*n.*) Something extraordinary, such as an eclipse or meteor. In 1751 Washington recorded,
"A prodigy in ye West appear'd towards ye suns setting abt 6 PM, remarkable for its extraordinary redness."

profane (*adj.*) **(1)** Secular. The 1726 *Ames' Almanac* referred to:
"the best of prophane history."
(2) Heathenish. William Bradford in 1630 referred to one as:
"being one of the profanest families among them."

professor (*n.*) One who makes public avowal of his religious beliefs and faith. In 1656 William Bradford wrote,
"Againe, when adultrie or sodomie is committed by professors or church members, I fear it comes too near ye sine of ye priests daughters."

profit (*n.*) A benefit. The 1668 royal patent to John Richbell entitled him to:
"all other profits, immunities and emoluments to the said parcel or tract."

prog (*n.*) Food obtained by begging or wandering about. Possibly from its sense of to poke about. Maj. John André, in his poem *The Cow Chase*, wrote,
"His horse that carried all his prog."

promiscuous (*adj.*) Undistinguished, common. In 1774 Philip Fithian:
"mixed with the Company in promiscuous conversation."

promote (*v.*) To act as an informer. A 1753 judge's commission included,
"The judge proceeded . . . on being promoted thereto by an informer."

prompt (*adj.*) Quick, bold. John Winthrop related,
"About the middle of this month a prompt young man, passing over the ice, fell in and was drowned."

pro patria A paper size, 8½" x 13½"; [from Latin 'for country']. The words appeared in the watermark in the paper on which Franklin wrote his *Autobiography*, first published in 1791. He said,
"It was a folio, pro patria size."

propound (*v.*) To offer for consideration. In 1638 in Massachusetts,
"Daniel Baxter propoundeth himselfe to be an Inhabitant."

proprietor (*n.*) The title of the owner of Pennsylvania. In the plural, the descendants of William Penn. In 1771 Franklin referred to the:
"True and Absolute Proprietaries of the Province of Pennsylvania."

propriety (*n.*) Ownership. In 1701 Cotton Mather advised,
"Never make any bargain with such as you suspect have no just propriety in what you go to purchase from them."

prorogue (*v.*) To recess the session of a legislative assembly. In Virginia in 1619,
"The Governor prorogued the said General Assembly to the first of March."

prospect glass A spyglass. In 1769 John Adams reported,
"You can see with a prospect-glass, every ship, sloop, schooner, and brigantine."

prothonotary (*n.*) A variant of *protonotary*, a clerk of a court. In 1776 John Adams reported,
"Mr. Francis Hopkinson . . . it seems is . . . a son of a prothonotary of this county."

protract (*v.*). To draw out with an instrument that measures angles. In 1719 the Massachusetts House of Representatives:
"Resolved, That the Land Protracted and Delineated in the said Plat, be Granted and confirmed."

proud (*adj.*) Of female animals, in heat. In 1768 Washington reported:
"a hound bitch . . . was proud."

provand (*n.*) Provender, provisions. An anonymous pirate in 1680 complained,
"Haveing our gunns Ammunition and knapsacks of provant to carry with us."

prove (*v.*) To verify. In a 1770 Virginia court,
"John McClure proved a certificate according to law."

proverbs (*n.*) A parlor game in which players try to guess proverbs. In 1715 William Byrd wrote,
"In the evening we played at little proverbs."

province (*n.*) A political unit of which the king appoints the governor; in contrast, in a colony the inhabitants elect the governor.

provost (*n.*) The superintendent of a jail. In 1780 Richard Varick told of one:
"detained in [the custody of] the provost."

prudentials (*n. pl.*) The discretionary concerns and economy of a town. The 1635 laws of Massachusetts provided:

"Their vote in the choice of selectmen for town affairs, assessment of rates, and other prudentials proper to the selectmen."

prunel (*n.*) A shortening of *prunella*, a member of the mint family. A corruption of *brunella*, a disease in which the mouth is covered with a brown crust, from medieval Latin *brunus* 'brown.' A brew from the leaves of this plant was gargled to check fungus of the mouth.

prunella (*n.*) A light-weight stuff for clergymen's gowns. From French *prunelle* 'sloe' in reference to its dark color. A 1783 Philadelphia newspaper offered:
"Prunellas and everlastings."

Prussian binding A coat binding with a twilled cotton back and a silk face, made in England. A 1775 Boston newspaper offered:
"Shalloons, 'Silver Prussian' bindings, children's Whimsey caps."

psalmody (*n.*) The singing of sacred songs. In 1737 Jonathan Edwards wrote,
"God was then served in our psalmody."

publisher (*n.*) The town crier. In 1695 Samuel Sewall lamented,
"Robt. Williams the Bell-Ringer, Publisher (crier) and Grave-digger died this morn."

puccoon (*n.*) An adopted Algonquian Indian word for 'bloodroot,' a plant that yields a red dye. In 1612 Capt. John Smith described:
"a woman fresh painted with pocones and oil."

pudder (*v.*) To poke, putter, or potter about. In 1647 Nathaniel Ward deplored those:
"as are least able are most busy to pudder in the rubbish."

pudding (*n.*) A protection for a child's head before he could properly walk. Resembling a *pudding* in its sense of a large sausage. A 1780 letter said,
"Mary is most wise with her child . . . She has little David in what she wore herself, a pudding and pinner."

puff (*n.*) An exaggerated statement; puffery. Of onomatopoeic origin. A 1776 song jeered,
"With puffs and flams and gasconade." Gov. Bernard of Massachusetts in 1768 wrote,
"Notwithstanding all the puff flung in the newspaper."

puffet (*n.*) A light cake. An anglicization of Dutch *puffertjies*. A 1776 New York inventory included:
"4 puffet pans."

puim (*n.*) An Indian game of chance. In 1634 William Wood recorded,
"The Indians . . . have two sorts of games, one called *Puim* the other *Hubbub*, not much unlike Cards and Dice, being no other than Lotterie."

puisne (*adj.*) Inferior in rank. In 1757 William Smith referred to:
"The puisne judges of the supreme court."

puke (*n.*) A medicine which causes vomiting; an emetic. Origin unknown. In 1780 Col. Israel Angell:
"took a puke."

pulicat (*n.*) A colored, cotton material for bandanas, from Pulicat, near Madras, India. In 1768 Philip M. Freneau wrote,
"Hum-hums are here . . . Bandanas, baftas, pullcats."

pull (*v.*) To pluck. A 17th-century cookbook directed,
"Take a fat capon & pull & draw it."

pull it To run. One version of *Yankee Doodle* went,
"She flew straight out of sight/ As fast as she could pull it."

pulse (*n.*) Edible seeds of certain plants, as peas, beans, etc. In 1737 John Brickell wrote,
"The Nanticoaks are another kind of Pulse."

pumpion (*n.*) A variant of *pompion* for pumpkin. In 1607 Capt. John Smith:
"daily feasted with good bread, Virginia Peas, pumpions and putchamins."

puncheon[1] (*n.*) A unit of liquid measure, generally 84 gallons, but could be 120.

puncheon[2] (*n.*) **(1)** A piece of timber placed upright. In 1722 William Byrd described:
"The fort . . . enclosed with substanial puncheons, or strong palisades about 10 feet high."
(2) A steel punch for stamping metals. In 1771 Franklin wrote that he:
"contrived a mould, made use of the letters we had as puncheons."

punk (*n.*) A prostitute. A character in a 1777 play said,
"Rolling along arm in arm with his punk."

pupton (*n.*) A variant of *pulpatoon*. A stew of rabbit and fowl similar to a pot pie. Mrs. Martha Bradley's *British Housewife* gives a recipe.

purchase (*n.*) Prey; plunder. In 1639 pirate Nathaniel Butler said that they went:
"to looke out for more purchase."

purgatory (*n.*) A narrow valley. Probably after St. Patrick's Purgatory in Ireland where, according to cave legend, Christ appeared to St. Patrick. In 1766 Manasseh Cutler:
"hunted in Purgatory . . . this afternoon."

Puritan (*n.*) A dissenter from the Church of England who professed to follow the *pure* word of God. They formed the bulk of the early New England population.

purpose (*v.*) To intend. In 1760 John Rowe wrote,
"I purpose a journey there very soon."

pursage (*n.*) A variant or misspelling of *parsonage*. John Winthrop referred to:
"Mr. Cotton's pursage and house."

push (*n.*) A trial, test. In 1774 John Harrower wrote,
"I put him to the push."

put along To put up, as for the night. A 1775 Massachusetts letter offered,
"If you cannot find a comfortable Retirement, I would have you put along here."

put out To protrude. A 1755 New Jersey newspaper announced,
"To be sold . . . A Plantation . . . about three Quarters of a Mile from a good Landing, that puts out of said River."

putrid fever Typhus. In 1774 Philip Fithian wrote,
"In this Town & in the neighboring Country rages at present a malignant, putrid Fever, & what is generally called the spotted Fever."

puttargo (*n.*) A variant of *botargo*, a kind of fish. In 1616 Capt. John Smith described:
"in abundance . . . puttargo."

pyd (*n.*) Probably an error in transcription for *pipe*. A document referred to:
"A pyd of wine" costing £16. Wine commonly came in pipes.

Pypowder, Court of An on-the-spot court to deal with infringements of rules at fairs. From French *pieds poudreaux* 'dusty feet.' A 1694 law for fairs in New York provided for:
"a Court of Pypowder."

pyrrhical (*adj.*) Describing a pyrrhic, an ancient Greek marital dance. In 1684 Increase Mather wrote,
"It is granted that pyrrhical or polemical saltation, i.e. when men vault in their armor to show their strength."

Q

quadrate (*v.*) To agree. Originally from Latin *quadrare* 'to square' In 1732 Jonathan Belcher wrote,
"I think nothing can be plainer than that it exactly quadrate with the charter."

quadrille (*n.*) A four-handed card game using forty cards; the remainder of the pack after tens, nines, and eights were removed. An adopted French word. Quadrille replaced ombre around 1725 as the popular card game; it was replaced by whist after 1755. In 1739 William Byrd:
"played piquet, quadrille and prayed."

qualify (*v.*) To ease. In 1775 Philip Fithian:
"Called for half a Gill of bitters to qualify my humours, & a dish of Tea to cheer me, & soon to Bed."

quarrel (*n.*) A square or diamond-shaped pane of glass. In 1685 Samuel Sewall deplored,
"The Window of Mother's Bed-Chamber next the Street hath many Quarrels broken."

quarry (1) (*n.*) A square or diamond-shaped pane of glass; a quarrel. In 1698 Gabriel Thomas said,
"The Glaziers . . . will have Five Pence a Quarry for their Glass."
(2) (*adj.*) Square, even. A 1730 song went,
"When two and two were met of old,/ Tho' they ne'er meant to marry./ They were in Cupid's book enroll'd/ And call'd a Party Quaree."

quartan (*adj.*) Occurring every fourth day. In 1748 Peter Kalm reported,
"No disease is more common here than that which the English call fever and ague, which is sometimes quotidian, tertian, or quartan."

quarter (1) (*n.*) A particular region of a town. In 1640 a New Haven, Connecticut, document referred to:
"every one of the 5 quarters whose proportion of meadow is under 8 acres."
(2) A cluster of slave cabins on a plantation; the slave quarter. In 1774 Philip Fithian wrote,
"Ben has gone to the quarter to see to the measuring of the crop of corn."
(3) Indulgence; mercy; treatment. In 1771 Franklin commented,

"But I give it fair quarter whenever I meet with it."
(4) (*v.*) In a military or naval sense, to send to stations and places for battle. In 1775 Franklin wrote of a man:
"who chose to stay upon deck and was quartered to a gun."

quarterage (*n.*) A quarterly allowance. In 1741 William Byrd wrote that a gambling lady:
"will venture her quarterage."

quarter cask A half-barrel; a quarter of a hogshead. In New Haven in 1683 it was recorded,
"One butt and one quarter cask of Malaga wine . . . was lately seized."

quarter day One of the four days marking a quarter of a year when quarterly payments fall due: March 25, Annunciation Day; June 24, Midsummer Day; September 29, Michaelmas; and December 25, Christmas. Before 1752, March 25 was the first day of the year. *See* **Gregorian Calendar.**

quartern (*n.*) A gill; a quarter of a pint. The word was used in a recipe for flip served at Abbott's Tavern at Holden, Massachusetts, in 1765.

queen's ware A, cream-colored china developed by Josiah Wedgwood in 1782 and named for Queen Charlotte (1744–1818), the wife of George III. It was fired at more than twice the heat of delft. A 1773 New York newspaper advertised
"blue and white Queen's ware."

quere (*v.*) A variant of Latin *quaere*, 'to ask'; preceded a question. In 1763 Washington wondered:
"Quere, has it [corn] time to make or Ripen"

quern (*n.*) A small, hand-turned grist mill. From Old English *cweorn*. In 1728 William Byrd wrote,
"He could make and set up quern stones very well."

questionist (*n.*) At Harvard College, a baccalaureate candidate during his final term; a word used in this sense at Cambridge University as early as 1574. Harvard records in 1654 have:
"The approved Questionists . . . after the usual examination . . . are made Bachelors at the beginning of Lent."

quick (*adj.*) Aware of the movement of a fetus. In 1709 William Byrd wrote,
"Mrs — taught me to reckon 20 weeks from the time a woman is quick when she will seldom fail to be brought to bed."

quickhatch (*n.*) A wolverine. An anglicization of Cree *kikkwahakes* 'hard to hit.' In 1743 Mark Catesby wrote,
"The Quickhatch . . . inhabits the very Northern Parts of *America*."

quick match A wick by which cannons were fired. *See* **match.** In 1776 Gen. Charles Lee wrote,
"Stores wanted to make up the Complement for the Cannon sent to Quebeck: Quick Match."

quickset (*n.*) A fence of live trees or bushes, especially of hawthorn. The 1642 instructions to the Governor of Virginia included,
"Fence either pales or quickset and dikes."

quicksilver (*n.*) Mercury. Taken internally, it promoted secretions, particularly saliva, and counteracted rheumatism. A deadly poison, it had other serious effects, too— over a period of time it made the teeth fall out. Its principal use was as a cure for

syphilis; it was absorbed through the skin. In 1731 Franklin observed,
"An imprudent use of quicksilver is the cure of the itch."

quick stock Livestock. A 1677 Long Island, New York, will stated,
"I Thomas Diament . . . bequeath unto my sonn . . . a double Share of ye Quick Stock wch I shall Leave behind me."

quick work The submerged planking of a ship. A 1773 letter to Delaware pilots used the phrase facetiously to imply that a man was fat,
"He has a good deal of quick work about him."

quiddany (*n.*) Quince marmalade. A 17th-century cookbook stated,
"You can make Quidony out of all kind of weak [soft] fruit."

quill (*n.*) In a medicinal sense, a curl of cinnamon bark. In 1782 in a Hartford, Connectcut, newspaper, Beardsley's & Hopkins offered:
"Quill, Jesuits Bark, Opium."

quilt (*n.*) A quilted petticoat. In 1775 Philip Fithian wrote,
"She [Priscilla Hale] is dresst in a white Holland Gown, cotton Diaper quilt very fine, a lawn apron."

quintal (*n.*) A hundredweight, 112 pounds, used for measuring fish. In 1759 John Rowe offered,
"I will send you two quintals of the Best Fish."

quitrent (*n.*) A rent, usually nominal, paid by a tenant to his overlord, which quit him from all other services. In New York, after the Revolution, the state assumed the position of the Crown until quitrents were abolished in 1823.

quotidian (*adj.*) Daily. *See also* **quartan**.

R

race (*n.*) A root of ginger, not pulverized. A 17th-century cookbook referred to:
"a race of ginger."

rack[1] (*n.*) **(1)** Short for *arrack*. In 1715 William Byrd:
"had rack punch."

rack[2] (*n.*) **(1)** A grate on which bacon is laid. In 1633 a Connecticut document read,
"An Inventory . . . 3 spitts, a jack, racks."
(2) A wooden frame for hay for horses or cattle. A 1652 Long Island deed noted,
"In the stable are Rack & manger."
(3) A fish trap. A 1735 Pennsylvania document stated,
"Racks are much greater Obstruction to Navigation than Wears."

rack[3] (*n.*) A horse's gait, either the pace or the singlefoot. A 1734 New Jersey newspaper advertised,
"Stolen . . . a black Horse . . . goes pretty fast on a rack."

racket (*n.*) A snowshoe, from its resemblance to a tennis racket. In 1704 a New Haven, Connecticut, document reported,
"They have upwards of 30 pr. of Snow Shoes and Racketts already."

radeau (*n.*) A sailing scow, variously rigged. From a French word meaning 'raft.' Cannon were mounted on them.

ragstone (*n.*) A rough silicious stone used for sharpening coarse tools. *Rag*, without the appended *stone*, means a 'hard stone.' A 1707 Boston newspaper advertised:
"Grindstones & Ragstones."

rail (*n.*) A daytime dress or cloak; later, a nightgown. In 1639 the Massachusetts General Court prohibited the wearing of:
"immoderate great sleeves, slashed apparell, immoderate great rayles, and long wings."

rally (*v.*) To treat with slight contempt. Gouverneur Morris in 1789 said,
"They rallied the friend for being so taken in."

rampant (*adj.*) Overleaping restraint. In 1727 William Byrd wrote, "bear meat: not a very proper diet for saints because 'tis apt to make them a little too rampant.''

random (*n.*) Short for *random line*, the base line of a survey. A 1745 New Jersey document said,
"You may then come back to the place where your random cutt Delaware."

range (1) (*n.*) A row of anything. In 1681 a Connecticut man bequeathed,
"On halfe of my great Lott in the westermost Rang of Lotts." A 1728 Boston newspaper reported,
"The Sealers of wood . . . are hereby Directed not to Seal any Rang of wood not Corded as aforesaid."
(2) (*v.*) An area patrolled by a ranger. *See* **ranger**.
(3) To rove over. In 1711 William Byrd recorded,
"A man came to be excused from ranging because his wife was sick."

ranger (*n.*) **(1)** A sworn officer of the crown to whom were granted rights such as the control of hunting. In a manor grant the lord was generally granted these rights. The 1697 grant for Cortlandt Manor, New York, appointed:
"van Cortlandt . . . to be our Sole and only Ranger."
(2) A man, usually mounted, hired to range an area. *See* **range**.
(3) In 1711 William Byrd wrote,
"Concerning the rangers in the upper county, he told me nobody would accept of that place because the pay was too little."
(3) A mounted soldier who gathered information and made hit-and-run raids. The best known, during the Revolution, were the Queen's Rangers under the command of Col. Robert Rogers.

ranis (*n.*) Frogs. A variant form from Latin *ranae* 'frogs.' They were dried, powdered, and combined with mercury for certain medicinal plasters.

rank (*adj.*) Luxuriant. From Old English *ranc* 'strong, proud.' In 1769 Washington commented,
"Wheat much better . . . being rank, better spread over the ground."

ransomer (*n.*) A hostage for a ship captured in wartime. In 1764 John Rowe wrote of one who was in:
"detention as a ransomer for the ship Prince George."

Ranter (*n.*) An Antinomian. The term originally applied to Antinomians. In 1656 Connecticut legislated,
"No Towne within this Jurisdiction shall entertain any Quakers, Ranters, Adamites, or such like notorious heretiques."

rape (*n.*) Turnip. In 1634 William Wood reported,
"This land likewise affoards Hempe and Flax . . . with Rapes if they bee well managed."

rappee (*n.*) A coarse kind of snuff, originally made by rasping a leaf of tobacco. In 1780 Baron von Steuben wrote,
"Send me 3 containers of good Maccuba tobacco or 3 pounds of good Rappe tobacco."

raree show A peep show carried in a box. In imitation of the foreign way of pronouncing *rare show*. In 1771 Franklin wrote,
"I produc'd a handful of silver, and spread it before them, which was a kind of raree-show, they had not been us'd to, paper being the money of Boston."

rareripe (1) (*n.*)   A kind of peach that ripens early. A 1722 Boston newspaper reported,

"Having in his Garden a plentiful Crop of Rare Ripes, he agreed with an Ethiopian Market Man."

(2) (*adj.*) Early ripe. A variant of *ratheripe*, 'ripening early,' from Middle English *rathe* 'quick.' In 1799 Washington wrote,

"All that part . . . is to be planted with rare-ripe corn."

rate[1] (*n.*) A local tax. In 1730 Samuel Sewall wrote,

"I gave you a Ten shilling Rate for your Minister."

rate[2] (*v.*) To chide, to berate. In 1703 Cotton Mather said,

"He would rate off Satan."

rater (*n.*) A tax collector. In Dorchester, Massachusetts, in 1633 it was decided:

"The Raters shall be Mr. Woolcott, Mr. Johnson."

ratoon (*n.*) A sprout from the root of sugar cane which has been cut. A 1779 Pennsylvania document reported,

"I then took each rattoon apart, and found it fastened to a joint of these last ones."

ratteen (*n.*) A thick, woolen stuff, twilled or quilted. A 1780 Connecticut newspaper advertised,

"Durants, Tamies, Ratteens."

rattinet (*n.*) A thinner, lighter ratteen used for lining clothes and curtains. A 1789 Connecticut newspaper advertised,

"Black Rattinet, Black Gimp, Black Lustrings."

rattle (*n.*) The croup. In 1744 Joshua Hempstead recorded,

"A Child . . . died of the Rattles or Throat Destemper."

rattlesnake root Any one of many plants used to treat epilepsy, gout, pleurisy, and, above all, rattlesnake bite. In 1682 Thomas Ash wrote,

"They have three sorts of the Rattle-Snake Root which I have seen."

ravensduck (*n.*) A fine quality, cotton sailcloth or a heavy, plain-weave fabric made in Russia. From German *Rabendtuch* 'raven cloth.' In 1765 in Boston Benjamin Faneuil, Jr., advertised,

"Ravens Duck, Ticklinberg, Oznabrigs."

real (*n.*) A small, Spanish, silver coin. The piece of eight.

realize (*v.*) To experience. In 1776 Abigail Adams wrote,

"To-night we shall realize a more terrible scene still."

recede (*v.*) To cede back; to return something to its former owner. In 1771 Frederick Chase thought,

"The lands on the west side [of the] Connecticut river might be receded back to New Hampshire."

receiver (*n.*) A sort of tobacco inspector. A 1793 Maryland document said,

"Tobacco did not undergo a public inspection as now—men skilled in that article were employed by the merchants (and who were called receivers) to view, weigh and give receipts to the planters."

recognizance (*n.*) A recorded obligation to perform some act: if it was not done, a sum was forfieted; for example, a posted surety bond. In 1767 South Carolina said the:

"Attorney General . . . may be empowered to prosecute on all recognizances given for the observance of the provincial laws."

reckon hook A variant of *rackan*, a hook for vessels in a fireplace. A 1649 Massachusetts accounting said,
"Estate of John Jarrat . . . Reckon hooks & some small things."

Recollect (*n.*) A Franciscan, for his recollection in God. In his surrender terms to the British at Montreal in 1775, Gen. Richard Montgomery said,
"The Continental troops shall take possession of the Recollect gate."

recorder (*n.*) A judge with criminal jurisdiction. The title is still used in London. In 1705 a Boston newspaper reported,
"Capt. John Tudor is appointed Recorder of the City of New York."

recruit (1) (*n.*) A new supply of anything that is wasted. In 1722 Samuel Sewall wrote,
"At last it fell to pieces and no recruit was made."
(2) (*v.*) To regain health. After being beaten up in 1769 in Philadelphia, tax collector William Shepherd said,
"When I had recruited a little I waited upon Mr. Williams."

recta in curia *Latin.* 'good standing in court.' The 1767 South Carolina *Remonstrance* said,
"All persons . . . are now admitted to give evidence, according to the mode of their profession, and stand recta in curia."

rectify (*v.*) To refine by repeated distillation. A 1721 Boston newspaper speculated,
"Whether rectified Spirit of Wine may be drank, when there is no Rum or other Dram to be had."

recusant (*n.*) A Roman Catholic who refuses to acknowledge the Church of England. In 1741 in New York there was passed:
"An Act for preventing Dangers which may happen from Popish Recusants."

redan (*n.*) A small fortification of two parapets pointing toward the enemy and open at the rear. An adopted French word. In 1776 Jared Sparks wrote,
"It was my intention . . . to throw up a great number of large fleches or redans."

redeem (*v.*) Regarding time, to use more diligence in the use of it. In 1643 at Harvard it was required of students:
"that they studiously redeem the time."

redemptioner (*n.*) One whose services are sold to a ship's captain in exchange for passage to America. He redeemed his passage by work. In 1786 Washington recorded,
"Received from on board the Brig *Ann*, from Ireland, two Servant men . . . redemptioners for 3 years service by indenture."

red money The paper money Maryland issued in 1781 and had four concentric red borders. A 1781 document stated,
"It is Projected to Give our Red Money a Value by making it a Tender in all Payments."

redoubt (*n.*) A small, completely enclosed fortification. A 1776 New York letter proposed to:
"make a chain of Ridouts from the North to the East River across the Heights of Harlem."

reduce (*v.*) To bring to a former state; in this case, to make them civilians. A 1763 proclamation proposed,
"We do hereby . . . empower . . . governors to grant . . . to such reduced officers as have served in North America . . . quantities of land."

reduct (*v.*) To deduct; subtract. In 1775 Capt. Burchmore agreed that the ship's owners would:
"supply my wife with 12 guineas which I will reduct from my wages."

reduction (*n.*) In algebra, placing all known quantities on one side of an equation, the
unknowns on the other. In 1754 Samuel Johnson, the first president, advertised
before it opened that the requirements for applicants to the College of New York
(which opened as King's College and is now Columbia) included:
"That they be well versed in the first 5 rules in arithmetic, i.e., as far as division
and reduction."

refiner (*n.*) One who refines metal. A 1776 Philadelphia newspaper advertised the sale
of:
"sundry negroes, viz. one a hammerman, one a refiner."

refractory (*adj.*) Obstinate; unmanageable. The 1745 rules at Yale College deplored:
"disobedient, or contumacious or refractory carriage toward his superiors."

refugee (*n.*) One who flees. The word first applied to a Huguenot (who fled persecu-
tion in France) and later to a Loyalist (who fled to the protection of British forces).
Some Loyalists became soldiers: Col. James DeLancey commanded the well-known
Refugee Corps. The word also applied to Canadians who came to help the rebels.

refuse (*adj.*) **(1)** As applied to slaves, worthless. A 1756 New York document
accounted for:
"Sale of 3 refuse slaves."
(2) As applied to fish, refused or rejected. In 1674 John Josselyn wrote,
"When they share their fish . . . they separate the best from the worst . . . the
second sort they call refuse fish, that is such as salt burnt, spotted, rotten, and care-
lessly ordered."

regale (*n.*) **(1)** A source of gratification. Washington described:
"a featherbed with clean sheets which was a very agreable regale."
(2) A refreshing drink. A 1768 song went,
"When in your own cellar you've quaffed a regale."

regaling (*adj.*) Refreshing; gratifying. Washington referred to:
"fine and regaling weather."

regeneracy (*n.*) The condition or state of being reborn. In 1630 John Winthrop
referred to:
"the law of gospel in the estate of regeneracy."

reglement (*n.*) A regulation. An adopted French word. In 1664 when the British took
Nieuw Amsterdam from the Dutch they adopted the previous:
"writings and records which concern the reglement of the church or poor."

regrating (*n.*) The act of buying and selling at a higher price at the same market or
fair. In a 1752 appointment of Justices of the Peace, Mayor Edward Holland listed
crimes including,
"Riots, Routs, Oppressions, Extensions, Forestallings, Regratings, Trespass."

regulator (*n.*) **(1)** A surveyor. In 1721 Philadelphia enacted,
"No person . . . lay the foundation for any building, before they have applied
themselves to the surveyors or regulators."
(2) One of a movement, from 1767 to 1771 in North Carolina, consisting of vigilan-
tes who banded together to regulate or control the area. The government, centered
on the seacoast, provided no protection from marauders inland.

remainder (*n.*) The ultimate disposition of an estate in fee simple. A 1737 New York deed included,

"And the revertion & revertions, remainder and remainders, rents, issues & profitts."

remarkable (*adj.*) Worthy of notice. In 1711 William Byrd:

"read some law and wrote the most remarkable part of it in a book." In 1771 Franklin:

"therefore filled all the little spaces that occur between the remarkable days in the calendar with proverbial sentences."

rem istam acu tangere *Latin.* To hit the nail on the head. In 1678 Charles Wolley wrote,

"Whether Adam or Eve sewed their fig leaves together with needle and thread is not my business to be so nice as *rem istam acu tangere*."

renate (*n.*) One born again. In 1662 Michael Wigglesworth said,

"Both the renate and the reprobate are made to die no more."

render (*v.*) To surrender. In 1636 John Winthrop hoped,

"he would render himself to one of the magistrates."

repair (*v.*) To go back to. The 1776 Virginia convention referred to:

"those who do not immediately repair to his standard."

reparation (*n.*) Repair. In 1642 the Governor of Virginia was instructed:

"that the said fort be well kept in reparation."

repine (*v.*) To be discontented; to complain. In 1730 William Bradford reported,

"The young men that were most fit for labor and service did repine that they should spend their time . . . without any recompense."

replication (*n.*) The plaintiff's answer to the defendant's reply to the plaintiff's plea. The 1765 Stamp Act referred to:

"plea, replication, rejoinder, demurrer."

reprize (*v.*) To repack tobacco more tightly. *See* **prize**[1]. A 1758 letter to Washinton reported,

"3 h[ogs]h[ea]d . . . was to[o] light & I Carried Tobco. from muddy hole and reprized. & maid one heavier."

reprobate (1) (*v.*) To reject. In 1775 the Continental Congress lamented British actions:

"which they know to be particularly reprobated by the very constitution of that kingdom."

(2) (*adj.*) Abandoned in sin. In a 1638 description of Harvard College we find,

"God may give them up to strong delusions, and, in the end, to a reprobate mind."

reserve (*n.*) A person or place kept for future use. In 1665, in Connecticut it is recorded:

"Mr. Matthew Allyn [was chosen] a reserue." In 1700 in Maryland mention is made of:

"Oliver's Reserve."

reserve, upon the Cautious in personal behavior. In 1744 Dr. Alexander Hamilton wrote,

"A trader from Jamaica . . . seized me for half an hour, but I was upon the reserve."

resolve (*n.*) A resolution. In 1778 Alexander Hamilton wrote,
"A late resolve directs George Washington to fix the number of men."

respectable (*adj.*) Convenient, appropriate. In 1773 J. Wentworth referred to:
"a place & spot most respectable to the college [Dartmouth]." Possibly a nonce use.

respite (1) (*n.*) Suspension of execution of a sentence.
(2) (*v.*) To suspend the requirement of payment temoporarily. In 1639 John Winthrop wrote,
"He should pay but £100, & the other should be respited to the further consideration of the next General Court."

Restitutionist (*n.*) One of a religious sect which believed in the "restitution of all things," putting the world in a holy and happy state.

return book A book in which official accounts of a military unit to a division commander are kept. In 1798 Gen. William Heath recalled,
"Gen. Lee asked to see the return-book of the division."

reversion (*n.*) The interest in property which may revert to the grantor if certain conditions are not complied with or upon expiration of a lesser estate created by the grantor. A 1737 New York deed included,
"and the revertion & revertions, remainder and remainders, rents, Issues & profitts."

Rhinegrave breeches A man's garment named after the Rhinegrave of Salm. They were kiltlike, or with divided skirts, and ornamented with ruffles, lace, and ribbons. A small apron of ribbon loops concealed the front closure.

rial (*n.*) A coin. Depending on where and when, an English gold coin first issued in 1465 or the Spanish *real*, the piece of eight.

ride (*v.*) To manage insolently. In 1767 back-country South Carolinians complained,
"This province being harder rode at present by lawyers than Spain or Italy by priests."

ridered (*adj.*) Having riders, or horizontal pieces of wood, to hold rails in place in a worm fence. In 1760 Washington lamented,
"Good part of my new Fencing that was not ridered was leveled."

ride rusty To be stubborn, obstinate. A variant of *resty*, which is in turn a variant of French *restif*, 'stubborn or obstinate.' In 1773 a letter to the Delaware pilots threatened,
"For so sure as he rides rusty, we shall heave him keel out."

riding (*n.*) An administrative district in the Province of New York from 1664 to 1683. Adopted from the three ridings in Yorkshire, England, Long Island was in the East Riding, Westchester County in the North. From Middle English *triding* 'third part.'

riding hood A cloak with a hood for women when they rode. Any color, including red. In a 1717 Boston newspaper a runaway was described as wearing a:
"red Camblet Ryding Hood faced with blue."

riding place A ford. A 1679 Connecticut document said,
"We went to the river . . . to the old rideing place."

rifle frock A rifleman's long shirt. A description of the aftermath of the Battle of Brooklyn in 1776 said,

"Rifle guns and rifle frocks will be as cheap in their camp tomorrow, as cods heads in New Foundland."

rift Split. The past participle of *rive*. A 1742 New York deed excepted:
"rift timber."

riggite (*n.*) A satirist. In 1771 Franklin described a man:
"esteemed to be a pretty good riggite, that is a jocular verbal satirist."

right (*n.*) A legal title to land. In 1710 William Byrd who was then Receiver General of the royal revenues in Virginia wrote,
"A man came from New Kent for rights . . . but had not money enough."

right, treasury The Colony of Virginia in 1699 granted the right to 50 acres to anyone who paid five shillings.

Rigid (*n.*) A member of an inflexible religious sect formed by Robert Browne (1550–1633), the founder of Congregationalism. In 1748 William Douglass wrote,
"The Rigids generally seceded from the more moderate, and removed with their Teachers or Ministers without the Limits . . . of the Colony."

rigolet (*n.*) A rivulet. In 1775 Bernard Romans commented,
"On this river they are not in such plenty at the freshes as below at the *rigolets*."

ring (*v.*) To fit a ring in a swine's snout. Mamaroneck, New York, town law required the howard [swineherd] if he found:
"any hog running at large in the town without being rung, to ring the same forthwith."

Riot Act A 1715 law of George I. It provided that if twelve or more people were gathered to disturb the peace, any justice of the peace, sheriff, or mayor could, after reading a specified portion of the act, order them to disperse. If, after one hour they did not, they were guilty of a felony. In Connecticut the law applied to as few as three. In 1769 in Philadelphia William Shepherd wrote:
"The collector . . . and a number of constables . . . the mob being so numerous. They ordered the constables off the wharf, though I think they tarried there long enough to read the Riot Act." *To read the riot act* 'to scold' did not come into usage until the late 1800s.

rising (*n.*) The act of closing a session of a legislative body (when it stops sitting). A 1700 Philadelphia document stated,
"After the rising of this assembly, he determines to send the laws for England."

River Brethren A Baptist sect in Pennsylvania which baptized only in rivers.

rix dollar A German silver coin. A *reichsthaler*, 'dollar of the realm.' The royal proclamation of 1704 regarding foreign currencies listed:
"Old rix-dollars of the empire—4s 6d."

roached (*adj.*) Curved upward. Origin obscure. A 1776 Boston newspaper advertised:
"Strayed or stolen, a sorrel horse—roach'd back, 3 white feet."

roach mane A horse's mane cut short so that it stands up. A 1781 Savannah newspaper advertised,
"A Black Horse, about 13 and an half hands high, half roach main."

road (*n.*) An anchorage. In 1697 Samuel Sewall reported,
"Johnson's ship was burnt in Charlestown Rode."

roanoke (*n.*) White shells used as money. An adopted Virginian Indian word. A 1634

letter from Maryland referred to:
"a large string of wampum or roanoke."

rochet[1] (*n.*) A woman's three- or four-cornered mantle.

rochet[2] (*n.*) A fish, the roach. In 1633 Andrew White reported,"
"Of the fishes, those that follow have already come to notice: sturgeons . . . rocket fish."

rock (*n.*) A distaff. The 1642 Massachusetts School Law provided that:
"children . . . be set to some other employment . . . as spinning upon the rock, knitting, weaving tape, etc."

rockahominy (*n.*) Hominy. An adopted Algonquian word. In 1705 Robert Beverley wrote,
"Each man takes with him a Pint or Quart of Rockahominie, that is, the finest Indian Corn parched, and beaten to a Powder."

roger (*v.*) To engage in sexual intercourse with. The noun is slang for 'penis.' From Roger, a name frequently given to a bull. In 1710 William Byrd:
"rose at eight o'clock having first rogered my wife."

Rogerene (*n.*) One of a Baptist sect in Connecticut which followed the teaching of John Rogers (1648–1721). In 1754 Joshua Hempstead recorded,
"A Co[m]pany of Rogerens . . . held their meeting after our meeting was over."

rogue (*n.*) A pirate ship. In 1689 Samuel Sewall wrote,
"Two Rogues to windward of us, which the Man of War keeps off but can't come up with them."

rolling house A tobacco warehouse. Hogsheads of tobacco were rolled in and out of it. In 1711 William Byrd:
"went to the Capitol where we read a bill concerning rolling houses."

romal (*n.*) A variant of *rumal*, silk cloth made in Bombay, India; also, a handkerchief made from it. From Urdu *ru mal* 'face wiping.' In 1699 Captain Kidd was quoted,
"The Narrator delivered a Chest of Goods, viz. Muslins, Latches, Romals and flowered Silke unto Mr. Gard[i]ner."

rood (*n.*) A unit of square measure, forty square rods; one quarter acre. The 1693 grant to Vredrick Vlypsen in New York included,
"six acres, three roods and eight perches."

room (*n.*) Place, stead. In 1744 a New York law appointed three men as highway commissioners:
"in the Room and Stead of" three others.

root (*n.*) A plant whose root is eaten, such as beets or carrots. A 17th-century cookbook instructed,
"Put ye pigeons in a pipkin with roottes."

rope dancing Tightrope walking. In 1734 in Boston,
"The Application . . . Praying for Liberty to Entertain the Town with the Diversion of Rope Dancing . . . [was] disallow'd."

ropewalk (*n.*) A shed in which twine was twisted into rope. Some were more than 1000 feet long. In 1723 a Boston newspaper reported,
"A Man and Woman [were] scuffling together in a jesting manner, at a Rope Walk at the South End."

roquelaure (*n.*) A tailored man's cloak with a vent in the back, worn while horseback

riding. *A Treatise on the Modes*, 1715 said,
"A short abridgement or compendium of a coat which is dedicated to the Duke of
Roquelaure."

rorismarin (*n.*) Rosemary. An alteration of Latin *ros marinus* literally 'sea dew.'

rosa solis (*n.*) A liquor flavored with sundew. Adopted from Latin 'rose of the sun.'
In 1637 Thomas Morton drank a toast and:
"confirmed that promise with health in good rosa solis."

rose (*n.*) The leaves and petals of the red rose are slightly astringent and were prescribed in the treatment of external ulcers.

rosemary (*n.*) A fragrant shrub. A brew of the tops of this plant stimulated the nervous system without affecting blood circulation.

rotten (*adj.*) Of ground, soft, unsound. In 1760 Washington complained that:
"the ground was vastly rotten."

round (*adj.*) In round numbers. A 1754 letter to Capt. David Lindsay instructed,
"In regard to the sale of your slaves, and if they will fetch £26 sterling per head,
round, you may dispose of them there."

Roundheads (*n.*) The Puritans, because they cropped their hair, so called by the Cava-
liers (who wore long ringlets). The 1649 Maryland Toleration Act banned,
"Roundhead, Separatist, or any other name or term in a reproachful manner relating to matter of religion."

roundlet (*n.*) A small, flat, round stone. In 1708 Ebenezer Cook wrote,
"the roundlet up he threw."

round robin A written petition, memorial, remonstrance, or other document signed
by writing names in a circle to conceal who signed first, that is, who the ringleader
was. The phrase appears in the disposition of Henry Bolton regarding William Kidd
in 1701.

round top A round platform at the head of a lower mast. John Winthrop wrote,
"In a passion, the deputy told the Governor that if he was so round he would be a
round top."

rout (*n.*) A clamorous party. In 1772 Anna Winslow:
"went directly from it to Miss Caty's rout."

rowen (*n.*) (1) The second seasonal growth of grass; aftermath.
(2) The stubble left of the first growth. In 1743 a resident of Holyoke:
"began to mow Rowens."

row galley A shallow-draft gunboat propelled by oars, used for harbor defenses. In
1776 Congress enacted,
"The General be authorized to direct the building of as many . . . row gallies . . .
as may be necessary."

royal (*n.*) (1) Another spelling of the Spanish *real*. A 1741 bill of sale referred to:
"eight royals of plate."
(2) A small mortar. In 1775 Gen. Richard Montgomery was:
"pleased to hear the 9 pounder and royals are arrived at your post."

Royal Train of Artillery The Fourth Battalion of The Royal Artillery Regiment. In
1766 John Rowe recorded,
"A transport ship bound from Halifax to Quebec has 70 people on board belonging to The Royal Train of Artillery."

royalty (*n.*) A right granted by a sovereign, used chiefly regarding mineral rights. The 1693 Cortlandt, New York, Manor grant included,
"Emoluments, Royaltys, profits."

rub (*v.*) **(1)** To excite, awaken. In 1710 William Byrd:
"could not forbear rubbing up the memory of them."
(2) To pass with difficulty. In 1771 Franklin wrote,
"We had together consumed all my pistoles, and now just rubbed on from hand to mouth."

rubstone (*n.*) A whetstone. In 1687 Samuel Sewall ordered,
"Send me for my own proper accountt . . . six doz of rub stones."

rudis indigestaque moles *Latin.* 'rough, disordered mass.' In 1763 John Adams quoted Ovid regarding the Caucus Club of Boston,
"Ruddock, Adams, Cooper, and a *rudis indigestaque moles* of others are members."

rue (*n.*) This herb, *ruta graveolens*, was taken as a powerful stimulant and as a gentle laxative. In 1679 Charles Wolley wrote,
"Every Country family understood the vertue of Rue . . . as a preservative against infectious Diseases."

rug (*n.*) A covering for a bed. Floor coverings were carpets. In 1685 a Connecticut will bequeathed,
"to my Cousen Martha Henderson . . . the rug that is on Cousen Steel's bed."

rum (*adj.*) Excellent. A 1698 song appealed to:
"Fortune biters,/ Hags, Rum-fighters,/ Nymphs of the woods."

run (*n.*) **(1)** A pair of millstones. In 1801 the sons of James Mott built a mill between New Rochelle and Larchmont, New York, with 12 runs of stones.
(2) A yarn measure. 1644 yards, almost a mile. A 1734 Connecticut law said,
"There shall also be paid . . . for every yard that is made of yarn that is eight runs to the pound, two shillings per yard."

runagate (*n.*) A vagabond. In 1619 the Virginia General Assembly concerned itself with anyone:
"found to live as an idler or runagate."

rundlet (*n.*) A small barrel of from three to twenty gallons. In 1636 John Winthrop mentioned,
"a rundlet of honey."

rung (*adj.*) A shortening of *running*. In 1773 Washington,
"touched upon the Drag of the rung-fox."

runtee (*n.*) A perforated shell disc ornament. A corruption of French *arrondi* 'rounded.' In 1705 Robert Beverley wrote of:
"wampum, runtees, beads and other such finery."

russel (*n.*) A twilled, woolen clothing fabric. Possibly from *Rijssel*, the Flemish name for 'Lille.' A 1774 Philadelphia newspaper offered:
"rattinets, shalloons, russells, bird-eye stuffs."

Russia duck A fine, imported, bleached linen used for summer clothing. A 1775 Boston newspaper advertised:
"children's Whimsey caps; Russia duck."

rut (*n.*) A misreading of *rot* 'decayed wood.' William Byrd's secret diaries were written in shorthand that had no vowels. A 1710 entry was transcribed as:
"caused all the rut to be cut away that lay at the wood pile."

S

Sabbatarian (*n.*) A Seventh Day Baptist who observed Saturday, the seventh day, as the sabbath. A 1725 Boston newspaper reported,
"Eight of the sect called Sabbatarians that committed the Murder of Capt. Symonds . . . were then executed."

Sabbati, Die *Latin.* Saturday, the 'sabbath day.'

sach. (*n.*) An abbreviation of Latin *saccharum* 'sugar,' used in prescriptions.

sack (*n.*) A sweet white wine from the Canary Islands. From French *sec* 'dry.' In 1608 Capt. John Smith wrote,
"The sack, *aqua vitae*, and other preservatives for our health."

sactia (*n.*) Probably a misreading of *saic* 'a ship similar to a ketch.' In 1755 the Georgia General Assembly levied a tax on:
"every snow, brig, polacre or sactia."

saffron (*n.*) A species of crocus, prescribed for coughs, asthma, and to control menstrual discharge.

sagamite (*n.*) A corn soup. An adaptation of an Algonquian word. In 1698 Louis Hennepin noted:
"a potful of Sagamite or Pottage of Indian Corn."

sagathy (*n.*) A kind of serge. In 1774 a Philadelphia newspaper advertised:
"bird-eye stuffs, cambletees, sagathies, masquerades."

sainfoin (*n.*) A plant cultivated for forage. An adopted French word from Latin *sanun foenum* 'wholesome hay.' In 1765 Washington:
"sowed four rows of St. foin."

saint (*n.*) **(1)** An early New England Puritan, a sardonic use. A 1736 letter stated,
"With Respect to Rum, the Saints of New England I fear will find out some trick to evade your Act of Parliament."
(2) One known for virtue. In 1727 William Byrd observed that:
"bear meat: not a very proper diet for saints because 'tis apt to make them a little too rampant."

St. Andrew's cross A plant with petals that look like St. Andrew's cross, a saltier, or "X". *Culpeper's Compleat Herbal* around 1650 said,
"Two drams of the seed in honeyed water purges choleric humours and helps the sciatica." In 1710 William Byrd took:
"a strong decoction of St. Andrew's cross."

St. Anthony's fire Ergotism. It was thought that ergotism could be cured by calling on St. Anthony. The Order of St. Anthony was founded in the 11th century to care for sufferers all over Europe. An 18th-century document in Virginia stated,
"My father was very unwell last night. High fever and I believe St. Anthony's fire."

St. Anthony's meal No meal at all. To dine with St. Anthony is to do without dinner. Around A.D. 305 St. Anthony founded a monastery, and sometimes he ate only once in three or four days. In 1728 William Byrd explained,
"While the commissioners fared sumptuously here, the poor chaplain and two surveyors . . . made a St. Anthony's meal, that is, they supped upon the pickings of what stuck in their teeth ever since breakfast."

St. Crispin, patronage of An apprenticeship as a shoemaker. St. Crispin, the patron saint of shoemakers, was a shoemaker in Gaul and was martyred around A.D. 287. In 1786 Josiah Flagg, Benjamin Franklin's grandson, confided to his grandmother that he had:
"spun out three years under the patronage of St. Crispin."

St. George's cross A Greek cross, like the symbol of the Red Cross. In 1744 Dr. Alexander Hamilton described a street intersection as being:
"in the shape of St. George's Cross."

St. John's wort This plant produced an oil, resembling turpentine, which was used to clean ulcers.

saker (*n.*) A small piece of artillery. From French *sacre* 'falcon'; another piece of ordnance named for a bird. In 1642 a Connecticut document said,
"[He] doth promise to lend the Country two peeces of Ordnance, Sakers or Minions."

sal (*n.*) *Latin.* 'salt.'

salient (*adj.*) Pointing outward, as:
"a strong redoubt with salient angles."

salivate (*v.*) To dose with mercury to cause an unusual secretion of saliva. In 1709 William Byrd regarding Jack's rheumatism:
"resolved not to have him salivated."

sallet (*n.*) A variant of *salad*. In 1634 a letter described Maryland:
"It abounds with vines & sallet herbs."

salmagundi (*n.*) A mixture of chopped meat and pickled herring with oil, vinegar, pepper, and onions. Adapted from a French word. A recipe for it appears in an 18th-century cookbook.

salon (*n.*) A misspelling of *saler*, 'salt cellar.' A 1776 New York inventory included:
"2 pewter salons."

salt (*n.*) Potash. A 1776 Boston newspaper announced,
"Cash given for wood-ash salts."

saltation (*n.*) An act of leaping; jumping. In 1684 Increase Mather referred to:
"spectators or actors in such saltations."

salter (*n.*) One who applies or sells salt.

salus populi *Latin.* 'welfare of the people.' In 1659 the Massachusetts General Court announced,
"These persons . . . become felons de se, . . . and the sovereign law salus populi been preserved."

salute (1) (*n.*) A blow. In 1710 William Byrd wrote,
"Prue with a candle by daylight . . . I gave her a salute with my foot."
(2) (*v.*) To address with kind wishes or courtesy. In 1720 Samuel Sewall went courting,
"I saluted her."
(3) To kiss. Sarah Knight wrote in her 1704 *Journal*,
"John . . . fumbled out his black junk, and saluted that."

salvatory bottle A pharmacist's container for ointment.

salve tu quoque *Latin.* 'hail to you, too.' In 1679 Charles Wolley wrote,
"The amaze [surprise] soon went [wore] off with a *salve tu quoque*, and a Bottle of Wine."

samare (*n.*) A variant of *cymar* a 'woman's garment.' Although more often found in this form, in different times and places it had many spellings and shapes. It could be tight- or loose-fitting, long or short, an under- or outergarment. A 1662 New York clothing inventory included:
"one black tartanel samare with tucker."

samp (*n.*) Crushed corn, boiled and eaten with milk. From Narragansett *nasaump*, same meaning. In 1643 Roger Williams wrote,
"From this the English call their Samp."

Sandemanian (*n.*) A follower of Robert Sandeman (1718–1771). A 1773 Massachusetts newspaper reported,
"The fire likewise was communicated to the Sandemanian Meeting House."

sanders (*n.*) A red sandalwood for coloring. A 17th-century cookbook instructed,
"Culler it with sanders or blood."

sannup (*n.*) An Indian husband. An adopted Abnaki word. In 1682 Mary Rowlandson wrote,
"A Squaw . . . spoke to me to make a shirt for her Sannup."

sap (*n.*) In military use, the process of undermining in attacking a fortification; digging beneath to place a mine. This work, and the construction of fortifications, was done by *sappers*.

sapodilla (*n.*) A fruit of the *Sapota achras* which also produces chicle, In 1751 Washington wrote,
"After Dinner was the greatest Collection of Fruits I have yet seen on the table was Granadello the Sappadilla Pomgranate."

sarcenet (*n.*) A gauzy silk twill. Also, *sarsenet*. A 1774 Philadelphia newspaper advertised,
"black peelongs, sarsanet, romalls."

sarsaparilla (*n.*) The smilax, a brew of the dried root of which promoted perspiration in the treatment of syphilis.

sass (*n.*) A variant of *sauce*, 'vegetables.' In 1775 in Massachusetts,
"Steven Barker come down and brought us som sas."

saturn (*n.*) Lead, its name in alchemy.

Saturnii, Die *Latin.* 'Saturday.' Referring to the Roman deity *Saturn*.

satyr (*n.*) A satire. *Poor Richard's Almanac*:
"Strange! that a man who has wit enough to write a Satyr, should have folly enough to publish it."

sauce (*n.*) Vegetables. In 1705 Robert Beverley wrote,
"Roots, Herbs, Vine-fruits, and Salate-Flowers . . . dish up . . . and find them very delicious Sauce to their Meats."

sault (*n.*) A waterfall. Pronounced *soo*. In 1600 Richard Hakluyt recorded,
"The Captaine prepared two boats to goe vp the great River to discover the passage of the three Saults or falles."

save (*v.*) To be in time for. In 1715 William Byrd:
"got there by one oclock and saved our dinner and I ate some young turkey."

save-all (*n.*) A pan on a candlestick to save candle ends. In 1684 Increase Mather wrote,
"He put out his lamp but in the morning found that the save-all of it was taken away."

savin (*n.*) The red cedar. In 1774 Philip Fithian:
"walked to see the Negroes make a fence. They drive into the ground chestnut stakes & then twist in boughs of savin."

savoy (*n.*) Short for *savoy cabbage*, named for Savoie, a region of France. In 1709 John Lawson wrote that there were:
"Coleworts plain and curl'd, Savoys" in Carolina.

Savoy Confession of Faith This statement of faith was declared in 1658 by the Congregational Church at the Savoy Palace in London and adopted by the Boston Synod in 1680. In 1700 Samuel Sewall wrote that:
"The Savoy Confession of Faith . . . has been lately printed here."

saw (*n.*) A saying, a proverb. In 1744 Dr. Alexander Hamilton referred to:
"old saws and Jack Pudding speeches."

sawyer (*n.*) One who saws timbers. It was one of the trades listed as needed in the Virginia colony in 1610.

say (*n.*) A kind of serge for linings or aprons. The Woollen Act of 1699 covered "says."

Saybrook Platform A platform of church conduct formulated in 1708 by the Connecticut Congregational Church at Saybrook.

scalade (*n.*) The scaling of a palisade by ladders. In 1722 William Byrd described:
"a strong palisade . . . and leaning a little outward to make a scalade more difficult."

scamo. (*n.*) An abbreviation of *scammony*. The gummy resin from the root of this herb was taken as a strong laxative.

scantling (*n.*) Sawn timber for house rails or studs. In 1781 in a New Jersey newspaper someone:
"wanted materials for errecting house: pine & oak scantling."

scarlet-in-grain (*n.*) A colored cloth, fast dyed, the red color being into the grain of the cloth. In 1757 William Smith wrote that five sachems wore:
"instead of a blanket a scarlet-in-grain cloth mantle."

Scarlet Whore The Catholic Church, after the woman St. John saw in a dream, believed to represent Rome and hence the Roman Church. In 1689 "A. B." wrote of:
"bigotry inspired unto them by the great Scarlet Whore."

schepel (*n.*) A Dutch measure, three-quarters of a bushel. In 1658 a Long Island, New York, document mentioned as a tithe
"one hundred schepells of wheate."

schepen (*n.*) An alderman in a Dutch city. In 1664 it was recorded,
"Jacob Kipp and Jaques Cosseau, are also Chosen to the Office of Schepens in this City of New Yorke."

schooner (*n.*) A two-masted, gaff-rigged ship originally developed around 1713 at Gloucester, Massachusetts. As a warship it carried from four to ten guns. In 1765 Washington wrote,
"My Carpenters had in all worked 82 days on my schooner."

schout (*n.*) The Nieuw Amsterdam official equivalent of sheriff. A Dutch word.

scoke (*n.*) The pokeweed. From Massachuset, *miskok* 'that which is red.' In 1778 Jonathan Carver wrote,
"Garget or Skoke is a large kind of weed."

sconce[1] (*n.*) A bulwark. From Dutch *schans* 'a small fortification.' In 1647 Nathaniel Ward wrote,
"to build a sconce against the walls of Heaven."

sconce[2] (*n.*) The skull or head. In 1772 Jonathan Trumbull wrote,
"Met fierce encount'ring every sconce, each void receptacle for brains."

scorbutic (*adj.*) Pertaining to scurvy. Robert Beverley's 1705 description of Virginia stated,
"Disorders grow into a cachexie on which the bodies overrun with obstinate scorbutic humours."

scorch (*v.*) A variant of *score* to 'cut.' A 17th-century cookbook directed,
"You scorch it to let out the gravie."

scot and lot A parish tax. A redundancy, as both words mean 'tax.' A 1683 New York petition requested that anyone who did not:
"keep fire and candle and pay Scott and Lott should lose his freedom."

scotch cloth A cheap imitation of lawn, from Scotland. In 1708 Ebenezer Cook referred to:
"shirts and drawers of Scotch Cloth."

scotch collops Veal or beef pieces sauteed and served with a sauce. *To scotch* is 'to score, to cut with shallow incisions,' hence scotch collops are scored, not Scottish. In 1739 William Byrd:
"ate Scotch collops."

scotch snuff A finely ground snuff. *Scotch* means to 'crush,' therefore this means crushed rather than Scottish. A 1733 Charleston, South Carolina, newspaper advertised:
"cut Tobacco, Scotch Snuff, and Pigtail."

scoterkin (*n.*) A false birth fabled to be produced by Dutch women from sitting over their fires. Thomas D'Urfey used the word in 1698 in *Mr. Lane's Magot*,
"Ye Jacobites As sharp as Pins,/ Ye Monsieurs and ye Scoterkins,/ I'll teach you all to dance." Maybe he meant *scatterling* 'wastrel.'

Scotts Pills *See* **Anderson's Pills.** In 1739 William Byrd complained,
"My head was much out of order for which I took two Scott's Pills."

scourge (*v.*) To whip severely. In 1776 Gen. William Smallwood related,
"We have twice stripped from these poltroons several of our soldiers coats and had them severely scourged."

scouring (*n.*) A cleansing with a drastic cathartic. In 1727 William Byrd told of a companion who:
"fed so intemperately upon bear that it gave him a scouring, and that was followed by the piles."

scouring rod A ramrod, used for scouring the musket bore. A 1740 inventory of gunner's stores included:
"2 Iron Schouranrod for the small arms."

scrag-tail whale A fin whale. In 1701 Charles Wolley wrote,
"A Scrag-tail is like another, only some what less, and his bone is not good, for it will not split."

screw (*v.*) To extort. This usage derives from the pressure exerted by thumb screws. In 1732 William Smith wrote about New York and:
"the excessive sums of money screwed from masters of vessels trading here."

screwed (*adj.*) Compressed. In 1789 Gen. William Heath told that:
"bundles of screwed hay were used in the work."

screw plate A thread-cutting die. In 1635 William Bradford referred to:
"screw plates to make screw pins."

scrivener (*n.*) A writer, one who drew contracts and other writings; a professional scribe. In 1771 Franklin wrote,
"The two first were clerks to an eminent scivener or conveyancer."

scruple (*v.*) To doubt; to question. In 1774 John Jay wrote,
"Pious and sober men through the land scrupled the mode of swearing on the book."

scrupulous (*adv.*) Doubtful, cautious. In 1756 Thomas Lloyd assured,
"You need not be Scrupulous on my former Follies for I am sensibly Fam'd."

scrutoire (*n.*) A writing desk. A shortened form of French *escritoire*, same meaning. In 1686 Samuel Sewall admitted,
"Have mislaid the Key of my Scritore and can't come at the papers."

scurvy grass The spoonwort which grows on rocks near the sea. It was taken to prevent scurvy. In 1630 John Winthrop wrote to his wife that he took with him:
"a gallon of scurvey grass to drink."

sea guard A coast guard. Regarding the reform of the customs service in 1763 it was said,
"The advantages of a sea guard . . . are sufficiently obvious."

sealer (*n.*) An officer who examines weights and measures and sets a stamp on such is a *sealer of weights and measures*; one who inspects leather and stamps such as good is a *sealer of leather*. In 1766 in Braintree, Massachusetts, it was recorded:

"Then the following officers were chosen by nomination, viz . . . Sealers of Leather."

seaming lace Lace to cover a seam. In 1684 an inventory included:
"A sheet with seaming Lace."

sea poose A passage from a bay to a millpond for water for a tidemill. Probably an adaptation of *purse* which gathers, as a *purse net.* In 1653 in Southampton, New York,
"Mr. Rayner & John White are appointed & left to agree (if they can) with the miller concerneing the alteration of his mill to ease the towne of the burthen of opening the sepoose."

search[1] (*n.*) A variant of *searce* 'sieve.' From Latin *saetaceus* [*pannus*] 'cloth made of bristles.' A 1647 Massachusetts inventory included:
"A search & a boxe."

search[2] (*v.*) To examine. In 1642 in Watertown, Massachusetts, two men:
"are appointed by the Towne to search & seal leather."

searcher (*n.*) **(1)** An inspector, as a *leather searcher, fish searcher,* etc. A Southampton, New York, document in 1689 recorded,
"Manassah Kempton Chosen sealer and searcher of leather."
(2) A customs officer who searches for dutiable goods or contraband. In 1661 in Portsmouth, New Hampshire, it was noted:
"Mr. Hinory Percey and Francis Braiton are Chosen Searchers for prohibited wine and strong water."

searse (*n.*) A variant of *searce* 'sieve.' A 17th-century doctor in Virginia listed:
"one box of medicines and 2 searses."

seat (1) (*n.*) A mansion, a dwelling. In 1704 Sarah Knight wrote of Mamaroneck, New York,
"Here were good buildings. Especially one, a very fine seat, wch they told me was Col. He[a]thcoats."
(2) (*v.*) To settle on as an inhibitant. To plant with inhabitants. A 1697 description of Virginia said,
"Everyone that takes out a patent . . . is . . . obliged to do two things. One is to seat or plant upon it within three years." And,
"Seating . . . is reckoned the building of a house and keeping a stock for one whole year." *Seated land* is settled land; a *seater* is one who seats.

second day Monday, among Quakers. In 1705 Samuel Sewall:
"referr'd them to second-day Morning Decr. lo to meet at the Secretary's office."

second degree A Master of Arts degree. A 1704 Boston newspaper reported that:
"Mr. Thomas Weld . . . took his Second Degree at Cambridge on the 5th Instant."

second table *See* **first table.**

secret (*n.*) A privy. A 1787 Baltimore newspaper offered:
"To be rented, a three story Brick House . . . with a large Smoke House & Secret, a large yard."

secrete (*v.*) To keep secret. In 1773 Franklin wrote,
"Encourage and reward these leasing men, secrete their lying accusations."

sectary (*n.*) One of a sect. In 1654 Edward Johnson wrote,
"All sorts of sectaries . . . should be tolerated."

sedan (*n.*) A portable chair or covered vehicle for one person, borne on poles by two men. In 1715 Samuel Sewall recorded,
"The Govr . . . was carried from Mr. Dudley's to the Town House in Cous[in] Dummer's Sedan."

seeker (*n.*) One of a sect that professed no determinate religion; many became Friends. In 1654 Edward Johnson commented,
"Familists, Seekers, Antinomians, and Anabaptists . . . are so ill armed that they think it best sleeping in a whole skin."

see the lions To go sightseeing. A *lion* is a 'fashionable thing or person.' In 1715 William Byrd wrote,
"When we got ashore saw the lions and drank a bottle of claret."

segar (*n.*) A variant of *cigar*. Cigars were popular in the West Indies and South America, but virtually unknown in the colonies, although a 1754 inventory of a ship included,
"1 Bag of Segars."

seize (*v.*) To take possession of. In 1710 William Byrd stated,
"My uncle Byrd came to speculate about seizing his things to secure himself in case the hour should come."

seizin (*n.*) The legal act of taking possession. In 1776 Sir William Blackstone commented,
"Immediately upon the death of a vassal the superior was intitled to enter and take seisen or possession of the land."

self hunt Of a dog, to hunt without being directed. Washington in 1768 wrote,
"The hounds havg. started a Fox in self huntg., we followed."

senna (*n.*) A shortening of *cassia senna*, a brew of the dried leaves of which was a strong laxative.

sennight (*n.*) A week, seven nights and days. Originally Old English *seofon nihta*. In 1629 John Winthrop wrote his wife that:
"the rest of our fleet will not be ready this sennight."

sensible (*adj.*) Aware. In 1756 Thomas Lloyd wrote,
"They'l lye in Ambush and Fire on us before we are sensible."

sensibly (*adv.*) (1) Strongly. In 1792 William Eddis wrote,
"Let not my sudden appearance affect your mind too sensibly."
(2) With intelligence or good common sense. In 1756 Thomas Lloyd assured,
"You need not be Scrupulous on my former Follies for I am sensibly Famed."

septennial (*adj.*) Lasting seven years. In 1776 Samuel MacClintock wrote,
"Would it prevent the abuse of that power by which the British Parliament made themselves septennial." In 1716 the Septennial Act provided that a Parliament might not last more than seven years.

seroon (*n.*) A bale of something wrapped in an animal hide. In 1745 the inventory of a ship included:
"669 Seroons Cocoa."

serpent (*n.*) A firework that squiggles along the ground. In 1701 Boston enacted,
"Nor shall any person hereafter fire or throw any . . . Rocket or Serpent, or other fireworks in any of the streets."

servant (*n.*) Generally, an indentured servant. *See* **indent**. In the south, a slave. In

1643 Virginia enacted,
"If any such runaway servants or hired freemen shall produce a certificate."

service (*n.*) **(1)** A fee. Because his doctor was a friend, William Byrd could not pay him directly, so in 1711 he gave a fee to his servant,
"I gave my service to Suky."
(2) Anything of interest. In 1709 William Byrd:
"asked the Governor if he had any service at Westover."

serving (*n.*) A serving man. In 1748 Peter Kalm wrote,
"This kind of servants the English call servings."

servitor (*n.*) A servant, an attendant, especially a table waiter. In 1753 Washington:
"hired four others as servitors."

set (*v.*) To put, as to set a person in prison. In 1764 John Rowe recorded that he:
"Saw John & Ann Richardson set in the gallows for cruelly & willfully starving their child."

set about Disposed to do. In 1768 Washington hired:
"Jonathan Palmer to come and work with my carpenters; either at their trade—Coopering—or, in short at anything that he may be set about."

set down (*v.*) To put on the ground. In 1717 William Byrd:
"went with Brig. Sutton and set him down and then went."

sett (*v.*) A variant of *set*, to 'lease.' In 1721 Philip Livingston and five Mayors of Albany:
"have demised sett and to farm Lett & by these presents do demise sett and to farm lett."

settable (*adj.*) Plantable; tillable; able to have seed set in it. In 1656 William Bradford instructed,
"They should only lay out settable or tillable land."

setting pole A pole for pushing a boat, often iron tipped. A 1645 Connecticut inventory included:
"2 owers, 2 setting poles."

settle[1] (*n.*) A high-backed bench with arms. In 1744 Franklin commented,
"They have no Comfort, 'till either Screens or Settles are provided."

settle[2] (*v.*) **(1)** To compose, to tidy up. In 1711 William Byrd wrote,
"In the afternoon I settled my library again."
(2) To establish. In 1734 William Smith wrote,
"Gov. Hunter recommended the settling a revenue." Also, in 1675 in Plymouth a document read,
"A case . . . will be defered to one of the Cettled Courts."
(3) To ordain. The South Carolinians in 1767 petitioned:
"that none but such settled pastors be allowed to teach."

set work Piece work; units done one at a time. In 1720 Samuel Sewall:
"bid him leave off working at his Trade of Set-Work Coopering."

Seven-day (*adj.*) Describing those who observe the sabbath on the seventh day, Saturday. A 1680 Connecticut document stated,
"There are 4 or 5 Seven-day men in our Colony."

Seventh-Day Baptist One of a religious sect organized in Rhode Island in 1671. A 1703 Pennsylvania letter referred to:
"One William Davis, a Seventh-Day Baptist."

sewant (*n.*) Indian shell money. Periwinkle beads the diameter of a straw, ⅓ of an inch long. From Narragansett *siwan* 'unstrung shell beads.' In 1650, six white beads or three black beads were worth one stiver, about two cents in today's money.

shaddock (*n.*) A large, spherical or pear-shaped citrus fruit; the pomelo. Named for a Capt. Shaddock who in 1696 brought seeds to Barbados from the East Indies where it was known as a 'pompelmoose.' In 1720 Samuel Sewall wrote,
"Mr. Cooper sends my wife a Present of Oranges and a Shattuck."

shade (*n.*) A woman's lace scarf. A 1738 Boston newspaper announced,
"Just imported . . . worsted Shades, Masks."

shag (*n.*) A kind of cloth with a long, coarse nap. A 1654 Massachusetts inventory included:
"one shagg wescoat & 3 cloath wescoats, 10s."

shagreen (*n.*) A leather made from fish skin. A 1754 Charleston newspaper advertised,
"John Paul Grimke Jeweller has just imported . . . tweeser cases, shagreen boxes."

shalloon (*n.*) A woolen stuff from Chalons, France, used mainly for linings. A 1775 Boston newspaper advertised:
"Persians, Missinets, Peniascoes, Shalloons."

shallop (*n.*) A small, two-masted vessel, usually schooner-rigged. From French *chaloupe* 'ship's boat.' A 1707 Boston newspaper reported,
"The Shallops give account of such a Ship seen this week."

share (*n.*) Short for *plowshare*. A 1664 Massachusetts inventory included:
"a shar & colter."

shaving mill A privateer. Derivation unknown. A 1781 Boston newspaper reported,
"A small boat, one of the noted Shaving-Mills, which continually infest our bay, was captured."

shay (*n.*) A chaise. A two-wheeled, one-horse, removable canvas-topped vehicle for two passengers. When the top was down it was a one-horse, open shay. In 1717 Samuel Sewall gossiped,
"The Governour went through Charlestown . . . carrying Madam Paul Dudley in his shay."

sheep walk A sheep pasture. The 1767 South Carolina backwoods petition referred to:
"the laying out of vineyards, sheepwalks."

sheldrake (*n.*) A canvasback duck. In 1710 William Byrd:
"ate some sheldrake for dinner."

shell (*adj.*) With a shell pattern. In 1774 Philip Fithian wrote,
"She [Betsy Lee] is drest in a neat shell Calico Gown."

shells (*n.*) Ground mussel shells were used medicinally, externally as a drying agent, and internally for promoting perspiration during fevers.

shepherdee (*n.*) A short, woman's garment. A 1756 poem, *The Petition* addressed to a painter, implored,
"Put her on a negligee,/ A short sack, or shepherdee."

shepherd holland A checked or plaid linen cloth. In 1693 Samuel Sewall ordered:
"One p[iec]e Shephard holland or course Bag-Holland."

sherbet (*n.*) A drink, usually water and lemon juice. In 1729 Franklin reported,
"Things served . . . a little Sweet-meat, a Dish of Sherbet."

shift (1) (*n.*) An effort. In 1711 William Byrd reported,
"We made a shift to agree the freight at £8 a ton."
(2) Expedients. In 1705 Robert Beverley recorded,
"But the single men were put to their shifts."
(3) A child's garment; a man's short undergarment; a woman's long undergarment. A 1707 Boston newspaper reported,
"Had on . . . a white Shift, as also a blue one with her."
(4) (*v.*) To change clothes. In 1717 William Byrd recorded,
"When I came home I shifted myself and drank some malmsey."

shifting (*n.*) Underclothing. A 1724 Rhode Island document told a story with a happy ending:
"Nathaniel Bundy . . . took ye widow Mary Palmister . . . in ye highway, with no other clothing but shifting, or smock . . . and was joined together in that honorable estate of matrimony."

shin wood The ground hemlock. In 1778 Jonathan Carver complained,
"Shin Wood proves very troublesome to the traveller, by striking against his shins."

ship of the line A battleship large enough to serve in the line of battle.

ship stuff Low-grade flour. In 1771 Washington:
"Sold all the flour I have left . . . ship stuff at 8/4 pr. Cwt [hundredweight]."

shire (*n.*) A county. In 1634 Virginia was divided into eight shires, to be governed like the shires in England. In 1648 they were called counties, as they are today in England.

shirtman (*n.*) A Virginia militiaman, because he wore a hunting shirt. A 1775 Philadelphia newspaper reported,
"The damn'd shirtmen, as they are emphatically called by some of his [the loyal governor's] minions."

shock pate A head covered by a shock, or thick bushy mass of hair. In 1771 Franklin wrote,
"A drunken Dutchman, who was a passenger too, fell overboard; when he was sinking, I reached through the water to his shock pate, and drew him up."

shoepac (*n.*) A moccasin. A redundancy, *shoe* plus Lenape *pacu* 'shoe.' In 1755 it was suggested to Washington,
"It would be a good thing to have Shoe-packs or Moccosons for the Scouts."

shook (*n.*) Enough staves for one cask, tied together. From the past participle of *shake*, to 'separate the staves of a cask.'

shop note A due bill, good for merchandise. A 1770 Maryland letter said,
"The following will Answer the Shop note you wrote for."

shop sugar Sugar from a shop, not homemade. In 1687 Samuel Sewall ordered,
"If the mony hold outt send a barrel or two of shopp sugar and 3 or 4 sugar loves."

shoreman (*n.*) A man involved with fishing, but who remained ashore, as a ship owner or a fish drier. A 1710 Massachusetts document stated,
"What fish was not utterly spoiled . . . was Carryed ashore & dryed by shoremen."

shorts (*n. pl.*) The bran and the coarse parts of meal. A 1742 Maryland letter directed,
"I desire you will send the Bran Shorts & Middleings."

short day A day in the near future. In 1740 Philip Dumaresq:
"prays . . . Court . . . that a Short Day may be assigned."

shortling (*n.*) A term used in grading wool. Shorts or shortlings were normally thrown away, yet they are included in the Woollen Act of 1699,
"no wool, wool-flocks, shortlings, mortlings."

shrub (*n.*) A liquor of sugared fruit juice. From Arabic *shurb* a 'drink.' A bill for liquor served at a 1738 New York election included,
"To a barill for Wine & Shrub £7 9s."

signalize (*v.*) To distinguish. A 1782 orderly book stated,
"The Colonel is persuaded that the officers wish to signalize themselves in every part of their duty."

signify (*v.*) To be of consequence; to matter. In 1771 Franklin related an occasion of some young men on the river and when one refused to do his share of the rowing, one of the others said,
"Let us row; what signifies it?"

sign manual The king's signature. The Revenue Act of 1767 starts,
"His Majesty . . . empowered . . . by any warrant . . . under his . . . royal sign manual."

signory (*n.*) A political division of a county in Pennsylvania and South Carolina. *See* **barony.**

silesia (*n.*) A species of cloth originally from Silesia, a province of Prussia. A 1741 Charleston, South Carolina, newspaper offered:
"Just imported . . . Silesias, Buckrams."

silk grass Any of three grasses whose fibers are strong and usable. In 1705 Robert Beverley wrote,
"Silk grass . . . whose fibers are as fine as flax and stronger than hemp."

silveret (*n.*) A silk-wool or silk-cotton fabric. A 1754 Charleston, South Carolina, newspaper offered:
"mantuas and other silks . . . silverets."

simnel (*n.*) A variant of *cymling*, a kind of squash. In 1675 Benjamin Thompson rhymed,
"When simnels were accounted noble blood/ Among the tribes of common herbage food."

sink (1) (*n.*) A privy; a drain for filthy water. Also used metaphorically:
"Nor would this Province be the sink as now it is of the refuse of other colonies."
(2) (*v.*) To diminish by payment. The Currency Act of 1764 included,
"Beyond the time fixed for the calling in, sinking, and discharging of such paper bills."

sippet (*n.*) A small sop, something dipped in milk or broth. A 17th-century cookbook advised,"
"See that the mutton broth have white toast sippets in it."

Sir (*n.*) The title given to a Bachelor of Arts. In 1763 Harvard:
"Voted . . . That Sir [Stephen] Sewall, B. A. (son of Samuel) be the Instructor in the Hebrew and other learned languages for three years."

Sir Reverence (*n.*) Human feces. From a facetious use of *save [your] reverence*, an apology. In 1740 William Byrd wrote,

"She [Prudencia] gets out of bed and plants her foot in the midst of a wholesome Sir Reverence."

Sir Richard A nickname for rum. The 1741 journal of the *Revenge* recorded,
"Sir Richard Gott fowl of some of Our hands." *John Barleycorn* was the personification of grain liquor.

Six Nations The confederation of Iroquois Indians plus the Tuscaroras. On September 26, 1726 Gov. William Burnet of New York wrote to the Lords of Trade that he met in Albany with:
"two Sachims of each of the Six Nations, named the Maquase, Oneydes, Tuscaroras, Onnondages, Cayouges & Sinnekes [Mohawks, Oneidas, Tuscaroras, Onondagas, Cayugas, and Senecas]."

skeel (*n.*) A variant of *keeler* a 'small, shallow wooden tub.'

skep (*n.*) A beehive made of straw. A 1658 Long Island, New York, document included:
"An Inventorie 2 pare of cards; 4 bee skeps."

skillet (*n.*) A vessel with a long handle. A 1644 Salem, Massachusetts, inventory included:
"One little skellett & one fryinge pann."

skilts (*n.*) A type of brown, tow trowsers. In 1845 antiquarian Sylvester Judd wrote,
"They wore checked shirts and a sort of brown tow trowsers known as skilts. These were short, reaching just below the knee, and very large, being a full half yard broad at the bottom."

skinner (*n.*) An outlaw with Rebel sympathies who skinned his victims of clothing in the Neutral Ground, Westchester County, New York, during the Revolution. In an interview in 1849 John Yerkes told John MacDonald,
"John Paine and Joseph Paine were from New England, both Skinners. John was hanged at North Salem for stealing a Continental officer's horse."

skipjack (*n.*) An upstart. A character in a 1776 play said,
"Many . . . skipjacks . . . fell that day."

skipple (*n.*) An anglicization of the Dutch measure *schepel*. In 1679 Charles Wolley wrote,
"Long Island wheat three shillings a Skipple."

skirret (*n.*) A water parsnip. From *skire wit* 'clear wit,' for its supposed medical properties. In 1737 John Brickell wrote,
"The Garden Roots that thrive here [North Carolina] are Parsnips, Carrots, Skirrets."

skirt (*n.*) The border, edge. In 1768 Washington recorded:
"people clearing the skirt of woods within ye fence."

slam (*n.*) The forerunner of whist. William Byrd played it. The word survives in the game of bridge for taking all, or all but one, of the tricks.

slang (*n.*) A strip. In 1658 a Providence, Rhode Island, document said,
"This meddow haueing a narrow slang goeth from it to the aforsaide Riuer."

slash (*n.*) A marsh. In 1799 Washington referred to,
"the slash by the Barn."

slashed apparel A garment with slits to show a different colored fabric underneath.

In 1639 the Massachusetts General Court prohibited the wearing of:
"slashed apparel."

sleeves (*n. pl.*) In the 17th century, sleeves were frequently separate and tied on with points to the doublet or jerkin, etc.

sley (*n.*) A weaver's reed. A 1648 Massachusetts will bequeathed:
"three slayes . . . three [spinning] wheels."

slice (*n.*) A baker's peel, or spatula. A 1641 Massachusetts inventory included:
"one spitt and slice."

slide groat An early form of shuffleboard. A groat was an English coin. May be the same as *shove ha'penny*.

slider (*n.*) A skid or runner. Franklin, in a 1757 letter to Dr. Fothergill, made a proposal for keeping streets clean:
"The scavengers be provided with bodies of carts, not plac'd high upon wheels, but low upon sliders."

slight (*v.*) To demolish. In 1732 William Smith wrote,
"Those who have any property in any houses in the fort . . . shall slight the fortifications there."

slipe (*n.*) A slip, a slice. In 1763 Washington referred to:
"a set of People which Inhabit a small slipe of Land.

slip shoe A felt slipper worn indoors. *Slip shoed* was 'slipshod.' In 1719 Samuel Sewall admitted,
"Going out to call the Fisherman in Slip-shoes, I fell flat upon the pavement."

slip-slops (*n.*) Liquid food. A character in a 1776 play:
"despised your slip-slops and tea."

slitting mill A mill where iron bars were slit into rods for making nails. In 1750,
"The colonists were forbidden to erect any more slitting mills."

slive (*n.*) A misspelling of *sleeve*. In 1774 John Harrower bought:
"a pair of silver slive buttons."

sloop of war A single-decked, one-masted warship with almost any rig and fewer than two dozen guns. In 1781 a New Jersey newspaper reported,
"two sloops-of-war, two tenders and one galley, all British."

slop basin A bowl for tea and coffee lees. In 1731 The Court for Reformation of Manners wrote of:
"A Set of China . . . such as Cups, Saucers, Slop-Bason, etc. proper for a modish Tea-Table."

slope (*n.*) A sloping cut in an animal's ear as a mark of ownership. In 1751 in Portsmouth, Rhode Island, it was recorded,
"The Ear mark is two Slopes one on each Ear."

slop seller Slops were loose, baggy trousers worn by sailors. By extension, *slop sellers* were those who sold any supplies to seamen; later it applied to the sellers of any cheap clothing. In 1681 William Penn wrote on the importance of navigation,
"This is followed by other depending trades, as slop sellers."

slur (*v.*) To conceal. In 1744 Dr. Alexander Hamilton:
"slurded a laugh with nose blowing as people sometimes do a fart with coughing."

slush (*n.*) Waste grease. In a 1776 play appeared:
"a handsome coat of slush and hog's feathers."

slut (*n.*) A girl of lower social standing. In 1774 Philip Fithian recorded,
"Fanny [a slave] towards Evening brought me half a *Water-Melon*. I accepted & thanked the pretty little slut, she seems so artless & delicate I esteem her exceedingly."

sluttish (*adj.*) (*n.*) Dirty. In 1682 Mary Rowlandson mentioned:
"a sluttish trick."

small beer (1) (*n.*) A weak beer. The Quartering Act of 1765 provided:
"that all . . . officers and soldiers . . . shall be furnished . . . with . . . small beer."
(2) (*adj.*) Trifling. In 1777 John Adams wrote,
"The torment of hearing eternally reflections upon my constituents, that they are . . . small beer."

small coal Wood coal, charcoal. An anonymous colonial song went:
"Gang of poor smutty souls,
Doth trudge up and down and cry small coals."

small way, in a In a humble condition. In 1711 William Byrd:
"went to visit Mrs. Harrison that I found in a small way."

smart (*adj.*) (1) Witty. In 1789 Gouverneur Morris reported that:
"we had a pretty smart conversation."
(2) Severe. In 1710 William Byrd:
"wrote a long and smart letter to Mr. Perry wherin I found several faults with his management."

smoky (*adj.*) Having the appearance of smoke, foggy. In 1775 Philip Fithian recorded,
"Mr. Carter returned, the day being smoky introduced at Coffee, a conversation on Philosophy, on Eclipses."

smooth stone Probably very much like freestone, which can be cut without flaking. In 1629 Francis Higginson wrote:
"For stone, here is plenty of slates . . . limestone, freestone and smoothstone and iron stone and marble stone."

smother (*n.*) A state of confusion; from the sense of 'dense, stifling smoke.' A 1776 version of *Yankee Doodle* included:
"They kept up such a smother."

snail trimming A corruption of *chenille trimming,* a tufted silk, cotton or wool cord. A 1778 Boston newspaper offered:
"India Dimothy, Buttons & Twist, Snail Trimmings."

snake streamed Referring to the Colonial flags depicting snakes, some coiled, some dismembered, some warning,
"Don't tread on me." In a 1776 play we hear,
"Her snake streamed ensigns."

snake weed The plant bistort. In 1630 Francis Higginson wrote,
"There are some serpents here called rattlesnakes . . . sting him so mortally. . . except . . . the root of an herb called snakeweed to bite in, and then he shall receive no harm."

snape (*n.*) A tapering tool. A 1651 inventory included,
"One Drawing knife 6 snape."

snaphance (*n.*) A flintlock. In 1658 in Rhode Island,
"Now it is declared, that both it and fyrelockes and snaphaunces with powder hornes bee allowed."

snarl (*n.*) A group. A 1776 broadside said,
"I see another snarl of men."

snath (*n.*) A scythe handle. In 1664 a bequest in Masssachusetts included,
"A seith & a snath."

sneaker (*n.*) A drinking vessel. In 1715 William Byrd:
"drank a sneaker of punch."

snib (*v.*) A variant of *snub* to 'check.' In 1675 Benjamin Thompson wrote,
"No sooner pagan malice peeked forth, but valor snibbed it."

snips, to go To share. In 1698 Lord Bellomont wrote to the Board of Trade,
"I conclude he [Brooks] went snips in so cheap a bargain."

snow (*n.*) A square-rigged ship similar to a brig, but having a supplemental mast with a try-sail. In 1753 Elias Merivielle wrote,
"We had a snow belonging to us . . . here last week from Gambia. We sold the greater part of her cargo at about £33 per head." She brought 135 slaves.

snug (*adj.*) Well off. In 1789 Gouverneur Morris referred to a lady as:
"an elegant woman and a snug party."

socage (*n.*) The holding of a lord's land by the payment of rent or by the rendition of certain husbandry services, generally nominal, other than knight's service. The 1701 patent to Caleb Heathcote for Scarsdale, New York, stated,
"to be holden of us . . . in free and common socage."

sociable (*n.*) A four-wheeled vehicle with seats facing each other and a box seat for the driver. An advertisement in a 1780 New Jersey newspaper:
"Wanted to exchange, a neat sulkey, almost new, for a sociable or handy one horse chair, equally good."

society (*n.*) A number of families united and incorporated to support public worship. In 1739 in Suffield, Connecticut,
"The Inhabitants of the West part of said Town . . . [ask] to be Set off into a District and seperate Society."

soft soap Liquid soap. In 1770 Franklin wrote,
"I sent you a receipt for making soft soap in the sun."

solemncholy (*adj.*) Melancholy. In 1773 Philip Fithian wrote,
"Being very solemncholy and somewhat tired, I concluded to stay there all night."

Solis, Die *Latin.* 'Sunday,' a direct translation.

somatic (*adj.*) Pertaining to the body, physical. Jefferson described walking as the
"culminating point of the human somatic forces."

sope (*n.*) A frequent spelling of *soap*. A *soap boiler* made soap. In 1771 Franklin wrote,
"At ten years old I was taken home to assist my father in his business, which was that of a tallow-chandler and sope-boiler."

sophister (*n.*) (1) A third- or fourth-year college student. In 1646 at Harvard,
"All Sophisters & Bachellors . . . shall publiquely repeate Sermons in ye Hall whenever they are called forth."

(2) An artful but insidious logician. Franklin wrote in 1771,
"One was a crafty old sophister and the other a true novice."

sorority (*n.*) Females. In 1645 Pagitt wrote,
"The Synod of New-England maketh not only the fraternity but . . . the sorority to be the subject of the . . . power of the keys."

sorrel (*n.*) An herb of the *Rumex* family. The roots and leaves were used medicinally in several mild treatments, one of which was as a substitute for wine when a patient craved it but wasn't permitted it.

sort (1) (*n.*) An individual piece of type. In 1771 Franklin wrote,
"I . . . had so many little pieces of private mischief done me, by mixing my sorts, transposing my pages."
(2) (*v.*) To terminate; to have success. In 1633 John Winthrop wrote,
"They delivered their several reasons which all sorted to this conclusion."

sot weed Tobacco, a stupefying weed. Many quotations herein are from Ebenezer Cook's 1708 poem *The Sot-Weed Factor.*

souchong (*n.*) A black Chinese tea. From Chinese *hsiao chung* 'fine sort.' A 1783 Philadelphia newspaper advertised:
"Tonkay, Congo, Bohea, Hyson, Soatchaun."

soul (*n.*) The one who gives life to something. In 1771 Franklin wrote,
"Dr. Mandeville . . . who had a club there, of which he was the soul."

soul driver One who drove slaves for sale from one place to another. In 1774 John Harrower deplored,
"Soul drivers . . . drove them through the Country . . . until they can sell them to advantage."

sound (*n.*) A fish's air bladder; a food dish. In 1789 Franklin wrote to his sister,
"I have lately wished to regale on Cod's Tongues and Sounds."

sounding (*n.*) A variant of *swooning*. A 17th-century cookbook prescribed,
"It is good for sounding or fainting fits."

souse (1) (*n.*) Parts of pig or other animal, especially the feet and ears, preserved by pickling. In 1709 William Byrd:
"ate cold souse."
(2) (*v.*) To pickle. In 1739 William Byrd reported,
"The Doctor had some soused fish."

sow iron Iron bars heavier than pig iron. In 1710 William Byrd recorded,
"At the same time no sow iron was imported."

Spanish bit A Spanish coin, one eighth of a Spanish dollar. Two bits are a quarter. In 1738 William Stephens, Governor of Georgia, wrote,
"One Smith . . . paying away a few Spanish Bits."

Spanish brown Earth, contaminated with iron oxide, used in paints. In 1784 storekeeper Justin Foote wrote,
"I shall send you by the Boat 10 Gallons Oil and one Ct. Spanish brown. I thought the oil and the paint to be necessary."

Spanish heavy dollar A Mexican silver dollar. The cargo of *La Virgen del Rosario* included:
"Six Thousand Nine Hundred and Seventy five Spanish Heavy Dollars."

Spanish milled dollar A dollar struck and milled in Spain; the *real*, which contained

77 oz. of silver. A 1775 Massachusetts Bay indented note required repayment in:
"lawful Money in Spanish Milled Dollars at five shillings each."

Spanish pistole A gold coin. In 1693 Samuel Sewall wrote,
"I have sent you three and twenty Spanish Pistolls."

spark (*n.*) A brisk, showy, gay (old meaning) man. In 1774 Philip Fithian commented,
"A young spark seemed to be fond of her [Dolly Edmundson]."

spatterdash (*n.*) The thigh-high leggings, worn for protection on horseback. In 1778 the Continental Congress authorized:
"Linen spatterdashes for soldiers." By 1802 both the garment and the word had shrunk to *spat.*

speck (*n.*) A disease of plants that causes seeds to shrivel. In 1771 Washington complained,
"My Wheat every where being much Injurd by the Speck or Spot."

speech belt An Indian wampum belt commemorating a meeting. In 1753 Washington recorded,
"The King . . . offered the French Speech-Belt which had before been demanded."

spelt (*n.*) *Triticum spelta,* also called 'German wheat.' In 1763 Washington planted:
"seven bushels of spelts in seven acres of corn ground."

Spencer wig A wig named after Charles Spencer, third Earl of Sunderland (1674–1722). In 1741 John Webb wrote,
"The Comp'y Gave the Capt. a Night Gown, a Spencer Wigg and 4 pair of thread Stock'gs."

spend (*v.*) To lose. John Winthrop recorded,
"Spent all her masts and had to be towed home."

spermaceti (*n.*) A waxy substance found in the head of sperm whales that was used to make beautiful white candles. In 1789 Congress imposed a tax:
"On all candles of wax or spermaceti, per pound, six cents."

spider (*n.*) A long–legged, iron frying pan. A 1790 Philadelphia newspaper advertised,
"William Robinson, Junr . . . Hath for Sale . . . bake pans, spiders, skillets."

spike (*v.*) To drive a spike into the touch hole of a cannon so that it cannot be fired.

spile (*n.*) **(1)** In a barrel, a bung; a wooden peg to stop a hole. In 1783 Michel Crevecoeur recorded,
"[They] employ themselves in . . . making bungs or spoyls for their oil-casks."
(2) In the water, a pile, a stake driven into the ground to protect a bank. In 1720 Massachusetts authorized:
"William Dummer . . . to secure the East and West Heads of Castle-Island . . . [by] driving in of spiles and timbers for a dock." Castle Island is now part of the mainland.

spiller (*n.*) A long fishing line with a number of hooks fastened to it. In 1705 Robert Beverley wrote,
"They also fish with Spillyards, which is a long Line staked out in the River, and hung with a great many Hooks on short Strings, fasten'd to the main Line."

spinster (*n.*) A woman or, rarely, a man, who spins. It had nothing to do with her, or his, marital status.

spirits of salt Hydrochloric acid. In 1711 William Byrd:
"took ten drops of spirits of salt" for his fever.

spit (*n.*) A little bit, hardly more than a mouthful. In 1768 Washington recorded,
"Cloudy and cold, with Spits of snow."

spittle (*n.*) A peel; a baker's spade-like tool. A 1648 Connecticut document said,
"Inventory . . . one broiling iron, one cleaver, 1 spittle iron."

spleen (*n.*) Melancholy. In 1715 William Byrd:
"lost three Guineas . . . which put me into the spleen very much."

splutter (*n.*) A bustle, a stir. A 1775 song included:
"added to the splutter."

spontoon (*n.*) A half-pike. In 1797 Gen. William Heath recalled,
"The officers went into battle at Stony Point with spontoons rather than firearms."

sportula (*n.*) A small, customary present or fee to a judge. A 1744 accounting billed,
"For Letters and Sportalage 7/6."

spotted fever Any of the various forms of purpura. In 1774 Philip Fithian wrote,
"A malignant putrid fever, & what is generally called the spotted Fever rages at present."

sprat (*n.*) Herring, *Culpea sprattus*. In 1740 William Byrd,
"with so much haggling get so many [13] sprats to the dozen."

sprekle (*adj.*) Probably, *speckled*. In 1679 Charles Wolley wrote,
"When its well dryed they parch it, as we [parch] sprekle Beans and Pease."

sprig (*n.*) A brad. A 1729 Maryland bill read,
"To 34 Quarries 7 sqrs & 7 foot [of glass] Repaired and sprigs, 0..11..1."

spring (*v.*) To crack, warp, or split or to cause to move out of its proper place. In 1766 John Rowe reported,
"Capt. Dashwood come in from St. Kitts having sprung his masts."

sprout (*n.*) A branch. A 1758 document stated,
"We cou'd get no further than . . . ye upper Mohaak Sprout."

spruce beer A beer flavored with spruce. In 1765 Jane Mecon wrote,
"I have brewed the spruce bear twice."

spun tobacco Twisted tobacco leaves. A 1706 Boston newspaper announced there would:
"be exposed to sale . . . twenty-nine half barrels of Leaf, and 40 Rolls of Spun Tobacco."

squadrant (*n.*) A square. In 1707 in the Cambridge, Massachusetts, records appears,
"The first Lott in ye Sixth Squadrant was layed out."

squadron (*n.*) A variant of *squadrant*. In 1658 in Watertown, Massachusetts, is found,
"The first Lott shall begin at the north Squadron."

Squantum (*n.*) *Narragansett.* 'a devil.' In 1630 Francis Higginson wrote,
"Their evil God whom they feare will doe them hurt, they call Squantum."

squib (*n.*) A firecracker; metaphorically, a sarcastic speech. A character in a 1776 play said,

"We have had such bad success with our crackers, that this is a proper time to throw your squibs."

Squire (*n.*) Short for *Esquire*, the honorific accorded a justice of the peace, later extended to any prominent person. In 1743 Franklin observed,
"We shall . . . discover in every little Market-Town and Village the Squire . . . [listening] to a Barber's news."

Squire's Elixir A panacea. *Squire's Original Grand Elixir* probably contained enough opium to make one feel better. It was taken for colds, coughs, asthma, stomach ache, and rheumatism. In 1739 William Byrd wrote,
"At night I took Squire's Elixir."

squitter (*v.*) To squirt. In 1738 William Byrd wrote that a skunk could:
"save himself by farting and squittering."

stack taker One employed to stack goods, wood, etc. A 1776 Philadelphia newspaper announced,
"To be sold by public vendue by Robt. McCorley Sundry Negroes, viz. One a hammerman, one a refiner, and one a stack taker or attender."

staddle (*n.*) **(1)** A small three- to four-year-old tree. A 1679 Connecticut document stated,
"We marked a white oake staddle."
(2) A frame for a stack of hay. A 1774 New York document said,
"Every person that owned staddles on said beach should have liberty to take them away."

stadt house The city hall. A 1695 New York document reported,
"When he arrived he went to ye Stadt House."

stag (*n.*) A castrated ox. In 1744 Joshua Hempstead:
"carryed my 2.2 yr old Steers and Staggs to the common pasture."

stage fight A fight in public. In 1687 Samuel Sewall wrote,
"After the Stage-fight in the even[ing], the Souldier [went] Shouting through the streets."

stalking horse A horse, real or fake, behind which a hunter conceals himself; hence, a pretense.
"[It] has been made a mask for a battery, a stalking horse."

stamen (*n.*) The support of the body; the bones. In 1679 Charles Wolley admitted,
"I, a person of a weakly stamen."

stamping mill A mill for breaking ore. The pestle in the mill which beats ore to a powder is called a *stamp*. In 1775 Silas Deane reported,
"The Stamping Mill is going."

stand (*v.*) To maintain a position. To *stand neuter* is to 'maintain a neutral position.' In 1757 William Smith wrote,
"We must . . . forsake our country and seek other habitation or stand neuter."

stand a poll To offer oneself for election. In 1770 Robert Mumford in the play *The Candidate* wrote,
"I was thinking you did not intend to stand a poll."

standaway (*n.*) Probably a separation rather than a divorce. In 1705 Sarah Knight deplored,

"These uncomely standaways are too much in vogue among the English in this indulgent colony [Connecticut]."

standing (*adj.*) Established. A 1748 Connecticut document reported,
"A controversy was then subsisting whether they ought to be acknowledged as belonging by Right to the Standing Church."

stand out To stand fast, not to yield. In 1774 Philip Fithian recorded,
"All the conversations is Politicks; but people seem moderate & yet settled in their determination to stand out."

Star Chamber, Court of An arbitrary court. After the King's Council which sat in the Star Chamber at Westminster (named from its star-decorated ceiling) from the 15th century until 1641; it abused its power. At the trial of John Zenger in 1735 Andrew Hamilton said,
"Informations for libels in a child, if not born, yet nursed up and brought to full maturity in the Court of Star Chamber."

start (*v.*) To rouse from concealment. In 1768 Washington complained,
"Never started a fox, but did a deer."

state (*v.*) **(1)** To grant. In 1661 a Massachusetts document said,
"The aforsaid fiue hundred acres of land is stated to the inhabitants of the Town . . . to share in the said common."
(2) To establish. In 1674 in Connecticut,
"There may be a roade stated between Connecticut Riuer and the upland."

States General The supreme parliament of the Republic of the Netherlands. It was made up of delegates from the seven provinces and represented the three estates: nobles, clergy, and commons. The 1627 *Freedoms and Exemptions* of The West India Company were issued:
"Under the supreme jurisdiction of their High Mightynesses the States-General."

statical chair A scale. In 1779 John Adams wrote a letter suggesting,
"Suppose you should make a statical chair and try whether perspiration is most copious in a warm bed, or stark naked in the open air."

station ship A ship appointed to a particular station. A 1715 Boston newspaper reported,
"His Majesties Ship the Rose . . . is to be the Station Ship for this port."

statutable (*adj.*) Governed by statutary law. In 1775 the Continental Congress referred to:
"all the easy emoluments of statutable plunder."

stave (*n.*) A lead bar from which bullets may be made. In 1683 Robert Livingston paid the Indians for land:
"Six Guns, fifty pounds of Powder, Fifty staves of lead."

stay hook A hook attached to stays on which a watch or locket might be hung. Alice Earle gives a 1743 reference to:
"Silver'd Stayhooks."

stays (*n. pl.*) A corset, generally stiffened with whalebone, worn by females. Style varied their size from time to time. In 1774 Philip Fithian described Betsy Lee,
"Her *stays* are suited to come to the upper part of her shoulders, almost to her Chin, and are swaithed around her as low as they possibly can be, allowing her hardly Liberty to walk at all." In 1734 stays were low, but in 1795 a New York newspaper commented,
"Corsetts about six inches long, and a slight buffon tucker of two inches high, are

now the only defensive paraphernalia of our fashionable belles between the necklace and the apron strings.''

steelyard (*n.*) A weighing balance. A 1774 Philadelphia newspaper advertised:
"pinchbeck, hand stilliards.'' And an anonymous song went,
"Who'll play at Billiards,
as fair as at Stillyards''

stepony (*n.*) A raisin wine with lemon and sugar added. Possibly from Stepney, a district of London. Recipes appeared in contemporary cookbooks.

sticcado (*n.*) A xylophone. From Italian *steccato* 'a palisade.' In 1786 Franklin's sister wrote to him,
"You may remember a man who made your stickado when you were last in Boston [1763].''

stinker (*n.*) A skunk. In 1738 William Byrd described,
"a little beast called a stinker, as big as a fox and shaped like a ferret.''

stinted (*adj.*) Restrained to a certain limit or quantity. In 1642 New Haven, Connecticut, decreed,
"The Neck shall be a stinted common for cattell.'' Also, the 1648 instructions to the Governor of Virginia included,
"Whereas your tobacco falleth every day more and more to a baser price, that it be stinted into a far less proportion than hath been made.''

stirrup hose An overgarment up to the waist for protection while on horseback.

stiver (*n.*) A Dutch coin, one twentieth of a gulden. In 1638 The Dutch West India Company offered:
"passage and board in the state-room, one guilder, in the cabin twelve stuivers, and between decks, eight stuivers, per diem.''

stock (*n.*) The main stem of a plant or the trunk of a tree. A 1634 letter from Maryland referred to:
"300 stocks ready grafted with pears, apples.''

stockfish (*n.*) Cod dried hard as wood in the air without salt. In 1664 William Browne testified,
"There was Aboarde the Shipe . . . Oakem, Stockfish, Some Coco.''

stock jobber Originally, a broker on the London Stock Exchange. Later one who speculated with public funds. In 1773 Franklin referred to,
"Prodigals who hve ruined their fortunes, broken gamesters, or stockjobbers.''

stockline (*v.*) To trim the branches from the trunk of a tree before felling it. In 1760 Washington:
"cleared the bushes from about a Poplar, stocklined it 10 feet long and hughed [hewed].''

stock lock A lock fastened in wood. L. P. Summer in 1780 wrote,
"The door is to be . . . furnished with a good and sufficient stock lock.''

stocks (*n. pl.*) The frame supporting a ship while it is under construction. A 1756 shipowner's letter referred to:
"a vessel on the stocks of about 90 Tons.''

stomach (*n.*) **(1)** An appetite. In 1711 William Byrd:
"ate some fish with a stomach.''

(2) A medicated plaster, applied to the five lower ribs on the left side toward the back. It was composed of laudanum, frankincense, cinnamon, mace, and mint.

stomacher (*n.*) An ornament or support, for men or women, made of an inverted triangular piece of cloth, sometimes stiffened with whalebone. The 1673 inventory of the *Providence* included:
"2 pa[ir]. parragon bodices and stomegers."

stomachful (*adj.*) Wilfully obstinate, stubborn. In 1774 Philip Fithian:
"corrected Harry this morning for telling me a Lie—stomachful & sullen as any youth."

stone (*n.*) (1) Could be bladder, kidney, or galstone. Franklin's was bladder. In 1784 he was:
"troubled with the Stone which sometimes gives a little pain."
(2) Testicle. In 1712 William Byrd:
"ate lamb stones for dinner."

stone horse A stallion, that is, one with *stones*. In 1711 William Byrd recorded,
"The mare was shut up with the stone horse."

Stone of Goa A fever medicine, composed of various drugs, formed into a hard pill. It was invented in the territory in Portuguese India by a lay brother of the Jesuits, Gaspar Antonio. In 1699 Capt. William Kidd declared,
"In his chest which he left at Gardiner's Island there was three small baggs or more of Jasper Antonio or Stone of Goa."

stool ball A game, possibly like croquet, in which a ball was driven from stool to stool. In 1656 John Winthrop deplored,
"In the street at play openly some pitching the bar, and some at stool-ball."

strain (*n.*) The generation, source. In 1801 Cotton Mather exhorted,
"Let obedience to God be the spring and the strain of all your business."

strappet (*n.*) A strip. In 1655 Springfield, Massachusetts, enacted,
"There is granted to John Lamb yt little strappet of land over ye river at ye hay place."

street roller One of a foot patrol for the prevention of robberies. One of Washington's General Orders in 1777 included:
"All C.O.s are strongly urged to make all their men . . . march in the ranks, for it is so great a reflection when all orders are disobeyed to see such a number of street rollers (for they cannot be called guards) with the wagons."

strenarum commercium *Latin*. 'vigorous business.' In 1679 Charles Wolley wrote,
"The English observed one anniversary custom . . . I mean the *strenarum commercium*, as *Suetonius* calls them, a neighbourly commerce of presents every New-Years day."

stricture (*n.*) A critical remark; a touch of criticism. In 1768 Benjamin Rush said,
"The rest of the professors don't deserve a stricture."

strig (*n.*) A stem. Origin obscure. A 17th-century cookbook instructed,
"Cherries, and pull out ye stones at ye top with ye strig."

strike (1) (*n.*) A dry measure; it varied from one to four bushels. A 1631 New Haven, Connecticut, document stated,
"Both the English and Indian corne beeinge at tenne shillings a strike."
(2) (*v.*) To level off the top of a container, as with a strickle. A 1641 Maryland docu-

ment said,
  "No attachm[en]t . . . may be layd upon tobacco afore it be struck in Cask."

stripes (*n. pl.*) Lashing, whipping. May be used metaphorically for severe criticism. In 1747 Polly Baker said,
  "That government that punishes my misfortunes with stripes and infamy."

stroke (*n.*) **(1)** A masterful effort. In 1703 Cotton Mather boasted,
  "My conversation . . . goes on with pure chaste noble strokes."
  (2) Manners; habits. A character in a 1770 play inquires after a man's wife with,
  "Does the good woman keep to the old stroke?"

strokings (*n.*) The rich milk gotten by stripping the udder. A 17th-century cookbook directed,
  "Take 6 quarts of stroakings or new milke."

stroller (*n.*) A vagrant, a vagabond. In 1775 Gen. Horatio Gates instructed,
  "You are not to enlist any . . . stroller, negro or vagabond."

strong water Whiskey. In 1709 four friends visited and William Byrd:
  "gave them some strong water."

stroud (*n.*) A coarse blanket cloth. From Stroud, in Gloucestershire, England. In 1677 part of the payment Stephanus van Cortlandt made to the Indians for land was,
  "6 fathoms stroud cloth."

strumpet colt A horse whose tail was docked. A misspelling of *strumple*, the 'fleshy stem of a horse's tail after docking.' In 1781 Lewis Morris wrote to his son,
  "As to your strumpet colt, you may remember you sold him."

stuff (*n.*) Textiles in general and especially a lustrous, English fabric of cotton or wool. A 1774 Boston newspaper advertised,
  "Light stuff cassock . . . and stuff breeches of one thickness."

stupe (*n.*) A cloth, usually flannel, dipped in a medicine and applied to an injury as a poultice. In 1709 William Byrd wrote of treating rheumatism by:
  "applying a hot dressing and stupe to the part affected."

subaltern (*n.*) A subordinate military officer below the rank of captain. In 1771 Franklin wrote,
  "Colonel Dunbar . . . represented to me his concern for the subalterns."

subduct (*v.*) To subtract. In 1729 William Douglas wrote,
  "Cambridge is . . . west of Paris (subducting . . . London's westing from Paris)."

subscription (*n.*) A paper with signatures subscribed. In 1705 Robert Beverley wrote,
  "They proposed that a subscription might pass through the colony to try the humour of the people."

subsist (*v.*) To be, to have existence. In 1771 Franklin wrote,
  "The Union Fire Company still subsists, though the first members are all deceased but one."

succade (*n.*) A fruit sweetmeat. From Old Italian *zuccata*, diminutive of *zucca* 'gourd.'

succahanah (*n.*) Water. From an Indian word, probably Virginia. In 1708 Ebenezer Cook:
  "soon got up To cool my Liver with a Cup Of *Succahana* fresh and clear."

succors (*n.*) Aid, help, assistance. In 1777 Alexander Hamilton wrote,
"The garrison and Steel's may be informed of these succours."

sucker (*v.*) To strip off shoots, or suckers. In 1774 Philip Fithian commented,
"Cotton . . . must be top't & suckered as Tobacco."

sucket (*n.*) A variant of *succade*. For transatlantic crossings,
"suckets and spices" were advised.

suffrage (*n.*) A vote. A 1769 North Carolina petition requested,
"That at all elections each suffrage be given by ticket and ballot."

sugar baker A sugar refiner. A 1725 Boston newspaper advertised,
"James Lubbuck Chocolate Grinder . . . opposite to Mr. Smith's[,] Shugar baker in Boston, sells the best Chocolate."

sulky (*n.*) A carriage for a single person. So called as the vehicle is for but one person: he wants to be alone. A 1780 Boston newspaper announced,
"An Elegant Sulky (or Windsor Chair) with its Harness compleat to be sold."

sulphur (*n.*) The chemical was used medicinally in various compounds, externally for skin eruptions and the itch, internally to loosen the bowels and to promote perspiration.

sum (*n.*) An amount of tobacco as a payment in kind. In some colonies taxes were levied and often wages paid in sums of tobacco. In 1666 a Maryland document stated,
"The Governour and Councell are hereby empowered to Levy . . . such Sume or Sumes of Tobacco."

Summer Islands The Bermuda Islands; for long known as Somers Isles for Sir George Somers, one of the founders of the South Virginia Company, who discovered them for England by being shipwrecked there in 1612. Administratively, they were part of Virginia. A 1625 royal proclamation stated,
"We hold those territories of Virginia and the Summer Islands."

sunck (*n.*) A queen of an Indian tribe. From Natick, *sonksq*. A 1663 Long Island, New York, document read,
"An agreement between the great Sunk squa[w] Quashawam, and the Indians of Shinecock."

supawn (*n.*) Hasty pudding; mush. From Natick, *sapaen* 'softened by water.'

supping (*adj.*) Soft, capable of being supped. In 1774 John Harrower complained he had not tasted:
"supping mate [meat]."

surety (*n.*) A godfather at a baptism. In 1760 James Reed, regarding Negroes, said,
"I baptize all those whose masters become sureties for them."

suretyship (*n.*) The obligation of one to answer for the debt of another. In 1584 Richard Hakluyt, regarding potential immigrants, wrote,
"Many men . . . overthrown by suretyship, by sea, or by some folly of youth."

surtout (*n.*) A long, close-fitting overcoat like that worn by stage drivers. From French *sur tout* 'over all.' The Board trying Maj. John André in 1781 recorded,
"that he had on a surtout over his regimentals."

sutler (*n.*) One who sells provisions, liquor, etc., to troops. In 1776 Congress recorded,

"General Schuyler [shall] be desired to encourage suttlers to attend the army in Canada."

swamp (*v.*) A milder version of *swear*. In 1764 Thomas Hutchinson wrote,
"He has in like manner . . . I swamp, and I vum, for I swear and I vow."

swamping (*adj.*) Impressive, striking. An adaptation of *swappin*, 'striking.' In 1775 *Yankee Doodle* went,
"There I saw a swamping gun." Also,
"He plays upon a swamping fiddle."

swanskin (*n.*) A fine type of flannel, thick and warm. A 1761 Newport newspaper offered,
"Just imported . . . And to be sold . . . white and striped swanskin."

swash (*n.*) A narrow channel between a sandbank and the shore. In 1785 Washington:
"examined a Gut, or swash, through which it is supposed the Navigation must be conducted."

sweat (*n.*) Any medication that would produce perspiration. In 1709, for a pain in a slave's side, William Byrd:
"gave him a sweat that worked abundantly."

sweet oil An edible oil, such as olive oil. A 1781 Boston newspaper offered,
"a few hampers of refined sweet oil."

swine pox Chicken pox. In 1774 Philip Fithian reported,
"Priscilla & Harriot are confined at Home of an erruptive Fever, some think it is Swine Pox."

swinger (*n.*) An animal that can swing its tail. In a song a mouse deplores that a frog has no tail,
"Uncle Rat, too so well known,/ That a swinger has on's own."

swingle (*v.*) To clean flax by beating it with a *swingle* 'knife-like instrument.' In 1774 John Harrower had:
"to break, swingle & heckle flax."

swivel gun A gun with a maximum bore of two inches, mounted on a pivot so that it might be turned in all directions; it was used more at sea than on land. During the French and Indian War, William Pote reported,
"We discharged one Cannon and one Swivel."

swizer (*n.*) Probably a variant of *switzer*, a 'mercenary Swiss soldier.' In 1705 Mungo Ingless writing about The College of William and Mary:
"Mr. Blair took full salary . . . and there remained no more money . . . no money no swizer so on salary no master."

tabby[1] (*n.*) A wavy, watered silk. In 1756 William Pepperell ordered a gown of:
"white watered *Tabby*, with *Gold lace* for trimming of it" for his daughter to be married in. The same word survives to apply to a striped cat.

tabby[2] (*n.*) A mixture of lime, stones, and shells which hardens; used as a building material. In 1775 The South Carolina Council of Safety ordered that Ft. Lyttleton be repaired with "tappy."

tabellion (*n.*) A public scribe. A 1752 Boston newspaper referred to:
"William Winter, Notary and Tabellion Publick."

table man A piece used in a game, checkers or backgammon. A 17th-century cookbook described:
"cakes about ye bigness of a table man."

tack duty In Scotland, rent. *See also* **tacksman.** In 1774 one of the reasons stated for Scottish immigration to America was:
"paying the extravagant tack duty."

tackle (*v.*) To harness a horse to a vehicle. In 1714 Samuel Sewall lamented,
"Our horses were forced to leap into the Sea. By that time had tackled them was duskish."

tacksman (*n.*) In Scotland, a tenant. *See also* **tack duty.** The same author referred to:
"the tacksman of Sir John Sinclair's estate."

tafia (*n.*) A distilled liquor similar to rum. In 1775 James Adair wrote,
"The French Alebahma Garrison had been . . . supplied pretty well with corrupting brandy, taffy and decoying trifles."

tag (*n.*) Something, usually paltry, added or tagged on. In 1744 Dr. Alexander Hamilton related,
"after some taggs of incoherent arguement."

tail (*v.*) To tie by the tail. In 1637 Thomas Morton described some people,
"as if they had been tailed one to the other."

take up To stop. In 1720 Samuel Sewall:
"was so taken up that I could not go if I would."

tale (*n.*) A reckoning, written account. In 1763 Washington counted:
"190 corn holes good Tale."

tale of a tub (*n.*) A fictitious tale, a cock-and-bull story. In 1744 Dr. Alexander Hamilton told,
"He was going on with this tale of a tub." The origin of the phrase is unknown, but it goes back to at least 1532, and was made famous by an article of this title by Jonathan Swift.

tales de circumstantibus *Latin.* 'such from those standing about.' A legal term applying to those added to a jury from those who happened to be at the courthouse rather than those summoned for that purpose. The 1641 Massachusetts Body of Liberties provided,
"As the challenger shall choose it shall be allowed him, and tales de circumstantibus impaneled in their room."

tallow chandler One who made and sold candles. John Urmstone's 1711 description of the North Carolina frontier stated,
"Men are generally carpenters, tallow-chandlers, and what not; women, soap makers."

tamarindae (*n.*) Tamarinds. In 1791 G. Motherby wrote,
"The pulp is useful in inflamatory and putrid fevers. When mixed with the laxative sweets, such as cassia and manna, it increases their action and prevents in a degree the flatulence which they occasion."

tambour (*n.*) A form of embroidery done on a spherical cushion. An adopted French word meaning 'drum,' for the shape of the cushion. A 1789 Maryland document described a lady:
"adorn'd with Pink Sattin Tambour muslin."

tammy (*n.*) A woolen stuff, used for curtains. A 1765 Boston newspaper advertised,
"Tammy, corded Paduasoy, Shalloons."

tampion (*n.*) A wooden stopper for a cannon. Several were included in a list of gunners' stores in 1740.

tandem (*n.*) A variety of linen. A 1741 Charleston newspaper offered:
"Just imported . . . wide garlix, tandem Hollands."

tansy (*n.*) A bitter-tasting plant. *Yankee Doodle* went,
"Sheep's Head and Vinegar,/ Butter Milk and Tansy."

tap (*v.*) To put a tap, a half-sole, on a shoe. In 1745 Joshua Hempsted:
"tapt & nailed Jont. Pierpoints shoes."

tapster (*n.*) One who taps, or draws ale or other liquor; a tavern keeper. In a 1673 New York document Balthazar Bayard was listed as the:
"Collector of Tapsters' excise."

tar (*n.*) A distillate of pine or fir sap. In estimating the annual produce of His Majesty's American colonies, Gov. Dinwiddie in 1740 included:
"pitch, pine trees or tar trees."

tar and feathers A punishment. In 1773 Capt. Ayers, master of the *Polly*, carrying tea from London to Philadelphia, was threatened with:
"ten gallons of liquid tar decanted on your pate with the feathers of a dozen wild

geese laid over that to enliven your appearance.'' Generally much less tar and the feathers of a single goose were used.

tare[1] (*n.*) The weight of a container, as contrasted with the weight of its contents. The 1725 Flour Inspection Law called for:
"well-seasoned cask the tare thereof thereupon marked.''

tare[2] (*n.*) A kind of vetch cultivated for fodder. In 1775 *American Husbandry* said,
"Pease, beans and tares are sown variously through the province.''

target (*n.*) A small, round, Indian shield. In 1610 Capt. John Smith wrote,
"They use targets that are round and made of bark of trees.''

taring (*adj.*) Tearing; grand, ripping. *Yankee Doodle* described,
"The flaming ribbons in his hat,/ They looked so taring fine ah.''

tarnal (*adj.*). Short for *eternal*, to avoid profanity. *Yankee Doodle* sang:
"So tarnal long, so tarnal deep.''

tarpaulin (*n.*) A sailor. In 1705 Robert Beverley described seamen who:
"cry in their tarpaulin language.''

tarrying (*n.*) Bundling. *See* **bundle.** In 1775 Andrew Burnaby commented,
"A very extraordinary method of courtship . . . is called Tarrying.''

tartanella (*n.*) A fabric of mixed cotton, linen, and wool. A 1662 clothing inventory included:
"one black tartanel samare with a tucker.''

tartar emetic Bitartrate of potash, the crystalline substance deposited in wine casks during fermentation. It was taken as an emetic. A 1779 Trenton, New Jersey, newspaper advertised,
"Jesuit's bark, Brimstone, Gum assafoetida, Tartar emetic.''

tattoo (*n.*) A beat of drum, a call to quarters. A character in a 1776 play said,
"He beat a tattoo for us all.''

teague (*n.*) A young Irish lad. An Anglicization of the Irish name *Tadhg*. In 1744 Dr. Alexander Hamilton told of a man:
"in company with an Irish teague.''

tell (*v.*) To count. In 1763 Washington recorded that he:
"told my sheep.''

tendency (*n.*) Receptiveness. In 1764 the Massachusetts Legislature wrote to the House of Commons,
"Your petitioners acknowledge with all gratitude the tendencies of the Legislature of Great Britain.''

tender (*n.*) A tether. In 1783 the Mamaroneck, New York, Town Board enacted,
"No horses to be commoners [on common ground] without hopples nor sheep without tenders.''

tenement (*n.*) Anything that may be held; it could be an office, a house, a franchise, an advowson, etc. The 1701 patent for Scarsdale, New York, included:
"Together with all and Every of the messuage, tennements, Buildings.''

tenor (*n.*) The value of a bank note or bill. In Massachusetts and Rhode Island, *new tenor* was valued in relation to silver and gold coin, *old tenor* was not. In 1762 John Rowe referred to:
"£2000 old tenor.''

tent (*n.*) A wine of a deep red color made near Rata, Spain. From Spanish *tinto* 'dark colored.' In 1686 Connecticut levied a tax on:
"Every butt or pipe of Sherry, Sack, Malaga . . . Tent."

terebinth. (*n.*) An abbreviation of Latin *terebinthus* 'turpentine.'

terror (*n.*) An act which causes terror. In 1778 the Fourth New York Regiment was ordered,
"You will immediately turn out a Corp. & 6 privates whom you can depend on, to go in quest of Torries at Crompond. The bearer will take such men as he knows best calculated for the terror."

tertian (*adj.*) Occurring every third day. In 1748 Peter Kalm wrote,
"No disease is more common here than . . . ague, which is sometimes quotidian, tertian, or quartan."

theriac Andromache Literally, the antidote against poison of the wife of Hector of Troy. Also known as *Venice treacle*. A concoction of 61 ingredients mixed with honey; the main ingredient was the flesh of vipers. As a cure-all it was no longer included in the *Pharmacopia* of the London College by 1791.

thickset (*n.*) A cotton cloth. A 1775 Boston newspaper advertised,
"Silk & worsted Sagathees; fustians & Jeans; thicksets."

thornback (*n.*) The stickleback. In 1630 Francis Higginson said,
"And besides bass we take plenty of skates and thornbacks."

thoroughbass (*n.*) A complicated musical bass enumeration; loosely used merely to mean an accompaniment. In 1774 Philip Fithian wrote,
"The Colonel at Dinner gave Ben & I a Piece of Music to prepare on our flutes, in which he is to perform the Thorough Bass on the forte piano."

thoroughfare (*n.*) A passage for ships between two bodies of water. In 1724 A. W. Read wrote,
"A Beach . . . on the side of a hill by the thorough fare of the Broad Run."

thribble bowl A punch bowl that held three quarts. A 1765 tavern bill included,
"To thribble Bowl Punch."

throw over To move over a body of water. In 1781 Washington wrote,
"Hazen's regiment being thrown over [the Hudson River] at Dobb's Ferry."

thrum (*v.*) To copulate.

thrummy (*adj.*) Fuzzy, hairy. In its sense of describing scraps of yarn. In 1740 William Byrd cautioned,
"Let her Maid be never so careful, when she pins up her Gown, she'll unavoidably run a calker into her thrummy Breech."

thwart saw A crosscut saw. In 1654 a Massachusetts man bequeathed,
"1 hand saw . . . . 2 thwart Sawes."

tickle (*v.*) To flog, jocularly or ironically. In 1774 Philip Fithian recalled,
"He told the master & then I was tickled . . . made my feet beat time to his lash."

ticklenburg (*n.*) A linen cloth from Tecklenburg, Germany. A 1765 Boston newspaper advertised,
"Ravens Duck, Ticklenburg, Oznabrigs."

tide waiter A customs officer who watched the landing of goods. In 1773 Franklin facetiously recommended,

"Convert the brave, honest officers of your Navy into pimping tide-waiters and colony officers of the customs."

tidingman (*n.*) *See* **tithingman.**

tierce (*n.*) A cask whose content is one third of a pipe; 42 gallons. A 1776 Boston newspaper advertised,
"20 Puncheons of old Jamaica Rum, 20 Tierces of sugar, 115 firkins of butter."

tiffany (*n.*) A thin, gauzelike silk. In 1651 *Sumptuary Regulations* in New England said,
"To declare our utter detestation and dislike that . . . women of the same rank to wear silk or tiffany hoods or scarves."

tiger (*n.*) A wild member of the cat family, such as an ounce, a cougar, or a wildcat. In 1709 John Lawson observed,
"Tygers are never met withal in the settlement; but are more to the Westward."

tilt hammer A heavy hammer used in forging iron. A 1750 Maryland document referred to:
"One Plateing forge with two Tilt Hammers."

tinman (*n.*) A manufacturer of tin vessels; a dealer in tin ware; a tinker. A 1782 Charleston, South Carolina, newspaper reported,
"His stock in Trade [includes] . . . Tin Man's Tools."

tithable (n.) A property subject to taxation. A 1770 Virginia court proceeding included,
"He, together with the titheables [taxable land] on both sides of the road."

tithe (*n.*) A tax. Originally a tenth part, the word came loosely to mean any small fraction.

tithe of mint and cumin An unimportant thing. This phrase was used metaphorically, as Jesus had used it, to criticize one, or a group, who paid more attention to detail than to larger, more important things. In 1625 Thomas Morton wrote,
"Much ado they keep about their church discipline. Tithes are banished from thence, all except the tithe of mint and cumin."

tithing (*n.*) An administrative district in Georgia, Maryland, or Pennsylvania. Originally, in England a tithing consisted of ten householders. In 1744 F. Moore wrote,
"Every ten houses make a tithing, and to every tithing there is a mile square."

tithingman (*n.*) In various colonies, various persons, such as a peace officer or one to keep good order in a church. In 1776 Braintree, Massachusetts, elected:
"Tithingman: Peter Adams."

tittle (*n.*) The dot over a lower case *i* or *j*. In 1740 William Byrd agreed that:
"protestations will all be performed to a Tittle." A *jot*, often used with *tittle*, comes from Greek *iota*, the smallest letter of the Greek alphabet.

tob (*n.*) Short for *tobacco*. Also seen as *toba, tobo,* and *tobco.*

tocknough (*n.*) *See* **tuckahoe.**

toll¹ (*n.*) A miller's payment in kind for grinding another's grain. In 1681 Bedford, New York, furnished the grain, Joshua Webb ground it, and received:
"the tole as in the law expressed."

toll² (*v.*) To tole, lure with bait. The 1767 South Carolina petition referred to:
"The laws concerning . . . tolling of horses."

tomkin (*n.*) A variant of *tampion*. An inventory of a gunner's stores c. 1740 included: "6 thomkans for great guns."

tonkay (*n.*) A tea from the province of Tonkin. It was then part of China; now, with Hanoi the capital, Vietnam. A 1783 Baltimore newspaper advertised, "Teas: Tonkay, Congo, Bohea, Hyson."

torentine (*n.*) A Taratine, an Abnaki Indian from Maine. John Winthrop wrote, "The Torentines came in 30 canoes."

torpedo (*n.*) An electric ray. In 1633 Andrew White reported from Maryland, "Of the fishes . . . come into notice . . . torpedoes."

toss 'em boys Chickens. Presumably, as they are run down by dogs set on them by the command, "Toss 'em boys." In 1775 Jonathan Boucher quoted, "At dinner, let me . . . toss 'em boys, and belly bacon see."

totidem verbis Latin. 'in so many words.' In 1775 Philip Fithian advised his successor, "You are not to tell them *totidem Verbis* that you understand . . . both the Latin & Greek Classicks."

toties quoties Latin. 'as often as occasion shall arise.' A 1697 description of Virginia said,
"The same seamen made oath that they had adventured themselves so many times into the country . . . and upon this they had an order for so many rights *toties quoties*."

totis viribus Latin. 'with all strength.' In 1735 William Smith wrote,
"The Connecticut agent opposed the King's confirmation of this act of *totis viribus*, but it was approved."

toto caelo Latin. 'in the whole of heaven,' i.e., completely. In 1775 Philip Fithian wrote,
"You . . . removing out of the Colony in which you was born . . . expected to find . . . peculiarities toto caelo different."

tragacanth (*n.*) The gum of the astralagus plant. From Greek *tragos akantha* 'he goat; a thorn.' It swelled in water to a gel and was used medicinally as a thickening agent.

train (*n.*) The process, regular method. In 1776 Gen. William Smallwood wrote, "I now find from the train they have kept their affairs in."

train band A company of militia, because they were trained. In 1697 Samuel Sewall wrote,
"As many Negro men as there are among us, so many empty places there are in our Train bands."

train oil Whale oil. From Dutch *traan* 'tear, a drop of oil.' A 1776 Boston newspaper advertised:
"40 new iron-bound Butts, 1200 gallons of Train oil."

trammel (*n.*) An adjustable pot hook. A 1639 Connecticut inventory included: "Tramels, Tongs, fier pan, bellowes."

transport (1) (*n.*) A grant or deed for land under the Dutch in New Netherland.
(2) Ecstasy, rapture. In 1762 Francis Hopkinson described:
"each patriot eye with transport glazed."
(3) (*v.*) To grant or deed land under the Dutch in New Netherland. In 1630 the grant for Swansdale on the Delaware River stated,

"have transported, ceded, given over and conveyed."
(4) To carry away with passion. In 1703 Cotton Mather alleged,
"the rage of that young gentlewoman . . . is transporting her."

trap (*n.*) A vehicle with two wheels, drawn by one horse. In 1774 Philip Fithian:
"rode thence by the trap five miles thence."

traverse (*n.*) A denial of what another party has put forth. The 1767 South Carolina petition requested,
"that no nolle prosequis or traverses be filed against informations made against transgressors."

trencher (*n.*) A wooden plate. In 1685 Harvard provided that:
"[there] shall be allowed to the butler thirty shillings for washing the Trenchers."

trepan (*v.*) To drill a hole, especially in the skull, with a boring device. In 1771 Franklin used the term figuratively:
"I used to work him [Keimer] so hard with my Socratic method, and had trepann'd him so often by questions."

Trinity Sunday In honor of the Trinity, the eighth Sunday after Easter. The Charter for Virginia specified,
"They should hold four assemblies a year on the next to last Wednesday of Hilary term, Easter, Trinity and Michaelmas terms."

truck (*n.*) Trading goods. In 1669 John Lederer advised,
"Your best Truck is a sort of course Trading Cloth . . . also Axes, Hoes, Knives, Sizars, and all sorts of edg'd tools."

try (*v.*) To purify by heating. A 1694 North Carolina document stated,
"[She] tryed up three Barrell of oyle out of the whale."

Tubal-cain (*n.*) A Biblical character who taught brass and iron workers. In 1710 William Byrd described an iron founder as:
"the Tubal Cain of Virginia."

tuckahoe (*n.*) The golden club or the floating arum. An adopted Algonquian word meaning 'it is globular.' The Indians made a bread from the dried, ground, and roasted roots. In 1612 Capt. John Smith recorded,
"In Iune, Iulie, and August, they feed upon the rootes of *Tocknough*."

tucker (*n.*) A modesty piece when a lady was decolleté. A 1662 New York inventory included,
"One black tartanel samare, with a tucker."

tuftaffety (1) (*n.*) A tufted taffeta.
(2) (*adj.*) Luxuriously dressed. In writing about the starving time in Virginia in 1614 Capt. John Smith facetiously wrote,
"We daily feasted with good bread . . . so that none of our Tuftaffety humorists desired to go to England."

tuly (*adj.*) Tulle, the light fabric, often used as a decorative trimming. The word is possibly derived from Tulle, France. A 1774 Philadelphia newspaper offered,
"brown Hollands, Marseilles quilting, tully garters."

tumbling dam A weir. In 1772 Washington mentioned a spot:
"next to the tumbling dam at Doeg Run."

tumbrel (*n.*) A two-wheeled dump cart, used to haul manure. In 1760 Washington

spread:
"a Tumbril load of dung."

tunnel (*n.*) A funnel. A 17th-century cookbook directed,
"put in with a tunnell."

turbith (*n.*) A vine *Ipomoea turpethum*. Its ground root was taken as a cathartic.

Turlington's Balsam A patent medicine. Robert Turlington received British patent No. 596 in 1774 for this concoction which contained 27 ingredients. It was taken to treat kidney and bladder stones and colic.

turner (*n.*) One who turns on a lathe. It was one of the trades Virginia had need of in 1610. *See* **cooper.**

turtogue (*n.*) The turtle. From Spanish *tortuga*. In 1767 John Rowe:
"dined on turtogue."

tutiae (*n.*) Tutty, zinc oxide. A medicinally used drying agent.

tweeling (*n.*) A twilled cloth. A 1777 Massachusetts document reported the selling of:
"Tweeling at 2s [shillings]."

twelve men In Massachusetts, the administrative body of a town. A 1637 Salem document reported,
"A towne meeting of the 12 men appointed for the busines thereof."

twice, at In two shifts. In 1775 Philip Fithian wrote,
"We were not throng'd at all, & dined all at twice." There were 105 guests, plus a ship's crew and servants.

twist (*n.*) A thread made by twisting strands. A 1778 Boston newspaper advertised,
"India Dimothy, Buttons & Twist, Snail Trimmings."

Tyburn tulips Candidates for hanging. A character in a 1776 play shouted,
"Clear the gangway there of them Tyburn tulips." From the 1300s until 1784, Tyburn was London's place of public execution. Marble Arch is now near the spot.

ubi libertas ibi patria *Latin.* 'where liberty is, there is my country.' It was the motto of James Otis (1725–1783).

ubi panis ibi patria *Latin.* 'where the bread is, there is the fatherland.' In 1782 Michel Crevecoeur wrote,
"Ubi panis ibi patria, is the motto of all emigrants."

uisquebah (*n.*) Whiskey. From Irish *uisge beatha* 'water of life.' In 1750 Gottlieb Mittelberger referred to:
"corn consumed in brewing uisquebah."

ulto. (*adj.*) Of last month. An abbreviation of Latin *ultimo* 'last.' In 1760 Washington wrote,
"Since the 28th Ulto."

underbed (*n.*) A pad under a feather mattress. In 1725 John Lovewell referred to:
"a feather bed and under bed and bed furniture."

underkeel (*n.*) A keel, red ocher, mark on the underside of an animal's ear. In 1713 a North Carolina document said,
"One . . . Cowe marked on the Right Eare with a Cropp and on the left with an under Keel."

underlive (*v.*) To live more frugally. In 1751 Franklin wrote:
"The Dutch underlive and are thereby enabled to underwork and undersell the English."

undertaker (*n.*) One who undertakes or engages in any project. In 1631 Thomas Dudley referred to:
"one of the five undertakers here, for the joint stock of the company."

underwood (*n.*) The small trees that grow among large trees. In 1669 John Lederer wrote,
"The ground is over-grown with underwood in many places."

underwork (*v.*) To work for less than normal. *See quotation at* **underlive.**

uneasiness (*n.*) A restlessness. In 1700 Samuel Sewall wrote,
"The numerousness of slaves . . . and the uneasiness of them under their slavery."

United Brethren Moravian Brethren.

United Colonies The four English colonies, Massachusetts Bay, Plymouth, Connecticut, and New Haven which, in 1643, pledged to protect each other. In 1676 Increase Mather recorded,
"The Commissioners of the united Colonies sat at Boston, in the latter end of September."

unprofitable (*adj.*) Useless. In 1710 William Byrd deplored,
"a man so tame as to be governed by an unprofitable and fantastical wife."

unseated (*adj.*) Not settled with inhabitants. *See* **seat, (2).** In 1662 a Virginia document said,
"The greatest part of the country [will be left] unseated and unpeopled."

upon the reserve Reserved. In 1744 in Philadelphia Dr. Alexander Hamilton mentioned,
"a trader from Jamaica . . . who seized me for half an hour, but I was on the reserve."

urtication (*n.*) The rubbing of a benumbed limb with green nettles to restore sensation. A 16th-century Virginia doctor prescribed,
"oxymel, ursicatories, defensives, oiles."

usher (*n.*) An assistant teacher. In 1711 William Byrd wrote,
"I desired him [John Randolph] to go to Williamsburg to present a petition to the Governor as Rector of the College that he might be an usher."

usurper (*n.*) The epithet by which some referred to Oliver Cromwell. They thought he had usurped royal powers. In 1705 Robert Beverley related,
"Thus, in the time of the Rebellion in England, several good Cavalier families went thither with their effects to escape the tyranny of the usurper."

vacuum domicilium *Latin.* 'empty home' and by extension 'empty homeland.' John Winthrop wrote,

"Their right appears to be good for they had taken up that place as *vacuum domicilium*."

vade mecum A manual or book that one always carries. Words adopted from Latin 'go with me.' In 1732 Daniel Henchman referred to:

"The Vade Mecum for America."

vagary (*n.*) A wandering from the subject. In 1720 Samuel Sewall wondered,

"if after a first and second vagary she would accept."

vakeel (*n.*) An agent. A 1695 letter referred to:

"Whom we intend to make our Vakeel to represent Our Cause to the King."

vale (*n.*) The earth; often in reference to *Othello,* III, iii, 265:

"I am declined into the vale of years." In 1701 Cotton Mather prayed,

"May I have the anchor of my hope cast within the vail."

valetudinary (*adj.*) Sickly, weak. In 1679 Charles Wolley complained that he had:

"a weakly stamen and a valetudinary constitution."

value (*v.*) To recommend. In 1775, Capt. Burchmore, a merchant captain, wrote,

"I thought it most for your interest to value myself on some merchant."

vamp (*v.*) To piece an old thing with a new part, to repair. In 1740 William Byrd wrote,

"A Second-hand Chariot is vampt up for these Sons of Fortune."

vandyke (*n.*) A woman's round handkerchief with a collar. So called from its frequent appearance in the paintings of Sir Anthony Vandyck (1599–1641). In 1783 Rufus Griswold wrote that:

"[the handkerchief] must be pinned to the top of the shoulders . . . as you would a girl's vandyke."

vapory (*adj.*) A hypochondriac. In 1771 John Adams deplored,

"Thirty people have been here today, they say;—the halt, the lame, the vapory, hypochondriac, scrofulous, &c. all resort here."

variance (*n.*) A disagreement. In 1655 Adraien Van der Donck described Indians in New Netherland:
"Chiefs . . . three or four wives . . . who live together without variance."

varinas (*n.*) A kind of tobacco named for a place in Venezuela. A 1745 ship inventory included:
"24243 lb. of Varinas Tobacco in packs."

varsal (*adj.*) Whole. A corruption of *universal*. In 1704 Sarah Knight wrote,
"I never see a woman on the Rode so Dreadful late in all my Varsall Life."

vault (*n.*) A privy. Capt. Thomas Preston told of an event shortly before the Boston Massacre in 1770,
"Two of the 29th going through Gray's ropewalk, the ropemakers insultingly asked them if they would empty a vault . . . from words they went to blows."

vedette (*n.*) A sentinel on horseback. Gen. William Heath refers to:
"a line of videttes" in his *Memoirs*.

velveret (*n.*) Cotton-backed velvet. A 1776 Boston newspaper advertised,
"Wilton, velverets, hair plush."

vendue (*n.*) A public auction sale. A 1775 Philadelphia newspaper announced,
"To be sold by James Kinnean at his vendue store."

Veneris, Die *Latin.* Friday. From the goddess Venus with whom Freya, the Norse goddess of love, was identified.

venetian (*n.*) A coin, the gold sequin of Venice. In 1698 Jeremiah Basse wrote,
"In their chestes are about seaven thousand eight hundred Rix dollars and Venetians."

venia testandi *Latin.* 'the right to dispose by will.' The 1627 *Privileges and Exemptions* of the West India Company provided that:
"there shall likewise be granted to all Patroons . . . venia testandi, or liberty to dispose of their aforesaid heritage by Testament."

Venice treacle *See* **theriac Andromache.** In 1711 William Byrd:
"gave [his] wife some Venice Treacle."

venire facias *Latin.* 'cause to come.' A writ ordering a sheriff to assemble a group of people for jury duty. The Massachusetts Government Act of 1774 provided,
"And all writs of Venire Facias, or other process or warrants."

vent (*n.*) An outlet. The Navigation Act of 1663 refers to the plantations beyond the seas as:
"a vent of English woole and other manufactures."

verdegrise (*n.*) Copper rust; used in an eye wash. Originally from Old French *vert de Grèce* 'green of Greece.' A 1782 Hartford newspaper advertised,
"Quill Jesuits Bark, Opium . . . Verdigrise."

verjuice (*n.*) A sour liquor squeezed from wild apples or sour grapes, used in sauces. Originally from Old French *vert jus* 'green juice.'

viaticum (*n.*) Provisions for a journey. In 1678 Charles Wolley noted,
"Indian Corn is their [Indians] constant Viaticum in their travels."

vicinage (*n.*) Neighborhood; vicinity. The 1774 Declaration of Colonial Rights and Grievances requested,
"being tried by their peers of the vicinage."

victus parabilis *Latin.* 'easy living.' In 1678 Charles Wolley wrote,
"Inhabitants of the Wood . . . had their *victus parabilis*, food that wanted no dressing."

vielle (*n.*) A musical instrument with four strings activated by a small wheel rather than a bow. Adopted from a French word which is also the root of *violin*. Gouverneur Morris related,
"We were entertained by an old woman who plays on the vielle and accompanies her instrument with loose songs."

vigneron (*n.*) A wine grower. In 1619 the Virginia General Assembly referred to:
"the instruction of some vigneron."

villeinage (*n.*) The holding of land by payment of *villein* service, in essence slavery. The 1641 Massachusetts Body of Liberties promised that:
"there shall never be any bond slavery, Villenage, or captivity among us."

vine dresser One who dresses, trims, prunes, and cultivates grape vines. One of the occupations needed in Virginia in 1610.

vinegar (*n.*) Vinegar was used medicinally as an antiseptic, a counter-irritant, and a gargle.

Virginia snakeroot An herb from which a brew was made to reduce fevers, to raise the pulse, and to promote perspiration.

virgin's wax Pure wax. A 17th-century cookbook instructed,
"Take a little quantity of virgin's wax."

virtue (*n.*) A strength, power. A 1773 handbill addressed to Capt. Ayers discussed,
"a trial of American virtue and resolution."

vis major *Latin.* 'greater force.' An accident arising from an act of God or inevitable force. In 1774 Gouverneur Morris asked John Penn,
"Then who is to decide the vis major?"

vitriol (*n.*) Copper sulfate. Blue or Roman vitriol was combined in many ways and used medicinally to produce an emetic or cathartic.

vizard (*n.*) A variant of *visor* 'mask.' In 1652 Roger Williams wrote,
"Pulling off their masks and vizards."

vizier (*n.*) The manager of a plantation. By extension from 'minister of state' in Turkey. In 1710 William Byrd:
"left the prudentest orders I could think of with my vizier."

vogue (*n.*) The custom; the way of living. In 1779 Franklin wrote home from Passy, France and described:
"the vogue I am in here."

voider (*n.*) A basket into which dishes are emptied of leftovers when clearing a table after a meal.

vomit (*n.*) Any of the many medicines that induce vomiting. In 1709 William Byrd confided,
"My brother took a vomit this morning which worked very well."

vulgar (*adj.*) Common; ordinary. In 1727 the College of William and Mary planned:
"to teach the Indian boys to read, and write, and vulgar arithmetic."

vum (*v.*) To vow. In 1764 Thomas Hutchinson wrote,
"He has in like manner . . . I swamp, and I vum, for I swear and I vow."

wadset (*n.*) A mortgage or mortgaged land in Scotland. A 1774 essay on Scottish immigration said,
"The land he possessed was a wadset of the family of Sutherland."

wafer (*n.*) A thin leaf used in sealing letters. A 1780 letter said,
"I enclose you mine to Wilson under flying seal, after perusing put a wafer on and send it to him." Envelopes did not come into use until the mid-19th century.

wag (*n.*) One who is inclined to engage in low sport. In 1711 William Byrd went:
"to see some Indian girls with which we played the wag."

wager of law The giving of surety by a man accused of a debt that on a certain day he would appear in court to deny it. The Navigation Act of 1660 stated,
"No essoin, protection or wager of law shall be allowed."

waif (*n.*) A piece of property of which the owner is not known. The 1701 patent for the Manor of Scarsdale, New York,
"doe further give and grant to ye sd. Caleb Heathcote . . . all waifs, estrays, deodands & goods of fellons."

wain (*n.*) A four-wheeled wagon for the transportation of goods. The 1693 grant to Vredrick Vlypsen referred to:
"one cart or waine way."

wainage (*n.*) Farm implements. The 1683 New York Charter of Liberties referred to:
"a husbandman saving him his wainage."

wainscot (*n.*) The best grade of straight-grain, knot-free oak for fine furniture, later used to line the walls of a room. In 1610 Peter Force wrote,
"The country yeeldeth abundance of wood, as Oake, Wainscot, Walnut tres."

waistcoat (*n.*) A woman's short undergarment as well as a man's vest. A 1639 Maryland document stated,
"To maid Servant [shall be given] one new petty coat and wast coat."

waiter (*n.*) (1) A customs officer. In the sense of one who watches. In 1648 Massachusetts Bay enacted,
"A deputy or deputies . . . shall be as searchers or waiters in severall places."

(2) A serving tray for tea cups and pot. A 1778 Boston newspaper advertised:
"Dutch Quills, Spinnet Hammers, Japan'd Waiters."

wait upon To visit on business or a ceremony. In 1760 Washington:
"waited upon the Governor."

Waldecker (*n.*) A mercenary soldier from the Principality of Waldeck. *See* **Hessian.**

walk (*n.*) A cattle or sheep pasture. A 1644 New Haven, Connecticut, document
stated,
"The Mohegin Indians have done much damage to them by setting their traps in
the walks of their cattell."

walking purchase Land, bought from the Indians, the bounds of which were fixed
by walking around it in a given length of time. In 1756 Franklin commented,
"It is said by many here that the Delawares were grossly abused in the Walking
Purchase."

wallet (*n.*) A knapsack. In 1738 William Byrd noted,
"Every man took care to pack up some buffalo steaks in his wallet."

walme (*n.*) The bringing of something to a boil twice. A 17th-century
cookbook advised,
"You put in ye chicken & give it a walme or two."

wampum (*n.*) Clam shell beads, used initially by the Indians as money. A shortening
of Narragansett *wampumpeague.* In 1647 John Winthrop complained,
"The wampom which he received for me never came to my hands."

wanch (*n.*) Short for *wanchance* 'misfortune.' *Wan* in its negative sense of 'mischance.'
In 1781 Col. Goose Van Schaick wrote his wife that:
"I am sorry you are so much plagued with the wanch."

wanton (*adj.*) Luxuriant. A poem in a 1775 Boston newspaper described a soldier as:
"seated under the wanton vine trees."

ward (*v.*) To guard. In 1620 William Bradford reported,
"And a watch kept; and when need required, there was also warding in the daytime."

warden (*n.*) A kind of large pear which kept for a long time. A cookbook explained,
"To make a Tart of Wardens. You must first bake your Wardens in a pot."

wardship (*n.*) A guardianship; the care and protection of a ward. The 1641 Massachusetts Body of Liberties stated,
"All our lands and heritage shall be free . . . from all heriots, wardships . . . upon
the death of parents."

warp (1) (*n.*) A rope attaching a harpoon to a post in a whaleboat. A 1667 New
York document lamented,
"But lost both, the iron broke in one, the other broke the warpe."
(2) (*v.*) To weave. In 1774 John Harrower:
"had six yards striped cotton warped for two vestcoats and two handkerchiefs."

waste gate A gate to let out surplus water from a mill pond. In 1774 Philip Fithian
noted,
"He [Mr. Carter] told me that his Wastegate as it stands alone cost him 95 £."

watch coat A heavy coat worn by one on watch, on either land or sea. In a poem in a
1775 Boston newspaper a soldier reflected,
"Warm me more effectually than my watch coat."

watching and warding Remaining watchful and on guard. The 1650 charter for Harvard provided,
"And that the same president, fellows, and scholars . . . exempted from all personal civil offices, military exercises or services, watchings and wardings."

watch someone's waters To keep a very close eye on. A character in a 1776 play said,
"I'll watch your waters."

waterman (*n.*) A boatman or ferryman. The Navigation Act of 1696 applied to:
"wharfingers, lightermen, watermen."

weather gage An advantage. From a ship's being to the windward, or aweather of another. A character in a 1776 play admitted,
"You've got the weather gage of us on this task."

webb (*n.*) *Algonquian.* 'wife.' In 1672 John Josselyn wrote,
"A Fisher-man . . . was healed again by an Indian Webb, or Wife."

welkin (*n.*) The sky, hence the air. To *let the welkin ring* is to 'fill the air with sound.' A song went,
"Huzza my Brave Boys, Ev'ry man Stand his Ground/ With Liberty's Praise Let the Welkin Resound."

well over Recovered. In 1630 Francis Higginson praised New England weather:
"Since he came hither he is well over . . . by the very wholesomeness of the air."

Welsh plains A plain flannel from Wales. Lt. Gov. William Bull in 1768 wrote that:
"One hundredweight of rice was often bartered for a yard or less of coarse Welsh plains."

wench (*n.*) A young woman. In 1711 John Urmstone wrote,
"With the assistance of a sorry wench my wife brought with her from England."

werowance (*n.*) An Indian chief; could be applied also to a white leader. From Virginian, *wirowantesu* 'he is rich.' A 1634 letter from Maryland included,
"When I heard that a werowance of the English was coming."

westing (*n.*) The distance westward. In 1729 William Douglas wrote,
"Cambridge is . . . west of Paris (subducting . . . London's westing from Paris)."

Westminster Confession of Faith The rules for Presbyterian churches promulgated in 1649 at Westminster, England. In 1745 regulations at Yale required,
"And the class shall . . . recite the Westminster Confession of Faith received and applied by the Churches in this colony."

wet (*v.*) To observe by drinking. In 1746 Joshua Hempstead recorded,
"Danl Starr wet his commission." The term is still used in England. A birth is celebrated by *wetting the baby's head.*

wether (*n.*) A castrated ram. In 1768 Washington:
"put my beeves & weathers to fatten."

wet the bush To celebrate the topping out of a new building, a tree was put on top and there were drinks all around. The Druids instituted the custom and it is still common.

whackets (*n.*) The blows given on the palm of the hand with a twisted handkerchief as a penalty for losing a game of cards. In 1782 Simeon Baldwin deplored,
"The others exercised themselves with the most disagreeable of Games *Whackets* which they made so ridiculously noisy it was disgusting."

whaleboat (*n.*) A boat used in warfare and in raiding; it was about 30 feet long, occasionally armed with a swivel gun at the bow, and propelled by from four to 20 oarsmen.

wharfinger (*n.*) The proprietor of a wharf or its caretaker. The Navigation Act of 1696 applied to:
"all the Wharfingers and owners of quays and wharfs."

wheel (1) (*n.*) A form of torture. The victim was tied to a wheel with arms and legs extended. His limbs were broken by striking them with an iron bar. There is no evidence that this was practiced in the colonies, although in 1750 Gottfried Mittleberger wrote,
"Pennsylvania is an ideal country for gallows and wheel customers."
(2) (*v.*) To move, as by a wheelbarrow. In 1771 Franklin related,
"Isaac Decow . . . told me that he began for himself, when young, by wheeling clay for brickmakers."

wheel band The band that operates a spinning wheel. In 1690 Cotton Mather described an alleged witch with:
"her hands tied together with a wheel band."

wherry (*n.*) A type of light passenger or cargo boat. In 1624 Capt. John Smith recorded,
"I intended with two Wherries and fortie persons to try [to cross] this [river] presently."

whet (*n.*) Something that stimulates an appetite. In 1708 Ebenezer Cook wrote,
"Who found them drinking for a whet,/ A cask of cider on the fret."

whiffler (*n.*) One who changes his opinion; a vacillator. A character in the 1770 play *The Candidate* said,
"To prefer such a one to any of your whifflers."

while (*prep.*) Until. In 1774 Philip Fithian noted,
"Mrs. Carter and myself sat while ten."

whimsey cap A child's fancy cap. A 1775 Boston newspaper advertised,
"children's Whimsey caps; Russia duck."

whipsaw (*n.*) A saw for use by two persons. In 1718 Joshua Hempstead recorded,
"Ye Goods were . . . 3 whip saws . . . & two Cases of bottles."

whisk[1] (*n.*) A woman's shoulder collar of cloth or lace. An advertisement in a London newspaper described,
"a cambric whisk with Flanders lace."

whisk[2] (*n.*) Millet. In 1757 Franklin wrote,
"I enclose you some whisk seed; it is a kind of corn."

whiskey (*n.*) A light, two-wheeled, one-horse carriage which whisked people around. In 1789 Gouverneur Morris said,
"Madame Dumolley takes me in her whiskey."

whiskin (*n.*) A wooden drinking bowl. In 1635 Thomas Heywood described:
"Carouseing . . . mazers, noggins, whiskins."

whist (*n.*) A card game, the forerunner of bridge. The earliest mention of the game is 1529. It was originally called *whisk*, possibly for the whisking of the cards off the table. Edmond ("according to") Hoyle wrote his *Short Treatise on Whist* in 1742. William Byrd recorded playing the game often.

Whitechapel needle A kind of needle, possibly made in the Whitechapel quarter of London, just east of The City. In 1774 two Philadelphia newspapers advertised, "Whitechapel & Glovers needles."

whitesmith (*n.*) One who finished tin, a tinsmith; in contrast to a blacksmith who forged it.

whitney (*n.*) A variant of *witney*, a loose woolen material for blankets made in Witney, Oxfordshire, England. A 1727 Boston newspaper advertised, "To be sold . . . Wadings, Whitney-Shaggs."

whoreson (*n.*) Precisely, a bastard; loosely used to apply to any low person. A 1768 song went, "Devil take such rascals, fools, whoresons and all."

wicket (*n.*) Probably cricket, which uses a wicket. In 1726 Samuel Sewall recorded, "Sam Hirst . . . went into the common to play at wicket." Croquet, which also uses wickets, did not become popular until the 1850s.

widow's peak A little, woman's cap with a point in front worn under a hood. Originally a sign of widowhood, but later worn by any woman.

wight (*n.*) A person. From Anglo-Saxon *wiht*, same meaning. A 1682 Massachusetts broadside stated, "Here lies interred a little weary wight."

wildfire (*n.*) Any flammable materials, primarily sulfur and pitch, used in warfare to spread fire. In 1647 John Winthrop reported, "Our captain shot a ball of wild-fire fastened to an arrow out of a cross-bow."

wimble (*n.*) A handtool; like a gimlet, for boring holes. A 1673 Massachusetts inventory included, "Wimble stocks, wimble bitts 2 saddles & bridles."

win (*v.*) To harvest. A 1774 paper described a Scottish farmer as: "cutting, winning, leading and stacking ten fathoms of peats yearly."

Winchester measure The standards for liquid and dry measure which were deposited in the Jewel Tower in Winchester, England, during the reign of Henry II (1154–1189). In 1764 John Rowe suggested, "The Advocate General should determine the method of gauging molasses whether it should be Winchester measure or wine measure."

Windsor bean A kidney bean. Named for the English town in Hampshire. A 1765 Boston newspaper offered: "marrow-fat peas, Leadman's dwarf peas, Windsor beans."

wings (*n. pl.*) A piece of apparel worn over the sleeves of a dress. In 1639 the Massachusetts General Court prohibited the wearing of: "long wings."

winter savory A kind of mint. In 1630 Francis Higginson said that in New England, "Excellent pot-herbs grow abundantly . . . as wintersavory."

wipe (*n.*) A severe sarcasm. In 1711 William Byrd: "gave him [Col. Frank Eppes] a wipe about hindering his son from going to Carolina."

wire card The card which guides the wires of a Jacquard loom. The 1769 Charleston Non-Importation Agreement said, "That we will upon no pretense . . . import wire cards."

wire man One who erects or repairs wire fences. In 1710 William Byrd:
"paid the wire man for what work he had done at Falling Creek."

wit (*n.*) Mental capacity. In 1632 Thomas Morton said,
"And the virtue of his father's nimble feet (being infused into his brains) might make his tongue outrun his wit."

withal (*prep.*) With the rest, together with. The 1642 Massachusetts School Law suggested,
"Some other employment withal as spinning up on a rock, knitting, weaving tape."

within flux and reflux of the sea High tide; between the flow and the ebb of the sea. In 1717:
"7 convicted and 6 hanged for piracy within flux and reflux of the sea" in Boston.

without mark A mark in the margin of a page.

wizard (*n.*) A male witch. A 1682 Salem, Massachusetts, document recorded,
"He heard the said Goody Jones call the said Walton a Wizard."

woad (*n.*) A plant whose leaves produces a blue dye. William Penn penned that among:
"the commodities that the country is thought to be capable of are . . . woad."

wolf hook A wolf trap. A 1636 Massachusetts document listed,
"20 wolfhooks for hanging."

wolfish (*adj.*) Like a wolf, fierce. In 1775 James Adair wrote,
"To keep the [Indian] wolf from our own doors, by engaging him with his wolfish neighbors."

wooden horse A military punishment. A most uncomfortable rail which a soldier was forced to straddle for a long period. In 1764 John Rowe wrote,
"One of the soldiers behaved saucily to his Captain upon which they called a Court Martial & ordered him to Ride the Wooden Horse."

wood measure Probably, a precise measure. A wooden pole was used in measuring rods, yards, and feet. A 1667 New York deed described a lot as:
"30 ffoote, wood measure."

woolang (*n.*) A fisher. From Abnaki *wulanikw* 'handsome squirrel.' A 1722 Massachusetts bill was for:
"3 fox skins and ½ a woolang skin."

wool card A hand tool with teeth with which to card wool. The 1769 Boston Non-Importation Agreement said,
"We will not send for or import . . . except . . . wool cards."

woold (*v.*) To wrap cables around a mast where it had been fished. An anonymous 1680 writer reported,
"His vessell being ould gave way in her boue that if shee had not been wolded, could never a he[ld] together."

wool fell A sheepskin. The colonies were prohibited from exporting:
"wool-fells" by the Woollen Act of 1699.

worm (*n.*) **(1)** Short for *worm fence*, a zigzag fence with the ends of rails laid on each other. In 1760 Washington:
"laid the worm around my apple orchard & made the fence."
(2) The spiral pipe in a still or condensor through which the vapor is passed for

cooling. In 1740 Robert Dinwiddie wrote,
"The value of their sugar works, mills, stills, worms, horses."
(3) The very destructive marine clam, *teredo navalis*, which burrows into ships' hulls. In 1677 Edward Randolph said of New England,
"There are many good harbors free from the worms."

wormer (*n.*) A screwlike device on the end of a ramrod for removing a charge from a muzzle-loading gun. A 1702 Massachusetts document listed,
"a gunne mallet . . . a wormer & scourer for small armes."

worm seed The fruit of the Mexican tea, a brew of which was ingested to expel worms from the bowel or intestines. In 1711 William Byrd:
"gave to all the sick people the worm seed because I believed their sickness proceeded from worms in some measure."

wormwood (*n.*) A European woody herb, *Artemisia absinthium*, from which absinthe is made. Wormwood is illegal in most countries because of its effect on the brain, but in Colonial days it was taken as a tonic, to produce menstrual discharge, and to produce uterine contractions.

wort (*n.*) A new, unfermented beer. A 17th-century cookbook instructed,
"Take 5 or 6 gallons of strong wort and boyle it."

wreck (*n.*) A variant of *rack*, the punishment. In a 1775 satire by Mercy Warren, she referred to:
"Wrecks, halters, axes, gibbeting and chains."

wright (*n.*) A workman. Generally used in a combined form as *boat—, cart—, house—, mill—, plow—, ship—, wagon—, wain—, wheel—*.

writ of assistance A search warrant, authorized in 1672, directing the sheriff to assist the king's collectors to look for smuggled goods. This writ was capriciously used in Massachusetts in the 1760s. The Revenue Act of 1767:
"authorized writs of assistance to authorize and empower the officers of His Majesty's customs to enter and go into any house, warehouse, shop, cellar or any other place."

writ of intrusion The legal document used by Gov. Andros in 1684 in Massachusetts Bay Colony to reclaim land for the crown that the settlers had thought they owned. An anonymous writer in 1689 penned,
"Yet we were everyday told that no man was owner of a foot of land in all the colony, accordingly writs of intrusion began everywhere to be served on the people."

yard (*n.*) A penis. Not 36 inches, but in the sense of a stick or rod, as the *yardarm of a ship*. In 1678 Charles Wolley wrote,
"As to the nature of a Whale, they copulate as Land-beasts, as is evident from the female Teats and Male's Yard."

yarrow (*n.*) The herb, milfoil, *Achillea Millefolium*. The leaves can be smoked as tobacco. In 1622 Mourt wrote of Plymouth,
"We found heere in winter . . . Sorrell, Yarrow, Caruell."

yaupon (*n.*) A species of holly, *Ilex vomitoria*. An adaptation of Catawba *yopun*. A brew from its leaves was used as an emetic or purgative.

yawl (*n.*) A ship's small boat usually rowed by four or six oars. A 1732 Charleston, South Carolina, newspaper reported,
"They came up with him & demanded the yawl out."

yaws (*n.*) A disease much like syphilis; the two were often confused. In 1728 William Byrd wrote,
"'Tis apt to improve into the yaws, called there very justly the country distemper."
The first example of syphilis reported in the colonies was in 1647 when a seaman returned to Boston after a long voyage and infected his wife.

ye (*art.*) The. The *y* here is a representation of the runic letter called 'the thorn' and it is pronounced "th."

year day and waste The king was entitled to the profits for a year and a day of land of persons guilty of petty treason together with the right to waste the tenements and restore the land to the lord. The 1641 Massachusetts Body of Liberties said:
"All our lands and heritages shall be free from all . . . year day and waste upon the deaths of parents or ancestors."

yeoman (*n.*) A small freeholder. A man of respected class, yet lower in rank than a gentleman.

ym (*pron.*) Them. *See* **ye.**

yt (*pron.*) That. *See* **ye.**

zequin (*n.*) A variant of *sequin*. In 1696 John Dann testified, ''In his pockets were 45 Zequins and 10 Guineas.''

zingiber *Latin.* 'ginger.' It was eaten to reduce flatulence and alleviate griping pain.

INDEX

INDEX

Entries Listed by Category

Entries Listed by Category

new land
old ground
outdrift
outhouse
overkeel
overlooker
oxgate
pan
pided
pitch
pit saw
plant patch
plumping house
point
pomace
prising
prize
proud
quarter
quickset
quick stock
race
rank
ragstone
ratoon
reprize
ridered
rift
roach mane
rolling house
rotten
rowen
rubstone
run
settable
share
sheep walk
ship stuff
shook
shortling
shorts
skep
slope
snape
snath
speck
staddle
stag
stock
stockline
stone horse
strumpet colt

sucker
swingle
tale
tell
tender
thwart saw
tob
underkeel
wainage
walk
waste gate
wether
whipsaw
wimble
win
wool fell
worm

Clothing

band
banyan
barvel
beaver
bib
binder
bishop
bodies
bolster
boothose
brace
bracket shoes
breast horn button
breeches
budget
bum roll
busk
calker
capuchin
cardinal
cassock
castor
chip hat
chitterling
chopine
coatee
coif
commode
cornet
corslet

cross cloth
demicastor
doublet
dowd
drawers
fall
farthingale
flappet
French fall shoes
Franch heel
frock
frost
furbelow
furniture
garter
girdle
gorget
hairbine
hips
hive
hood
hosiery
jack boot
jerkin
jockey
joseph
jump
kilmarnock
mandillion
mantelet
mantle
mantua
mask
match coat
mob cap
monmouth cap
mourning
muftee
napkin
necklet
nightgown
patten
peak^2
pelerine
perizomata
petticoat
petticoat trousers
pinner
pocket
poke^2
polonaise
pudding

Fauna and Flora

eddo
eelpout
English corn
English grass
Englishman's fly
Englishman's foot
English potato
eryngo
feist
female Hemp
fennel
fenugreek
feverbush
fimble
fitch
flag
flare
flatting
flint corn
flower-de-luce
fowl meadow grass
frankincense pine
French bean
frenchman
frost fish
fustic
galeberry
gallberry
gallinipper
glutton
granadilla
green seed cotton
ground leaves
ground nut
guinea corn
haw
hen
herb of grace
hog corn
hoopwood
hortage
hotspur peas
hyperic
Indian weed
karl
lap
liverwort
logwood
loup-cervier
lupine
luzerne
maccarib

macock
madder
maize thief
marjoram
marrow fat
marshmallow
medlar
melocoton
milo
milter
Mississippi nut
monack
mullein
musquash
nanquitoche
nanticoke
nave wood
New Jersey tea
oil nut
orignal
oringo
oronoco
pele fish
pellitory
pennyroyal
pepperidge
Persicaria
petchamin
phocina
pig nut
pinkroot
pistia
plantain
platan
point coupee
poke[1]
pompion
poor Robin's plantain
prunel
puccoon
pulse
pumpion
puttargo
quickhatch
rape
rareripe
rattlesnake root
rochet[2]
rosemary
rue
saffron
sainfoin

St. Andrew's cross
St. John's wort
sapodilla
sarsaparilla
savin
savoy
scoke
scrag-tail whale
scurvy grass
shaddock
sheldrake
shin wood
silk grass
simnel
skirret
snake weed
sorrel
sot weed
spelt
sprat
staddle
stag
stinker
stone horse
tamarindae
tansy
tare[2]
thornback
tiger
tob
tocknough
torpedo
tuckahoe
turtogue
Virginia snakeroot
wether
whisk[2]
Windsor bean
winter savory
woad
woolang
wormwood
yarrow
yaupon

Food and Drink

allize
anagreeta
apple leather

Entries Listed by Category

Games, Dances, Musical Instruments

Household Contents

burgair
cag
candlewood
capcase
chafing dish
charger
cheesefat
cheesepan
chimney glass
clavel piece
closet
coal dish
comb fry
commode
compotier
cord
cottrel
cowl
creeper
crisping pin
cuttoe
cyttle
distaff
double bowl
dressing glass
dumb betty
Dutch oven
elbow chair
faggot
fire slice
fire stick
flasket
form[1]
furnace
gallows balk
gallows crook
gilefate
gilt
gourd
gudgeon
hake
hale
hand iron
hastener
heater
housewife
hussy
hutch
jack
jagg
jiggin iron
joint stool

keeler
kimnel
kit
lanthorn
leach[1]
light
lightwood
loggerhead
lug pole
lumber
malkin
mawkin
mazarine
mazer
mingo
monteith
nick
noggin
pier glass
piggin
pillow bere
pinking iron
pipkin
plate
posnet
quarrel
quarry
queen's ware
quern
rack[2]
recon hook
rock
rug
salon
save-all
scrutoire
search[1]
searse
settle
skeel
skillet
sley
slice
slop basin
sneaker
soft soap
sope
spider
spile
spittle
stock lock
thribble bowl

trammel
trencher
tunnel
underbed
voider
waiter
wheel band
whiskin
Whitechapel needle
wimble
wool card

Law and Punishment

abuse
advowson
alien
allodial
amerciament
apostle
appurtenance
Assembly of the XIX
assignation
assize
Assize, Court of
assumpsit
average
bailiwick
barony
bath
behoof
benefit of clergy
bilboes
bill
billa vera
Bill of Rights
Board of Trade and
    Plantations
Body of Liberties
bolts
bond slave
boodle
book
boot
borough town
brand
breviate
bridewell
broad seal

Occupations

feather merchant
fellmonger
fence viewer
fire ward
fiscal
fletcher
foot post
foremastman
fowler
fuller
ganymede
gauger
gayhead
gazetteer
general assistant
general recorder
General sergeant
gilder
goffer
granny
grasier
graver
grazier
gut scraper
hammerman
handler
hayward
hewer
hog howard
hogreeve
horner
horse leech
house joiner
husbandman
impost master
improver
intendant
iron man
japanner
jockey
joiner
journeyman
keep
land jobber
land layer
landwaiter
letter founder
lighterman
limeburner
lorimer
lot layer

lucina
malster
mantua maker
marker
mathematician
measurer
merchant
messenger
mineral man
minister
money maker
mother
nailer
nurse keeper
ordinary
overlooker
paroch
pawawe
peace maker
peace officer
picaroon
pilate
pinder
placeman
plater
platman
postillion
posture master
poulterer
powwow
prizer
proctor
prothonotary
provost
publisher
ranger
rater
receiver
recorder
refiner
regulator
St. Crispin, patronage
    of
salter
sawyer
schepen
schout
scrivener
sealer
searcher
serving
servitor

shoreman
slop seller
soul driver
spinster
stack taker
stock jobber
sugar baker
sutler
tabellion
tallow chandler
tapster
tide water
tidingman
tinman
tithingman
turner
usher
vakeel
vigneron
vine dresser
vizier
waiter
waterman
werowance
wharfinger
whitesmith
wire man
wright

Places and People

Albion
Algerine
Anamaboe
Avalon
Bayman
Birching Lane
bristowman
Brunswicker
Carlisle Road
Eastland merchants
Ebo
Five Nations
Gold Coast
Goodwin Sands
Hessian
High German
Ind.

pillar
pipe[1]
pistareen
pistole
pole
pon
pottle
proclamation money
puncheon[1]
pyd
quarter cask
quartern
quintal
real
red money
rial
rix dollar
roanoke
rood
royal
run
rundlet
schepel
seroon
sewant
shook
skipple
Spanish bit
Spanish heavy dollar
Spanish milled dollar
Spanish pistole
stiver
strike
tenor
tierce
venetian
wampum
Winchester measure
wood measure
zequin